The Point Is To Change It

Antipode Book Series

General Editor: Noel Castree, Professor of Geography, University of Manchester, UK

Like its parent journal, the Antipode Book Series reflects distinctive new developments in radical geography. It publishes books in a variety of formats – from reference books to works of broad explication to titles that develop and extend the scholarly research base – but the commitment is always the same: to contribute to the praxis of a new and more just society.

Published

The Point Is To Change It
Edited by Noel Castree, Paul Chatterton, Nik Heynen, Wendy Larner, and Melissa W. Wright

Practising Public Scholarship: Experiences and Possibilities Beyond the Academy
Edited by Katharyne Mitchell

Grounding Globalization: Labour in the Age of Insecurity
Edward Webster, Rob Lambert and Andries Bezuidenhout

Privatization: Property and the Remaking of Nature-Society Relations
Edited by Becky Mansfield

Decolonizing Development: Colonial Power and the Maya
Joel Wainwright

Cities of Whiteness
Wendy S. Shaw

Neoliberalization: States, Networks, Peoples
Edited by Kim England and Kevin Ward

The Dirty Work of Neoliberalism: Cleaners in the Global Economy
Edited by Luis L. M. Aguiar and Andrew Herod

David Harvey: A Critical Reader
Edited by Noel Castree and Derek Gregory

Working the Spaces of Neoliberalism: Activism, Professionalisation and Incorporation
Edited by Nina Laurie and Liz Bondi

Threads of Labour: Garment Industry Supply Chains from the Workers' Perspective
Edited by Angela Hale and Jane Wills

Life's Work: Geographies of Social Reproduction
Edited by Katharyne Mitchell, Sallie A. Marston and Cindi Katz

Redundant Masculinities? Employment Change and White Working Class Youth
Linda McDowell

Spaces of Neoliberalism
Edited by Neil Brenner and Nik Theodore

Space, Place and the New Labour Internationalism
Edited by Peter Waterman and Jane Wills

Forthcoming

Space of Environmental Justice
Edited by Ryan Holifield, Michael Porter and Gordon Walker

Working Places: Property, Nature and the Political Possibilities
of Community Land Ownership
Fiona D. Mackenzie

The Point Is To Change It

Geographies of Hope and Survival in an Age of Crisis

Edited by

**Noel Castree, Paul Chatterton, Nik Heynen,
Wendy Larner and Melissa W. Wright**

A John Wiley & Sons, Ltd., Publication

This edition first published 2010
Chapters © 2010 the Authors
Book Compilation © 2010 Editorial Board of Antipode and Blackwell Publishing Ltd
First published as volume 41, supplement 1 of *Antipode*

Blackwell Publishing was acquired by John Wiley & Sons in February 2007. Blackwell's publishing program has been merged with Wiley's global Scientific, Technical, and Medical business to form Wiley-Blackwell.

Registered Office

John Wiley & Sons Ltd, The Atrium, Southern Gate, Chichester, West Sussex, PO19 8SQ, United Kingdom

Editorial Offices

350 Main Street, Malden, MA 02148-5020, USA
9600 Garsington Road, Oxford, OX4 2DQ, UK
The Atrium, Southern Gate, Chichester, West Sussex, PO19 8SQ, UK

For details of our global editorial offices, for customer services, and for information about how to apply for permission to reuse the copyright material in this book please see our website at www.wiley.com/wiley-blackwell.

The right of Noel Castree, Paul Chatterton, Nik Heynen, Wendy Larner and Melissa W. Wright to be identified as the authors of the editorial material in this work has been asserted in accordance with the Copyright, Designs and Patents Act 1988.

Library of Congress Cataloging-in-Publication Data

The point is to change it : geographies of hope and survival in an age of crisis/edited by Noel Castree ... [et al.].
    p. cm. – (Antipode book series)
Includes index.
"First published as volume 41, supplement 1 of Antipode."
ISBN 978-1-4051-9834-9 (pbk. : alk. paper) 1. Geography. I. Castree, Noel, 1968-
G62.P65 2009
320.01′1–dc22

                                2010002766

Library of Congress Cataloging-in-Publication data is available for this book

A catalogue record for this book is available from the British Library.

Set in 10.5pt Times
by Aptara, New Delhi, India
Printed in Singapore
by Markono Print Media Pte Ltd.

01 2010

Antipode

Volume 41   Supplement 1

CONTENTS

The Point Is To Change It

Introduction:
The Point Is To Change It

Noel Castree
School of Environment and Development, University of Manchester, UK

Paul Chatterton
School of Geography, University of Leeds, UK

Nik Heynen
Department of Geography, University of Georgia, USA

Wendy Larner
School of Geographical Sciences, University of Bristol, UK

Melissa W. Wright
Department of Geography, Pennsylvania State University, USA;
mww11@psu.edu

The title we have chosen for this book, borrowed from one of Marx's most famous injunctions, is an invitation to think and a provocation to act. We're in the midst of some exceptionally challenging, complex and momentous changes to the global economy, polity, society and ecology. Disease, starvation, malnutrition, hunger, poverty, torture, unlawful imprisonment, poverty, marginalization, racial discrimination, cultural chauvinism, ethnic prejudice, gender inequality, religious intolerance, sexual discrimination, and environmental destruction are all signature features of the early twenty-first century. Democracy, in its various imperfect actually existing forms, is something that only a small minority of the world's people enjoy. Material wealth exists in abundance, but is commanded disproportionately by an elite of financiers, land developers, property tycoons, commodity traders, corrupt politicians and owners of various transnational corporations. "Uneven development" is, today, extreme in both social and geographical terms. Equality of opportunity (never mind outcome) is still an idealist's dream in most of the twenty-first century world.

Antipode Vol. 41 No. S1 2009 ISSN 0066-4812, pp 1–9
doi: 10.1111/j.1467-8330.2009.00713.x

Militarism is also writ-large: the legal and illegal trade in weaponry helps
to sustain the economies of supply countries and underpins seemingly
endless conflagrations in the global South. Geopolitical tensions bubble
under the surface where they are not already made manifest. Virtually
all of the world's problems have an international dimension to them, yet
cross-governmental efforts to enact joined-up policy—such as the Kyoto
protocol—are routinely foiled or attenuated. On top of this, the new
powerhouses of capitalism—such as China and India—seem to be
following a Western road to development, with all this implies for the
world's ecology. And we haven't even mentioned the effects of the recent
world financial crisis. But like any crisis moment, the late noughties are
also a crossroads, a crucial interregnum of immense opportunity and
new possibilities.

The essays in this volume have been commissioned to mark the 40th
birthday of *Antipode: A Radical Journal of Geography*. The journal was
founded during an extraordinary period in modern history, one in which
hopes for progressive change were exceedingly high. Four decades on,
and Leftists have an awful lot to contemplate. We think this is especially
true for those of us who work with ideas and books, abstractions and
words, among the sundry tools of the academic trade as we are faced with
the task of using them to engage with the world in progressive ways.
Plying the tools of our trade to reveal more effectively the multiple
relations of power along with bolstering efforts for thwarting these
relations continues to be an urgent challenge confronting academic
leftists. It is the challenge that *Antipode* has embraced since its founding
in 1969 as its many contributors endeavor to generate knowledge
and pedagogy that sustain resistance to all manner of injustice and
exploitation in a world in which the best ways to do so are not patently
clear.

Engaging with this challenge is the de facto obligation of any journal
that proudly claims the word "radical" in its masthead. Linguistically,
the term originates from the Latin word, *radix*, meaning "root" that
links the term to the idea of foundational truth, as is commonly used
in mathematics, chemistry and also in politics, as radicals seek to
expose political truths and not shy away from the consequences of
doing so. Political truths in this meaning of the term "radical" are
twinned always with subversion. As Rosa Luxemburg notably opined:
"The most revolutionary thing one can do always is to proclaim loudly
what is happening." Or as Gloria Steinem quipped: "The truth will
set you free, but first it will piss you off." Whether advocating for
political rights under fascism or for a woman's right to control her
own body within limited democracies, the point is not only to expose
the many truths concerning how power corrupts all manner of social
relationships. The point of radical leftist academic work, as Karl Marx
famously announced, is also to conjoin revelation with revolution, not

necessarily of the violent variant, but in its most basic sense of turning power around, however and whenever it corrodes the bonds of justice and humanity. As Antonio Conti, the Italian autonomous Marxist, said: "The goal of research is not the interpretation of the world, but the organization of transformation." We are in this game to change things, directly or otherwise.

As a journal of radical geography, *Antipode* was founded with this point in mind. When it was the birth-child of a handful of Left-wing academics and graduate students at Clark University in 1969, the journal was the only one of its kind within the field of human geography, and not only because it was produced on a shoestring and eschewed the conventions of normal "academic" writing. It was the only geography journal that called itself "radical" at a time when universities were expunging faculty and expelling students so-labelled. By calling some four dozen pages "a journal", the founders of *Antipode* created an outlet for the publishing of work that was unapologetically critical of the status quo and dedicated to ideals of social justice. And with this opening, the journal joined an incipient list of others across a variety of fields to turn the topics and approaches within its pages into legitimate academic concerns. Over the last four decades, *Antipode* has played an important role within and beyond geography in making capitalist exploitation, social justice, radical movements, gender inequality and other such topics into staple intellectual themes. But as *Antipode*'s contributors to this volume agree, now is not the time to settle into some middle-aged complacency. Around the world there is clearly a desperate need for progressive scholars and activists to challenge the notion that "business as usual" is not acceptable—and that we are willing to work as hard as we can, and in concert with others, to change things for the better.

Addressing this challenge is what we had in mind when we invited some 14 contributors (as we said in our letter to them) "to offer informative, illuminating and sophisticated analyses of 'the state of the world' in the early twenty-first century and how it might be changed for the better". In response, we have received a collection of essays that seek to align commitments to social and environmental justice to political strategies for addressing complex political realities and our roles as radicals within the academy. This volume is topically and intellectually diverse, reflecting the microcosm of the broad Left comprised by our authors. The contributors speak to multiple concerns and use diverse examples to illustrate their assessments. And yet, they all converge around a common desire to unravel the meanings of power, inequality, injustice and progressive politics in the current period. While we do not want to impose an artificial interpretation that finds common ground across a wide-ranging set of essays, there is a coherent call within this volume for refining of conceptual tools that can be better used as instruments of political change in specific places and in response to specific issues in the world today. The essays are not oriented toward polemics or for theorizing for its own sake. They, rather, seek to hone and craft ideas into implements of progressive change.

Toward this end, the authors address the following sets of questions: How do our conceptions of justice contribute to social justice activism in diverse parts of the world? How do our analyses of social and economic crises assist those who are struggling against mean-spirited processes of neoliberalization, the ravages of privatization and the biopolitics of international development? How can we apply our analytical insights in ways that are accessible beyond our narrow disciplines and specialties and that address the devastation of racism and xenophobia? How can we on the left continue to be effective as we do our jobs in institutions that are conservative and corporate? How can we make the principal medium of our craft—the written and spoken word—more accessible to international publics that do not have access to our publications or to the languages of our medium and to less educated populations who are eager to engage our radical theory? How can we reach the youth of today who read less and communicate through Twitter and Facebook? How can we be relevant from our places of privilege to the people whose outrage, suffering and political commitments provide the material of our conjoined political and academic interests?

In raising such questions, the authors brought together in this collection are agreed on the continued need for radical scholarship. Less clear, however, is the form radical scholarship should take in the current period. Whereas 40 years ago when *Antipode* was founded there may have been a broad consensus that variants of Marxism offered the best intellectual platform on which challenges to injustice and exploitation should be based, this is no longer the case. While Marx, Polanyi and Gramsci remain key theorists for many of our authors, we also see clearly in these contributions how the challenges of, and ongoing encounters with, feminist, postcolonial, "green" and poststructural theorizing have indelibly reshaped the contours of radical scholarship. Even those who remain committed to a Left theoretical orthodoxy no longer take for granted the centrality of the industrial worker as the potential revolutionary subject, the economism of some Marxian frameworks, or the nation-state as the container within which capitalism operates. In addition to a more internationalist stance, there is also a new emphasis on plurality, contingency and a richer sense of the validity of multiple political sensibilities. Indeed, overall there is a notable reluctance to be overly prescriptive about the forms that left alternatives should or could take in the current period.

Then there are those who aspire to even broader conceptualizations of radical politics. Foucault, Negri, Latour, Plumwood, Said, Nancy, Ranciere, Agamben and Haraway, among others, are also part of the conceptual repertoire on which our contributors draw to the effort to understand and address the challenges of the present. Such accounts are attempting to develop new ways of thinking about politics that are genuinely progressive, but move away from the revolutionary ideals and utopian desires that have tended to characterize leftist accounts. This often takes the form of more specific and situated approaches, in which already existing politics and practices are reframed and interrogated for their transformative potential. Whereas economies, states and markets tend to feature as the dominant categories in more conventional leftist political-economic analyses, spatialized, gendered and racialized bodies become more visible in these alternative accounts, as do geographically specific processes and practices of imagination and assembly, and the micro-politics of emotion, affect and ethics. There is also a politics of prefiguration flagged-up here ("be the change you want to see" as Ghandi said), which aims to build achievable future aspirations in the present through an accumulation of small changes. It is about embracing "power together" rather than power over.

There is, of course, a variety of views herein about the analytical and political utility of these diverse theoretical positions, and also of the actual and potential relationships between them. We would not wish it to be otherwise. However, what we do want to do is foster the linking of these critical analyses to contemporary political struggles, understanding that these struggles encompass, among others, issues such as finance, poverty, environment, indigeneity, enclosure, work, education and citizenship. None of these struggles are new foci in broader political ambitions to further economic and social justice. However, in the present political-economic conjuncture they may appear to be taking on new characteristics both because the world itself has changed—in both epochal and quotidian ways—but also because we are coming to understand this changing world in new ways.

Radical scholars have taken many cues from the emergence of anti-globalization activism often inflected with a strong anti-capitalist sentiment. The term "movement of movements" is often used to describe this latter turn, a vibrant hydra-like disorganization with no clear centre, defined through the idea of "one no, many yeses", and which has networked groups across the world and mobilized large international days of action. The spaces opened up by this new anti-capitalist internationalism are fraught with tensions, disagreements and conflict, often reflecting the well worn divisions on the Left between majoritarian and minoritarian politics—or the horizontals and the verticals. Part of this is because it represents a clear tension and desire for a break with traditional models of Left political organizing, a rejection of ideological dogma in favour of fluid, creative and more shifting political affiliations. Well-worn routes to political change—central committees, organized marches and the ballot box—are rejected or questioned, and a much more complex definition of the enemy, political programmes and relations to state power are embraced. In the writings and actions of leftist scholars, there is a recognition that taking on capitalism is far from a simple process. Social change is usually not well organized, coherent and easily defined—and nor should it be. We are simultaneously in, against and beyond capitalism.

The contribution of this collection is not simply "academic". Indeed, our initial intention was that these essays not be overly introspective, and certainly not simply exercises in rehearsing philosophical, theoretical, methodological or evidential debates. We asked the authors for pieces that offer informative, illuminating and sophisticated analyses of "The state of the world" in the early twenty-first century and how it might be changed for the better. We encouraged them to use concepts and evidence unselfconsciously and imagine a readership keen to know about the why and wherefore of twenty-first century power, inequality, injustice and progressive politics in all their complexity. In all cases, we sought essays which can both offer diagnosis and say something about political strategy and tactics looking into the future. We were not seeking polemics but, rather, well argued and evidenced assessments of our current conjuncture and the short-to-medium-term future.

Each of the authors asks us to think about changing the world in provocative and instructive ways. We open with Michael Watts, who recalls the context in which this journal was born and the aspirations of its founders. At the moment of *Antipode*'s inception, he reminds us that there was never a single understanding of the term "radical", and that the tensions between liberalism, social democracy and socialism were always apparent within even its early pages. What can we take from this account as we consider the political possibilities of the current conjuncture? For Watts there is no going back to the political certitudes and orthodoxies of the 1970s; however, he concludes that a key reference point for the contemporary Left continues to be a critical stance towards capital. This is a reference point shared by all our contributors, even as they differ as to how this critical stance might be made manifest.

Hugo Radice is concerned to recuperate the tenets of socialism for the present, arguing for an "authentic and popular socialism" that reckons with the failures of the actually existing socialisms of the last century. He stresses the need for an internationalist vision of social justice based on radical egalitarianism, which begins in day-to-day workplace interactions. Concerns about the quality of work, the need for a new internationalism of labour, and calls for workplace democracy might allow the building of a new socialist commonsense that might realize the radical potential he saw in the events of 1968. Neil Smith has an even grander vision. He argues that we have lost the political imagination (and perhaps the intellectual ambition?) to think outside of capitalism. One consequence of this is that, until recently, revolutionary change was no longer seen as viable. Today, however, in the context of an apparent global economic crisis, social change and political transformation have once again become possible. This crisis, he emphasizes, is fundamentally a crisis of capitalism. Returning to Marx, he argues that just as feudalism was eventually replaced by capitalism so too might we be finally witnessing the difficult birth pangs of a new way of organizing social life.

Tania Murray Li is agreed that we should re-read Marx, but for her it is his analysis of spatial and temporal unevenness that gives us insight into the current conjuncture. In her analysis of rural dispossession, she's concerned to show how both capitalist development strategies and biopolitical programmes need to be examined in their historical and spatial specificity. Unlike Smith, however, she's not convinced there is a capitalist master-plan but rather regards political economy as "assemblages pulled together by one set of social forces, only to fragment and reassemble". Consequently, she seeks the advancement of social justice in specific sites and conjunctures that are only very occasionally revolutionary.

Jamie Peck, Nik Theodore and Neil Brenner are also concerned with uneven spatial development, but in the context of a discussion about the analytical and political status of neoliberalism and postneoliberalism. While using the financial crash of 2008 to ponder what a postneoliberal order might entail, Peck, Theodore and Brenner are quick to urge us that progressive postneoliberal projects need to think deeply about the entrenched forms and processes that led to neoliberalism in the first place. Their astute political economic analysis offers much by way of insights regarding the next steps toward toppling these hegemonic forms. Just as Gillian Hart emphasizes the difference between "Development" as a postwar international project, and development as a creative project of creation and destruction, so too do Peck and his co-authors highlight the distinction between Neoliberalism as a fully formed political agenda, and neoliberalization as a polymorphous, relational, process that involves ongoing reconstructions and reorientations.

Robert Wade underlines this point in his discussion of the resilience of the globalization consensus, showing that even though much of the evidence mobilized to justify the deregulated market model is surprisingly weak, this may not lead to a decline in the dominance of finance capital. He emphasizes the importance of the politics of the policy-making process in determining the future of dominant economic narratives. Similarly James Ferguson makes an analytical distinction between the ideological project of neoliberalism and the politics of social policy and anti-poverty initiatives. Provocatively, he suggests that while certain political initiatives and programmes may appear to be aligned with the ideological project, they can also be used for quite different purposes than the term usually implies. Using the examples of Basic Income Grants and Food Aid and Cash Transfers, he shows how these might create situations in which markets play a redistributive role. Importantly, he stresses that this focus on the mundane real world debates around policy and politics is not simply to engage in reformist strategies, but rather illustrates that the need to develop new progressive arts of governing.

The next four essays focus on the so-called "neoliberal heartlands". Noel Castree focuses on the coincidence of economic and environmental crises, and is interested in the possibility of post-neoliberal futures. Taking the case of the UK's domestic politics and European Union emissions trading scheme, he's concerned to identify the barriers to creating a new political-economic and social order. He argues that the legacies of neoliberalism are such that while progressive ideas abound the conditions to make them flesh are currently absent— even in a moment of apparent "crisis". John Agnew and Katharyne Mitchell highlight distinctive features of the US financial and racial economy respectively. Agnew is also focused on the so-called global financial implosion of 2008, arguing it signals the decline of US-led Anglo-American model of global capitalism. He speculates about the emergence of new currency regimes, arguing that the world economy created and enforced by the USA is no longer sustainable. Mitchell is concerned with processes of racialization and new modalities of surveillance that—not for the first time—belie the classic American ideals of personal liberty and freedom.

Juxtaposed, Agnew and Mitchell's essays depict an America whose slow decline on the global stage is accompanied by intensified domestic control and repression. Paul Cammack echoes Agnew, but with a twist. His account of institutions of global economic governance post-Bretton Woods suggests that mainstream and radical commentators alike have over-emphasized US dominance. Cammack shows that new hegemons and blocs have been in-the-making for some time, emerging under the aegis of globalizing capital and a transnational capitalist class.

Our last group of contributors emphasize the new cartographies of justice, conceptions of political agency, processes of subjectification, and solidarity demanded by contemporary political economies and ecologies. Nancy Fraser focuses on what a post-Westphalian notion of community and justice should look like. As she says:

> a viable approach must valorize expanded contestation concerning the 'who', which makes thinkable, and criticizable, transborder injustices obscured by the Westphalian picture of political space. One the other hand, one must grapple as well with the exacerbated difficulty of resolving disputes in which contestants hold conflicting views of who counts. What sort of justice theorizing can simultaneously meet both of those desiderata?

Her essay provides an extended answer to this critical question.

Erik Swyngedouw emphasizes how the financialization of both nature and affect are giving rise to new forms of capitalism that in turn demand that we rethink the meaning of communism. Rather than being a claim taking the form of demands for self-management and self-government that would eliminate the need for the state, he calls for a reinvention of the communist hypothesis based on "equal, free and self-organizing being-in-common". In this context we have deliberately given J.-K. Gibson-Graham and Gerda Roelvink the last word. Theirs is the most profound political challenge offered by the assembled authors in that they move even further away from the human-centred conceptions of human agency found in the other essays in the book and explicitly argue for a new economic ethics appropriate to a world in which the being-in-common of both humans and more-than-humans is recognized. While the language of their contribution draws from Marxism, the hybrid research collectives they call for demand radically new conceptions of political agency that proliferate actions and identities that may give rise to as yet barely visible progressive futures.

We believe that this volume is a fitting way to mark *Antipode*'s 40th year in existence. Perhaps in another four decades there will be no need for a "radical" journal in geography or any other field—but we doubt it.

Now and Then[1]

Michael J. Watts

Class of 63 Professor of Geography and Development Studies,
University of California, Berkeley, CA, USA;
mwatts@berkeley.edu

Abstract: *Antipode* was launched into the firmament of the 1970s. We might reflect upon how well the journal and its contributors fully appreciated the historical gravity and weight of what was surrounding the project to create "a radical journal of geography". What sort of radicalism was on offer? The language was "social relevance" from "a radical (Left) political viewpoint". In writing to celebrate *Antipode*'s birthday, this time in another, and similar, firmament there is still the need to confront the challenge of radicalism and its meanings. Whether we agree with Perry Anderson that the last vestiges of the 1960s have been finally swept away, that the "fluent vision" of the Right has no equivalent on the Left and that embedded liberalism is now as remote as "Arian bishops", where do radical alternatives stand in relation to the fractured hegemony of neoliberalism? At the very least the need for alternatives is more pressing than ever. David Harvey has proposed rethinking the idea of "the right to the city". But what other rights might we rethink? I reflect upon this question by returning to the 1960s and 1970s and Marxist debates over the law, and by thinking about the possibilities offered by this Polanyian moment.

Key words: radicalism, commons, law, Magna Carta, markets

One does not easily isolate ideas for study out of that mass of facts, lore, musings, speculations which we call the thought of an age or of a cultural tradition; one literal tears and wrenches them out. There is nothing disembodied about them, and the cut is not clean...Large bodies of thought thus appear, at first, like distant riders stirring up modest dust clouds, who, when they arrive, reproach one for his slowness in recognizing their numbers, strength and vitality (Clarence Glacken 1967:12).

Antipode was launched into the firmament of the 1970s: an imperialist war in southeast Asia, a troubled American Fordism feeling the pressures of global competition, class struggles over the future of embedded liberalism, the Nixon dollar devaluation and the turn to global financialization, massive volatility in commodity markets especially food and oil, a robust Third World nationalism ultimately hobbled by balance of payments deficits, massive public sector debt and Cold War "low-intensity conflict" and proxy wars, the popular energies unleashed by the environmental movement, and not least, the first stirrings of what was to become, to quote Perry Anderson (2000), the global neoliberal

Antipode Vol. 41 No. S1 2009 ISSN 0066-4812, pp 10–26
doi: 10.1111/j.1467-8330.2009.00714.x

"grand slam". *Antipode* came on the heels of the 1960s, and of the genuinely revolutionary moment of 1968, and was tempered by a decade in which some theoretical and political flesh was placed onto the bones of the social and cultural libertarianism that passed as the radicalism of the *soixtante-huitards*. The 1970s, in this sense, launched a ferocious debate within the Left and among Marxisms of various stripes, it gave birth to a number of vital political experiments, not the least of which were various Third World socialisms, and commenced, partly as a result of the failures of '68, what Antonio Gramsci called the "long march through the institutions". From the perch of the present, there have been some remarkable personal trajectories through this period and beyond—one thinks of Joschka Fischer, Bernard Kouchner, Daniel Ortega—and they are not always salutary. A country which loses its hippies is, says Israeli playwright Salman Tamer (cited in Mamet 2009:12), in deep trouble. But I digress.

With the power of hindsight we can now appreciate the watershed nature of the decade into which *Antipode* was born, and indeed we might reflect upon how well the journal and its contributors fully appreciated the historical gravity and weight of what was surrounding the project to create a "radical journal of geography". Perhaps it is too easy—or are my expectations too high?—to acknowledge what we did not take full account of in the 1970s, but I have a profound sense that in some respects history was operating behind our backs.

What sort of radicalism was on offer? The language was "social relevance" from "a radical (Left) political viewpoint" (I take this from the journal's mission statement). But this launches us immediately into the complex historical semantics of the word radical. Here is Raymond Williams:

> Radical has been used as an adjective in English from C14, and as a noun from C17 from...*radix*, Latin—root. Its early uses were most physical...[but] the important extension to political matters...belongs specifically to lC18, especially in the phrase Radical Reform...[The word then has] a curious subsequent history. Radical...was by the second half of C19 almost as respectable as *liberal*...there was by lC19 a clear distinction between Radicals and Socialists...(Williams 1976:251).

The tensions between liberalism, social democracy and socialism inevitably surface from the very onset of *Antipode* in 1969 and of course in the founding text—David Harvey's 'Social justice in the city'. Reflecting upon radicalism and radical geography led me to return to something I had published in *Antipode* as a graduate student (Drysdale and Watts 1977, but drafted in 1975 and 1976), a piece written with Sandy Drysdale (a political geographer now at the University of

New Hampshire), which reflected (inevitably) the sorts of Antipodean debates as they were configured locally in Ann Arbor in the early and mid 1970s. We were part of a special issue (edited by Dick Peet and Milton Santos) devoted to underdevelopment (a term that has now become obsolete!) and the notion of a "socio-economic formation". It was admirably international—contributions by Venezuelans, Mexicans, Argentines, Tanzanians, Brazilians, Egyptians and so on—in a way that arguably has been diluted in the journal over time. Sandy and I opined on geography and modernization theory. We provided a madly inclusive *tour d'horizon* of social protest movements of various sorts— something missing as we saw it in the clinical and frictionless world of modernization surfaces—including banditry, millenarian movements, cargo cults, peasants rebellions and so on, all of which represented an "indigenous" critique" of an "alien ideology and total system". In my recollection Sandy and I were not exactly on the same page as regards what was reclaimable about this alien system and what the alternatives to underdevelopment were. At the very least, there is a staggering lack of attentiveness in our piece to the political projects rolled together— New Guinean cargo cultists, Vietnamese peasant communists, and Italian renegade bandits—in the name of resistance and "indigenous communication". The essay is held together in theoretical terms by the work of Karl Polanyi and by the teaching of Mick Taussig (in the days prior to the emergence of his book of commodity fetishism). It was, at the end of the day, a sort of weak-wristed anti-market radicalism.

I am writing once more, but now to celebrate *Antipode*'s birthday, this time in another firmament and still confronting the challenge of radicalism and its meanings. On its face the parallels between now and then are striking: another imperialist war-making adventure (prosecuted not in the name of anti-communism but of global democracy and anti-terrorism), another round of oil and food volatility, another space-ship earth moment (this time detonated by the spectre of global climate change), seething nationalisms (or proto-nationalisms and communalisms of multifarious stripe) in the global South in reaction to decades of structural adjustment and "economic realism", an anti-imperialism issuing not from the secular or revolutionary Third Worldist left but in the name of political Islam, and, of course, a deep crisis of capitalism of a deeply Polanyian sort triggered by the wreckless commodification of money and monetized assets. This time around one might say that the firmament is defined by the catastrophic consequences of the capitalist project *launched* in the 1970s. First time tragedy, second time farce.

One needs to say immediately that the contrasts between the 1970s and the current conjuncture are as striking as are the resemblances or repetitions. Nobody would question the observation that US hegemony, from the vantage point of 2009, looks much more fragile. China now appears as a profound counterweight to the American sense of a Pacific Century. The EU is now rather more than a figment of the imaginations of Jean Monnet and Robert Schuman. The US militarization of its program of global financialization (military neoliberalism) exceeds virtually anything encompassed by the term military Keynesianism or permanent war. Whether we agree with Perry Anderson (2002) that the last vestiges of the 1960s have been finally swept away, that the "fluent vision" of the Right has no equivalent on the Left and that embedded liberalism is now as remote as "Arian bishops", neoliberalism does rule undivided across the globe. In this sense, Polanyi's belief that free-market liberalism was finally dead and gone (he wrote at the end of the Second World War) was horribly wrong. It is back with a vengeance, but transmuted into a plethora of national (even sub-national) forms (Prasad 2006). The particular confluence of territorial and capitalist logics of power have produced a setting for Antipode's next decade for which we cannot simply fall back on the 1970s and what we did or not get right.

Nevertheless, reading Antipode's birthday against the current moment of danger does have the advantage of framing the question of what a radical project might mean at this moment, and the contours of what Edward Said memorably called the "endless search for alternatives". Inevitably a huge amount of ink over the last seven or eight years has been spilled on the question of militarism and American empire. In a world in which fictitious commodities have run amok, much energy now is (and will be) devoted to whether, as The Wall Street Journal (2008) put it, "we're all Keynesians now" or whether, as some on the Left have suggested, this is "the end of neoliberalism"—surely the answer to both must be no (I am ignoring the call of the American Enterprise Institute that Obama's project endorses the idea "we are all socialists now" and the Governor of Texas's latest attempt to rally the Republican faithful around a tax revolt predicated ultimately on secession from the Union). In virtue of the composition of the Obama administration, these questions from this side of the Atlantic would only lead one to believe that, at best, the jury is still out.

What is striking to me personally is that it is not at all clear, in view of the events since late 2001, what is the standing of that old staple of the Left "the crisis of legitimacy"? In the wake of the Enron collapse, the run of travesties surrounding the American adventurism in Mesopotamia, the massive assault on civil and political liberties, and now a collapse of credit that disqualifies any sense of credibility within the sector of US capitalist power . . . one wants to ask where is a politics of counter-hegemony congruent with the gravity of these massive and serial legitimation crises, any one of which (yet alone collectively) represents a fundamental challenge to the edifice of capitalist legitimacy.

I fully appreciate I am reading out of this narrative the 20 million who protested in the streets in March 2003 in advance of the US invasion of Iraq, the growing powers of the World Social Forum and so on, but one might surely ask: what did this get us? Was not the voice of the multitude ignored by the leaders of the world? Why should we not expect that from the ruins of Lehman Brothers will be a new financial architecture good for the bankers and bad for those foreclosed? At the very least the need for alternatives is more pressing than ever. David Harvey (2009) has proposed rethinking the idea of the right to the city? But what other rights might we rethink?

I want to spend a little time reflecting upon this question by returning to the 1960s and 1970s and to something Drysdale and I refer to in our *Antipode* essay, namely the May Day Manifesto written by Stuart Hall, Raymond Williams and Edward Thompson in 1967 and which spawned an ultimately failed National Convention of the Left in 1969, and to their notion of the masking and unmasking of the "real costs" of the making of a modern society.

The 1970s Again

After a decade, an interminably protracted piece of litigation was finally heard in October and November 2008 in the northern California District Court in San Francisco. Chevron v. Bowoto et al pitted the unimaginably poor and disenfranchised against the unthinkably rich and powerful; the wretched of the earth against the Olympian powers of corporate behemoths, the biggest of Big Oil. Fourteen villagers from some of the most isolated and desperate communities on the Nigerian oilfields brought a class action lawsuit charging Chevron/Texaco Corporation with gross violations of human rights including extrajudicial killings, crimes against humanity, and cruel, inhuman, and degrading treatment. In May 1998, roughly 150 Ilaje villagers occupied Chevron's Parabe Platform 8 miles offshore, demanding to meet with senior executives of the corporation to discuss resources for community development and compensation for environmental destruction associated with oil and gas exploration and production along the Atlantic coastal littoral and especially across the deltaic creeks from which most Ilaje eke a miserable existence. The occupation of a barge and platform—populated by a rainbow coalition of expatriate and Nigerian oil workers—came on the heels of what the Ilaje saw as a history of serial neglect and abuse. A deep well of local resentment and frustration seeded, inevitably, an unstoppable surge of political energy. Direct action against oil installations was a way of drawing the attention of senior oil executives, a class holed up in their corporate compounds in Port Harcourt and Lagos for whom the only Nigerian constituency to appear on their Blackberries was a venal and corrupt political class presided over by a military psychopath, President Sani Abacha. Even though negotiations between the protestor's leaders and representations of Chevron Nigeria Ltd (the subsidiary of Chevron Corporation) appeared to be making headway and a tentative agreement reached, on the morning of 28 May, a group of the protestors were shot (some in the back) and killed by Nigerian government security forces and Chevron security personnel transported to the platform on Chevron-leased helicopters. The plaintiffs sought a compensation injunctive and other relief under the federal Alien Tort Claims Act (ATCA, 28 U.S.C. 1350)—a statute two centuries old, framed as part of the original Judiciary Act—which provides a sort of testing ground within the federal court system on which victims against individuals or corporations that commit human rights violations outside of US territorial jurisdiction can have their day in court.[2]

Much could be said about the details of the trial and its own particular mix of drama, soap opera and tragedy. In the 6-week battle between the Davids and Goliaths of the oil world, Chevron only put on three live witnesses, not one of them connected with the San Francisco Bay area defendants; they also chose to reveal expatriate oil workers' testimonies (most of whom are outside the jurisdiction of the Court so plaintiffs could not subpoena them to appear from Texas, Louisiana, and elsewhere) through videotaped depositions taken years earlier, resulting in an inability to effectively cross-examine key witnesses live; Chevron did not introduce one single fact to rebut either the "agency claim" that the Nigerian subsidiary is the US defendants' agent, or the "ratification claim" that press statements by Chevron of the sort "we categorically deny we paid the military a dime" flew in the face of thousands of documented payments by the company to the military. Chevron won, fully exonerated on all claims in a unanimous jury verdict rendered on 1 December 2008 after barely 1 day of deliberation.

I should probably say that I provided expert testimony in the case in the course of which Chevron subpoenaed 50,000 pages of material, 5 years of field notes, 5000 photos, copies of speeches (and videotapes) of speeches I had delivered at various political events, protests and rallies, and not least a *tranche* of email correspondence. On the basis of some of the latter, I was grilled in my deposition by Chevron's counsel as to why I had referred to a Nigerian colleague as "comrade" (it was the same counsel who also questioned my credentials as a geographer since my only qualification as an expert witness was the fact that I read books and essays and expressed opinions about them). It was deeply unpleasant and unsettling (when was the last time you had a posse of smart Harvard and Yale trained lawyers pore over every word you had written in an essay published two and a half decades ago, teasing apart every poorly worded sentence and interrogating every slippage in meaning and timbre?). In the closing and summary remarks by legal

counsel on both sides, my testimony was invoked in favor of each of the
opposing sides. You have to wonder.

All of this took me back to the 1970s to E.P. Thompson's *Whigs and
Hunters* (1975) and the Black Acts, the boisterous debate over matters
of law, state, power and ideology by, among others, Louis Althusser
and Nicos Poulantzas, and not least Perry Anderson's ferocious, and
ferociously intelligent, engagement with Thompson's *Poverty of Theory*
(1979) and English Marxism. One thread in these debates was something
called "the rule of law" and whether the judicial sphere was anything
more than "an instrument of class power *tout court*" (Thompson
1975:262). Reading now through this body of committed political
writing—drafted at a moment when talk of "proletarian democracy
embodying a new and insurgent sovereignty" would solicit no fear of
embarrassment—is a salutary exercise, penned as it was in the very
early days of the neoliberal revolution. We can now see clearly with
the powers of hindsight, that coeval with the internecine squabbles
over Marxist rectitude lay the origins of the radical right's ascendancy
and its evisceration of the institutions of parliamentary democracy.
The long march from the founding of Friedrich von Hayek's chummy
club of free-market utopians at Mont Pelerin to the collapse of the
Berlin Wall took about 40 years, by way of the Chicago Boys in
Chile, the IMF–IBRD–Treasury complex, and the Reagan–Thatcher–
Kohl dispensations. As Gramsci might have put it, there has been a
Hayekian "passive revolution" from above. We have witnessed what the
Left's great pessimist Perry Anderson (2002) called the most successful
ideology in world history. Resistances are like "chafe in the wind",
and the Left can only "shelter under the skies of infinite justice". The
goonsquads and salesforces of neoliberalism had taken, one might say,
the commanding heights. Well perhaps, or perhaps not.

But before I return to Anderson's synoptic account of the irresistible
rise of a radical *right*—and what this might imply for being radical (of
an altogether different hue) today—let me dwell for a moment on the
law and what the 1970s Marxists had to say about it. Thompson's (1975)
magisterial examination of the Black Acts—an omnibus statute passed
over 4 weeks in 1723 which in defending the rights of the propertied
classes contained a criminal code with an unprecedented scope and
breadth of capital provision—argued that its very hegemonic capacity
depended upon the credibility of rules which in turn imposed limits and
restraints on its manipulability by the dominant classes.[3] The dialectics
of class and law made the juridical sphere a "genuine forum within
which certain kinds of class conflict were fought out" (1975:265) and
even producing reversals and interruptions in the operations of state
power. The rule of law imposed "effective inhibitions upon power and
the defense of the citizen from power's all intrusive claims" (266).

Anderson (1980) in turn responded that it was not the "rule of law" that performed such work as such, but rather the popular defense of specific civil liberties as part of a wider set of differentiated juridical rules and processes (constitutional and criminal law for example). Yet at the same time the legal procedures for the substantive codes of legal conduct—applied differentially over time and space—were drawn together in common institutions not the least of which was jury by trial. And it was here in the jury, a custom that predated the feudal epoch in England, that resided, said Thompson, a "stubbornly maintained democratic practice . . . a lingering paradigm of an alternative mode of participatory self government, a nucleus around which analogous modes might grow" (1978, cited in Anderson 1980:202).

Whether, as Anderson believed at the time, *Whigs and Hunters* offered an analysis that "has gone wrong" (1980:200), or represents a "movement to the right" (201) or, horror of horrors, is a "defensive strategy" for Left politics (203), remains a matter of judgment. I want to return to Thompson's claim that "the immense capital of human struggles over the previous two centuries" was, as he put it, "passed down as a legacy to the eighteenth century . . . where it gave rise to, in the minds of some men, of an ideal aspiration toward the universal values of law" (1975:269). The Chevron case stands surely as part of this inheritance, passed down as the accumulated capital of human struggles over several centuries. The Alien Tort Claims Act after all was signed by George Washington in 1789, now put to the service of addressing the contradictions of making contemporary law congruent with the realities of a gentry, class power and a state that operate with and through a lethal mix of transnational capital flows, "poor governance", privatized security forces, and military neoliberalism.

Construed in this way—that is to say as a bequest which speaks to the positive and popular inheritance of struggles for civil liberties— Chevron v. Bowoto represents a radicalism (for my purposes I shall call it *radicalism writ small*) which places its feet at the confluence of two streams of political practice. One returns us to the original foundational definition of radical as root. It speaks to an enduring sense of civil liberty and the preservation of civil liberties, a *longue duree* of human struggles now confronting the class perogatives of a different cast of "oligarchs and great gentry", a set of corporate personalities equally "content to be subject to the rule of law only because this law was serviceable and afforded to their hegemony the rhetoric of legitimacy" (1975:269). The Chevron case represents, at risk of universalizing a precedent-setting but nevertheless tightly circumscribed case of human rights violations and torture, an exemplar of a radical politics placing the defense of civil liberties as a bulwark against the relentless march of the commodity in its various guises. Law remains a forum in which certain sorts of class conflict—whose armies are drawn from the boardrooms of global capital and the slum worlds of the Third World proletariat—are fought out in classic Thompsonian fashion.

The other stream discloses, to return to Thompson once again, the potentiality for alternative modes of participatory self-government in the town halls, factories, villages and streets (this is what I shall call *radicalism writ large*). The untold story of the plaintiffs in the Chevron litigation was that, under conditions of extraordinary differences in class power and among dispersed and isolated villages at the margins of the modern world system, they forged a robust solidarity spanning 43 communities (the Concerned Ilaje Citizens). To suggest that the Ilaje plaintiffs were the socially dispossessed brought to the juridical center ignores, of course, the central fact that the enclosure of *their* commons by a non-local gentry and oligarchy—Big Oil—was preceded by two *other* rounds of primitive accumulation: three centuries of the slavery trade, followed by an other lubricant of industrial capitalism, palm oil. What matters surely is that across the great arch of this long theft, the vast capital of human exploitation and struggle came to claw its way into the judicial hallways of the federal courts standing at the heart of American empire. The jury, confronted with 60 pages of jury instructions of mind-numbing complexity, rendered a decision based on a parsimonious account of Nigerian political economy and a defense pandering to the basest sorts of white fears, racial violence and African primitivism ("juju" was the term of art). The villagers lost and the gentry won. Class power was expressed, registered and executed through forms of law. And yet there is a sort of residue, a legacy, because the law is, and yet is more than rhetoric, it is not merely fraud or force by another name. After all the case was heard and more will follow in another case—Shell versus Wiwa et al, addressing Shell's alleged involvement and complicity in the hanging of Ogoni activist Ken Saro-Wiwa and his compatriots in November 1995—in the New York federal court in June 2009[4] to be precise (and other cases are lined up waiting on judges dockets). What links radicalism writ small with radicalism writ large, I want to suggest, is a politics of scaling up—through a raft of modalities, the law being only one element within the arsenal—producing a sort of counter-hegemonic politics which turns for want of a better word on enclosure, or resisting enclosure and placing other commoning activities in the way of corporate capital. That is to say, rejecting the logic and expressions of the commodity in its drive to privatize everything.

The Magna Carta Manifesto

To focus on the commodity—surely the root of contemporary capitalism, the cell form of the modern as Marx understood it—necessarily returns us to the setting for the neoliberal grand slam, since it provides a horizon for any discussion of radical potentialities. Here I want to start with the observation that we are living through a Polanyian counter-revolution on the backs of a Hayekian revolution. Karl Polanyi's *The Great Transformation* and Friedrich Hayek's *The Road to Serfdom* were both published in 1944. Hayek, an Austrian economist trained at the feet of Ludwig von Mises but forever associated with a largely non-economic corpus produced at the London School of Economics and the universities of Chicago and Freiburg between 1940 and 1980, is widely recognized as one of the leading intellectual architects of the neoliberal counter-revolution.[5] Hayek's critique of socialism—that it destroys morals, personal freedom and responsibility, impedes the production of wealth and sooner or later leads to totalitarianism—is the *ur*-text for market utopians. In the Hayekian universe collectivism was by definition a *made* rather than a *grown* order: it was, Hayek said, constructivist rather than evolutionary, organized not spontaneous, a "taxis" (a made order) rather than a "cosmos" (a spontaneous order), an economy rather than a "catallaxy", coerced and concrete rather than free and abstract (see Gamble 1996:31–32). Its fatal conceit was that socialism (and social democracy for that matter) admitted the "reckless trespass of *taxis* onto the proper ground of *cosmos*" (Anderson 2005:16).

The other half of Hayek's project was a robust defense of western civilization—that is to say of liberty, science and the spontaneous orders that co-evolved to form modern society ("Great Society" as he termed it). It was a buttressing of the liberal (unplanned) market order from which the preconditions of civilization—competition and experimentation—had emerged. Hayek, like Max Weber, saw this world as an iron cage constituted by impersonality, a loss of community, individualism and personal responsibility. But (contra Weber) Hayek saw these structures, properly understood, as expressions of liberty. From the vantage point of the 1940s this (classical) liberal project was, as Hayek saw it, under threat; what passed as liberalism was a travesty, a diluted and distorted body of ideas corrupted by constructivist rationalism (as opposed to what he called evolutionary rationalism). Hayek was neither a simple conservative or libertarian, nor a voice for *laissez-faire* ("false rationalism" as he saw it). He identified himself with the individualist tradition of Hume, Smith, Burke and Menger, thereby providing a bridge that linked his short-term allies (conservatives and libertarians) to classical liberals in order to make common cause against collectivism (Gamble 1996:101). To roll back the incursions of taxis required a redesign of the state. A powerful chamber was to serve as guardian of the rule of law (striking all under 45 years off the voting roll), protecting the law of liberty from the logic of popular sovereignty. As Anderson (2005:17) notes, the correct Hayekian formula was "demarchy without democracy".

Polanyi conversely was a Hungarian economic historian and socialist who believed that the nineteenth century liberal order had died, never to be revived. In the Polanyian account, by 1940 "every vestige" of the international liberal order had disappeared, the product of the necessary adoption of measures designed to hold-off the ravages of the self-regulating market (market despotism). It was the conflict between the market and the elementary requirements of an organized social life that made some form of collectivism or planning inevitable. The liberal market order was, in sharp contrast to Hayek, not "spontaneous" at all but rather a planned development, and its demise was the product of the market order itself. A market order could just as well produce the freedom to exploit as it could the freedom of association. The grave danger, in Polanyi's view, was that liberal utopianism might return in the idea of freedom as nothing more than the advocacy of free enterprise, the notion that planning is nothing more than "the denial of freedom" and that the justice and liberty offered by regulation or control becomes nothing more than "a camouflage of slavery" (1944:258). Liberalism in this reading will always degenerate, ultimately compromised of an authoritarianism that will be invoked as a counter-weight to the threat of mass democracy.

At the heart of Polanyi's account is the ideology of the self-regulating market and the relentless drive to commodify virtually everything. Even to commodify those realms—the environment, labor, land, money—not produced for sale by conferring a price upon them:

> [L]abor and land were made into commodities... they were treated as if they had been produced for sale. Of course, they were not actually commodities, since they were either not produced at all (like land) or, if so, not for sale (like labor). Yet no more thoroughly effective fiction was ever devised. Because labor and land were freely bought and sold, the mechanism of the market was made to apply to them... Accordingly, there was a market price for the use of labor power, called wages, and a market price for the use of land, called rent. Labor and land were provided with markets of their own, similar to those of the proper commodities produced with their help... [Yet] labor is only another name for man, and land for nature" (Polanyi 1944:10).

Labor is simply human activity, land is simply nature, and money is simply an account of value, all indispensable parts of the market economy, and yet not produced as commodities. All these fictitious commodities resemble forms of commons that are subject to the logic of commodification (Bollier 2003; De Angelis 2007; Frederici 2004). Through the fiction of particular commodities, Polanyi provides an alternative "tragedy of the commons", one that renders the ruination of capitalism and human sociability—rather than as Hardin suggests reflecting the ineluctable logic of self interest.

The evil twin to enclosure or loss of the commons is the frontier and its closing. Here the process implies a sort of opening or opening up, but it is necessarily a sort of closure (fencing, displacement), a space of violent and lawless primitive accumulation (Redclift 2006). In his brilliant account of the rise of Jacksonian democracy, Mike Rogin points out that primitive accumulation is the "heroic stage of capitalism" (1975:13), linking ideology and psychology to sanctify capitalist hegemony. The loss of Indian land through a particular confluence of law and power was central to the wreckless and wholesale dispossession of the American frontier (Banner 2005). The oil frontier in the Niger delta is a twenty first century variant of this heroic moment. It is a heroism not of individual psychic regression as in the case of Jackson as he marched westward but of the heroic petro-nationalism of the Nigerian military junta.

Modern capitalism contained the famous "double-movement" in which markets were serially and coextensively "disembedded" from, and re-embedded in, social institutions and relations—what Polanyi called the "discovery of society". In particular, the possibility of a counter-hegemony to the self-regulating market could be found in resistance to the commodification of the three "fictitious commodities" (land, labor and money); such reactions represented the spontaneous defense of society (Arrighi and Silver 2003). A textbook case of spontaneous defense to a fictitious commodification gone awry is the utter spectacle of the Wall Street—and now mainstreet—crisis of big finance capitalism. The stimulus package, TARP (the Troubled Asset Relief Program) and the new financial regulations released on 17 June 2009 by the Obama administration which confers enhanced powers upon the Federal reserve, is precisely a sort of reactive defense to re-embed the fictitious world of money. The chicanery of the credit–default swap, the Potemkin villages otherwise know an investment banks, Ponzi schemes run by small armies of physicists and mathematicians turned money managers, and the depravity of CEO's going cap in hand to Washington to defend not just their salaries but the next *tranche* of government bailouts, can only be read as the excretions of a form of disembedding that Polanyi himself would have a hard time getting his head around. In the Polanyian universe a crisis arises necessarily because a fully realized market utopia would eviscerate and dissolve all forms of sociability. All of which is to say that capitalism is in the business of continually and simultaneously creating commodities and as it were negating them. What distinguishes, even makes, the uneven displacements and rhythms of capitalist development—what we call economic history—is the relative and defining weight of each.

The logic of commodification (Williams 2005) is of course deeply contradictory. The freedom of the market demands a state to impose its market will whether of state-backed dispossession of the sort described by David Harvey (2005) or state interventions to provide a juridical and institutional ground on which markets, property rights and contracts can operate and flourish. That is to say capitalism destroys the commons and yet needs (and the capitalist state must help create) commons too. Violence and the state—and hence law and the means of organized force—are central to the dialectics of the commons. Parliamentary enclosures in England marked the long and drawn out demise of the commons through the *force* of law (Neeson 1993).

But if private property (and labor power) stands as the obverse of collective rights (and commoning), the capitalist system of private property and individual rights can become too much of a good thing. There can be, as Michael Heller (2008) shows, *too many* private property rights—which demands a "recollectivization" (or perhaps more aptly the reconstitution of certaion sorts of commons)—for capitalism to function (see also Boyle 2008). Heller provides an example of the tragedy of the "anti-commons"—for example the privatization by the Federal Communications Commission in 1980 of the airwaves commons granted 734 licensed territories for cell phone service which produced a fragmented space of discontinuous wireless broadband service. Privatization "overshoot" creates "the gridlock economy". Solutions to these market inefficiencies are "co-operative". Commons are made or perhaps remade across history. Technology (for example how flight makes airspace a particular sort of commons within global space) and techno-science tends to produce new sorts of commons that are subject to new rounds of enclosure. The logic of commodification demands that agents—the state, capitalists, property owners—reassert certain sorts of commons in order that accumulation can continue. The commons are made and unmade just as primitive accumulation is recursive (De Angelis 2007).

In the same way that commodification proceeds along many fronts including the world of the image and the spectacle (as T.J. Clark says body, desire, war, community, subjectivity all become fully fungible abstractions) to the same extent de-commodification, the politics of resisting the commodity form and decoupling from the market, must proceed in multiple registers. They all in some sense carry the potential to assert or delimit a *commons*; that is to say to resist enclosure (RETORT 2005; Williams 2005). Indian peasants resist the state-backed takeover of land for export processing zones or massive highway construction; governments re-nationalize banks (albeit in a variety of ways and forms); the global commons are defended by a multiplicity of state and non-state actors in the name of human survival; workers contest the privatization of public pension funds; and the Ilaje struggle to retain customary control of coastal lands appropriated by fiat through powers vested in the Nigerian state and ecologically obliterated by its joint venture corporate oil partners.

There is good reason to place the commons on a very deep historical template as Peter Linebaugh suggests in *The Magna Carta Manifesto* (2008). He traces the Charters of Liberties framed by the armistice of the English civil war. What was signed at Runnymede was ignored at the dawn of modern capitalism and then rehabilitated in its modern form as a protector of individual rights and of free trade. Linebaugh is concerned to trace the uneven history (and survival) of the Magna Carta as a founding document (a constitution) for both communing activities—rooted in his account in a particular ecology, labor process, collectivity and independence form the state—and of a set of principles rooted in basic liberties: namely, neighborhood, subsistence, travel, anti-enclosure and reparations. Linebaugh sees recent radical traditions as "staying away from the Magna Carta" (2008:274) and in so doing neglect not only the politics of anti-enclosure but of neglecting too the deeper tradition of restraining state power.

> The communing of the past, our forebear's previous labor, survives as a legacy in the form of capital and this too must be claimed as part of our constitution. Chapter 61 [of the Magna Carta] giving liberty to *communa toitus terrae* provides the right of subsistence to the reality of a planet of slums, gated communities and terror without end (Linebaugh 2008:279).

The Charters of Liberties do not yearn for nostalgia or early modern restoration but rather of a fulfillment of their promise and potential.

Commodity Dialectics

> After the ideological and institutional adventures of the twentieth century, with their terrible record of oppression in the name of redemption, much of humanity may have reason to be wary of proposals to reorganize society. It may prefer to resign itself to small victories in the defense of old rights . . . The discipline of ruling interests and ideas has allied itself with a skepticism that masquerades as realism . . . creating a sense of closure (Unger 2005:169).

To assume that anti-enclosure (or commoning) politics are all of a piece or indeed are necessarily left or anti-capitalist would be to fall prey to the same logic that all anti-imperialist movements (al-Qaeda, the quit-India movement, Mr Chavez and his happy band of "chavistas") are somehow an unqualified good. My point is rather different. It is to suggest that a radicalism with credible claims to be representative of the Left must have as a reference point a critical stance toward capital, a formulation which sees a resistance to the commodity world as a refusal of capitalism's basic impulses. Whether these radicalisms writ small, often geographically dispersed and fragmented, can amount to radicalism writ large (an organized politics of anti-enclosure) remains a large question.[6] They might at least—whether anti-slum displacement movements in New Delhi, land reform struggles in Brazil or back to the land "commune" movements in northern California—be profitably understood in the same terms that Edward Thompson invoked the jury as a harbinger of self-government. But it is worth bearing in mind that even if these movements collectively do not easily map onto the landscape of revolutionary working class politics in the trans-Atlantic capitalist states, seen globally the picture looks rather different as a perusal of Sebastiao Salgado's massive photo-compendium *Workers* testifies. The neoliberal counter-revolution and the new enclosures have produced an entire planet of slums in the global South. The figures are hard to comprehend; in the final buildout of humanity the new megacities will perhaps contain 20 billion people by the year 2030. These sinks of informal labor, says Mike Davis (2006), constitute the "fastest growing and most unprecedented social class on earth", and he poses the questions: "To what extent does an informal proletariat possess that most potent of Marxist talismans: 'historical agency'? . . . Or is some new, unexpected historical subject, *a la* Hardt and Negri, slouching toward the supercity?" There is plenty of enclosures to be had here, and in global terms a massive proletariat perhaps less duped by the fetishism of commodities than drugged by the fetishism of Islam and evangelical Christianity.

My point would not be that the commodity provides the only ground on which radical can draw meaning and significance. Surely nation and war are, for better and worse, as important. But my purpose has been to sketch what potential might reside in resisting commodity forms and the deadly solicitations of the market. And as my comrades in RETORT have suggested, radical politics necessarily encompasses the image war in which contemporary spectacular capitalism is nothing more than capital accumulated to the point at which it becomes an image (Debord 1995). Resisting and transforming the logic of the competitively produced commodity is to endorse a certain sort of collectively and therein lies a resistance to enclosure. The fronts along which this enclosure now proceeds of course are multiple from the human genome, to the airwaves to the annexation of the Arctic.

But perhaps this is a strength rather than a weakness. Anti-enclosure holds out the prospect of what breaking through the barrier of what Roberto Unger (2005) calls "the dictatorship of no alternatives" and the need to direct the Left out of the sullen *cul de sac* of having, in his view, no palpable alternative or set of ideas beyond a reversion to a narrow (and conservative) social democracy. The Left, says Unger, has no central agent. He proposes a prophetic project to democratize the logic of the market, to deepen democracy through a high-energy deliberative politics, each of which contributes toward a cumulative reorganization of economy and state. I am not entirely sure that Unger's primary driving force in his schema—the desire of workers to become petit-bourgeois—provides an unambiguous alternative to class struggle, or that democratizing the submersion of everyone into the market in the name of democracy holds out much promise either. But my radicalism writ small and large—with the insinuation that it might operate rather like polyps in the construction of a reef—may suffer from the implication of a global popular frontism. Nonetheless, I believe that the prospect of resisting enclosure and commodification presents an opportunity not, as we are seeing currently, to rehabilitate J.M. Keynes, but to endorse a project worthy of the appellation alternative.

If we are to map the larger landscape, resistance to neoliberalism must, as Polanyi noted, take account of divergent national responses and global reactions. Here there is perhaps reason to be less gloomy than Anderson suggests. Fong and Wright's (2004) work on "empowered participatory governance" has the very great strength of linking participatory budgeting in Brazil with decentralized planning in India with school reform in Chicago (see also M. Williams 2005). Such "vigorous underground experimentalism" as Unger (2000) puts it may represent a counterweight to the Hayekian revolution in its multiplicity of forms. But we should also reflect upon Andrew Gamble's concluding observation in his exemplary book on Hayek himself, namely, that Hayek has most to offer socialists. His analysis of knowledge, coordination and institution revealed that the most effective forms of social organization were decentralised and democratic. Hayek's own elitism and classical liberalism predisposed him to a sort of political despotism, but it is perhaps the traditional Left goals of solidarity and equality that might benefit most from Hayek's ruminations on dispersed knowledge, co-ordination, and spontaneous orders. Geographers should have much to say about such a project.

Endnotes

[1] Some of these ideas are explored in an essay in a forthcoming book edited by Jonathon Pugh entitled, *What is Radical Politics Today?*

[2] The plaintiffs also sought compensation under the federal Racketeer Influenced and Corrupt Organizations Act (RICO) and California state law.

[3] There is an irony in the fact that this position bears family resemblances to Nicos Poulantzas's (see Martin 2008) Althusser-inspired writing on the law.

[4] The case was settled on June 8th 2009. Shell's payments totaled $15.5 million providing funds for a trust and "compassionate payment" to the plaintiffs.

[5] Margaret Thatcher famously pronounced that "this is what we believe" as she slammed a copy of Hayek's *The Constitution of Liberty* (1978) onto the table at Number 10 Downing Street during a Tory Cabinet meeting.

[6] This is of course the project of London-based anarcho-Marxists who operate under the sign of *The Commoner*; see http://www.commoner.org.uk/

References

Anderson P (1980) *Arguments Within English Marxism*. London: Verso
Anderson P (2000) Renewals. *New Left Review* 1:5–24
Anderson P (2002) Internationalism: A breviary. *New Left Review* 14:5–25
Anderson P (2005) *Spectrum*. London: Verso
Arrighi G and Silver B (2003) Polanyi's double movement. *Politics and Society* 31(2)
Banner S (2005) *How the Indians Lost their Land*. Cambridge: Harvard University Press
Bollier D (2003) *Silent Theft*. London: Routledge
Boyle J (2008) *The Public Domain*. New Haven: Yale University Press
Davis M (2006) *Planet of the Slums*. London: Verso
De Angelis M (2007) *The Beginning of History*. London: Pluto
Debord G (1983) *The Society of the Spectacle*. Detroit: Black and Red
Drysdale A and Watts M (1977) Modernization and social protest movements. *Antipode* 11(1):40–56
Fong A and Wright E (eds) (2004) *Deepening Democracy*. London: Verso
Frederici S (2004) *Caliban and the Witch*. Brooklyn: Autonomedia
Gamble A (1996) *Hayek: The Iron Cage of Liberty*. Boulder: Westview
Glacken C (1967) *Traces on the Rhodian Shore*. Berkeley: University of California Press
Harvey D (2005) *A Brief History of Neoliberalism*. London: Clarendon
Harvey D (2009) The right to the city. *New Left Review* 53
Hayek F (1944) *The Road to Serfdom*. Chicago: University of Chicago Press
Heller M (2008) *The Gridlock Economy*. New York: Basic
Linebaugh P (2008) *The Magna Carta Manifesto*. Berkeley: University of California Press
Mamet D (2009) Wall: A monologue. *New York Review of Books* 30 April
Martin J (ed) (2008) *The Poulantzas Reader*. London; Verso
Neeson J (1993) *Commoners*. Cambridge: Cambridge University Press
Polanyi K (1944) *The Great Transformation*. Boston: Beacon
Prasad M (2006) *The Politics of Free Markets*. Chicago: University of Chicago Press
Redclift M (2006) *Frontiers*. London: Routledge
RETORT (2005) *Afflicted Powers*. London: Verso
Rogin M (1975) *Fathers and Children*. New York: Knopf
The Wall Street Journal (2008) We're all Keynesians now. 18 January, http://online.wsj.com/article/SB120062129547799439.html (last accessed 8 July 2009)
Thompson E P (1975) *Whigs and Hunters*. London: Allen
Thompson E P (1979) *The Poverty of Theory*. London: Merlin
Unger R (2000) *Democracy Realized*. London: Verso
Unger R (2005) *What Should the Left Propose?* London: Verso
Williams C (2005) *A Commodified World?* London: Zed Books
Williams M (2005) "Democratic communists: Party and class in South Africa and Kerala, India." Unpublished PhD dissertation, Department of Sociology, University of California, Berkeley
Williams R (1976) *Keywords*. New York: Oxford University Press

The Idea of Socialism: From 1968 to the Present-day Crisis

Hugo Radice

Life Fellow, School of Politics and International Studies,
University of Leeds, UK
h.k.radice@leeds.ac.uk

Abstract: In 2008 the 40th anniversary of that iconic year, 1968, was celebrated in the media in relation to student uprisings and cultural revolts, largely neglecting the very significant movements of workers and peasants who were challenging power structures around the world at that time. This omission reflects the failures of socialism in the twentieth century, which are explored in this essay. Beginning from a more complete picture of 1968, the essay examines the history of socialism, identifying the main sources of failure in its theory and practice, in particular that of the revolutionary left. If the failure lies in the elite character of socialist politics and its focus on distribution rather than production, it is to be remedied by a firm focus on the politics of the workplace and the goal of substantive equality. The concluding section reviews the prospects for such an alternative in the current circumstances of global crisis.

Keywords: socialist politics, Leninism, class, equality, global crisis, workplace democracy

Introduction

> In every country in the world a huge tribe of party-hacks and sleek little professors are busy "proving" that Socialism means no more than a planned state-capitalism with the grab-motive left intact. But fortunately there also exists a vision of Socialism quite different from this. The thing that attracts ordinary men to Socialism and makes them willing to risk their skins for it, the "mystique" of Socialism, is the idea of equality; to the vast majority of people Socialism means a classless society, or it means nothing (George Orwell, *Homage to Catalonia*, London 1938:104)

The attention that was paid during 2008 to the events of 1968 indicated the importance of that year in shaping our understanding of how humanity has navigated the past four decades. Since memory is always constructed from the present, and continually reconstructed as time goes by, we are now necessarily remembering 1968 from today, and doing so in ways that suit our own particular needs and purposes. My own underlying purpose today is the development of a socialist politics

Antipode Vol. 41 No. S1 2009 ISSN 0066-4812, pp 27–49
doi: 10.1111/j.1467-8330.2009.00715.x

that can address the manifold problems of war, poverty, oppression, inequality and environmental degradation that now confront us.

Whatever we may find to celebrate in 1968 as a year of awakening and rebellion, the collective memory that has evolved since then has entailed also a forgetting—namely, forgetting the idea of socialism, and more specifically socialism in relation to the self-activity of the working class, and as the classless society envisaged by Orwell. I will explain this by examining the development of socialist politics in the twentieth century, and the reasons for the evident failure of socialists to achieve their goals up to the present. I will go on to argue in particular that we need to break once and for all with the failed trajectories of "revolutionary" socialism, which sought to achieve its goals through the destruction of the existing social, economic and political order.

To begin with, however, it may be helpful to say what I mean by the term socialism. It has been understood in many different ways since its first use in the 1830s, varying according to the political agenda of both supporters and opponents. One common understanding equates socialism with collective state ownership of the means of production and central planning; this is based primarily on the economic model that governed the Soviet Union from 1928 to 1991, but can also refer to the extensive public ownership found in many otherwise capitalist economies for 40 to 50 years after World War II. There have been prolonged arguments about whether this "economic socialism" can possibly be as productively efficient as a capitalist system based on private property and market relations. Advocates of this sort of socialism may either reject the methodological individualism of capitalism's supporters, or alternatively believe that it is possible to design a "market socialism" in which collective ownership can be efficiently combined with freedom of choice at least in markets for consumer goods and services.[1] The Marxist–Leninist tradition offers a variant on this theme, arguing that socialism in this sense is a transitional form, to be superseded by a "higher stage" (usually termed communism) in which human nature has changed sufficiently from the capitalist norm for society to achieve Marx's famous condition of "from each according to his ability, to each according to his need".

There is, however, a very different tradition, as old as that of state socialism, which emphasises social relations of power at least as much as the economic system. This tradition has always questioned whether the replacement of private ownership by state ownership necessarily changes the lot of ordinary members of society, if they continue to have no voice in the disposition of society's resources. The anarchist answer is to envision a society without a central state authority, but more commonly, socialists who reject the statist model argue instead for the creation of forms of organisation that vest effective power in society at large, in other words forms of egalitarian democracy.

Because of the central importance of production in meeting society's material needs, many socialists have argued for structures of economic management based on workers' control over production: this tradition includes syndicalism, in which trade unions are the key organisations; guild socialism, in which economic management is organised by branch of production; and council communism, in which central planning is combined with democratic control within each workplace.[2]

Since 2007, what at first appeared to be a credit crisis limited to the US housing market has turned into a major and unforeseen economic crisis affecting all countries and all sectors of the economy. Given the global hegemony of the "free market" neoliberal form of capitalism in recent decades,[3] it is not surprising that socialist ideas of all kinds are in vogue again, along with more modest proposals for returning to the more regulated form of capitalism that prevailed during the golden age of 1945–71. But after some 30 years of political retreat, the left is everywhere struggling not only to understand why the crisis has occurred, and to articulate convincing alternatives, but also to gain any political traction. Given the widespread disillusion with liberal democracy, as evidenced by declining electoral participation and media cynicism about the motives of both politicians and public servants, it is hard to know where to begin.

Many on the left have long since given up any aspiration to a singular socialist politics, which they regard as irredeemably tainted by the Soviet experience, and instead settled for engagement with a multiplicity of social movements, each pursuing a different issue. But the present crisis has come upon us at a time when it is increasingly clear that humanity as a whole faces the possibility of major social collapse—literally, the end of civilisation as we know it—as a result of anthropogenic climate change. In these circumstances, it seems essential that we return to a politics that is universal in scope and aspiration, embracing all aspects of society's self-organisation but focused on the provision of livelihood.

The Left in 1968 and Today

The *prima facie* evidence that socialism, as a movement of and for the working class, has been written out of 1968 can be found readily enough in the contemporary written and broadcast media in Britain.[4] The Tet offensive is remembered as the moment when the USA began to understand that it faced defeat in Vietnam, rather than as the dawn of victory for the people of that country. In the recollection of Enoch Powell's speech on immigration, we remember the workers who marched in support of Powell, but not the simultaneous opposition to capitalism within organised labour, and especially the then-influential shop stewards' movement. The May events in France are now seen simply as a student rebellion on the Left Bank, forgetting the millions of workers all over the country who occupied their factories, initially in solidarity with the students but rapidly formulating their own demands. The Prague spring is likewise seen as primarily a movement of intellectuals and artists pressing for political change within the Czechoslovak Communist Party, while the vital role of factory-based committees, in supporting reform and later in defending its leaders, is pushed aside. And if some of the most cited events of 1968, like the assassinations of King and Kennedy, the Democratic Party convention in Chicago, and the Tlatelolco massacre in Mexico City, had less direct connection to workplace and union politics, they too encouraged many radical students to look for such connections with a view to broadening the base of their opposition to those in power.

For some of us who were involved in radical student politics at the time,[5] this was not just a matter of identifying romantically with an idealised and reified working class. Rather, the sheer variety of events and their global range impelled us to inquire much more broadly into their historical origins, and thereby towards a renewed interest in socialist political ideas. However, this renewal took place in a very specific context, that of the Cold War. The international relationship between capitalism and communism—West and East— always contained elements of accommodation as well as confrontation, especially in the context of "mutually assured destruction" by nuclear weapons. Equally, the domestic struggle in the West against communism was based not exclusively on aggressive opposition (as envisaged by the theory of totalitarianism), but also on the more subtle arguments of convergence theory, which included the theses of (post)-industrialism, technological determinism and the end of ideology. As for the working class, by 1968 it was widely argued among progressive liberal intellectuals that it had become "embourgeoisified" by consumerism and the security provided by the welfare state.[6]

In this context, when we as students protested against injustices within the West, or perpetrated in our name by Western leaders, the mass media labelled us either spoilt children, or communists. The "spoilt children" label of course had some justification: we had grown up in a period of unparalleled and uninterrupted prosperity that embraced the vast majority of those attending university. Remember that only 10–15% of our age group in Britain undertook higher education of any kind, although a greater proportion of students at that time were from families headed by manual workers compared to the present day. Remember too that we were pretty much guaranteed admittance to a professional or managerial career. However, the Robbins Report,[7] which framed the development of the new universities founded in Britain in the 1960s, had drawn its rationale from the general philosophy of the postwar welfare state: higher education was an entitlement, not a privilege, and one which did not require, and could no longer enforce, social and ideological conformity.

As for communism, since the Soviet invasion of Hungary in 1956 the "Moscow line" had lost any serious influence on the left in most Western countries, and the great majority of 1968ers regarded the Soviet system as capitalism's evil twin. Instead, we burrowed into the history of socialist ideas and practice in search of a renewal of purpose, trying to reconstruct collective memories of past struggles and rescue them from the ossified mantras of Marxism–Leninism and social democracy alike. We also responded creatively to the increased prominence of areas of struggle less obviously related to production, especially those of gender and race. In addition, the realisation that postcolonial independence had by no means ended imperialist domination of the Third World served to expand our political horizons, and to revive the tradition of internationalism that had been so compromised by the Cold War (actually hot, in many parts of the Third World).

In Britain, most student activists were drawn towards one of three political organisations that saw themselves as promoting the interests of workers: the Communist Party, the International Socialism group (precursor to the present Socialist Workers' Party), and the Labour Party. The CP had by 1968 recovered some of its vitality since the débacle of 1956, and the influx of new student members contributed substantially to the process of renewal that led to a "Eurocommunism", which increasingly distanced itself from the USSR.[8] The IS at that time was a relatively open and democratic group, which had escaped from the suffocating conspiratorialism of the tiny Trotskyist tradition: it recruited many students with more libertarian tendencies, although they mostly left during or after the purges that preceded the creation of the SWP in the mid 1970s. In the Labour Party, the left was emerging from the stultifying anticommunism that is one of the forgotten legacies of the so-called golden age of Attlee, and Labour students could link up with a new generation of more radical trade union leaders, as well as the parliamentary left around the weekly *Tribune*. In addition to this range of more conventional opportunities for political engagement, radical students could also discover the delights of anarchism, syndicalism, situationism, Maoism, Trotskyism (all 57 varieties, as we used to say), or indeed any number of "Eastern" or otherwise esoteric mysticisms, with or without illegal substances. Even if we were not spoiled, we were certainly spoiled for choice.

Forty years on, what is left (in both senses) of all this? It is easy enough to look back to 1968, and across to the students of 2008, and conclude that the answer is: very little indeed. In London, Paris, Rome, Berlin, we may have struggled, but we evidently did not win.[9] However, that would be to short-change ourselves. In rejecting the ossified polarities of the Cold War, we were able to shape a new political agenda for the 1970s, centred on (in no particular order) equality, human rights, international peace and disarmament, and the protection of the environment. It was precisely the challenges from below around these issues that led the ruling elites, of West, East and South alike, towards the liberal revival that went from strength to strength from 1979 to 1991 and beyond.

The important question is why did neoliberalism succeed? One answer is that offered by those who have abandoned their past socialist views and embraced the new right, nearly always some variant of the hoary old "human nature" argument. The working classes rejected our idealism because they are naturally lazy, racist, sexist and above all interested only in material advancement—usually in directions despised by the intelligentsia, who can therefore happily enjoy their vastly greater wealth and autonomy with a clear conscience. A second answer is to go on holding faithfully to the same political agenda, regardless of the passing years, in the continuing hope that eventually the masses will see the light: hence the continued survival of the tattered remnants of communism, Trotskyism, and the Labour left. A third is to embrace social movement politics[10] and the cognate ideas of post-modernism: this is based on rejecting the old class conflict politics as reductionist. Workers, it is argued, are lots of other things as well—citizens, parents, consumers—and wearing those alternative hats, we can define a progressive political agenda.

Many 1968ers are, however, neither apostates, nor diehards, nor postmodern revisionists: we may often be cynical and world-weary, but we are still guided by our old socialist ideals when faced with egregious wickedness from our rulers, and we still see capitalism as a divided and unjust form of society. We are however realistic enough to know that there is no point repeating supposedly revolutionary mantras that have fallen on deaf ears for 40 years. Some of us still tend to look elsewhere for inspiration and hope: *New Left Review* continues as ever to bring us the latest radical intellectual ideas from around the world, and we all cheer when any remotely progressive government takes office in Brazil or Spain or Nepal. Some of us even take some comfort from the idea that our key mistake was over timing: with a nod to the much despised Russian Mensheviks, we may think that 1917 was hopelessly premature, and that capitalism has not yet completed its world-historical mission. But still, we want to do more than wait around until the situation has "matured".

The failures of twentieth-century socialism[11]

For those still looking to replace capitalism with an authentic and popular socialism, the starting point has surely got to be a reckoning with the abject failure of all socialist movements in the twentieth century.

A hundred years ago, there were of course many different visions of socialism on offer, and as many paths being followed towards them. But a minimal common understanding existed, that the gulf between rulers and ruled in capitalist society centres on their relation to the means of production. Capitalists are the owners of the means of production, and draw their livelihood from the exploitation of wage labour; this in turn is provided by the great majority of the society, through the sale of their labour power. Socialism was envisaged as a form of society in which this division no longer existed: instead, the free association of producers would determine the deployment of available resources, natural and human, to meet the needs of all.

In Europe, the period from the defeat of the Paris Commune to the outbreak of World War I saw the emergence of organised political parties with overtly socialist objectives, based for the most part on two new features in the socio-economics of capitalism: mass trade unions and nascent welfare states. These provided respectively the brawn and the brains for the new parties.

The unions brought together countless millions of workers, especially in the manufacturing industries, around their shared positions in the labour market and in the workplace. Workers paid the price exacted by the cyclical rhythms of capital, drawn into employment in the boom and discarded in the bust. Structural changes in the longer term destroyed whole communities and built up new ones as industries rose and fell. Within the workplace, "scientific" management watched and measured, intensifying the pace of work and constantly seeking to reduce or subvert the skills upon which workers relied in bargaining for a living wage. But on the highly practical basis of struggling to resist these tendencies, wider perspectives were constructed: in fighting against unemployment or appalling working conditions, the unions agitated in the streets and in the press, and pursued legislation that would further their collective interests.

The beginnings of the welfare state may be seen in large part as a considered response by the ruling classes, designed to meet demands from below without compromising the structures of economic and political power. But it also resulted in a substantial growth in the ranks of the urban intelligentsia. This was fuelled by the expansion in state apparatuses to meet the needs of education, housing, public health, colonial administration and war, which meant that the activities and the outlook of the professional, technical and managerial strata were increasingly shaped by public rather than just private interests.

Socialist politics thus drew in not only activists and leaders from the unions, but also "public" intellectuals from the professions— lawyers, doctors, engineers and teachers. It was the latter who provided the leadership cadres, as this politics increasingly took the form of membership-based political parties. Parties, as opposed to loose alliances of elected representatives, were a recent political phenomenon; much like the welfare state, they could be regarded as a means of channelling, and thus controlling, potentially dangerous impulses from below. Both the unions and the professions prided themselves on having complex internal structures that educated their memberships, established norms of behaviour and shaped their agendas. Such an approach could readily be transferred to explicitly political parties, with their executives, committees, local representative bodies, conferences, electoral candidates and publications. While workers might through periodic eruptions formulate demands for justice, the purpose of the political party was to transform those demands and bring them into the electoral and legislative arenas of the state.

By the mid 1920s, socialist politics was irremediably divided into two wings, those of reform and revolution. The reformist wing— eventually typically dubbed "social democratic"—espoused a gradualist agenda, centred on the pursuit of electoral success followed by legislation within the overall framework of liberal-capitalist governance. The revolutionary wing—eventually for the most part "communist"— advocated the overthrow of the capitalist state, and the radical transformation of the economic order as well, to one based on state or social ownership: for revolutionaries, participation in conventional bourgeois politics was in essence a tactical question, and took second place to agitation in factories and working-class communities.

To cut a long story short, by the end of the twentieth century both wings had utterly failed to achieve their original objectives.[12] The reformist social-democratic parties had long given up any eventual socialist purpose: in the context of the triumph of neoliberalism, they were everywhere content merely to mitigate the social and environmental depredations of capitalism. In some countries, such as Britain, this has entailed a conscious and deliberate ideological turn towards economic liberalism, while in others the shift was more pragmatic or even reluctant. The social-democratic segment of the political elite is now drawn naturally from university-educated professionals in law, management, education, health, even on occasion science and engineering. Since the same is true of senior union officials and top business executives as well, the political elite as a whole is now overwhelmingly what is called "middle class" (a term to which we will return later). The main achievement of social democracy, the welfare state, has meanwhile mutated from the postwar model of social justice and universal entitlement, to one of selective and limited redistribution and social provision, all geared increasingly to the demands of capital for employable labour. In parallel with this trajectory in advanced capitalism, the non-aligned movement that dominated the postcolonial world for some 30 years was cowed by the global debt crisis of the 1980s and submitted willingly or not to neoliberalism.[13]

As for the supposedly revolutionary wing, all that is left of communism as it actually existed in the Soviet Union and its progeny are the impoverished and embattled remnants of North Korea and Cuba. Neoliberalism holds sway in Eastern Europe, robber barons in Russia and much of the former USSR, and authoritarian state capitalism in China and Vietnam. The Communist Party of Italy has managed to go from 30% of the seats in the Chamber of Deputies in 1948—when the right was lavishly supported by US money—to a handful of seats in a centre-left coalition in 2008, defeated for a third time by a third-rate populist charlatan.

There remains the question of why. I am not so concerned here with why social democracy failed, for its functioning was explicitly shaped first by a rejection of revolutionary change, and later by the rejection of socialism by any means. But why did the revolutionary wing fail? To answer this, we have to look at how the revolutionaries understood capitalism, and how that helped to shape their actions.

That understanding of capitalism developed explicitly on the basis of Marx's critique of political economy. The singular success of the international communist movement in Russia in 1917 stamped Lenin, in particular, as the fount of all wisdom, and ensured that the understanding of Marxism developed by the Communist Party of the Soviet Union would dominate the theoretical formulations of the revolutionary left. The first key element of the resulting orthodoxy concerned the nature and trajectory of the capitalist economic system, centred on the evolutionary sequence from competitive to monopoly to state monopoly capitalism, and on the theory of imperialism. These theories, elaborated by Hilferding, Bukharin and Lenin,[14] were constructed by applying an economistic reading of Marx to the empirical studies of the German historical school of political economy, and their British counterpart Hobson. Since the most important conclusion of the orthodoxy was that capitalism was by then a decaying system in which the forces of production had outgrown the relations of production, the robust revival of capitalism after 1945 and the moderation of its tendency to periodic crisis dealt these theories a severe blow. Attempts were made to update communist economic theory, mostly by merging it with progressive Keynesian thinking on the basis of a shared focus on capitalism's tendency to stagnation,[15] but this proved a dead end once mainstream Keynesianism crumbled beneath the monetarist assault of the 1970s.

The second key feature of communist orthodoxy was the role of the revolutionary party as the necessary agent of revolution. Some communists (eg Luxemburg and for a time Gramsci) proposed that workers might make their own revolution,[16] but after the Kronstadt uprising in 1921, this leftist "infantile disorder" (as Lenin termed it)[17] was confined to the dissident fringes of communism: indeed, the two main opposition movements within world communism, first Trotskyism

and later Maoism, were no less authoritarian and undemocratic than
the CPSU. One-party rule under "democratic centralism" led directly
to Stalin's purges and the *gulag*, and the revisionism that followed
Khrushchev's secret speech never addressed the underlying issue of the
relation between party and class—that is, democracy.

In any case, with the Soviet invasions of Hungary in November
1956 and Czechoslovakia in August 1968, the world communist
movement had entered its own ineluctable process of decay, rejecting all
opportunities for a real democratic reform that could appeal to ordinary
working people living under the Soviet system, or for that matter those
living under capitalism.

What is to be undone?

The key problem remains that most of those who have not abandoned all
hope of revolutionary change remain trapped in Lenin's legacy.[18] Hence
the repeated efforts to establish a "new" socialist party, each group
believing that it can come up with a programme that will galvanise the
working class into action. Given the self-evident failure of all such efforts
thus far, is it not time, once and for all, to bury not just poor Lenin's
mummified corpse, but the entire corpus of Leninist thought? Instead,
let us look to some of the many alternative challenges to capitalism
over the last two centuries, challenges that one way or another start
from the self-activity of ordinary people, and their own articulation of
social needs that capitalism has been unable to meet, whether through
the market or through the state.

Here 1968 can again provide a way in. A common principle of our
politics in 1968 was that all forms of authority needed to be permanently
questioned. This is what attracted us to the Chinese cultural revolution,
although it took some of us a very long time to wake up to its brutal
realities and to the cynical manipulation of youthful idealism by the
Chinese party élite. Closer to home we students questioned authority in
the university: we wanted our teachers to address the issues of the day, to
respect our right to hold our opinions and to question their own, and to let
us participate in university decision-making and management. But we
also connected this to other arenas in which power was being contested,
whether it was the power of management over workers, of men over
women, of dictators over citizens in southern Europe, or of colonial
and postcolonial rulers over the Third World. The idea of *autonomy*
fundamentally challenged all the cant with which the powerful tried to
justify the grotesque inequalities of wealth and power which we saw all
around us.

The drive to question everything took us into the hidden histories
of resistance. We asked why the promise of gender equality had not
progressed beyond the formal sphere of legal and political rights, and

uncovered a history of economic, social and cultural struggle that inspired the women's movements of the 1970s. In direct response to the civil rights and black power movements in the USA and to Powellism in Britain, we read Fanon and Cleaver and Rodney, linking the fight of ethnic minorities for recognition and empowerment to our national history of slavery and colonial exploitation. The strikes and factory occupations that spread across the centres of industrial capitalism during that time were, we realised, as much in defiance of the unions' established routines of class compromise as against the employers' drive for profits: we found that the issue of workers' control had been repeatedly if fleetingly raised in the global history of capitalism.[19] Even university occupations could lead not merely to much-derided nonsense about "red bases", but to the meticulous analysis of creeping corporate control over higher education (and how right we were about that).[20]

For the subsequent 10 years or so, the political establishments of East and West responded defensively to these challenges from below. The postwar settlements on either side had been struck on terms dictated by the disasters of 1914–45, and centred on the provision of a substantial measure of economic security through active economic management and the universal welfare state. Ideologically, economic liberalism had apparently been replaced by a depoliticised "industrialism", in which an enlightened state worked with a new professional managerial élite in industry to maximise employment, growth and innovation. Yet, as *The Times* had famously predicted in 1944, once the stick of unemployment was removed, capital lost its most basic source of power over labour. At the same time, the confidence of citizens in their new social rights undermined the old deference towards their rulers, the forelock-tugging and the cultural cringeing. A parallel story can be told in the East, of how once the instrument of universal terror was foresworn in 1956, communist rule came to depend on the ability of the party state to meet the ever-increasing demands of workers for not only material welfare, but also democracy and human rights.

In this perspective, the resurgence of the old economic liberalism, dated variously between 1976 and 1982 (from Healey's IMF moment to Mitterrand's capitulation to global finance), should be seen as indicating not the weakness, but the *strength* of the challenge that 1968 posed.[21] Of course we can see that in the economic Golden Age of 1945–76, liberalism was always there under the surface: for example, in the West German model of the "social market economy", the social was always subordinated to the market (the Bundesbank got its independence in 1957, not 1997 like the Bank of England). But the threat posed by our attempts to push forward the boundaries of equality and redistribution was a very real one, because there was no automatic mechanism in the postwar Western capitalist order that could set any limit to our challenges. In place of the rule of the market, the law of value, capital had to rely directly on *political* rule—and in the 1970s it became abundantly clear that, short of putting an end to liberal democracy as such, in favour of some form of fascism, this simply did not work. For capitalism has yet to produce a social theory that can reliably and acceptably justify the *direct* appropriation of society's wealth and power by a ruling élite.

The restoration of economic liberalism has resolved this problem by reinstating capitalism's most fundamental premise: the enforced separation of economics and politics, and the concomitant supremacy of property rights over human rights. The result has been, in the economic sphere, a return to the pre-war order. Limits to the redistributive purposes of democratic government are now openly set by the masters of global finance, just as Keynes had feared.[22] Trade unions have seen their legal rights removed, while the public sector is parcelled up and sold off to the highest bidder. But political democracy too has been transformed. Political parties have become groups of professionals who compete with each other for the right to manage society for business: as Anthony Downs (1957) argued in the US case already 50 years ago, party programmes are constructed by compiling an agenda in which enough "interest groups" get their demands included to give the party an electoral majority. This is of course combined with the buying of all significant political parties by the super rich, and the complacency of a prostituted mass media.

Back to Basics

There is no shortage of pundits who chart this process of economic and political degradation. But what has gone completely, from academia and the mass media alike, is any underlying and unifying political concept from which to build an alternative. Indeed, the currently dominant approach among the intelligentsia holds that "unifying political concepts" are the problem, the inevitable outcome being totalitarianism. Perhaps it is time to suggest that we could benefit from a return to some straightforward social theory.

The concept of the working class, as elaborated by Marx especially in *Capital*, is not difficult to grasp. It consists of those who rely for their livelihood on the sale of their labour power. It is a relational concept, and its correlative is the capitalist class, those who own sufficient property to be able to live off the returns that it yields. What a worker produces—whether it is the piston rings that go into the making of a petrol engine, or the legal documents that are required to complete the sale of a house—matters not a jot. The conventional idea of "working class" and "middle class", distinguished until recently as blue versus white collar and now largely by educational attainment, is based upon an occupational classification related to what is produced, rather than the social organisation of production: it is really a division *within* the working class as just defined. The fact that many workers apparently own a stake in their pension fund, which is in turn invested in shares, bonds or other forms of tradable property, in no way makes them into capitalists. Indeed, the function of pension funds, as with all forms of workers' savings, is fundamentally to provide a pool of money capital which can be by various mostly legal means expropriated by capitalists for their own purposes. As for the "professional and managerial classes"[23] (a quarter of UK workers, going by job titles), they provide a pool of relatively more educated workers from whose ranks the capitalist class can renew itself, when the hereditary principle is insufficient to keep up its numbers.

Workers in higher education provide a suitable case study. The apparently autonomous professional teacher has been subordinated to a "new managerialism" which, like the old managerialism, amounts to the unfettered rule of those in authority. In Britain, our workplaces may not have been legally privatised, but organisationally and culturally, and above all in our minds, we have no more autonomy than a clerk or a factory worker. Across all the supposedly "higher" professions— law, accountancy, medicine, engineering, even management itself—a relentless process of differentiation has taken place, in which the great majority have become workers, while a tiny minority are now able to generate sufficient wealth to be able, when leveraged by external finance, to aspire to becoming capitalists.[24]

Among the possible sources of opposition to neoliberalism, the social movements whose origins are so often attributed to 1968 have never generated a united and singular movement. Of course they can count some significant successes, for example with regard to gay rights and environmental awareness. But from a capitalist standpoint, their greatest success has been to *conceal* as a potential foundation of opposition the one really universal condition of humanity under capitalism—wage labour. The responsibility for this lies precisely with the intellectuals of 1968. We sit and wring our hands about gang culture and TV reality shows and the egregious crimes of corporations and states alike, but we have forgotten the one possible way out of it all, namely to recognise our own selves for what we are—a section of the working class that has been not merely complicit, but active in perpetuating the conditions of poverty and dependence that most of the world's workers endure. We prattle on about equality of opportunity, because it means that we can pretend that grotesque inequalities of wealth and power are down to human nature or "effort" or just chance.

But they are not: they result from political choices that we make. We can instead begin from basic principles of social justice—equality, solidarity and the freedom of *all* individuals rather than the propertied alone. We can hold that every human life has equal value, and that this gives to all the right not to mere subsistence, but to a fully developed social existence, an equal share of society's material resources and equal participation in all of society's mechanisms of decision-making and administration. This implies a radical transformation of education so that it produces citizens broadly equal in their capacity for mental as well as manual labour, confident to express their opinions and eager to discover new and better ways to fulfil their own need for creative expression, as well as for the consumption of goods and services. In an egalitarian approach to education, resources would be distributed in inverse rather than direct proportion to achievement—as health resources were to be distributed under the founding principles of Britain's National Health Service. Furthermore, this radical egalitarianism is intrinsically global in character: my solidarity does not stop at the borders of Britain or the European Union.

In proposing such a vision of socialist politics, the place to start is not in special political spaces, in elections and governments and parties, but in our day-to-day social existence, and first and foremost in the workplace. For there, in what Marx called the hidden abode of production (1954 [1867]:172), we do all work together for a common purpose, and in pursuit of self-fulfilment as well as a livelihood. For all that the new managerialism commands, prescribes, monitors and rewards from above, employers cannot escape the need for their workers to collaborate freely and creatively across the divisions of occupation, skill and status.[25] But precisely because capitalism places such a barrier between the workplace and the wider world, between "economics" and "politics", we do not realise that our capacity for creative communication and the reconciliation of different interests and opinions could be deployed for purposes now deemed political.

In the twentieth century it was precisely at moments of the most acute societal breakdown that collective action of this kind emerged—and invariably it emerged not from self-proclaimed political parties created by and for intellectuals, but from ordinary people in their factories, farms, offices and communities. In the collapse of Tsarism, it was such self-activity that created the dynamic and sweeping changes that the Bolsheviks corralled, after 1921, into their grotesque parody of socialism. In Barcelona in 1937, in the liberated areas of Europe and Asia after World War II, in Budapest in 1956, in French factories in 1968 and Polish ones in 1970, 1976 and 1980, we find the same story, one of people impelled by circumstances to work together to meet social needs. In the history of the left, the movements of guild socialism, syndicalism and council communism[26] placed the self-activity of workers in their workplaces at the centre of their theory and practice, drawing inspiration also from the Levellers and the Diggers of the English Civil War, and from the cooperatives and the utopian communities of the mid-nineteenth century. In this history, perhaps, lie the foundations for a renewal of the sort of socialism that Orwell envisaged, but identifying them requires a dispassionate examination of our present circumstances.

Responding to the present crisis

As the present economic crisis has deepened,[27] so the potential agenda for political change has steadily broadened. Indeed, with feverish suggestions in the British press of a potential "middle-class revolt", some may envisage precisely the sort of social breakdown just discussed. But while that might, as in the cases mentioned, hasten the growth of democratic engagement in social change, it seems equally likely from the history of the twentieth century that it would fuel the nationalist and authoritarian politics that has been recently boosted by the war on terror and widespread Islamophobia. How, then, to fashion a response that might help eventually to build support for democratic socialism?

At the time of writing (March 2009) the most urgent task for governments and the general public to address is how to minimise the economic and social impact of what has become the most severe global downturn since the 1930s. In this context, the main task for democratic socialists is to address the question of how the costs of the crisis are distributed, and to argue for the strengthening of social safety nets to protect those thrown out of work. Beyond these immediate issues, public debate has moved from an initial focus on the most egregious scams and blunders of the financial sector, towards wider concerns about whether the crisis is in fact a crisis of the modern neoliberal order (Radice 2009), and it is here that there are real opportunities to shape the political agenda.

The most obvious agenda concerns the financial system, at all levels from the local to the global. Proposals for the re-regulation of finance have been supported right across the political spectrum. These include the restoration of the separation of investment banking from retail or "utility" banking;[28] the reform of international accounting and reporting standards for banks;[29] the strengthening of national regulation of finance, which has been seriously weakened by 20 years of deregulation (so-called "light-touch" regulation), and the international harmonisation of national regulation; a global commitment to the abolition of tax havens; and restrictions on the mobility of speculative capital, for example through the imposition of a Tobin Tax on transactions. Given that the costs of this global economic crisis fall most heavily everywhere on the poor, socialists should give all the support they can to such reforms with a view to avoiding future breakdowns in the financial system.

Beyond the realm of finance, however, the crisis has reinvigorated debate across a wide range of issues over which we can expect much sharper struggles. First, the question of how the burden of the crisis is shared, not to mention the public's response to revelations about the bonuses of financial moguls, has transformed debate about taxation: it is now feasible to press for the restoration of much higher tax bands, and the integration of tax and benefit systems that would remove some of the more egregious anomalies that affect people moving in and out of employment. Secondly, there has been widespread support for taking banks into public ownership, at least on a temporary basis, rather than simply pumping public money into them; and that in turn has allowed us to challenge the juggernaut of privatisation that has rolled across the globe for the past 25 years.[30] Thirdly, the widespread stimulation of economies through increased public spending has led to public debate about the direction of that spending, with especially strong support for infrastructure projects, in areas such as public transport, energy, housing, health, education and training. Such projects provide important opportunities for addressing the ever-increasing threat of severe climate change. Fourthly, in that context also it is increasingly possible to challenge the entire ideology of economic growth, entailing a significant shift in employment towards social care and leisure activities, together with the restoration of resource-efficient local networks of exchange. Finally, the global character of the crisis emphasises the necessity of international coordination in addressing these issues.

All these potential areas of change can be addressed in ways that seek primarily to retain, broadly speaking, the present social order: that is, the distribution of wealth and power both within and between nations. But equally, they can be addressed from the standpoint of radically challenging that order. In line with the analysis so far, such a challenge needs to centre on productive labour and livelihood. If the core social relation of capitalism is the separation of most people from ownership of the means to ensure their livelihood, then the core of a socialist alternative is equal access to resources and to the processes of decision-making over their use. Since history tells us that to organise this through a state set over society is to exchange one form of tyranny for another, we have to fashion participatory forms of organisation that can successfully guarantee equality and democracy, starting from workplaces and communities and building upwards.

In Britain, radical thinking and initiatives from the 1960s through to the early 1980s offers valuable lessons and examples: the shop stewards' movement and worker cooperatives, community newspapers and bookshops, campaigns for inner-city redevelopment, squatting, and the whole panoply of activism on issues of gender and racial equality, protection of the environment, and so on.[31] Such activities struggled to continue as Thatcherism took its toll, and continued to do so under New Labour. Public funding dried up, or channelled energies into structures and processes controlled by the state.[32] Yet the same creativity has been displayed by the anti-globalisation and climate change movements in the past decade, in much more difficult circumstances, and the same range of bottom-up initiatives, independent of official political parties and structures, continues to generate debate and scholarly study.[33]

Given the centrality of the workplace as the primary locus of production, socialisation and control in capitalism, this is surely the most vital area if we are to envisage a real transformation towards socialism. The headlong decline of trade unionism in the last 25 years, at least within the private sector, means that there is little in place on which a movement for workers' control can be built. Rank-and-file resistance to closures and redundancies is nevertheless rapidly spreading as the economic crisis deepens, even if, as in the UK, unions are hampered in any effort to widen support by legal constraints. It remains a big step from objecting to the impact of market forces on employment—the staple diet of unions from their origin in the nineteenth century—to challenging capitalist control.

However, there are three potential avenues of advance. In the first place, as argued in the last section, there has been an increasing concern about the quality of work and its intrinsic meaning in our lives. This affects workers in all sectors and at all levels of pay and responsibility, and thus offers an important way of uniting disparate groups. Such concerns can also be presented in terms of their consequences for the social cost and efficiency of production, as well as for the wellbeing of individuals. The "job enrichment" movement of the 1960s began from management experiments, but was taken up and transformed by workers[34], and the same could happen to the present-day "economics of happiness" movement.

Secondly, the heightened focus on international cooperation in dealing with the crisis contains a largely hidden dimension, namely the international flows of capital and of labour that have been such a central part of globalisation. As transnational corporations reel from declining sales and profits, history would suggest that they close their foreign operations and retreat home; but given the spread of network structures of production, the complex intra-corporate division of labour, and the universal liberalisation of policies on inward investment in recent decades,[35] this is significantly less likely today. The increased mobility of labour, particularly skilled labour, is also hard to reverse through a return to protectionist policies. But these issues raise the broader question of the real significance of the capitalist shibboleth of free trade: it represents freedom for capital, while labour as a whole is less free than ever before to obtain security of employment and livelihood. This can and must provide the basis for a new internationalism of labour.

Thirdly, the issue of workplace democracy inevitably raises the question of ownership. In the mid 1970s Rudolf Meidner of the Swedish trade union federation LO proposed that workers should use their pension funds to gain control over the enterprises employing them, by taking the employers' pension fund contributions in the form of shares.

This idea has recently been taken up by Robin Blackburn in the UK in the context of addressing the looming crisis in funding adequate retirement pensions (Blackburn 2007:83; 2009:134). However, the Meidner plan precipitated a revolt by the Swedish bourgeoisie against the political consensus that had prevailed since 1933, and the Social Democratic Party refused to endorse it (Wilks 1996). Clearly, given the immense political power of high finance in Britain, such a proposal would require a long campaign of mobilisation within workplaces transformed into centres of democratic debate and initiative.

The question that unavoidably arises from this agenda is that of political agency. In keeping with the arguments of this essay, the lesson from the history of socialism thus far is that we cannot rely on political parties as traditionally conceived. Social democratic governments, whatever their often considerable achievements in mitigating the worst effects of capitalism, have always shrunk from challenging the property rights of capital in its heartland, the business enterprise: following the global privatisation drive of the last 30 years, they are less likely than ever to do so. Regimes ostensibly pursuing revolutionary goals have raised new political élites over society at large, and reduced workers' rights to an entirely fictional rhetoric, which explains why in their moment of crisis, workers did not defend the Soviet bloc party-states. This of course does not rule out continued attempts at revolution from above: the jury is still out, in particular on the Bolivarian revolution in Venezuela. It also does not deny the role that can still be played, especially in disseminating information, ideas and solidarity, by the fringe parties of the left that remain wedded to the Leninist tradition. But they show little evidence of wider appeal in terms of membership growth and public recognition.

The last section concluded with the suggestion that popular initiatives have flourished most visibly at times of economic and social breakdown. Although this might lead us to imagine that the present crisis offers just such an opportunity, the crisis has thus far not seriously challenged the legitimacy of the dominant model of democratic capitalist governance. On the contrary, the most likely outcome in the short to medium term is that, as in France after the May 1968 events, ruling classes will successfully promote the replacement of unreliable centre-left governments by right or centre-right parties as soon as possible. Yet if there is little sign of popular rejection of parliamentarianism and party rule, this does not signal positive approval, but rather the marginalisation of any alternative forms of government. It has become commonplace to point to declining electoral participation and party membership, often as part of a broader decline in "civil" society,[36] and to the imperviousness of government to public dissent, for example over the 2003 US/UK invasion of Iraq.

It seems necessary, therefore, to insist that there are no short cuts available, and that we must begin from whatever forms of association that we find to hand: in this respect, our situation is no worse than it was 200 years ago. But foremost among the building blocks are surely workplaces and, where they still function, trade unions. The present crisis has certainly revealed how far we are from having the means to challenge capital's rule from below, but still worker occupations have taken place even in neoliberalism's Anglo-Saxon heartlands. In the USA there is real hope that after decades of union decline, the Obama administration may ease the legal restraints on union recruitment, while French workers have shown their customary flair in the new tactic of bossnapping. Interest is once more increasing in worker cooperatives and other forms of common ownership; within the public sector the visible exhaustion of the new managerialism, with its cant about efficiency and performance, has opened some space for strategies of democratic community control.[37] From a starting point in the workplace, linkages to resource suppliers and to customers or clients provide an available transmission belt for widening such initiatives.

What this amounts to is not some magic wand, nor a rallying cry to rouse the masses and overthrow the state. It is the modest aim of building a socialist commonsense around the aspirations and grievances of colleagues, friends and neighbours: a socialism of the water cooler and the workbench. In this way, perhaps, we could begin to realise the true promise of 1968.

Acknowledgements

This article is based on an essay originally written in the summer of 2008, which was jointly awarded the Daniel Singer Millennium Prize for 2008. The original version is available at www.danielsinger.org. For comments on that version I am very grateful to Logie Barrow, Anthony Barzey, Ian Bullock, Ingo Cornils, Pat Devine, the Leeds *Soundings* group and the Transpennine CSE Working Group.

Endnotes

[1] In the "socialist calculation" debates of the twentieth century, the critics of socialist planning such as von Mises and Hayek argued that centralised state decision-making would inevitably be unable to match the invisible hand of the market in terms of cost and efficiency. However, drawing on the work of Neurath, O'Neill (2006) has recently argued that the superiority of the market cannot be established simply on the basis of the informational requirements of central planning.

[2] On syndicalism see Linden and Thorpe (1990); on guild socialism, see Wyatt (2006); on council communism see Pannekoek (2002 [1950]) and Rachleff (1976).

[3] On neoliberalism see especially Harvey (2007) and Saad-Filho and Johnston (2005).

[4] One of the few recent scholarly accounts of the international student movement in the 1960s, Horn (2007), does discuss in some detail the relation between student and worker struggles in continental Europe, and that between the "new" left and the traditional Leninist parties.

[5] To be specific, I was a student in England from 1965 to 1971.

[6] On post-industrialism and convergence, see Bell (1974); on embourgeoisement, Goldthorpe et al (1969).

[7] See Committee on Higher Education (1963).

[8] See eg Boggs and Plotke (1980), Ross (1982).

[9] This refers to the common slogan of 1968, "Dare to struggle, dare to win!".

[10] Ruggiero and Montagna (2008) provides a wide-ranging introduction to the history and practice of social movements, and different views on their relation to conventional politics.

[11] The following section provides a heroically abbreviated account of the history of socialism since 1870, and given the purpose of this account detailed referencing would be superfluous. The best introduction remains Lichtheim (1983).

[12] So much so that for many, the rebuilding of a feasible socialism had to go back 150 years to the *Communist Manifesto*: see Panitch and Leys (1998).

[13] See Radice (2008a).

[14] The classic texts are Bukharin (1927 [1918]), Hilferding (1981 [1910]) and Lenin (1970 [1917]).

[15] See notably Baran and Sweezy (1966). This tradition still flourishes in the journal *Monthly Review*: see the recent collection of essays on the current credit crisis by Foster and Magdoff (2009).

[16] See Luxemburg (1961), and on Gramsci and the Turin factory councils, Schecter (1991).

[17] Lenin (1964 [1920]). On the process by which the Bolshevik Party established its dominance over the Russian working class between 1920 and 1924, see Pirani (2008).

[18] Early efforts to come to terms with the fall of communism in 1989–91 included Blackburn (1991), Miliband and Panitch (1991), and later Cox (1998). Despite such efforts, Leninist sects continue to exercise substantial influence over what remains of world socialism. As Judt puts it, "The Left has long shied away from confronting the Communist demon in its family closet. Anti-anticommunism—the wish to avoid giving aid and comfort to cold warriors before 1989, and End-of-History triumphalists since—has crippled political thinking in the Labor and Social Democratic movements for decades; in some circles it still does" (2008:126). Or more succinctly, "the historic failure of Bolshevism weighs like a nightmare on the brains of the living" (Panitch and Leys 1998:36).

[19] See eg Brinton (1975), Goodrich (1975 [1920]), Montgomery (1979) and Schecter (1991).

[20] For a British example see Thompson (1970).

[21] A thorough comparative account of capitalism from 1945 to the late 1980s is provided by Armstrong et al (1991). On the demise of Keynesianism see Clarke (1988), and on contemporary global neoliberalism see Radice (2008a).

[22] See Bonefeld and Holloway (1995).

[23] See notably Ehrenreich and Ehrenreich (1979).

[24] On the British university sector see Radice (2008b) and references therein; on the legal profession, see Ackroyd and Muzio (2007).

[25] The need for meaningful work is highlighted by Overell (2008).

[26] See the references in footnote 2.

[27] For an account of the crisis up to November 2008 see Radice (2008c).

[28] That is, restoring something like the US Glass-Steagall Act of 1933.

[29] The Basel II accords, developed and maintained by the Bank for International Settlements, are seen by many as contributing to the credit crisis by regulating outcomes rather than behaviour.

[30] In the UK, the Private Finance Initiative, under which projects within the remaining public sector were bled dry through the guaranteeing of profits for private investors, has completely collapsed: absurdly, the government is contemplating lending public funds to private investors so that the PFI can be kept alive.

[31] A clear picture of the momentum that built up in the women's movement is given by Rowbotham, Segal and Wainwright (1979).
[32] The problematic relationship between social activism and the state was explored by the London-Edinburgh Weekend Return Group (1980).
[33] A good example is Panitch and Leys (2000).
[34] To such an extent that it was soon abandoned by management; for discussion of its ambiguities see Thompson (1989:138–142).
[35] These trends have been tracked by Peter Dicken in the successive editions of his excellent *Global Shift*: see Dicken (2007).
[36] Notably in Putnam's influential account (2000), and in the so-called communitarian critique (Etzioni 1995).
[37] For an account of an exemplary recent union-led initiative within Newcastle City Council see Wainwright (2009).

References

Ackroyd S and Muzio D (2007) The reconstructed professional firm: Explaining change in English legal practices. *Organisational Studies* 28(5):729–747
Armstrong P, Glyn A and Harrison J (1991) *Capitalism Since 1945*. Oxford: Basil Blackwell.
Baran P A and Sweezy P (1966) *Monopoly Capital: an Essay on the American Economic and Social Order*. New York: Monthly Review Press
Bell D (1974) *The Coming of Post-Industrial Society*. London: Heinemann
Blackburn R (ed) (1991) *After the Fall: the Failure of Communism and the Future of Socialism*. London: Verso
Blackburn R (2007) A global pension plan. *New Left Review* 47:71–92
Blackburn R (2009) Value theory and the Chinese worker: A reply to Geoff Mann. *New Left Review* 56:128–135
Boggs C and Plotke D (1980) *The Politics of Eurocommunism: Socialism in Transition*. London: Macmillan
Bonefeld W and Holloway J (eds) (1995) *Global Capital, National State and the Politics of Money*. London: Macmillan
Brinton M (1975) *The Bolsheviks and Workers' Control, 1917–1921: The State and Counter-Revolution*. Montréal: Black Rose Books
Bukharin N (1927 [1918]) *Imperialism and World Economy*. London: Martin Lawrence
Clarke S (1988) *Keynesianism, Monetarism and the Crisis of the State*. Aldershot: Edward Elgar
Committee on Higher Education (1963) *Higher Education*. London: HMSO, Cmnd.2154
Cox M (ed) (1998) *Rethinking the Soviet Collapse: Sovietology, the Death of Communism and the New Russia*. London: Pinter
Dicken P (2007) *Global Shift: Mapping the Contours of the World Economy*. 5th ed. London: Sage
Downs A (1957) *An Economic Theory of Democracy*. New York: Harper & Row
Ehrenreich B and Ehrenreich J (1979) The professional-managerial class. In P Walker (ed) *Between Labour and Capital* (pp 5–45). Hassocks: Harvester Press
Etzioni A (1995) *The Spirit of Community: Rights, Responsibilities and the Communitarian Agenda*. London: Fontana
Foster J B and Magdoff F (2009) *The Great Financial Crisis: Causes and Consequences*. New York: Monthly Review Press
Goldthorpe J H, Lockwood D, Bechhofer F and Platt J (1969) *The Affluent Worker in the Class Structure*. Cambridge: Cambridge University Press

Goodrich C L (1975 [1920]) *The Frontier of Control: a Study in British Workshop Politics*. London: Pluto Press

Harvey D (2007) Neoliberalism as creative destruction. *Annals of the American Academy of Political and Social Sciences* 610:22–44

Hilferding R (1981 [1910]) *Finance Capital: A Study of the Latest Phase of Capitalist Development*. London: Routledge and Kegan Paul

Horn G-R (2007) *The Spirit of '68: Rebellion in Western Europe and North America, 1956–76*. Oxford: Oxford University Press

Judt T (2008) *Reappraisals: Reflections on the Forgotten Twentieth Century*. New York: Vintage

Lenin V I (1964 [1920]) *Left-Wing Communism: An Infantile Disorder*. In *Collected Works* Vol 31 (pp 17–118). Moscow: Progress Publishers

Lenin V I (1970 [1917]) *Imperialism, the Highest Stage of Capitalism*. Moscow: Progress Publishers

Lichtheim G (1983) *A Short History of Socialism*. London: Fontana

Linden M van Der and Thorpe W (1990) *Revolutionary Syndicalism: An International Perspective*. Aldershot: Scolar Press

London–Edinburgh Weekend Return Group (1980) *In and Against the State: Discussion Notes for Socialists*. London: Pluto Press

Luxemburg R (1961) *The Russian Revolution* and *Leninism or Marxism?* Ann Arbor: University of Michigan Press

Marx K (1954 [1867]) *Capital* Vol I. Moscow: Progress Publishers

Miliband R and Panitch L (eds) (1991) *Communist Regimes, The Aftermath: Socialist Register 1991*. London: Merlin Press

Montgomery D (1979) *Workers' Control in America: Studies in the History of Work, Technology and Labor Struggles*. Cambridge: Cambridge University Press

O'Neill J (2006) Knowledge, planning and markets: A missing chapter in the socialist calculation debates. *Economics and Philosophy* 22:55–78

Orwell G (1938) *Homage to Catalonia*. Secker and Warburg: London

Overell S (2008) *Inwardness: The Rise of Meaningful Work*. London: The Work Foundation (Provocation Series 4:2)

Panitch L and Leys C (eds) (1998) *The Communist Manifesto Now: Socialist Register 1998*. London: Merlin Press

Panitch L and Leys C (eds) (2000) *Necessary and Unnecessary Utopias: Socialist Register 2000*. London: Merlin Press

Pannekoek A (2002 [1950]) *Workers' Councils* (R F Barsky ed). Oakland: AK Press

Pirani S (2008) *The Russian Revolution in Retreat, 1920–24: Soviet Workers and the New Communist Élite*. London: Routledge

Putnam R (2000) *Bowling Alone: the Collapse and Revival of American Community*. New York: Simon and Schuster

Rachleff P J (1976) *Marxism and Council Communism: the Foundation for Revolutionary Theory for Modern Society*. New York: Revisionist Press

Radice H (2008a) The developmental state under global neoliberalism. *Third World Quarterly* 29(6):1153–1174

Radice H (2008b) Life after death? The Soviet system in British higher education. *International Journal of Management Concepts and Philosophy* 3(2):99–120

Radice H (2008c) What kind of crisis? *Red Pepper* 163:18–21

Radice H (2009) Neoliberalism in crisis? Money and the state in contemporary capitalism. *Spectrum: Journal of Global Studies* forthcoming

Ross G (1982) *Workers and Communists in France: from Popular Front to Eurocommunism*. Berkeley: University of California Press

Rowbotham S, Segal L and Wainwright H (1979) *Beyond the Fragments: Feminism and the Making of Socialism*. London: Merlin Press

Ruggiero V and Montagna N (eds) (2008) *Social Movements: A Reader*. London: Routledge

Saad-Filho A and Johnston D (eds) (2005) *Neoliberalism: A Critical Reader*. London: Pluto Press

Schecter D (1991) *Gramsci and the Theory of Industrial Democracy*. Aldershot: Avebury

Thompson E P (ed) (1970) *Warwick University Ltd*. Harmondsworth: Penguin Special

Thompson P (1989) *The Nature of Work*. 2nd ed. London: Macmillan

Wainwright H with Little M (2009) *Public Service Reform . . . But Not As We Know It*. Hove: Picnic Publishing

Wilks S (1996) Class compromise and the international economy: The rise and fall of Swedish social democracy. *Capital and Class* 58:89–111

Wyatt C (2006) A recipe for a cookshop of the future: G.D.H. Cole and the conundrum of sovereignty. *Capital & Class* 90:93–123

The Revolutionary Imperative

Neil Smith

Center for Place, Culture and Politics, Graduate Center,
City University of New York, New York, NY, USA;
nsmith@gc.cuny.edu

Abstract: In the last three decades in the advanced capitalist world, the idea of revolution has largely slipped from political view. The neoliberal moment seemed to smother any political possibility other than capitalism, but with that historical phase now itself fading, it may be a good time to revive the idea of revolution if for no other reason than that revolutions do happen. Certainly, the political right is concerned about the possibility of revolts resulting from the social privation resulting, in turn, from the global economic crisis. This essay attempts to explore and reanimate the notion of revolution, both historically and in the present context.

Keywords: revolution, capitalism, neoliberalism, crisis

If one may say of the revolutionary period that it runs wild, one would have to say of the present that it runs badly (Søren Kierkegaard, 1846).

He only earns his freedom and his life who takes them everyday by storm (Goethe, *Faust*)

People are either not familiar with their history, or have not yet learned that revolution is but thought carried into action (Emma Goldman, *Anarchism: What it Really Stands For*, 1910)

Søren Kierkegaard is generally seen as a religious philosopher rather than a social or political revolutionary, but it must be admitted that his diagnosis of the pitiful state of social affairs, just 2 years before the widespread revolutionary upheavals of 1848, are eerily familiar today. In the global economic and social crash that began unfolding in 2007, presaged by many protracted albeit largely unheeded warning signs, one could hardly find better evidence that, as regards contemporary capitalism, things are running very badly. Of course, this is hardly news to the majority of the world's population for whom things running badly is the daily bread (or lack thereof) of capitalism. In their very different ways the widespread (if largely unreported) revolts of sub-continental India and the movements that brought Chavez and Morales to power in Venezuela and Bolivia, the uprisings in the Parisian *banlieue* and in the streets of Greece, give heft to Kierkegaard's wry observation, but they

Antipode Vol. 41 No. S1 2009 ISSN 0066-4812, pp 50–65
doi: 10.1111/j.1467-8330.2009.00716.x

also verify the conclusions of Red Emma, as Goldman was known, that "revolution is but thought carried into action".

A Bad Time for Revolution?

In a world hypnotized by the raptures of the neoliberal moment, the very idea of revolution has, in the global North at least, not just fallen out of fashion but removed itself to the infinite horizon of never-never land—excepting of course those historical revolutions such as the American and French that underpin and are championed by bourgeois rule. Just as there are good Muslims and bad Muslims, there are good revolutions and bad revolutions. We know George Washington today as a hero of American independence over the tyranny of European feudal monarchy; we do not remember him as a terrorist bent on tearing down the prevailing social order. With the exception of those revolts that established capitalist societies, revolution is simply erased from the memory banks of future social possibility. The various ideologies of the period marched in not-so-surprising lockstep with such denial. Margaret Thatcher's much reviled yet brilliantly proscriptive assessment that there is no alternative (to free market capitalism) may have become the mantra of the political right, but it also became the unspoken defeatism of much of the left who, while we fought it, had no effective response to the dissolution of social choice into market necessity. Her follow-up claim that there is no such thing as society, only individuals, seemed to seal the impossibility of any social action outside the rubric of free market capitalism—everyone to their own lifeboat in neoliberal seas. Meanwhile, Frances Fukuyama's 1989 assessment that the end of history is nigh, although now largely renounced, not least by Fukuyama himself, equally set the ideological mood for the last decades of the twentieth century: if indeed we are at the end of history—capitalism über alles—what in the world could revolution mean? The very possibility of revolution was rendered ideologically absurd. Even to retain the possibility of revolutionary change was widely perceived as a hopelessly irrelevant utopianism.

In retrospect we will probably find the violence to the political imagination wrought in the last three decades quite exceptional if not unfathomable. The visceral fury of neoliberalism, from the torture of bodies to the torture of continents, obviously undergirds this assault on political imagination. The tragedy is less the political onslaught by the right than the political non-response of the left. Thus Donna Haraway, precisely because she is such an imaginative, creative, original and self-reflexive thinker, once voiced our predicament directly, drawing a collective gasp from a 300-person audience: "I think the most difficult problem that I face, if I own up to it", she said, "is I have almost lost the imagination of what a world that isn't capitalist could look like. And that scares me" (Harvey and Haraway 1995:519). To put it this way is a testament to Haraway's brilliance and in no way a critique; it is an indictment of us all. And since then, things have only become worse. We have, almost all of us, largely lost the political imagination of a different future, at best holding on to the empty shell of revolutionary possibility, and this very much expresses the conceptual and political violence of the last few decades. But it is not historically unique. Thus from 160 years ago, Kierkegaard follows his pithy remark on revolutionary times with a stinging rebuke that might well have been written today:

> Indications are, indeed, the only achievements of the age; and its skill and inventiveness in constructing fascinating illusions, its bursts of enthusiasm, using a deceitful escape from some projected change of form, must be rated as high in the scale of cleverness and of the negative use of the strength of the passionate, creative energy of the revolution in the corresponding scale of energy. But the present generation, wearied by its chimerical efforts, relapses into complete indolence. Its condition is that of a man who has only fallen asleep towards morning: first of all come great dreams, then a feeling of laziness, and finally a witty or clever excuse for remaining in bed (Kierkegaard 1962 [1846]:33–34).

Reading Kierkegaard today serves as a powerful invite to scrounge our collective political imaginations for some projected change of form.

If revolutionary change is largely perceived as utopian today, this is a judgment that emanates from the left as much as the right. Postmodernism, in retrospect, posed left but was in many ways a child of neoliberalism. But in a more serious vein, the indictment of left utopianism gets a much more sustained life in the power of the contemporary poststructuralist sensibility. Emanating primarily from Europe, this sensibility has grown to dominance on the left alongside and not entirely disconnected from the rise of neoliberalism. With clear echoes from the 1960s, the central political implication of this admittedly variegated new left sentiment is that aspirations for revolutionary change are outmoded, patent failures, and unrealistic in the present age, and with its emphasis on discourse (rather than, for example, ideology) the implication of much post-structuralist work would seem to be that one changes the world first and foremost by changing how we think and talk about it. This goes along with a greater or lesser rejection of political parties as vehicles for change and a rejection too of the state as a target for political action (cf Holloway 2005). In the case of Antonio Negri and Michael Hardt's *Empire* (2001), and subsequent work, this is quite explicit: the multitude is already always in power, the state slips from focus, and the only political task that remains is for the multitude to realize the power it already possesses. In the meantime, while the axe of anti-utopianism is so often aimed at the neck of the left—even from within the left—it is important to note that the most blatantly utopian project of the last 30 years is, quite obviously, neoliberalism and its progeny, globalization. The initial promise of a flat playing field (ie global equality of capitalist opportunity) has quite predictably evaporated into a world of steeper social and economic gradients than anything witnessed since the Great Depression: for every new entrepreneur from Bangalore, Silicon Valley or Shanghai, there is deeper poverty in the slums of Lagos, immigrant communities of Los Angeles, or hovels of Kolkata. As lamentable, certain left academic streams, whether influenced by poststructuralism or by a more nihilist utopianism, have followed the same broad road in search of flat (or blank) ontologies.

There are exceptions. In their various ways, the anti-globalization left at the turn of the century and the anarchist groupings which have a longer history and still work in opposition to neoliberalism, globalization and capitalism have all tended to have a far more powerful sense of a different social future. Both before and after Seattle (1999), on all continents, the hopefulness and indeed the successes of these movements, even as they were being repressed, were crucial in announcing the bankruptcy of neoliberalism. They took on the centers of global power in a way that few others did. Whether the various strands that have developed out of this now-fragmented global opposition grow into a revolutionary movement remains to be seen, but at present its ethos is not especially revolutionary, even as it strives for fundamental social change. For all of the organization that is involved, sufficiently so to draw extraordinary police infiltration and repression around the world, and recognizing the extraordinary diversity of these networks, its primary focus seems to be on events and the spectacle more than revolutionary organizing.

Given that history is scattered with revolutions of every stripe, how could this broader loss of political imagination have come about? It is not simply a question of ideological but also practical political change. Several events have been crucial. First, the implosion of the so-called socialist world is often seen as the fulcrum of the post-socialist transformation. The capitalist turn in China after 1978 and the implosion of the Soviet Union and Eastern bloc after 1989 are obvious markers, and it has to be said that globalization as we know it and the wars in Iraq (at the very least) could not have occurred without the integration of the Chinese economy and the dismantling of the USSR. And yet it also has to be said that the USSR had become its own political disaster by the 1930s and had largely denounced any revolutionary intent that was not explicitly supportive of Moscow—socialism in one country. Second and just as important, the widespread defeat of anticolonial movements and national liberation revolts from the 1960s onward fueled the sense that revolution was futile. Some revolutions were overthrown from outside, others imploded, still others were coopted, while others yet devolved into internal chaos. Often some amalgam of all these forces was at work. The Nicaraguan revolution of 1979, for example, was viciously undermined by CIA-sponsored contras but this should not disguise internal problems; the Iranian revolution of the same year began among oil workers as an ouster of the US-backed Shah but was co-opted by Muslim clerics; attempts at postcolonial reconstruction in Central Africa, from Rwanda to Chad, not to mention parts of India, have devolved into genocidal bloodshed that still owes significantly but by no means wholly to the arbitrary and malicious colonial carving up of the postcolonial landscape. Frantz Fanon was extraordinarily perspicacious in this respect. Even in the belly of the beast, revolutionary Black Power was watered down into a pro-capitalist subsumption of politics into the halls of Washington DC (Johnson 2007).

Third, the stage for the ideological victories that vanquished revolution from the tableau of the possible was set in significant part by the defeat of the revolts of the 1960s. These were nothing if not transnational from Paris to Mexico City, Tokyo to Prague and quite apart from the indictment of capitalism they broadly represented a rejection of any kind of Stalinist politics which was seen as corrupt, violent, and a sign of the failure of utopianism. But they were also eclectic: student revolts here, workers revolts there; feminist and environmental struggles alongside anti-racist and civil rights revolts; the anti-Vietnam War movement and much more, all shot through to a greater or lesser extent with hippie libertarianism. The proto-revolution of 1968 eventually imploded not just under the weight of state repression, which spanned from the state murder of students in Mexico City to the assassination of Black Panthers in the USA, but it also collapsed into a self-made vacuum of inadequate organization and, yes, a certain utopianism of its own.

Neoliberalism is badly wounded today, dominant but dead we might say (Smith 2008), but whether it is fatally wounded or not remains to be seen. Naomi Klein's *Shock Doctrine* (2007), although explicitly not a revolutionary book, probably provides the most damning indictment. Poststructuralism, as any kind of oblique ideological alternative, is also ailing, faltering under the weight of its own utopian anti-utopianism. Although many of its progenitors deserve better, this wide-knit intellectual tradition has, especially in the English-speaking world, engendered the implicit assumption that to change the world it is necessary first and foremost to change the discourse. In the face of global social- and political-economic crisis, this presumption seems increasingly lame. It is a very particular moment. An old Soviet-era joke has it that the history of the future is fixed; it is the history of the past that keeps changing. We could make the same observation today about the history of neoliberalism, even (or perhaps especially) as its ideological power fades. Whereas 10 years ago, the future seemed fixed and change impossible, the global economic meltdown and recession have wrecked this neoliberal certainty, and the social and political future suddenly looks radically open.

A Good Time for Revolution

The global economic crisis has been blamed on many things, but as the meltdown deepened in late 2008 and incredulity passed into blanket denial and confusion among the captains of industry and finance it became popular to put the blame on a certain psychological collapse by business (Sen 2009:29). The market, by such an account, would be a bit like an economic ouija board whose power is entirely dependent on the faith of participants. So far, no one has actually believed this explanation sufficiently to propose that in order to solve the world's global economic crisis, such psychological collapse should be addressed by having the world's bankers all submit to group psychological therapy.

The contemporary atrophy of neoliberalism is due to at least five causes.[1] First, the 1997–1999 Asian economic crisis exposed the failure of neoliberalism on its own economic terms, convincing several high-profile adherents from Jeffrey Sachs to Joseph Stiglitz to launch withering critiques and mea culpas. Second, trenchant political opposition, especially in Latin America, challenged the economic, social and political ideas and quite brutal practices that were foisted on that continent. This began famously with the US-supported 1973 coup (11 September) overthrowing democratically elected Salvador Allende and the subsequent involvement of the Chicago Boys (Chicago economists including most prominently Milton Friedman) with Pinochet's murderous and fascist regime. This culminated most visibly in the election of leftist regimes from Venezuela to Brazil to Bolivia but also in the building of social movements across the continent. Third, the anti-globalization movement of the late 1990s and early 2000s from Vancouver to Genoa, Seattle to Cancun also exposed the brutality and hypocrisy of neoliberalism; while it soon fragmented, that movement deserves considerable credit for translating the discontented indictment of neoliberalism into an open global challenge. Fourth, the Iraq War led by the USA and the UK, which only served to reveal the geoeconomic imperialism behind the so-called war on terror, was a drastic diplomatic mistake even in the Bush administration's own terms, not to mention the brutal incompetence with which it was prosecuted. By the first years of the twenty-first century, then, an already stagnating neoliberalism was, at best, filling in the social and geographical interstices of a project that had already stalled. The economic collapse that gathered after 2007 with the US subprime crisis, and the consequent global economic meltdown, was only the final and fifth nail in the neoliberal coffin. Although an easing of the stock market decline in mid 2009 encouraged some economists and politicians to predict an attenuation of the crisis, others looking more globally at the drop in industrial production and global trade detect an even steeper decline than in the Great Depression beginning in 1929 (Eichengreen and O'Roorke 2009). As ever, of course, the depth and extent of economic decline is highly uneven across the globe, and its future course is unpredictable.

Neoliberalism may be dead yet still dominant, but its self-immolation opens up real political possibilities. One of the greatest violences of the neoliberal era was the closure of the political imagination. Even on the left, perhaps especially so, the sense became pervasive that there was no alternative to capitalism. Revolutionary possibility was generally confused with utopianism, the history of revolutions notwithstanding, and revolution was collapsed into a caricature of inevitable failure. The history of the Russian revolution in particular was widely reduced to a story of utopian affront to human nature, a Sisyphian challenge to the inevitability of human greed that undergirds capitalism. For many too, revolution became equated with a conspiracy of some vanguard party. This is not the place for a detailed evaluation of Lenin's notion of the vanguard party, nor for a recount of the history of the Russian revolution. Suffice it to say that even a cursory history would show that the 1917 revolution was not invented by the Bolshevik Party. Rather, in the summer of 1917 Lenin was squeamish about the immediate prospects of revolution, calculating that the Russian working class simply did not have the power or ability to carry it out. Only 3 months before the uprising happened, when it was clear that the wider proletariat gave not a whit for Lenin's conservative judgement, did the Bolsheviks realize that the fury of the working class and peasantry was so complete and so visceral that they had no choice but to catch up. Lenin's *State and Revolution*, published in August 1917, marked the Bolshevik transition to an engaged revolutionary posture.

By 2009 the global economic crash and its destruction of business as usual put the question of revolution back on the agenda for many. Wouldn't the economic crisis potentially lead to revolt in cities around the world? Even before the crisis, the Chinese government conceded that in 2005 there were an extraordinary 74,000 violent uprisings and demonstrations in that year alone, presumably making China not only the epicenter of capitalist expansion on the planet but also of class struggle. While the left may be tentative about recovering the prospect of political revolt in response to the social deprivations of economic crisis, the right has no such reticence. The fear of revolt is actually a deep-seated dread for the world's ruling classes. In a Canadian interview in 2009, Niall Ferguson, the Harvard apologist for the British Empire, predicted that before the crisis was resolved, "There will be blood". Before it is all finished, he continued: "It will cause civil wars to break out, and it will topple governments . . . and bring in governments that are extreme . . . " (quoted in Scoffield 2009). In fact, the governments of Latvia and Iceland were early casualties of the economic crisis with others faltering. Civil unrest, domestic and otherwise, is also on the minds of the CIA and Britain's MI5 and on the minds too of the militaries of both countries. Accordingly, the CIA in 2009 added the global economic crisis to its list of top security threats.

The political right, this would suggest, understands that the future has become radically open, and not necessarily in an auspicious way for them. The left needs to catch up with this same recognition and grasp the opportunity. Since the 1970s, the left in much of Europe and North America has not only been in retreat but has broadly bemoaned its own lack of power, focusing instead on the viciousness of top-down state and corporate might, treating workers and peasants all too often as little more than victims. As anger at the economic crisis builds, as old movements remake themselves, and as new movements emerge around (and often combining) issues as diverse as immigrant rights and police brutality, environmental destruction and labour organizing, decimated social services and indigenous rights, a political reconstruction of the left is urgent.

In the wake of the anti-globalization movement and the subsequent rise of various anarchist political tendencies, and building on critiques of the old left, it is often argued that a politics appropriate for the present era should not focus on the state. A poststructuralist sensibility vaunting the interstitial power of daily social interaction displaces the state as a crucial focus of political revolt. The conquest of state power for many is accordingly a misguided strategy (cf Holloway 2005) and the focus instead should be on creating political disruptions that can translate into social openings and spontaneous political change, thereby expressing a power that already exudes from the populace (Hardt and Negri 2001, 2004). The problem with this approach seems to be twofold. In the first place, it misconceives the goal of revolution as simply taking power over the state, the replacement of one regime with another. Only a willful misreading of marxist political theory could make such an elementary mistake. It not only disavows a whole history of revolutionary thought but it also conveniently erases Engels and Lenin's argument about the withering away of the state. This precisely at a time when neoliberals from Wall Street to the City of London were trumpeting their own withering away of the state. Such an argument hides the political target, whether that target be the state, corporate class power, or other sources of power, and it finds an uncomfortable parallel in the anti-state doctrines of neoliberalism. Second, the invocation of political spontaneity as a means to a different future conjours up its own utopianism. A revolution of the discursive self is necessary, whether connected to political movements or not, but it is not a sufficient means to revolutionary social change. "Change yourself and the world will change with you" was a hopeful

1960s slogan which had its genuine uses, but the need for political organization is not thereby dissolved. It takes a considerable idealism, however, to trust the discursive self to dissolve the power of the state—military, ideological, economic, political—as an impediment to social change.

At the same time, it is equally necessary to eschew any cheap economism. An all too common mistake on the left has assumed that economic hardship automatically brings political uprising in its trail: the more people are squeezed economically the more they will revolt. In reality, the question of political revolt is much more complicated. For sure, people do not tend to revolt when times run well, and political organization is certainly vital for bringing revolts to fruition. But economic hardship in no way guarantees revolt, and it can in fact bring about its opposite as happened in the wreckage of Weimar Germany leading ultimately to fascism. Political organization is necessary but in and of itself it is not the sufficient condition for successful revolt. People generally revolt for two reasons: they revolt if they are so desperate that they feel they have nothing to lose; or they revolt if they think they can win.

"Revolutions . . . come like a thief in the night." So wrote Trinidadian revolutionary C L R James in his book, *Beyond a Boundary*, which reads the history of imperialism through an autobiography of his cricket life (James 1993:239). The debates between Lenin and Luxemburg in the lead-up to the Russian and eventually German revolution focused on exactly this tension between organization and spontaneity. Unfortunately codified in the Marxist tradition, these debates need to be put in historical and geographical context as arguments about the immediate prospects and means for revolution from Munich to St Petersburg, from 1917 to 1919. Many years later, Henri Lefebvre makes a complementary point which speaks to the present and simultaneously rehabilitates a sense of utopian possibility. For Lefebvre (2003) utopian thinking steps back from the real without losing sight of it. Given the violence done under neoliberalism to our sense of political imagination and possibility, although this observation was first made in 1970 it seems a powerful and appropriate corrective today. We could do a lot worse than to return to the Russian revolution and reassess the forgotten history of social, cultural, political and economic innovation and imagination that took hold, even amidst the worst of political and wartime conditions from architecture to film, poetry to painting. As Lefebvre once observed: "Between 1920 and 1930, Russia experienced a tremendous burst of creative activity. Quite amazingly, Russian society, turned upside down through revolution, managed to produce superstructures (out of the depths) of astonishing novelty" (Lefebvre 2003:183–184).

And yet our poststructuralist sensibility today is still wary about revolution. In the English-speaking world especially, poststructuralism has come to be treated as an antidote to Marx and Marxism. It is not too much of an exaggeration to say that Foucault in particular has been raised to the status of the anti-Marx. If anyone can be posited as a progressive political alternative to revolution it is surely the author of *The Order of Things*. But this represents a gross disservice not only to Marx but to Foucault whose political sensibility was nowhere so confined. Indeed, Foucault revealed himself on at least one occasion as a proponent of revolution. Writing about the 1979 Iranian revolution, in a piece entitled *Useless to Revolt?* Foucault (2000) was quite explicit about the ineluctability of revolution. "Revolts belong to history", he observed, "but in a certain way they escape from it. The impulse by which a single individual, a group, a minority, or an entire people says, 'I will no longer obey', and throws the risk of their life in the face of an authority they consider unjust seems to me to be something irreducible.... People do revolt; that is a fact, and that is how subjectivity (not that of great men, but that of anyone) is brought into history, breathing life into it." Revolution here is a quite practical affair. As Lefebvre (2003:19) put it earlier, "Revolutionary events generally take place in the street."

Of New Deals and Stealth Neoliberalism

Social change and political transformation are not optional but a fact, and the status quo, as it used to be said, is not much to quo about. The only question is the form that social and political transformation will take. Sometimes it can be gradual, sometimes cataclysmic, often somewhere in between, but it is always the subject of power struggles, explicit or muted. The global economic meltdown after 2007 has already brought political and economic changes that would have seemed impossible only months earlier. Heavily bound up in financial capital, the Icelandic economy crashed virtually overnight; banks in Britain and the US have been nationalized; Citicorp alone had by early 2009 received $60 billion of taxpayers' money with another $340 billion of loan guarantee on the table; meanwhile the Spanish bank Santander, broadly immune from the global banking crisis, is buying up smaller banks around the world including the USA; two of the three largest North American auto companies have gone bankrupt, with the union and the US and Canadian governments owning the majority of the restructured companies. In the case of General Motors, in the first phase of reconstruction, only 10% of the reconstructed company remained in private hands. Through various bailouts and stimulus plans, the US government had by April 2009 committed an estimated $12.7 trillion in guarantees, a figure that almost matches that country's annual gross domestic product (*New York Review of Books* 2009). In the UK, it is estimated that government spending now accounts for almost 50% of national income, with the national debt approaching £1000 billion (Giles and Briscoe 2009). Change can and does happen quickly: the question is, in whose interests?

Various national governments have introduced economic stimulus plans very much after the model of the Keynesian New Deal of the 1930s. A Keynes revival is in full swing. The US plan has been to date the largest; the plans in Europe and European economies are generally smaller; while the Chinese plan emphasizes infrastructure development. The call for a New New Deal has also been picked up by many on the left as a realistic response to the global crisis. There is clearly a sense that capitalism has changed fundamentally, indeed in early 2009 French President Nicolas Sarkozy hosted a high-powered symposium entitled "New World, New Capitalism". Nobel prize winning economist Amartya Sen (2009:27) argues that the most forceful question today concerns the nature of capitalism and whether it can be changed. Sen reviews Keynes' arguments from the 1930s and his advocacy of state economic stimulus policies, yet finds the British economist of limited use. He clarifies a broad historical misconception by reminding us that Keynes was not especially concerned with such social issues as inequality, welfare and social services. (On the latter issue he makes the point that even Otto von Bismarck had more to say on social services than Keynes; Sen 2009:29; see also Cowen 2008.) Looking to the present, Sen argues that in the US context, the single most effective stimulus might involve state health care spending, and he proposes the models of China and the southern Indian state of Kerala as working models. In the end, however, Sen rejects the call for a new capitalism, going so far as to say that capitalism may no longer be a useful term.

Others on the left have not relinquished the language of capitalism, and for good reason, yet have also embraced, however tentatively, the notion of a New New Deal (cf Harvey 2003:210). But doesn't the aspiration for a New New Deal seem quite unambitious and in fact get the cart before the political horse? This becomes clear from a glance back at the original New Deal. In the first place, the US New Deal of the 1930s, with Keynesian variants around the world, was not always a great deal for everyone. To take just the example of housing, the creation of the Federal Housing Authority mortgage insurance program was supposedly intended to open up home ownership to a larger section of the lower middle and working classes. In fact, over more than three decades, it operated as a means to foster white suburbanization; out of several hundred thousand successful applications for mortgage insurance a small minority were in cities and an even more minuscule number went to African American families (Checkoway 1980). The folly of the New New Deal also becomes clear from the fate of the Obama administration's early efforts in 2009.

Second it is important to recall that the New Deal was not a product of Franklin Roosevelt's supposed altruism, regardless of the liberal accounts that tilt the received histories in that direction. On the contrary, the patrician Roosevelt knew well that a revolt was brewing as a result of the Depression. Unemployment was rocketing, labour strikes were on the rise, the Communist Party was building, many socialists were also on the streets, Hoovervilles (shanty settlements housing the homeless) were mushrooming in cities around the country. The New Deal represented first and foremost a response to the political pressure thrown up by the Depression and the threat of open revolt. It is also important to remember that the original New Deal, whatever its putative social benefit, came with a widespread and often vicious corporate and state repression throughout the 1930s, aimed especially at strikes by unionized workers.

It is in this sense that the call today for a New New Deal gets the Democratic Party policy horse before the organizing cart. The response to global economic crisis has played out quite differently in different countries, but the US response, given the economic, military and cultural predominance of the country, deserves special attention. As the capitalist bailout and stimulus plans of the Obama administration's first year make clear, without political pressure, indeed without the threat of revolt, any supposed effort at a New New Deal is likely to accomplish even less than the original New Deal achieved in the 1930s, namely to buttress existing class and social relations. The New Deal was an instrument of class struggle insofar as it quite deliberately contained the growing revolt in the name of keeping a capitalist hegemony alive. With the Obama strategy, the optimistic mobilization that swept him to power failed to become a movement, at least in the first year of his administration, and as a result the kinds of policies emitting from his administration emphasized bailing out banks, bankers and car executives, often providing failed CEOs with multi-million dollar bonuses and severance packages, while workers suffered concessions and the victims of subprime mortgage corruption were generally faced with foreclosure, propelled back into poverty. In the meantime, despite the multi-trillion stimulus and bailout subsidies to corporations, capital effectively went on strike, refusing to provide capital to homeowners or small businesses. Much as the 1990s leadership by nominally socialist leaders such as Tony Blair or Lula or Schroeder amounted to a stealth neoliberalism, especially compared with the pugilism of George W. Bush, Obama's response to the global economic crisis represents class struggle by stealth. In truth, given the lack of opposition and revolt, in the USA and Europe if demonstrably not in China, very little stealth was required.

While we might disagree with Amartya Sen's conclusion to jettison the language of capitalism, his thoughtful piece on the future of capitalism makes some vital arguments. In particular, he suggests that the economic crisis demands a new understanding of older ideas

(Sen 2009:30). In particular, he has Adam Smith in mind, and he is undoubtedly correct. A latter-day hero of neoliberalism, Adam Smith's work is powerful precisely because it provides an account of the social economy, the economy before economics was divided out ideologically from its social integument. Much as she lionized Adam Smith, Margaret Thatcher denied him, along with a denial of society. Smith's work is preternaturally social even as it vaults the economic. Sen is right about the salience of Smith, a point too little conceded on the left by many of us who have stopped reading formative work from the eighteenth century. Still Smith was not so much a theorist of capitalist crises as he was an analyst of emerging national economies. Karl Marx, his successor a century later, by contrast, was very much a theorist of the systemic nature of economic crises in capitalist societies, the endemic disequilibrium of capitalism, and he is another whose older ideas deserve a new understanding.

This is especially important today because so much has been made of the fact that by the mid 2000s as much as 41% of officially declared US corporate profits emanated from finance capital (*New York Review of Books* 2009:76). Profit in other words was being generated as interest on investments, paper and electronic capital passed around, rather than on any profitability from the social production of value. Marx's analysis of capitalism, strewn not just throughout the volumes of *Capital* but also elsewhere, both explains and predicts such a crisis, demonstrating that such events are simultaneously cyclical and endemic to capitalism. They come from a mix of three interrelated causes: first, an underconsumption crisis in which consumption lags; second, an overaccumulation crisis in which too much commodity is produced for a market that cannot consume it; third, a longer term crisis in the profit rate which sends capital out of the productive sector into real estate and eventually finance. When the conditions are right, it is easier, cheaper and faster to make money by lending it overnight or for a week or for a year with a guaranteed rate of interest than it is to build streets, offices and factories. For Marx this is a cyclical pattern: as the expansion of the productive economy becomes increasingly competitive and capital moves elsewhere, the crisis accumulates and the financial sector becomes flooded with capital (hence the focus during this crisis on the role of securities, derivatives, and debt/security instruments). With less and less capital devoted to the production of social value, and more and more capital devoted to the legalized gambling of the financial system, the discrepancy between the paper value of capital and its social value in terms of actual work is increasingly wide. At some point, the claims that paper capital makes to produce social value—claims in the form of stocks, bank accounts, hedge funds, securities, bonds, derivatives, debit-credit swaps, currency and so forth—have to be rationalized with the actual social value produced; paper claims to value and real value have to be brought back into commensurability, generally requiring a massive devaluation of paper capital. A crisis of capitalism is the quite predictable outcome.

So, if we understand that the capitalist mode of production per se not society, or politics, or economics, not to mention "psychology" is the problem, how do we respond? Why is capitalism such a problem? The problem is that the systemic disequilibrium of capitalism is rooted in that mode of production's DNA. There are three central components to this. First, and crucially, there are the *social relations of production between classes* where some own the means of production and others have nothing to sell but their labour power. Certainly there are many middle classes, not least many academics and other professionals, but the defining relationship in capitalist societies pits capitalists against workers. There is no rule that says societies have to be organized this way, however. Second, we have *private property*, a comparatively new historical invention, which takes the things made and possessed and occupied in common and donates them to individuals. Third, the social relations between owners of the means of production are governed not by collective or cooperative agreements for productive social ends but by *economic competition*, abetted by the state. The amalgam of these three foundational pillars of capitalism—class relations, private property and competition—creates a mode of social production in which capital accumulation, economic growth with no sense of the social or environmental cost, and outright individual greed are rendered the society's highest social values.

How did this come about? Actually, the historical victory of capitalism came about through multiple revolutions. The American and the French in the eighteenth century are the obvious candidates, opening both countries up to an unfettered capitalism that supersedes an exhausted, corrupt and unjust feudalism. The British revolutionary wars a century earlier had a similar if less immediately definitive effect. Various other European revolutions and postcolonial struggles from nineteenth century Latin America (1810s) and Europe (1848) to twentieth century Asia and Africa, and indeed 1990s Eastern Europe whatever the cross-border exploitations and oppressions involved, have equally contributed to the making of global capitalism.

Even as the proletarianization of academic labour expands from the ranks of graduate students to adjuncts to contract workers, most tenured or senior First World academics lead relatively comfortable lives, part of the middle classes and generally out of the direct firing line between exploited workers and the capitalist classes, between capital accumulation and environmental destruction. This in no way legitimizes a self-interested analytical laziness that refuses to acknowledge the severity of crises and the severity of its effects on so many people. The future is indeed radically open in a way unprecedented just months ago, and it would be intellectually shiftless not to anticipate social upheaval of some sort. But it must be recognized too that any move toward a New New Deal, either nationally or globally, is likely to come, as with its 1930s predecessor, with a heavy dose of repression, this time deploying the entire repressive architecture put in place after September 11, 2001. Personally, as academics, especially in wealthier countries but also in wealthier classes, many of us may avoid the resulting clampdown, but insofar as the larger society will be heaved up, there is little global intellectual or political security in that judgment.

It may not be premature to suggest that a capitalist way of organizing social life, like feudalism before it, has become exhausted, corrupt and unjust and therefore expendable. Social theorist Slavoj Žižek early sensed the ideological violence to our political imagination wrought by neoliberalism. With an eye on the prospect of planetary environmental destruction or nuclear meltdown, Žižek observes that "it seems easier to imagine the end of the world than a far more modest change in the mode of production"—the overthrow of capitalism (1994:1). Revolution may, as James (1993) suggests, come like a thief in the night, but if there is going to be a heist on capitalism, the thief needs to come with a few tools. Some tools are intellectual ideas; others are tools of the imagination about other possible worlds; still others are our human bodies, but most importantly they are social and political organization for a more humane future. Or as Goethe put it, "one earns one's freedom and life when one takes them everyday by storm".

Acknowledgements

Gracious thanks to Deborah Cowen who as ever contributed sharp and challenging ideas to this piece, introduced me to the Kierkegaard text, but bears no responsibility for the result.

Endnote

[1] This paragraph is adapted from Smith (2009).

References

Checkoway B (1980) Large builders, federal housing programs and postwar suburbanization. *International Journal of Urban and regional Research* 4:21–44

Cowen D (2008) *Military Workfare: The Soldier and Social Citizenship in Canada.* Toronto: University of Toronto Press

Eichengreen B and K H O'Rourke (2009) A tale of two depressions. http://www.voxeu. org/index.php?q=node/3421&ref=patrick.net Accessed 11 June 2009

Foucault M (2000) Useless to revolt? In J D Faubion (ed) *Essential Works of Foucault 1954–1984, Volume 3: Power* (pp 449–453). New York: New Press

Giles C and S Briscoe (2009) The state of Britain. *Financial Times* 22 June

Hardt M and Negri A (2001) *Empire.* Cambridge MA: Harvard University Press

Hardt M and Negri A (2004) *Multitude.* London: Penguin

Harvey D (2003) *The New Imperialism.* Oxford: Oxford University Press

Harvey D and Haraway D (1995) Nature, politics, and possibilities: A debate and discussion with David Harvey and Donna Haraway. *Environment and Planning D: Society and Space* 13:507–527

Holloway J (2005) *Change the World Without Taking Power*. London: Pluto

James C L R (1993) *Beyond a Boundary*. Durham NC: Duke University Press

Johnson C (2007) *Revolutionaries to Race Leaders*. Minneapolis: University of Minnesota Press

Kierkegaard (1962 [1846]) *The Present Age*. New York: Harper and Row

Klein N (2007) *Shock Doctrine*. London: Penguin.

Lenin (1935 [1917]) *State and Revolution*. Moscow: Progress

New York Review of Books (2009) The crisis and how to deal with it. 11 June

Scoffield H (2009) There will be blood. *The Globe and Mail* 10 April: A1

Sen A (2009) Capitalism beyond the crisis. *New York Review of Books* 26 March

Smith N (2008) Neoliberalism is dead, dominant, defeatable—then what? *Human Geography* 1(2):1–3

Smith N (ed) (2009) *After Neoliberalism. Cites under Systemic Chaos*. Barcelona: MACBA

Žižek S (ed) (1994) *Mapping Ideology*. London: Verso

To Make Live or Let Die? Rural Dispossession and the Protection of Surplus Populations

Tania Murray Li

Department of Anthropology, University of Toronto, Canada;
tania.li@utoronto.ca

Abstract: A biopolitics of the population, when it succeeds in securing life and wellbeing, is surely worth having. It has become urgent in rural Asia, where a new round of enclosures has dispossessed large numbers of people from access to land as a way to sustain their own lives, and neoliberal policies have curtailed programs that once helped to sustain rural populations. At the same time, new jobs in manufacturing have not emerged to absorb this population. They are thus "surplus" to the needs of capital, and not plausibly described as a labour reserve. Who, then, would act to keep these people alive, and why would they act? I examine this question by contrasting a conjuncture in India, where a make live program has been assembled under the rubric of the "right to food", and Indonesia, where the massacre of the organized left in 1965 has left dispossessed populations radically exposed.

Keywords: Asia, labour, land, social protection, biopolitics, governmentality

My essay concerns the politics of making live, or letting die, and the struggles that shape the way the equation is resolved for different segments of the global population. While Foucault highlighted the general historical conditions for the emergence of biopolitics, that is, an orientation to intervene in populations to enhance their health and wellbeing, he had little to say about when or how this orientation would be activated.[1] Nor did he say much about the politics of let die scenarios: why governing authorities would elect not to intervene when they could, or select one subset of the population for life enhancement while abandoning another.

Letting die, I want to stress, is not a counterfactual. Abysmal life expectancy, below 55 in much of sub-Saharan Africa and in parts of Asia is sad testament to the fact that letting die is here (World Bank 2006b:292, 300). Discrepancies within one city are another indicator: African–Americans on the south side of Chicago are "let die" at around 60 years, while the mostly white, middle-class residents on the city's northwest side can expect to live until the age of 77.[2] Letting die is also signalled by the presence of a billion people in the global South who must try to survive on less than a dollar a day, a sum that leaves them chronically short of food, shelter and health care. Letting die is not an

Antipode Vol. 41 No. S1 2009 ISSN 0066-4812, pp 66–93
doi: 10.1111/j.1467-8330.2009.00717.x

apocalypse. It is not a media event, like a massacre, an earthquake, or a famine that kills large numbers in a compressed period of time. Nor is it a Malthusian problem of inadequate global food supply. It is a stealthy violence that consigns large numbers of people to lead short and limited lives.

Both letting die, and making live, have a politics, but I reject the idea that the two are in some kind of functional equilibrium—that it is necessary to select some to die, in order for others to live. No doubt such selections are made, according to a whole range of rationales (race, virtue, diligence, citizenship, location, age, gender, efficiency, affordability; see Sider 2006) but if "the point is to change it", we cannot concede that selection is necessary. It is possible for social forces to mobilize in a wholly make live direction.

Make live possibilities are highlighted by conjunctures such as the one that emerged in the state of Kerala in India, which has a predominantly rural population and no special natural endowments, yet has achieved an average life expectancy of around 73, 10 years longer than the all-India average of 63. This effect was produced by decades of investment in public health and education, together with rates of pay for agricultural workers that are 100% higher than elsewhere in India for the same tasks.[3] The social forces that put this regime in place included a strong labour movement, and a communist party held accountable through democratic elections. The way these forces came together in Kerala is the product of a struggle with its own, unique history that cannot be replicated in modular fashion. Further, the gains in Kerala are fragile, and incompletely realized (Paraiyil 2000; Steur 2009; Tharamangalam 2006). Nevertheless, Kerala confirms that "making live" is more than a counterfactual—it too is here, and not just in the welfare states of the global North.

Make live interventions become urgent when people can no longer sustain their own lives through direct access to the means of production, or access to a living wage. In large parts of rural Asia, my focus in this essay, these conditions have become widespread as a result of two sets of forces: a new round of enclosures that have dispossessed large numbers of rural people from the land; and the low absorption of their labour, which is "surplus" to the requirements of capital accumulation. For the 700 million Asians who live on less than a dollar a day, tiny incomes are ample testament to the fact that no one has a market incentive to pay the costs of keeping them alive from day to day, or from one generation to the next. Yet I am not convinced that their chronic under-reproduction is, as Araghi (2009:119) has argued, "a strategy of global capital". I see their perilous condition, rather, as a sign of their very limited relevance to capital at any scale. If the population rendered surplus to capital's requirements is to live decently, it will be because of the activation of a biopolitics that places the intrinsic value of life—rather than the value of people as workers or consumers—at its core. But what are the social forces that would activate such a politics? And why would they do so? I return to these questions later in this essay. First, however, I want to consider more fully the implications of the concept of surplus population.

Surplus Population

When I use the phrase surplus population, my intention is to provoke some hard thinking. It is, of course, offensive to suggest that some people are surplus, yet as I argued above, the truth is that large numbers are in fact abandoned. Some are kept alive in prisons, refugee camps and ghettos, but they are not being prepared for work, as they were in the workhouses of industrializing Britain (Bauman 2004). The key to their predicament is that their labour is surplus *in relation to* its utility for capital.

Marx used the term "relative surplus population" (Marx 1986:574–606), with the term "relative" serving, first, to distinguish his concept from that of Malthus, who argued that population would outstrip resources; and second, to highlight the continuous tendency of capital to concentrate labour's productive capacity into labour-displacing technologies. Among the relative surplus population, Marx further distinguished between the floating part, people who were cyclically unemployed; the latent part, namely rural people not fully integrated into capitalist production; and the stagnant part, including people who are elderly or injured, and among whom the lowest stratum "dwells in the sphere of pauperism". Pauperism, Marx argued, "is the hospital of the active labour-army and the dead weight of the industrial reserve army. Its production is included in that of the relative surplus-population, its necessity in theirs; along with the surplus-population, pauperism forms a condition of capitalist production, and of the capitalist development of wealth. It enters into the *faux frais* of capitalist production; but capital knows how to throw these, for the most part, from its own shoulders on to those of the working-class and the lower middle class" (Marx 1986:603).

Whether or not the pauperized population of the global South fulfils the same function in relation to capital as the paupers of industrializing England, described by Marx, is an urgent question. To answer it fully would require trying out his categories to see what they reveal, or what they occlude, in a range of contemporary conjunctures.[4] Minimally, we have to recognize that the spatial and temporal unevenness of capital investment, already present in Marx's time, is far more prominent today, as capital incorporates some places and peoples, and ejects or rejects others. James Ferguson (2005) captures part of this dynamic with his image of transnational investment capital "hopping" over Africa's useless people and places (*Afrique inutile*) to land in the few spots where superior profits can readily be made. There is another dynamic, however, that is potentially more lethal: one in which places (or their resources) are useful, but the people are not, so that dispossession is detached from any prospect of labour absorption. This is the dynamic that forms the core of my analysis in this essay.

Too often, hard thinking about the predicament of surplus population is avoided by the repetition of some remarkably resilient narratives about agrarian transition that assume a linear pathway, and a predictable set of connections. According to these narratives there will be—sooner or later—a transition from agriculture to industry, country to city, and peasant to entrepreneurial farmer or wage worker.

A recent example of the transition narrative is the World Bank's World Development Report (2008), *Agriculture for Development*, which organizes the nations of the global South along an axis that heads resolutely towards the city. According to the report, the principal task of governments in the "transforming countries", a category that includes most of Asia, is to manage transitions out of agriculture for rural populations whose labour is surplus to the requirements of a more efficient agricultural sector, and to supply targeted "safety nets" for a residual few who cannot make this transition, namely the old and the infirm. Jarringly, despite the report's recognition of a globalized regime of agricultural production and consumption, its framework for analyzing agrarian transition is national, as if rural dispossession and the generation of new jobs naturally occur within the same national frame, and unmarked, generic citizens have equal access to national jobs. Generalized welfare provisions to keep the dispossessed alive do not figure in the report. A full chapter on "Reducing vulnerability and chronic food insecurity", anticipated in the report outline, is not in the final version. Somehow, the report assumes hundreds of millions of deeply impoverished rural people will find their way onto the transition path.

A competing version of the agrarian transition narrative, which takes its inspiration from Marx, relates dispossession to the emergence of capitalism through three effects: a grab for land and other resources that furnish initial capital, so-called "primitive accumulation;" the production of proletarians; and the formation of a labour reserve (Glassman 2006; Harvey 2003; Moyo and Yeros 2005). In a recent re-statement of this narrative, that takes in a global scale, Farshad Araghi links "enclosure-induced displacement" to "camps of surplus labour in urban locations", and the conditioning of partially dispossessed peasantries as "a potential reserve army of migratory labour", or labour power freed "for global consumption" (2009:111–112, 134–135). Yet Araghi's narrative short circuits an important question: how much of this labour is really necessary for accumulation?

Confronting the concept of surplus population challenges the residual functionalism sometimes embedded in the concept of a labour reserve. In order to fulfil the functions of a labour reserve—that is, to depress wages, and be ready to work when needed—the population must not die. Yet accounts that stress the utility of a labour reserve for capital often fail to specify the causal mechanisms that would keep the members of this "reserve" alive, even on a minimal basis. The case for a labour reserve can be made, and the Bantustans of South Africa were a clear example: dispossession was designed to generate labour for the mines, and Bantustan land and remittances served to reproduce the reserve population (Wolpe 1980). But the Bantustans also became dumping grounds, warehouses for surplus populations whose labour would never be required. To assume a link between dispossession, and the (re)production of a labour reserve is not just too linear, it is dangerously complacent.

Several scholars have provided useful correctives to linear notions of transition that link dispossession too directly, and too quickly, to employers' need for workers. Henry Bernstein (2004:204–205) describes the failure of the generalized capitalist system to provide a living wage to the dispossessed as the central agrarian question of our times. Cautioning against apocalyptic images of disposable humanity, Michael Watts (2009:283) argues for a "nuanced and place-specific mapping" of formations of labour, and the different ways in which capital takes hold. Jason Read (2002) argues persuasively for a non-teleological or "aleatory" reading of capitalism, also present in Marx's own historical writings, which examines how capital and "free" labour connect—or fail to connect—at particular conjunctures (see also Akram-Lodhi and Kay 2009:16–17). Read points out that the movement to enclose agricultural land, which began in England in the fifteenth century, was driven by "improving" landlords, a social group quite distinct from the manufacturers who would later profit from the availability of landless people desperate for waged work. The class that required proletarians was different from the one that evicted peasants, and separated in time by several centuries. Examined retrospectively, it is true that capital and labour encountered each other. But looked at historically, a particular capitalist might struggle to find labour, and not all aspirant labourers were able to find capital.

For the dispossessed who needed to work but failed to encounter capital, the situation was dire. As Marx observed, state powers were used both to secure evictions and to discipline "vagabonds", yet these two interventions were not coordinated. Instead, legislation punishing paupers and obliging "vagabonds" to return to their places of origin seemed to assume that they could resume working under the old agrarian conditions, although these conditions no longer existed (Marx 1986:686). As I will later show, fantasies about returning surplus populations to "the village" recur repeatedly in colonial and contemporary Asia, where they play a similar role in legitimating abandonment.

In colonial Asia, as Jan Breman (1990) has explained, the potential disconnect between dispossession and rural labour absorption was both temporal and spatial. The major sites of industrial employment for unskilled, "coolie" labour were plantations and mines. These industries were situated in rural areas, where they dispossessed the in situ populations, but they seldom employed the same people they displaced. Instead, they set up elaborate systems to recruit tens of thousands of workers from afar, often across vast distances of land and sea, people whose social isolation and dependence made them easier to discipline.[5] The migrant labourers in these massive enterprises had been dispossessed "at home" through processes quite unrelated to their eventual employment. For the most part, Breman stresses, new recruits were already involved in "coolie" labour, in city or country, having been landless or near-landless for several generations. Some were dispossessed by the contingencies of illness, bad weather and failed harvests that drove them into debt in their places of origin. Some were members of minority or "tribal" group that were dispossessed by migrants who grabbed their land by force, and cast them out, or entrapped them in bondage. Some were deliberately dislodged by colonial policies, especially taxes. Just as often, however, colonial authorities had little direct role in their dispossession, and their eventual employers, thousands of miles away, had even less. Employers and officials did have control over their fate, however, since they could turn off particular recruiting streams at will, abandoning would-be migrants and their families, out of sight, and out of mind.

Contingency plays a part in these misconnections between capital and labour, and for populations rendered "surplus" at a particular place and time, misconnection can be fatal. But it is not the case that anything goes. Tim Mitchell puts the matter this way: "A term like "capitalist development" covers a series of agencies, logics, chain reactions, and contingent interactions, among which the specific circuits and relations of capital form[ed] only a part" (2002:51). In these chain reactions, one set of events establishes the conditions of possibility for another set, but whether the possibilities will be realized depends on "a series of agencies" that do not necessarily pull in the same direction.

Rural Dispossession in Asia circa 2000

There are three main vectors of rural dispossession in Asia today, none of which has any intrinsic link to the prospect of labour absorption. One is the seizure of land by the state, or state-supported corporations, a practice that is widespread in China, India, and Southeast Asia. The second is the piecemeal dispossession of small-scale farmers, unable to survive when exposed to competition from agricultural systems backed by subsidies and preferential tariffs. The third is the closing of the forest frontier for conservation. I will discuss each of these, briefly discussing China and India before focusing on Southeast Asia, where all three vectors are operating in a kind of pincer movement, dispossessing rural people to a degree that is unprecedented in this region.

Land seizures have been widespread in China since the passing of a new land regulation in 1987. The result, according to Kathy Le Mons Walker (2008), has been an "'enclosure movement' of unprecedented proportion worldwide, resulting in the dispossession—and in many cases impoverishment—of tens of millions of peasant households." Official government statistics report that 40 million rural households had lost their land by 2005, while other experts find the number closer to 70 million, or about 315 million people (2008:472). Rural township officials are centrally involved in these seizures, backed by business allies and the private, mafia-style criminal organizations they employ as enforcers. The dispossessed do not go quietly. Mass protests are widespread, and violent on both sides: according to a government report, protestors attacked or killed 8200 township and country officials in 1993 alone (Walker 2008:469). A great many peasants—up to 150 million by 2003—were absorbed as temporary labour migrants in the booming manufacturing sector, where employers prefer this highly exploitable labour force over workers with legal "urban" status, who are entitled to welfare benefits. In Shenzen, for example, with a defacto population of eight million people, "unofficial" rural migrants comprise a staggering seven million (Chan 2009:208). However, large numbers of dispossessed peasants have not found work. They call themselves "a new 'class' of 'three nothings'—no land, no work, no social security" (Walker 2008:476). Chinese farmers have also been devastated by competition from cheap imported cotton, soybeans and sugarcane, as the government removed tariffs to increase global market access for Chinese manufactures (Walker 2008:465–466). Despite these dire conditions, 20 million migrant workers were returned "home" to the countryside in the 2008–2009 recession (Chan 2009), as if there was land and a thriving agriculture ready to reabsorb them.

In India, rural landlessness has been entrenched for several centuries, but a new round of dispossession is currently under way, as investors eye land for conversion into "special economic zones", or simply hold it for speculation (*Inter Press Service News Agency* 2009). Among small-scale farmers, dispossession by debt has also intensified, resulting in an epidemic of farmer suicides. Farmers who had been encouraged to buy productivity-increasing inputs on credit faced ruin when state subsidies were abruptly removed. As a result of the rollback of state support for farmers, and a 58% rise in the price of grain, the percentage of rural people consuming less than 2400 calories per day increased from 75% in 1994, to 87% in 2004 (Davis 2006:171; Patnaik 2008). As I noted earlier, the World Bank recommends that farmers unable to succeed in high-value agriculture should exit. It suggests, further, that "in India, the low level and quality of education of most rural workers is mainly responsible for their inability to find jobs in the booming services sector" (World Bank 2008:36), as if everyone with a suitable education could find work in a call centre. In reality, much of the impressive growth in India over the past decade has been virtually jobless, as high-productivity manufacturing and service work absorb very few workers.[6] Partha Chatterjee puts the point bluntly: "large sections of peasants who are today the victims of the primitive accumulation of capital are completely unlikely to be absorbed into the new capitalist sectors of growth" (2008:55). Irrelevant to capital, only make live provisions could save them—if such provisions were actually made.[7]

Landlessness in Southeast Asia has historically been high in the fertile lowland deltas and valleys, but overall, it has been less severe than in China or India as a result of a relatively sparse population, and a relatively open forest frontier (Boomgaard 2006:117; Elson 1997; Fisher 1964:5 n7). Today, however, dispossession is progressing rapidly in Southeast Asia, through all three vectors I named earlier—large-scale enclosures for agricultural expansion and conservation, and the piecemeal dispossession of farmers through debt.

The biggest enclosure for agricultural expansion has occurred in Malaysia and Indonesia, where oil palm has expanded rapidly from 3 million ha in 1990 to 9 million in 2003, with much more planned, stimulated by high prices and anticipated demand for biofuels. About 60% of the oil palm area is under direct management by private corporations or parastatals, with the balance managed by smallholders, mostly under contract.[8] The legal status of much of the land converted to plantations is disputed, and tens of thousands of local landholders have been evicted, or incorporated on coerced terms, as protest movements attest. Many smallholders have embraced oil palm, however, especially where they have been able to retain control over their own land and sell the crop freely to a processing mill, or negotiate contracts for land development from a position of strength (Barney 2004; Cramb 2007; Potter in press). Rubber is another plantation crop that is expanding rapidly, especially in Cambodia and Laos, where corrupt officials in league with transnational investors and the military dispossess customary landholders who have little recourse (Barney 2008; Shi 2008; World Bank 2006a). The land area involved is not so huge, but the impact is severe because the potentially arable land is limited by rugged topography, especially in Laos.

Replicating the colonial pattern traced by Jan Breman, the people employed in Southeast Asia's new plantations are seldom the people who were dispossessed on site. Instead, migrant labour is imported over large distances. As in the colonial period, labour importation is justified by myths of the "lazy native"—a reluctance to work, lack of skill, and failure to understand the requirements of labour discipline (Dove 1999; Potter in press). In Laos, the racialized stigma attached to highland minorities by the lowland Lao works against their employment on the plantations that now occupy their land, and when they are employed, the terms are coercive (Shi 2008). Almost all the oil palm work in the Malaysian state of Sabah is carried out by migrants from Indonesia, many of them illegal. On the Indonesian side of the border in Kalimantan, workers are pulled in from other Indonesian islands, recruited by brokers to whom they are bound by debt, in the colonial style Breman describes. The Javanese often arrive through transmigration schemes that promise them title to a plot of land planted with oil palm, after debts for the cost of land development are paid off, effectively bonding them to the oil palm scheme. Javanese also work as contract labourers on privately owned plantations, with no promise of land. Often, they find themselves in conflict over land and jobs with the local population (Potter in press).

Oil palm plantations, it must be noted, absorb little labour. Ten thousand hectares of oil palm together with a processing mill employ 1000 workers, one person per 10 ha, much less than tea (two to three people per ha) or rubber (one to two people).[9] Thus in the case of oil palm, the disconnect between land and labour is profound. For decades to come, the huge swathe of land under oil palm is guaranteed to generate very few jobs, and it is doubtful that much could be done with the land after the oil palm boom ends, so severely is the land modified by the bulldozers, chemicals, and intensive mono-cropping.

Smallholdings of oil palm are also powerful vectors of the "everyday" form of dispossession that works through debt. Many smallholders have prospered through oil palm, but it is not a crop for the poor. Unlike rubber, which will continue to produce at a low level even when neglected, oil palm requires constant attention and a high level of chemical input. Smallholders without the necessary capital quickly fall into debt, and their land is bought up by their more successful neighbours. They end up as wage labour, or indeed, out of work (*Jakarta Post* 2008b). This is a familiar trajectory that occurs whenever subsistence crops fail, or when the price fetched by cash crops does not match costs, and farmers are compelled to borrow money or mortgage their property as they enter a downward spiral (Hall 2004). Ruling regimes can intervene by calibrating tariffs, prices, taxes, rents, wages, and interest to adjust the rate at which farmers hold on to, or lose, their land. Put another way, the conditions governing the so-called "free market" are always set. When they are set to work against small-scale farmers, currently the case in much of the global South, the result is pervasive land loss and "depeasantization" (Araghi 2009; Bryceson, Kay and Mooij 2000).

Large-scale enclosures in Southeast Asia took a new twist in 2008 when the global hike in food prices provoked China and other rich but food-insecure countries, especially Japan and the Gulf states, to buy or lease land in Cambodia, the Philippines, Indonesia, Burma and Laos. The largest of these new enclosures, 1.6 million ha in West Papua, was acquired by Saudi Arabia to grow rice, the preferred food of the Asian migrant workers on whom the Saudi economy depends.[10] But as Jennifer Clapp (2008) points out, the so-called "food crisis" was not caused by changes in demand for food, or the food supply, and Malthusian talk of global population outstripping food supply was misplaced. The main driver of the price hike was large institutional investors switching out of dollars and into commodities, among them oil and food. Nevertheless, as the "food crisis" receded, it left behind a powerful rationale for a new set of global land seizures brokered directly between governments, or initiated by corporations, and supported by the IFIs. Food-insecure governments argued that they could no longer put their populations at risk of hunger by relying on food imports; they had to engage directly in offshore food production to guarantee their supply. Corporations joined in these ventures in the expectation that increasing global food demand would yield profits. The World Bank increased its pressure on national governments to relax laws on landownership, arguing that foreign investment would bring development (GRAIN 2009:8).

The re-alignment between capital, land and labour in these offshore production regimes signals a new form of disconnect. The purpose is to control offshore land and resources. Offshore labour is optional. Some of the Chinese government's offshore plantations export Chinese labour to do the work (GRAIN 2009:3, 10). China has also exported Chinese labour to staff mines in Papua, and proposes to do the same in Canada. Chinese corporations that have acquired Canadian mines argue that skilled mineworkers are in short supply, and they want permission to import Chinese mineworkers en bloc, so they can work as "an entire mine crew" (Ernst & Young 2008; *Mines and Communities* 2007; *The Globe and Mail* 2009). They hope to make use of the Temporary Foreign Worker Program, initially designed to enable Canadian agribusinesses to import Mexican and Caribbean migrant workers for seasonal farm work under harsh contracts that would not be legal, or acceptable, for Canadian labour. In the farm worker program, the low price of the imported labour is key. Without it, Ontario farmers would stop producing tomatoes. If Chinese mineworkers are imported into Canada, however, the logic would be different. No doubt the use of Chinese workers would make the mines more profitable. But the critical shift brought about by the use of Chinese workers is the way it clarifies the disconnect between the Chinese government and the Canadian population. The

Chinese government's biopolitical priority is the provisioning of its own population. It is not responsible for the lives of Canadian mineworkers, or the Southeast Asian farmers dispossessed by its offshore enclosures.

Forest conservation is another field in which the disconnect between land and labour is profound. Conservation is supported by transnational donors and NGOs as a biopolitics of planetary survival. Although surrounded by a legitimating discourse of poverty reduction, the reality is that conservation routinely implicates donors in poverty production on a shocking scale. Globally, the number of people evicted from protected areas and deprived of access to land and former sources of livelihood over the past few decades has been estimated at 8.5 million (Cernea and Schmidt-Soltau 2006:1818). Obviously, conservation absorbs little or no labour, and the very presence of surrounding populations is viewed as a threat to conservation objectives. Yet conservation agencies and the donors that fund them make no commitment to resettle, compensate, or identify alternative livelihoods for the people their programs dispossess. They seem to assume these people will find somewhere else to go, and something else to do. Donors further sidestep their responsibility by devolving it downwards, onto the national governments that "volunteer" to extend their conservation enclosures, and the communities that "choose" to participate in "community-based conservation", overlooking the role of donor incentives in creating the conditions under which national or local elites become implicated in dispossession (Li 2007b).

Race is a crucial dimension of dispossession in Southeast Asia, as ethnic minorities are most often the ones accused of forest destruction, and conservation becomes yet another reason to evict them (Lohmann 1999; Vandergeest 2003a, 2003b; Wittayapak 2008). The most egregious contemporary, life-threatening instance of racialized, conservation-backed eviction is Laos, where a program to demarcate forest boundaries in highland villages has forced the population to seek refuge "voluntarily" in lowland resettlement sites, where arable land is extremely scarce, there is little work, and hunger and disease prove fatal for many. Nevertheless, donors continue to support the resettlement program on grounds of conservation and for the benefit of the highlanders, since it will increase their access to services and markets. The phrase "policy-induced poverty" has entered the critical discourse that circulates among some donors in Laos, but it has not interrupted the resettlement agenda (Baird and Shoemaker 2007; Vandergeest 2003a; Goldman 2005).

There is a further, dispossessory dimension to contemporary conservation enclosure in Southeast Asia that merits attention. This is the knock-on effect of cutting off access to the forest frontier that has long provided a "safety valve" for the dispossessed—a place to find land and start over. Until the 1980s, many governments across the region either accommodated or made deliberate use of this "safety valve" to meet peasant demands for land (De Koninck 2006). Resettling landless people to the forest frontier was a way to avoid redistributive land reform, while abating a communist threat. Life on these frontiers was far from egalitarian: whether they arrived through state-sponsored programs or on their own initiative, migrants with little capital were soon entrapped in new relations of debt by land "pioneers", traders and money lenders, a problem already observed in the colonial period (Elson 1997). Nevertheless, the existence of these frontiers in much of Southeast Asia enabled people ejected from lowland agriculture to survive, and sometimes to prosper. The possibility of exit also gave the landless lowland population some bargaining power. Although there were forest boundaries dating from the colonial period, in many parts of the region these were poorly enforced until the advent of donor dollars supporting conservation.

What happens to Southeast Asians dispossessed from the land? Opportunities for work are highly uneven, both between countries and within them. In Vietnam, for example, manufacturing has absorbed large numbers of former peasants, while in Indonesia, manufacturing never quite recovered from the effects of the 1997 Asian economic crisis, and competition from China casts a long shadow. Demographer Graeme Hugo (2007) describes Indonesia as "a quintessential labor-surplus nation". In 2006, "an estimated 11 percent of Indonesian workers (11.6 million) were unemployed, and underemployment was over 20 percent (45 million workers)". Disparities within Indonesia are also marked. Manufacturing is concentrated in Java, but a person ejected from the rural economy in West Papua or Kalimantan has little chance of securing a job in Java, where competition is fierce and exclusionary barriers of ethnicity, locality and kinship keep labour markets closed. There are, in short, no generic citizens, or generic jobs.

Cross-border migration is an important outlet for labour, but as with domestic migration, its circuits are specialized and uneven. Recruiting agents select one village, or one ethnic, class, gender or age group, leaving others stranded. In 2008, two million Indonesians were working in Malaysia, mainly in plantations and construction, at least half a million of them illegally. In the Mekong region, 1.5 million Burmese and 0.5 million Laotians and Cambodians were working in Thailand, mostly in agriculture, and most of them illegally (*Migration News* 2008, 2009). Illegality makes workers especially vulnerable. A report on Indonesian plantation workers in Sabah described their conditions as "bonded labor . . . a modern kind of slavery" (*Jakarta Post* 2008a). In Thailand, as the global economic crisis of 2008–2009 caused a decline in the price of rubber, the response of plantation owners was to cut the wages of their Burmese workers by half, from two dollars per day to one (*Migration News* 2009). Needless to say, these plantation workers are barely able to stay alive. They do not send home remittances, or take home savings for their old age. The only benefit to the sending household is one less mouth to feed.

Migration has its success stories. A large number of Filipinos have been able to parlay their education and English language skills into the transnational migration circuit; young people from across the region endowed with a secondary school education, who long to escape village life, find their way into urban employment. These successes are not random. Studies show, with unsurprising regularity, that the outcomes of labour migration are directly related to the land and capital assets of the migrant's family (Rigg 2006, 2007; White, Alexander and Boomgaard 1991). People who are dispossessed or marginalized in their villages of origin do not have access to the high-income circuits. When they migrate, they do so on the most adverse terms, wholly dependent on labour brokers, and vulnerable to being cheated, trapped in debt, coerced, segregated, injured, and imprisoned in their places of work. Although these brokers offer them no security, would-be migrants attach themselves loyally, because the alternative—having no broker, and no work—is even worse (Mosse 2007; Rigg 2007).

The processes of dispossession I have outlined in this section, when combined with the limits on labour absorption and some catastrophic misconnects affecting particular spatialized, racialized, or otherwise stigmatized populations, have produced the pattern of human suffering I outlined earlier: 700 million Asians who live very precariously, on less than a dollar a day. One obvious response to the problem of dispossession is to stop it in its tracks—not to add to the numbers. Much of the popular mobilization and some of the social movement activism in Asia is focused, rightly, on this goal. There are also attempts to reclaim land through distributive land reform, although the experience is that reform beneficiaries often lose their land again through the "everyday" mechanism of debt. For most of the people who have been dispossessed, and have no access to living wage, a different kind of solution is needed. In the next section, I consider some biopolitical assemblages that might address this problem, and use a recent example from India to think through the conditions under which a make live politics can be activated.

Biopolitical Assemblages and the Protection of Surplus Populations

A biopolitical program, as I have argued in other work, can usefully be viewed as an assemblage of elements, pulled together at a particular conjuncture, in relation to a given ensemble of population and territory (Li 2007a, 2007b). Just as the connection between capital and labour that constitutes "capitalist development" needs to be examined in all its historical and spatial specificity, so does the emergence of a biopolitical program that seeks to sustain life. Although situated within the broad historical trajectory Foucault (1991) described as the emergence of "government", that is, the grounding of the rationale for rule in techniques for knowing and improving the condition of the population, the deployment of biopolitical programs to secure life is uneven, suggesting that a range of social forces is involved. What are these forces?

Karl Polanyi (1944) offers an underdeveloped but still fruitful way of thinking about the social forces involved in protecting life. He rejected an analysis based on a narrow view of class interest, or a concept of capitalism on auto-pilot that cannot be tamed or directed. Instead, he highlighted the role of cross-class alliances in promoting life-enhancing interventions, their adoption by European regimes across the spectrum from left to right, and their emergence under authoritarian conditions as well as democratic ones. He also pointed out that many interventions arose as pragmatic responses to particular problems such as unemployment, and crises in public health. While the extension of market relations was planned, he argued, planning was not (1944:141). There are multiple social forces at work in a make live conjuncture. Polanyi wrote, for example, of the meeting of the justices of Berkshire at the Pelican Pub in Speenhamland in 1795, when they ruled that parishes should subsidize wages on a scale related to the price of bread, thereby countering the emergence of a "free" market in labour, and inventing the "right to live" (1944:77). He also traced the social forces behind this event, and this invention. Similarly, we can understand the emergence of Britain's post-war welfare state as an assemblage of elements: post-war patriotism, the shameful exposure of malnutrition in the urban underclass, memories of suffering in the depression, pressure from organized labour, fears of the potentially revolutionary consequences of mass unemployment, and new expertise in planning, among others.

Sadly, the desolate data on life expectancy I cited earlier gives ample reason to question Polanyi's confidence that "society as a whole" (1944:152) is equipped with a homeostatic capacity to protect "itself" from the risk of destruction. Clearly, in the history of life-preserving interventions, social protection has been racialized and spatialized. Not everyone has been able to claim a "right to live". In the "late Victorian holocausts" described by Mike Davis (2002), market fundamentalism in colonial India dictated that Indians should be valued only as units of labour. There would be no Indian Poor Law. If there was no demand for Indian labour, Indians should be allowed to die, as they did in vast numbers in 1876–1878 and again in 1896–1902, about 20 million people in all. Colonial authorities banned charitable efforts to supply food to these people as interference in the natural law of the market. Such interference, the experts argued, would only make matters worse, not only for the British whose coffers would be drained, but also for the

Indians, whose development would be diverted from its natural—though deadly—path. Letting die was not an oversight. It was a calculated decision, rationalized in terms of the greater good.

Echoing the late colonial holocausts, as Davis (2006:174) observes, the structural adjustment programs of the 1980s and 1990s deliberately exposed rural populations of the global South to the full blast of market discipline, while withdrawing social protections. "Letting die" was part of this biopolitical triage, not in its rhetoric—one of economic growth and development—but in its results. In the period 1990–2003, 21 countries experienced a decline in the Human Development Index, which includes factors such as life expectancy and infant mortality (UNDP 2003). The effects of structural adjustment were horrendous, and policies of a similar kind are still promoted. Yet death and destruction were not everything. Even at their height, neoliberal attacks on social protection were tempered by countermoves such as safety nets, employment schemes, and Millennium Development Goals that pulled in the other direction. Likewise, colonial regimes often had protective aspirations that coexisted in uneasy tension with the search for profit, the need for stability, and other agendas (Li 2007b, in press). How can we understand these contradictory formations?

One approach to the contradiction between dispossession and protection would be to look at how it is sustained by quotidian practices of compromise that enable, at the end of the day, a monstrous disavowal (Mosse 2008; Watts 2009:275). Or we could approach it as a matter of bad faith: dispossession is real, protection is just talk. Or protection is real but minimal, self-serving, and disciplinary: its purpose is to manage the chaos created by dispossession, and stave off revolt (Cowen and Shenton 1996; Peck and Tickell 2002). Another approach, the one I took in *The Will to Improve* (Li 2007b), is to take make live aspirations at their word, while acknowledging the contradictions that cause them to fall short. There is, from this perspective, no master plan, only assemblages pulled together by one set of social forces, only to fragment and reassemble.

Some of the elements of a make live assemblage are located within the state apparatus. Writing about the rise of neoliberalism in Europe in the 1980s and 1990s, Pierre Bourdieu (1998:2) distinguished between what he called the "left hand of the state, the set of agents of the so-called spending ministries which are the trace, within the state, of the social struggles of the past", and the "right hand of the state", often headquartered in ministries of finance. In a democratic system, and within the container of the nation state, tensions between productivity and protection may be worked out by means of the ballot and embedded in laws that define entitlements and—just as important—a sense of entitlement that is not easy to eradicate. In the UK, as in France, decades of neoliberal government did not eliminate public expectations about the provision of public services, especially state-mediated social security for people facing hard times. As Janet Newman and John Clarke (2009) argue, announcements of the "death of the social" have been premature. Nevertheless, under increasingly globalized conditions, it is less obvious that nation states provide containers for cross-class settlements, or command the resources to engage in projects of productivity *or* protection, as contradictory pressures operate at multiple scales (Swyngedouw 2000).

Echoing the left-hand/right-hand split at a transnational scale, the UN system, with its Declaration on Economic and Social Rights, including a right to food, and a "rights-based approach" to development, sits awkwardly alongside the IFIs, convinced that sacrifice is necessary in order to promote growth, from which the poor will eventually benefit (Kanbur 2001; United Nations 2007). The IFIs, unable to admit that their own policies are implicated in dispossession and abandonment, attempt to pass the responsibility on to national governments, obliged to prepare poverty reduction strategies as a condition of receiving funds. Many national regimes, in turn, have been radically reconfigured by decentralization measures, making it difficult for them to deliver on national commitments, and devolving responsibilities downwards to districts, "communities", groups of "stakeholders" and other weakly territorialized units with uncertain mandates and capacities (Craig and Porter 2006). To the left-hand/right-hand mix, then, is added the problem of territorial jurisdiction and scale, and the further problem of population mobility. As a result, it is often very unclear who is responsible for the fate of which ensemble of population, and what resources they could command to make the dispossessed live better.

The attempt to govern through communities, and make them responsible for their own fate, has been prominent in the era of neoliberalism, especially in the form of micro-credit schemes that require the poor to supply their own employment as entrepreneurs (Elyachar 2005). Variations on the theme of community self-reliance have reappeared with regularity in Indonesia for 200 years, and appeared again in the 1997–1998 economic crisis, when some experts argued that there was no need to supply a "safety net" for displaced urban workers since they could be reabsorbed into the village economy. There was a program to supply them with one-way tickets "home" (Breman and Wiradi 2002:2–4, 306; Li 2007b). The World Bank subsequently glorified this event with a label, "farm financed social welfare", heralded as a remedy for "urban shocks" (World Bank 2008:3). The same discourse arose in 2009, as global recession set in. A news report about job losses in Thailand anticipated an "exodus of workers back to the family farm", waxed lyrical on the "bright green rice terraces", coconut groves, and fishponds dotting "an exceedingly fertile countryside", and quoted the country director of the Asian Development Bank on the virtues of the Thai countryside as a "social safety net" (*International Herald Tribune* 2009). A critical flaw in these observations, however, is that a large number of those who exit rural areas have no farms, and some of them have been landless for multiple generations. If "farm-financed social welfare" works at all, it works for prosperous landowners. For the poor it is a mirage, with potentially lethal effects.

In his recent book, Mark Duffield (2007:19) draws a stark contrast between "insured life" in the global North, and "non-insured surplus life" in the global South. The goal of transnational development intervention, he argues, is not to extend northern-style social protections to the population of the global South, but to keep the latter in their place—ensconced in their nations, communities and families, where they must be self-sufficient, and not make demands. I think the distinction between insured and uninsured life is accurate enough as a description of the status quo, but it is not the end of history. As I noted earlier, some parts of the development apparatus talk in terms of rights and entitlements, even though they do not have the means to secure them. More significantly, Duffield's North–South division underestimates the aspiration for broader forms of social justice that exists within some nations of the global South, is nurtured in unions, social movements, left-leaning political parties and the "left hand" of the state apparatus, and can sometimes assemble a protective biopolitics, despite the odds. In the next section, I examine one such assemblage in India, that aspires to secure the "right to food" on a national scale, and contrast it with the situation in Indonesia, where movements for social justice are truncated, and the myth of village self-sufficiency leaves the dispossessed seriously exposed.

The Politics of Entitlement

The "right to food" initiative in India took off in 2001, when a group of public interest lawyers from Rajasthan sued the government for its failure to meet its legal obligation to supply famine relief to people afflicted by drought, although government warehouses were well stocked with grain. The lawyers and their allies inside and outside the state apparatus then expanded the legal case to cover the much more pervasive problem of hunger and malnutrition, arguing that in permitting these conditions to persist, the government was in violation of its constitutional obligation to protect and enhance the life of its citizens. The Supreme Court responded by *confirming* that citizens of India do indeed have a constitutionally guaranteed "right to food". In so doing, it enfranchised the staggering 380 million people (35% of India's population) whose income—less than a dollar a day—leaves them chronically short of proper nourishment. The Court then appointed commissioners, and oversaw the development of national programs designed to follow through on the "right to food", including free lunches for every school child, subsidized food for qualified applicants, pensions for the elderly, special care for the destitute and so on. It also implemented a system of "social audit" in which failures to comply at any level of the system would be made known to the court and redressed (Right to Food India 2005).

Needless to say, implementing a nationally guaranteed "right to food" in India involves numerous difficulties, among which the relative autonomy of India's 31 states looms large. Some states have refused to acknowledge or act on the Supreme Court's orders. There are problems in identifying and registering appropriate beneficiaries; problems of corruption and quality control; and collusion between politicians, bureaucrats and labour contractors to exclude claimants or steal their allocation (Cheriyan 2006). There are also problems in reaching destitute families, since destitution strips away political personhood, while survival strategies (begging, prostitution, and itinerant trading) and vagrancy are criminalized, casting the destitute into the category of the undeserving and licensing brutal treatment (Harriss-White 2005; Mosse 2007). So the aim of "making live" hundreds of millions of deeply impoverished Indians is very difficult to accomplish. It would be easy enough to give up, on the grounds that the situation is hopeless.

A close look at one of the "right to food" programs, the guarantee of a "right to work" for 100 days per year on a public works project at the official minimum wage, or receive an unemployment allowance in lieu of work, will give an indication of the social forces at work in this assemblage, and why it is still moving ahead. The government passed the National Rural Employment Guarantee Act (NREGA) in 2005, as a result of hard lobbying from activists and crucial support from the left political parties that used their leverage inside and outside parliament. Government officials have also been active in the assemblage, in some rather surprising ways. I was struck by a document on the "right to food" website, a report by the Government of India's Second Administrative Reforms Commission, a body dedicated to mundane (and neoliberal) matters of efficiency, accountability and audit in public service. Why, I wondered, would the commission select this potentially radical Act as a "case study" for *administrative* reform? The preface to the commission's report notes that the areas of rural India with the highest concentrations of famine and destitution are sites of "extremism and Naxalism" (Government of India 2006:preface). Yet there is little evidence that the Naxalites pose a serious threat to the wealthy population of India, or its ruling regime; nor are they holding back India's remarkable economic growth. So why should administrative reformers get involved? Speculatively, I can list a few factors that may have been at work here.

First, the fragility or, in some cases, the total absence of the supposedly standard, national bureaucratic apparatus in India's "backward districts" might offend bureaucratic sensibilities, while extreme social hierarchy, predatory labour contractors, and violent attacks that keep government officials away challenge liberal notions of citizenship that link individuals directly to the state. The report notes the importance of delivering the program with at least "a modicum of success in these backward regions" (Government of India 2006:1). NREGA rules specifically ban the use of contractors, and administer the program through village councils (*gram panchayats*), highlighting the role of state as benevolent provider (Dreze and Khera 2009). Second, the report heralded NREGA as a path-breaking demonstration of the government's new approach to poverty, one that would replace the inefficient rationing systems of the past with a universal entitlement. Everyone who presents themselves for work is guaranteed 100 days. The report anticipates the use of computerized tracking, and a future in which program participants would swipe a card to log each transaction. Third, the program would be a pilot for a new relationship between national and state governments, in which the center supplies the funds, while making the state governments responsible for performance according to national standards. Responsibilization is a common tactic of neoliberal rule, as I noted earlier. Effective ways to monitor the performance of the government apparatus at each level, from the state to the village, were the main topic of the scores of detailed protocols in the tightly printed, 111-page report. Here was audit culture turned loose, in the service of the poor. Finally, and most broadly, if famine was the scandal that started the "right to food" movement, it was a scandal only because an entitlement to famine relief was already established in India. When the Supreme Court raised the stakes on what the government is obliged to deliver, it also increased the number of fronts on which the government could be found wanting, and embarrassed by public exposure. Indeed, the supreme court's insistence on "social audit" was designed for this purpose.

Early reports on the fate of the program, which is now being implemented, show that the uptake is uneven (Poorest Areas Civil Society nd). The states in which the program is working well are those that have a track record of distributive intervention, sustained by strong support from the organized left, and traditions of popular mobilization. The states where these social forces are lacking have not implemented the program, or implemented it in a desultory and corrupt fashion. These tend to be the states with high concentration of poverty. Although no doubt they have "left hands" within them, the ruling regimes in these states are not very responsive to Supreme Court orders, national law, media exposure, or even the threat of the Naxalites, who are active in these same places. Votes matter, but even when lower caste groups are well represented in parliament, entrenched inequalities prove difficult to shift (Jeffrey, Jeffrey and Jeffrey 2008). Partha Chatterjee (2008) argues that "Indian democracy" and fear of producing "dangerous classes" will ensure that India's dispossessed are protected, but I do not think this outcome can be assumed. As the activists of the right to food movement clearly appreciate, establishing a national "right to food" and some mechanisms to implement it is merely a first step. Making that right real across national space will be a long hard struggle (Dreze and Khera 2009).[11]

The social forces behind the "right to food" movement in India are strikingly absent in Indonesia. There is a specific historical reason for this. There was a clandestine but organized left stream in Indonesian politics from the 1920s, and visions of social justice were prominent in the anti-colonial struggle. In the 1950s, the Communist Party was legal, and was the biggest outside China and the Soviet Union (Cribb 1985). All this ended in 1965, when the army engineered the massacre of about half a million people, mainly members of the communist party or affiliated unions, and peasants involved in struggles to reclaim land. Leftists in the media, education and related fields were killed or imprisoned. These massacres, and the repression that followed, created a crucial gap in the parliamentary system and in public debate that has still not been filled, more than a decade after the end of General Suharto's rule. There is remarkably little national debate about social justice or citizen entitlements. There is little faith in the parliamentary system as a vehicle to bring about change.[12] Important social movements have emerged to defend the land rights of people threatened with eviction, but these movements have stopped short of articulating a comprehensive program for social justice. There is no functioning welfare system, only some provisions for the hand-out of subsidized rice put in place as a "safety net" at the time of the Asian economic crisis, and renewed to balance the increased prices for fuel and food under structural adjustment (Husken and Koning 2006). In stark contrast to Kerala, where the poorest people are centrally involved in the defense of social rights and assume the "taken-for-granted legitimacy of making redistributive demands on the state" (Steur 2009:31), the Indonesian villagers I have come to know complain bitterly about corruption, and their exclusion from a share of poorly targeted state largesse, but they have little sense of entitlement.

As I noted earlier, an important rationale offered by ruling regimes in Indonesia for *not* providing protection for the rural poor is the notion that villagers have their own mechanisms to support their weaker members. Although many scholars have worked hard to rupture assumptions about the harmonious, moral and caring character of village life in general, and Indonesian villages in particular, the village myth is stubborn. Even Mike Davis falls under its spell, when he contrasts the vicious competition among the poor in urban slums to what he calls, far too optimistically, "the subsistence solidarities of the countryside" (2006:201). Clifford Geertz (1963) bears some responsibility for the problem. His much cited description of rural Java as an oasis of "shared poverty" and infinite labour absorption, where everyone is assured of a place, misrepresented Java in the 1950s and 1960s, before the green revolution (Alexander and Alexander 1982; Husken 1989; Husken and White 1989; Pincus 1996; White 1983). It would also have been an inaccurate description of village life early in the nineteenth century, when an estimated 30–50% of the population of Java had no land. Villages were stratified into caste-like estates, in which landholding families organized production by incorporating landless farm servants as permanent dependents, and employed roving bands of "free" coolie labour when needed. Thus in Java, as in India, a large section of the rural population has been landless, and living precariously, for many generations. Yet colonial officials clung doggedly to the village myth, and proceeded with dispossessory policies on the comfortable assumption that villagers would take care of their own (Breman 1983).

To further the rupturing effort, I will take the reader briefly to the highlands of Sulawesi, among indigenous farmers, the kind of people often assumed to value collective harmony above individual profit. Since 1990, I have been tracking a process of dispossession initiated from below, when highlanders privatized individual plots from their common pool of ancestral land in order to plant a new boom crop, cacao. They had their reasons. Far from living in a state of primitive affluence, they felt their lives were insecure due to periodic drought, famine, and lack of medicine. They were also ashamed of living in unchanging poverty from one generation to the next, and more so as they saw others around them begin to prosper. Class formation proceeded with remarkable speed. By 2006, some of the highlanders had accumulated significant landholdings while their kin and neighbours became landless and mired in debt. The new landlords occasionally hired their kin, but did not feel obliged to do so, and readily replaced labour with chemical herbicides which, they argued, were more efficient. For the dispossessed, the only employment option for men was hauling rattan and timber out from the forest on a piece rate that barely covered the cost of their own food, and left them exhausted and often injured. Women, children and old people stayed in the hills, in their tiny huts, perched on borrowed land, eating very little.

My point in telling this story is that it is situated and specific, but not exceptional. As I noted earlier, colonial officials routinely reported rapid class formation on Southeast Asia's forest frontiers, when people started to plant cash crops and became indebted to co-villagers and traders. The story has echoes of that told by James Scott (1985) about a Malaysian village at the point when production was mechanized. As soon as combine harvesters made the labour of their co-villagers surplus to requirements, landlords stopped acting as patrons. On close inspection, patronage routinely includes an economic calculus centered on labour: if labour is short, especially at peak seasons, it may be necessary to bear the costs of reproducing that labour throughout the year, or across the generations. But if labour is not needed, or supply is super-abundant, the landlord has no need to reproduce it. It becomes surplus. As Jonathan Pincus (1996) showed, in his remarkable comparative study of the introduction of green revolution technologies in three adjacent villages on Java, there were important variations in how the gains from increased productivity were distributed, but these had more to do with the capacity of workers to act collectively than with shared values binding villagers into a moral economy, complete with subsistence guarantees.

Conclusion

Although I began this essay with a critique of the linear narrative of agrarian transition, I want to stress that I do not counterpose transition to a rural utopia, in which people reject new products and labour regimes in favour of locally oriented production on small family farms. As my own field research in Sulawesi demonstrates very clearly, and other studies confirm, the transition narrative corresponds closely to a popular desire to leave behind the insecurities of subsistence production, and enjoy the fuller life that better food, housing, education and health care can offer (Ferguson 2005; Rigg 2006). Yet the sad truth is that this desire is frustrated, especially for the poorest people, who are routinely dispossessed through the very processes that enable other people to prosper. Far too many of them cannot even access a living wage, because their labour is surplus to capital's requirements.

Whose responsibility is it to attend to the welfare of surplus populations? "No purely selfish class", wrote Karl Polanyi, "can maintain itself in the lead" (1944:156). I fear this is not true, at the extreme. Burma's military junta is utterly selfish, and has maintained itself for more than four decades. Most regimes, however, wrestle with a more complex sense of "leadership" that involves some degree of balance between contradictory agendas (productivity, equity), and an obligation to make live that has become integral to the modern sense of what it means to govern. Transnational agencies, charitable foundations, activists, experts, and social reformers of many kinds share in this sense of obligation. How the obligation is met, and for which sectors of the population, is a matter that is worked out in specific sites and conjunctures through means that are sometimes grandiose, and occasionally revolutionary, but just as often pragmatic, and unannounced. These conjunctures are worth attending to, however, because as Gillian Hart (2004:95) observes, "the ongoing tension between pressures for 'economic freedom' and the imperatives of welfare arising from their destructive tendencies opens up a rich vein of critical possibilities". These possibilities are both analytical and political, and my essay has offered but a small glimpse of them.

Acknowledgements

Thanks for critical input from Gavin Smith, Derek Hall, Kregg Hetherington, John Clarke, Craig Jeffrey, John Harriss, Haroon Akram-Lodhi, Urs Geiser and members of the Markets and Modernities symposium at the Asian Institute, University of Toronto, especially Jesook Song, Katharine Raskin, Ken Kawashima, Frank Cody and Tong Lam and colleagues in the Challenges of Agrarian Transition in South east Asia (ChATSEA) project. Teaching release to enable me to work on this project was provided by the Canadian Social Sciences and Humanities Research Council.

Endnotes

[1] The four terms, let live/make die, associated with the right of sovereigns, and make live/let die, associated with "government" are discussed in Foucault (2003:239–264).

[2] http://www.chicagoreporter.com/index.php/c/Cover_Stories/d/Health_Watch:_Life_Cut_Short_for_City's_Minorities

[3] http://labourbureau.nic.in/WRI-03-04table%20no-12(a).htm.

[4] For example, Quijano Obregon (1980) argues that people surviving at the "marginal pole" of Latin American cities during the 1970s contributed to capital accumulation through their savings, by providing cheap goods and services, and by consumption. But not all marginal populations contribute in these ways, so his analysis cannot be generalized.

[5] Estimates of long-distance migration of Indian workers 1846–1932 range from 10 to 45 million (Breman 1990:14).

[6] For discussion of India's jobless growth see Harriss (unpublished). Jeffrey (2009) and Dasgupta and Singh (2005).

[7] Harriss (unpublished) and Patnaik (2008) find Indian government claims about welfare hollow.

[8] http://www.pecad.fas.usda.gov/highlights/2007/12/Indonesia_palmoil/

[9] Tunku Mohd Nazim Yaacob (email 23 January 2009) supplied this data based on actual numbers from Malaysian plantations. Indonesia's oil palm lobby claims the industry employs five people per ha (Indonesian Palm Oil Board 2007:21). The numbers for rubber and tea are from the International Labour Organization (1991:43). The high-tech, genetically modified soy colonizing South America uses even less labour (Hetherington forthcoming; Teubal 2009).

[10] See GRAIN (2009:10). Laos is reported to have signed away 15% of its viable farmland (*The Guardian* 2008).

[11] Agarwala (2006) describes demands for state-sponsored welfare as a front of class struggle, since 93% of India's labour force is "informal" and cannot press claims directly against employers.

[12] In the 2009 elections, 30% of registered voters did not vote, and 15% cast spoiled ballots. http://www.pemiluindonesia.com/pemilu-2009/jumlah-golput-hampir-50-juta-orang.html

References

Agarwala R (2006) From work to welfare: A new class movement in India. *Critical Asian Studies* 38(4):419–444

Akram-Lodhi A H and Kay C (2009) The agrarian question: Peasants and rural change. In A H Akram-Lodhi and C Kay (eds). *Peasants and Globalization: Political*

Economy, Rural Transformation, and the Agrarian Question (pp 3–33). London: Routledge

Alexander J and Alexander P (1982) Shared poverty as ideology: Agrarian relationships in Colonial Java. *Man* 17(4):597–619

Araghi F (2009) "The invisible hand and the visible foot: Peasants, dispossession and globalization". In A H Akram-Lodhi and C Kay (eds). *Peasants and Globalization: Political Economy, Rural Transformation, and the Agrarian Question* (pp 111–147). London: Routledge

Baird I and Shoemaker B (2007) Unsettling experiences: Internal resettlement and international aid agencies in Laos. *Development and Change* 38(5):865–888

Barney K (2004) Re-encountering resistance: Plantation activism and smallholder production in Thailand and Sarawak, Malaysia. *Asia Pacific Viewpoint* 45(3):325–339

Barney K (2008) China and the production of forestlands in Lao PDR: A political ecology of transnational enclosure. In J Nevins and N L Peluso (eds). *Taking Southeast Asia to Market: Commodities, Nature, and People in the Neoliberal Age* (pp 91–107). Ithaca: Cornell University Press

Bauman Z (2004) *Wasted Lives: Modernity and its Outcasts*. Cambridge: Polity

Bernstein H (2004) "Changing before our very eyes": Agrarian questions and the politics of land in capitalism today. *Journal of Agrarian Change* 4(1–2):190–225

Boomgaard P (2006) *Southeast Asia: An Environmental History*. Santa Barbara: ABC-CLIO

Bourdieu P (1998) *Acts of Resistance: Against the Tyranny of the Market*. New York: The New Process

Breman J (1983) *Control of Land and Labour in Colonial Java*. Dordrecht: Foris Publications Holland

Breman J (1990) *Labour Migration and Rural Transformation in Colonial Asia*. Amsterdam: Comparative Asian Studies, Free University Press

Breman J and Wiradi G (2002) *Good Times and Bad Times in Rural Java*. Leiden: KITLV Press

Bryceson D, Kay C and Mooij J (2000) *Disappearing Peasantries? Rural Labour in Africa, Asia and Latin America*. London: ITDG

Cernea M and Schmidt-Soltau K (2006) Poverty risks and national parks: Policy issues in conservation and resettlement. *World Development* 34(10):1808–1830

Chan K W (2009) The Chinese *Hukou* system at 50. *Eurasian Geography and Economics* 50(2):197–221

Chatterjee P (2008) Democracy and economic transformation in India. *Economic and Political Weekly* 19 April:53–62

Cheriyan G (2006) *Enforcing the Right to Food in India*. United Nations University, World Institute for Development Economics Research

Clapp J (2008) Responding to food price volatility and vulnerability: Considering the global economic context. Paper present at the International Governance Responses to the Food Crisis workshop, Waterloo, Ontario, 4–5 December 2008

Cowen M and Shenton R (1996) *Doctrines of Development*. London: Routledge

Craig D and Porter D (2006) *Development Beyond Neoliberalism? Governance, Poverty Reduction and Political Economy*. London: Routledge

Cramb R (2007) *Land and Longhouse: Agrarian Transformation in the Uplands of Sarawak*. Copenhagen: NIAS Press

Cribb R (1985) The Indonesian Marxist tradition. In C P Mackerras and N J Knight (eds) *Marxism in Asia* (pp 251–271). London: Croom Helm

Dasgupta S and Singh A (2005) Will services be the new engine of Indian economic growth? *Development and Change* 36(6):1035–1057

Davis M (2002) *Late Victorian Holocausts: El Nino Famines and the Making of the Third World*. London: Verso

Davis M (2006) *Planet of Slums*. London: Verso

De Koninck R (2006) On the geopolitics of land colonization: Order and disorder on the frontiers of Vietnam and Indonesia. *Moussons* 9:35–59

Dove M (1999) Representations of the "other" by others: The ethnographic challenge posed by planters' views of peasants in Indonesia. In T M Li (ed) *Transforming the Indonesian Uplands: Marginality, Power and Production* (pp 203–229). London: Routledge/Harwood

Dreze J and Khera R (2009) The battle for employment guarantee. *Frontline* 26(1), http://www.flonnet.com/fl2601/stories/20090116260100400.htm Accessed 1 July 2009

Duffield M (2007) *Development, Security and Unending War: Governing the World of Peoples*. Cambridge: Polity

Elson R (1997) *The End of the Peasantry in Southeast Asia: A Social and Economic History of Peasant Livelihood*. London: MacMillan Press

Elyachar J (2005) *Markets of Dispossession: NGOs, Economic Development, and the State in Cairo*. Durham: Duke University Press

Ernst & Young (2008) Labour shortage threatens Canada's mining industry. 23 June, http://www.ey.com/global/content.nsf/Canada/media_-_2008_-_Mining_ Human_Capital Accessed 12 March 2008

Ferguson J (2005) *Global Shadows*. Durham: Duke University Press

Fisher C A (1964) *South-East Asia: A Social, Economic and Political Geography*. London: Methuen

Foucault M (1991) Governmentality. In G Burchell, C Gordon and P Miller (eds) *The Foucault Effect: Studies in Governmentality* (pp 87–104). Chicago: University of Chicago Press

Foucault M (2003) *"Society Must be Defended": Lectures at the College de France 1975–1976*. New York: Picador

Geertz C (1963) *Agricultural Involution: The Processes of Ecological Change in Indonesia*. Berkeley: University of California Press

Glassman J (2006) Primitive accumulation, accumulation by dispossession, accumulation by "extra-economic" means. *Progress in Human Geography* 30(5):608–625

Government of India (2006) *Unlocking Human Capital: Entitlements and Governance—A Case Study*. Delhi: Second Administrative Reforms Commission, Government of India, http://www.righttofoodindia.org/data/goi2006 adminreformscommissionnregareport.pdf Accessed 19 January 2009

Goldman M (2005) *Imperial Nature: The World Bank and Struggles for Social Justice in the Age of Globalization*. New Haven: Yale University Press

GRAIN (2009) *Seized! The 2008 Land Grab for Food and Financial Security*, http://www.grain.org/go/landgrab Accessed 19 December 2008

Hall D (2004) Smallholders and the spread of capitalism in rural Southeast Asia. *Asia Pacific Viewpoint* 45(3):401–414

Harriss J (unpublished) "Reforms guided by compassion and justice"? The tempering of neo-liberalism in India?

Harriss-White B (2005) Destitution and the poverty of its politics—with special reference to South Asia. *World Development* 33(6):881–891

Hart G (2004) Development and geography: Critical ethnography. *Progress in Human Geography* 28(1):91–107

Harvey D (2003) *The New Imperialism*. Oxford: Oxford University Press

Hetherington K (forthcoming) *Guerrilla Auditors: The Politics of Transparency in post-Cold War Paraguay*. Durham: Duke University Press

Hugo G (2007) Indonesia's labor looks abroad. *Migration Information Source*, http://www.migrationinformation.org/Profiles/print.cfm?ID=594 Accessed 13 January 2009

Husken F (1989) Cycles of commercialization and accumulation in a central Javanese village. In G Hart, A Turton and B White (eds) *Agrarian Transformations: Local Processes and the State in Southeast Asia* (pp 303–331). Berkeley: University of California Press

Husken F and Koning J (2006) Between two worlds: Social security in Indonesia. In J Koning and F Husken (eds). *Ropewalking and Safety Nets: Local Ways of Managing Insecurities in Indonesia* (pp 1–26). Leiden: Brill

Husken F and White B (1989) Java: Social differentiation, food production, and agrarian control. In G Hart, A Turton and B White (eds) *Agrarian Transformations: Local Processes and the State in Southeast Asia* (pp 235–265). Berkeley: University of California Press

ILO (1991) *Recent Developments in the Plantation Sector*. Geneva: International Labour Organization

Indonesian Palm Oil Board (2007) *Sustainable Oil Palm Plantation*. Jakarta: Indonesian Palm Oil Board

Inter Press Service News Agency (2009) Special economic zones, path to massive land grab. 2 June, http://www.ipsnews.net/print.asp?idnews=34732 Accessed 8 June 2009

International Herald Tribune (2009) Unemployed Asians return to villages. 28 January

Jakarta Post (2008a) Palm oil plantations linked to child slavery and prostitution. 17 July

Jakarta Post (2008b) Surfing and crashing in the Indonesian oil palm boom. 28 March

Jeffrey C (2009) Fixing futures: Educated unemployment through a North Indian lens. *Comparative Studies in Society in History* 51(1):182–211

Jeffrey C, Jeffrey P and Jeffrey R (2008) Dalit revolution? New politicians in Uttar Pradesh, India. *Journal of Asian Studies* 67(4):1365–1396

Kanbur R (2001) Economic policy, distribution and poverty: The nature of disagreements. *World Development* 29(6):1083–1094

Li T M (2007a) Practices of assemblage and community forest management. *Economy and Society* 36(2):264–294

Li T M (2007b) *The Will to Improve: Governmentality, Development, and the Practice of Politics*. Durham: Duke University Press

Li T M (in press) Indigeneity, capitalism, and the management of dispossession. *Current Anthropology*

Lohmann L (1999) Forest cleansing: Racial oppression in scientific nature conservation. *Corner House Briefing* 13

Marx K (1986) *Capital: A Critique of Political Economy* vol 1. Moscow: Progress Publishers

Migration News (2008) Southeast Asia, http://www.migration.ucdavis.edu/mn/comments.php?id=3445_0_3_0 Accessed 8 June 2009

Migration News (2009) Southeast Asia, http://www.migration.ucdavis.edu/mn/comments.php?id=3495_0_3_0 Accessed 8 June 2009

Mines and Communities (2007) Coal company wants to hire Chinese workers for B.C. mine. 28 May, http://www.minesandcommunities.org//article.php?a=3880 Accessed 18 June 2009

Mitchell T (2002) *Rule of Experts: Egypt, Technopolitics, Modernity*. Berkeley: University of California Press

Mosse D (2007) *Power and the Durability of Poverty: A Critical Exploration of the Links between Culture, Marginality and Chronic Poverty*. CPRC Working Paper 107. Manchester: Chronic Poverty Research Centre

Mosse D (2008) International policy, development expertise, and anthropology. *Focaal—European Journal of Anthropology* 52:119–126

Moyo S and Yeros P (2005) The resurgence of rural movements under neoliberalism. In S Moyo and P Yeros (eds) *Reclaiming the Land: The Resurgence of Rural Movements in Africa, Asia and Latin America* (pp 8–64). London: Zed Books

Newman J and Clarke J (2009) *Publics, Politics and Power: Remaking the Public in Public Services*. London: Sage

Poorest Areas Civil Society (nd) Poorest Areas Civil Society (PACS) programme, http://www.empowerpoor.com/bottom.asp Accessed 18 June 2009

Paraiyil G (ed) (2000) *Kerala: The Development Experience*. London: Zed Books

Patnaik U (2008) Neoliberal roots. *Frontline* 25(6), http://www.flonnet.com/fl2506/stories/2008038250601700.htm Accessed 18 June 2009

Peck J and Tickell A (2002) Neoliberalizing space. *Antipode* 34(3):380–404

Pincus J (1996) *Class Power and Agrarian Change: Land and Labour in Rural West Java*. London: MacMillan Press

Polanyi K (1944) *The Great Transformation*. New York: Farrar & Rinehart

Potter L (in press) Agrarian transitions in Kalimantan: Characteristics, limitations and accommodations. In R De Konink (ed) *Territories in Transition: Borneo in the Eye of the Storm*. Singapore: National University of Singapore

Quijano Obregon A (1980) The marginal pole of the economy and the marginalized labour force. In H Wolpe (ed). *The Articulation of Modes of Production* (pp 255–288). London: Routledge

Read J (2002) Primitive accumulation: The aleatory foundations of capitalism. *Rethinking Marxism* 14(2):24–49

Rigg J (2006) Land, farming, livelihoods, and poverty: Rethinking the links in the rural south. *World Development* 34(1):180–202

Rigg J (2007) Moving lives: Migration and livelihoods in the Lao PDR. *Population, Space and Place* 13:163–178

Right to Food India (2005) Supreme Court orders on the right to food: A tool for action http://www.rightofoodindia.org/data/scordersprimer.doc, Accessed 1 July 2009

Scott J C (1985) *Weapons of the Weak: Everyday Forms of Peasant Resistance*. New Haven: Yale University Press

Shi W (2008) *Rubber Boom in Luang Namtha*. Vientiane: GTZ RDMA

Sider G (2006) The production of race, locality, and state: An anthropology. *Anthropologica* 48(2):247–263

Steur L (2009) Adivasi mobilisation: "Identity" versus "class" after the Kerala model of development? *Journal of South Asian Development* 4(1):25–44

Swyngedouw E (2000) Authoritarian governance, power, and the politics of rescaling. *Environment and Planning D: Society and Space* 18:63–76

Teubal M (2009) Peasant struggles for land and agrarian reform in Latin America. In A H Akram-Lodhi and C Kay (eds). *Peasants and Globalization: Political Economy, Rural Transformation, and the Agrarian Question* (pp 148–166). London: Routledge

Tharamangalam J (ed) (2006) *Kerala: The Paradoxes of Public Action and Development*. New Delhi: Orient Longman

The Globe and Mail (2009) China's new empire. 3 January

The Guardian (2008) Rich countries launch great land grab to safeguard food supply. 22 November, http://www.guardian.co.uk/environment/2008/nov/22/food-biofuels-land-grab/print Accessed 8 June 2009

UNDP (2003) *Human Development Report*. New York: UNDP/OUP

United Nations (2007) *Human Rights in Development: Rights Based Approaches*, http://www.unhchr.ch/development/approaches-07.html Accessed 13 December 2008

Vandergeest P (2003a) Land to some tillers: Development-induced displacement in Laos. *International Social Science Journal* 175:47–56

Vandergeest P (2003b) Racialization and citizenship in Thai forest politics. *Society and Natural Resources* 16:19–37

Walker K L M (2008) From covert to overt: Everyday peasant politics in China and the implications for transnational agrarian movements. *Journal of Agrarian Change* 8(2–3):462–488

Watts M (2009) The southern question: Agrarian questions of labour and capital. In A H Akram-Lodhi and C Kay (eds). *Peasants and Globalization: Political Economy, Rural Transformation, and the Agrarian Question* (pp 262–287). London: Routledge

White B (1983) "Agricultural involution" and its critics: Twenty years after. *Bulletin of Concerned Asian Scholars* 15(2):18–31

White B, Alexander P and Boomgaard P (eds) (1991) *In the Shadow of Agriculture: Non-farm Activities in the Javanese Economy, Past and Present*. Amsterdam: Rural Tropical Institute

Wittayapak C (2008) History and geography of identifications related to resource conflicts and ethnic violence in Northern Thailand. *Asia-Pacific Viewpoint* 49(1):111–127

Wolpe H (1980) Capitalism and cheap labour-power in South Africa: From segregation to apartheid. In H Wolpe (ed). *The Articulation of Modes of Production*. London: Routledge

World Bank (2006a) *Justice for the Poor? An Exploratory Study of Collective Grievances over Land and Local Governance in Cambodia*. Phnom Penh: Center for Advanced Study, World Bank

World Bank (2006b) *World Development Report: Equity and Development*. Washington: World Bank

World Bank (2008) *World Development Report: Agriculture for Development*. Washington: World Bank

Postneoliberalism and its Malcontents

Jamie Peck
Department of Geography, University of British Columbia,
Vancouver, BC, Canada;
peck@geog.ubc.ca

Nik Theodore
Urban Planning & Policy Program, University
of Illinois at Chicago, Chicago, IL, USA;
theodore@uic.edu

Neil Brenner
Department of Sociology, New York University, New York,
NY 10012-9605, USA;
neil.brenner@nyu.edu

Abstract: The onset of the global financial crisis in 2008 has been widely interpreted as a fundamental challenge to, if not crisis of, neoliberal governance. Here, we explore some of the near-term and longer-run consequences of the economic crisis for processes of neoliberalization, asking whether we have been witnessing the terminal unraveling of neoliberalism as a form of social, political, and economic regulation. In many ways a creature of crisis, could neoliberalism now be falling to a crisis of its own making? Answering this question is impossible, we argue, without an adequate understanding of the nature of neoliberalization and its evolving sociospatial manifestations. These are more than definitional niceties. The prospects and potential of efforts to move genuinely beyond neoliberalism must also be considered in this light.

Keywords: postneoliberalism, neoliberalization, economic crisis

The free-market project is on the ropes. Never before has the question of neoliberalism's political, economic, and social role—culpability might be a better word—been debated with such urgency, so globally, and in such a public manner. The financial crash of 2008 has already brought about, inter alia, ostentatious repudiations of the free-market credo from across the political spectrum; staged acts of contrition and public humbling (punctuated by the occasional indictment) among financial and corporate elites; the abrupt erasure of a decade or so of stock-market and real-estate appreciation; the failure of entire economies, including Iceland, Hungary, and "Detroit"; untold suffering as a result of successive waves of layoffs and mortgage foreclosures, lost savings and decimated pensions; and street riots and political mobilizations around the world, not least at the April 2009 gathering of the Group

Antipode Vol. 41 No. S1 2009 ISSN 0066-4812, pp 94–116
doi: 10.1111/j.1467-8330.2009.00718.x

of 20 (G20). While previous crises of the neoliberal era, such as the wave of debt defaults across Latin America and the Asian financial collapse, may have been (problematically) "managed" by way of a series of midcourse adjustments in neoliberal governance, discourse, and strategy, the current crisis threatens, perhaps fatally, to undermine the political legitimacy of neoliberalism. It may also—though this is certainly not the same thing—finally overwhelm the adaptive capacity of neoliberalism, as a flexibly mutating regime of "market rule". The uniqueness of the present threat lies not simply in the scope and scale of the crisis, though this is daunting enough; above all, it strikes at the heart of the project—the nexus of malregulated finance and American power. The ideological and institutional response to what seems certain to be a protracted crisis, Brand and Sekler (2009a:5) are surely correct to observe, will be "among the most important political and social questions of our times". Already, while socialism is hardly back, crisis-driven forms of Keynesian reflation, seat-of-the-pants industry policy, and even pseudo-nationalizations already are. Are we entering a "postneoliberal" world?

Exploring this question, we reflect here on the analytical and political status of neoliberalism, albeit from a vantage point in the midst of the crisis. "Oft-invoked but ill-defined" (Mudge 2008:703), neoliberalism's crisis may have arrived before there was even a shared understanding of the term's meaning. On the other hand, there is arguably no better time to seek to understand the meaning, *and consequences*, of neoliberalization as a project of sociospatial transformation. Here, we ask whether neoliberalism has, as many have suggested, encountered its own "Berlin Wall moment" of irretrievable collapse. In this context, it is important to recall, appropriating an old economics joke, that seven of the last three crises of neoliberalism were predicted by critical analysts. Moments of crisis always reveal a great deal about the nature of neoliberalization as an adaptive regime of socioeconomic governance, though recent historical experience suggests that they do not necessarily foretell imminent disintegration (cf Peck and Tickell 1994). This calls for an assessment, in the context of the present conjuncture, of the mutually constitutive relationship between neoliberalization and crisis. We have no interest in exhuming neoliberalism for its own sake. Instead, we reflect critically on some of the talk that has been circulating around neoliberalism's (supposed) wake, and some of the claims that are being made about its legacy. This leads us to some preliminary conclusions in the emergent debate over postneoliberalism. An underlying theme of the essay, both analytically and politically, is that of uneven spatial development, which we will suggest is central to understanding not only the sociospatial form of neoliberal hegemony, but also the prospects and potential of efforts to move genuinely *beyond* neoliberalism.

Neoliberalism, R.I.P?

Long before the advent of the globalizing financial crisis of 2008–2009, neoliberalism had become a rascal concept. Largely a critics' term, it had been circulating, simultaneously, as an oppositional slogan, a zeitgeist signifier, and an analytical construct. Partly as a result of this contradictory pattern of usage and signification, the life of this keyword has always been controversial. And the uneven development of neoliberalism, coupled with the intensification of uneven development *through* neoliberalization, further complicated the picture. Ostensibly global in reach—in material, social, and explanatory terms—"neoliberalism" was apparently associated with an almost bewildering array of local trajectories, contingent forms, and hybrid assemblages. So while some could see (or thought they could see) the hegemonic traces of neoliberalization all over the place, others focused just as insistently on the limits, exceptions, and alternatives to neoliberal rule. If neoliberalism is inescapably found in hybrid assemblages (Ong 2006), or in parasitical co-presence with other social formations (Peck 2004), apparently some were inclined to see the glass half empty (focusing on processes of creeping, but never-complete, neoliberalization), while others saw it half full (focusing on the resilience, relative autonomy, and potential of *extra*-neoliberal forms). The *necessary* incompleteness of neoliberalism as a social process ensured that the analytical and political questions around the project's hegemony, or otherwise, were destined to remain unresolved. Should contemporary China, for example, be seen as a key frontier in a mutating neoliberal project, or as a state of such bold exception as to render demonstrably incoherent "global" conceptions of neoliberalization? Answers to such questions (see Wang 2003; Harvey 2009; Wu 2009) serve as a kind of radical Rorschach test, separating those prone to divine neoliberalizing tendencies (however contingently expressed) from those inclined to focus on the kinds of exceptions that ostensibly disprove the (neoliberal) rule.

These underlying differences and tensions have been aggravated by the rude ascendancy of neoliberalism in analytical and political discourse. Even though the phenomenon of neoliberalization itself is hardly new, its relatively recent diffusion as a critical keyword has been nothing short of explosive. Neoliberalism's history as an explicit ideational project, distinct from classical liberalism, can be traced back at least as far as the 1920s, while its traction as a program of state restructuring dates back to the 1970s (Harvey 2005; Mirowski and Plehwe 2009; Peck 2008; Turner 2008). Yet curiously, the term only entered widespread circulation in the last decade. It is difficult to reconstruct accurately neoliberalism's passage into public discourse. The *New York Times* used the neologism intermittently from 1939, and fairly regularly after the Reagan ascendancy, but 44% of the citations occurred in the last decade.[1] Among activists, it was the first of the Zapatistas' "encounters" with neoliberalism, in 1996, that placed the term in global circulation. In academic discourse, explicit deployment of neoliberalism is a strikingly recent phenomenon: of the 2500 English-language articles in the social sciences that cite "neoliberalism" as a keyword, 86% were published after 1998. And any glance through the pages of *Antipode* in the past few years reveals an intensive engagement with the politics of neoliberalization. The journal has published 96 articles dealing with "neoliberalism" since 2000, but in the previous decade carried only one.[2]

On this evidence, neoliberalism might be considered to be a "post-globalization" keyword, one that has found wide currency since the late 1990s, as a means of *denaturalizing* globalization processes, while calling attention to their associated ideological and political constructions. Ironically, the term itself seems to have been subject to a form of globalization, the ubiquitous applications and promiscuous affiliations of which have led John Clarke (2008:137), among others, to question whether it has been degraded into a "next-generation 'globalization' concept", possibly due for "retirement". Aiwa Ong (2007) continues to find utility in refined concepts of neoliberalism, when applied in close-focus studies of mobile technologies of rule, although she distances herself from what are characterized as "big-N" formulations of neoliberalism, which variously assert or presuppose some hegemonic or systemic form (cf Hardt and Negri 2000; Harvey 2005). Gibson-Graham (2008:62) goes further still, portraying the preoccupation, among radical geographers in particular, with "studies of neoliberal this and that" as a politically counterproductive and ultimately disempowering form of "strong theory", the invocation of which is diagnosed as a kind of structuralist paranoia, inadvertently reproducing the self-same dominant order that it seeks to critique. In a similar vein, Barnett (2005:9) has railed against the "consolations" of neoliberalism for left analysts, abruptly contending that "there is no such thing as neoliberalism!"

Then, in an apparent case of life imitating art, the Wall Street crash of 2008 has been widely interpreted, across broad swaths of the political and intellectual spectrum, as a terminal moment for neoliberalism. French President Nicolas Sarkozy publicly mused, at the onset of the crisis, that "a certain idea of globalization is dying with the end of a financial capitalism", yielding a seemingly unambiguous ideological conclusion: "Self-regulation, to fix all problems, is over. Laissez-faire is over" (quoted in Erlanger 2008:C9). World Bank chief economist turned globalization critic, Joseph Stiglitz, promptly arrived at a similar judgment:

The world has not been kind to neo-liberalism, that grab-bag of ideas based on the fundamentalist notion that markets are self-correcting, allocate resources efficiently, and serve the public interest well. It was this market fundamentalism that underlay Thatcherism, Reaganomics, and the so-called "Washington Consensus" in favor of privatization, liberalization, and independent central banks focusing single-mindedly on inflation... Neo-liberal market fundamentalism was always a political doctrine serving certain interests. It was never supported by economic theory. Nor, it should now be clear, is it supported by historical experience. Learning this lesson may be the silver lining in the cloud now hanging over the global economy (Stiglitz 2008:1–2).

Of course, radical analysts of macrohistorical trends had been predicting this moment for some time.[3] Wallerstein (2008:2) was arguing in early 2008, for example, that, "The political balance is swinging back. Neoliberal globalization will be written about 10 years from now as a cyclical swing in the history of the capitalist world-economy." It should be noted, however, that these accounts are primarily concerned with long-run geoeconomic and geopolitical dynamics, rather than with the particularities of neoliberalization as a political project, an ideological construct, or an institutional matrix. Premonitions of structural crisis represent a recurrent theme in this literature, reflecting its concern with quasi-tectonic shifts in the economic "fundamentals". But there is an appropriate degree of circumspection concerning the timing and consequences of real-time crises (cf Wallerstein 2003, 2008). In Foster and Magdoff's analysis, for example, neoliberalism is portrayed as the "main legitimating ideology" of what is characterized as a phase of monopoly-finance capitalism, a manifest crisis in the latter representing a *de facto* crisis of the former (Foster and Magdoff 2009; WIN Magazine 2009). Here, the historical dynamics of financialization are explained in the language of Marx, Kalecki and Keynes, while the monetarism of Friedman, Greenspan and Bernanke is exposed for what it is—a credo, in effect, of neoliberalism itself (cf Gowan 2009). In this respect, it is misleading of Stiglitz to argue that neoliberalism was "never supported by economic theory"; particular *forms* of economic theory clearly played a constitutively central role in the project.

It was not just a credit bubble, then, that burst so spectacularly in 2008. Anticipating a structurally induced depression and global deflation, Wallerstein (2009) remains convinced that the world will be a very different place "when we emerge from the cellar", although whether it will be a better or worse one, ultimately, will be a matter for political struggle. Eric Hobsbawm's interpretation has been similarly circumspect: the conditions seem ripe for transformative change, but probably not revolutionary transformation; more likely, in his view, is a crisis-induced and pragmatically guided return to various forms of "mixed economy". Invited to talk to the BBC in the early weeks of the crisis, the venerable historian was asked if he felt "vindicated". Above that, Hobsbawm nevertheless confessed to a twinge of schadenfreude:

> It is certainly the greatest crisis of capitalism since the 1930s . . . The last 30 years [have witnessed] a sort of theological free-market ideology, which all the governments have taken to in the West . . . [It is] the end of this particular era. No question about it. There will be more talk about Keynes and less talk about Friedman and Hayek . . . This is the dramatic equivalent, if you like, of the collapse of the Soviet Union. We now know that the era has ended. [But] we don't know what's going to come (Hobsbawm 2008).

While the events of late 2008 may indeed have represented a kind of theological crisis for the neoliberal belief system (cf Bourdieu and Wacquant 2001), "what's going to come" remained an open question for Hobsbawm. His read in the Fall of 2008 was that forces of the right might be better placed to capitalize on the fallout of the economic crisis than those of the left, although the ruptural break with the immediate neoliberal past would surely amount to a moment of historical significance, akin to the collapse of state socialism. This was an argument that Naomi Klein had taken to the University of Chicago, of all places, just a few days earlier, where she contended that the financial crisis "should be for Friedmanism what the fall of the Berlin Wall was for authoritarianism: an indictment of ideology" (2008:2). Equally sacrilegious sentiments were also to be found in Vienna, another symbolic birthplace of neoliberalism's ideational project, where the former Federal Chancellor, Alfred Gusenbauer (2008:1), echoed the increasingly pervasive interpretation that "the fall of Wall Street is to neo-liberalism what the fall of the Berlin Wall was to communism".

Looking over the Wall

There are at least three reasons to be wary of mobilizing Berlin Wall metaphors in the heat of this ostensibly postneoliberal moment. The first concerns the character and form of neoliberalism itself, the social order for which last rites are being read; the second relates to what it is, ideologically speaking, that is on the other side of the wall; and the third caution refers to the metaphorical wall itself, as the concretized divide between neoliberalism and its "others". On all three grounds, we will raise some critical questions about the salience of collapse metaphors, using these as points of departure for thinking through some of the causes, characteristics, and consequences of the crisis. In the spirit of the emergent debate around "postneoliberalism"—the roots of which lie in Latin American politics, but which have acquired a new salience in the wake of the crisis in the North (see Brand and

Sekler 2009a; Macdonald and Ruckert 2009)—we venture into this territory with a view to constructive provocation rather than incautious prediction. After all, while crisis periods often vividly expose underlying power structures, connectivities, tensions, and contradictions, they are also moments of paralysis and panic, opportunism and obfuscation, visionary experimentation and catastrophic failure (Jessop 1992; Peck and Tickell 1994).

Beginning with the first of our reservations, the allegedly analogous relationship between the crisis of state socialism and that of neoliberalism, while the former may have fallen like a proverbial house of cards, in an almost simultaneous collapse of an entire ideological, institutional, and political complex (see Offe 1997; Przeworski 1991), recent events have been taking a rather different course. There may never, in fact, be a single moment that catalyzes and crystallizes the current crisis. The opening acts of the crisis *qua* crisis reach back at least as far as the initial failure of Bear Stearns hedge funds, based on securitized mortgages, in July 2007, and it has since been characterized by a quite unprecedented series of bailouts, stimulus packages, recovery plans, and multilateral summits . . . all against a backdrop of a now-global macroeconomic slowdown and glimpses, here and there, of "green shoots". Already, it seems that the slow "death" of neoliberalism, if that is what we are witnessing, is taking on melodramatic dimensions. Meanwhile, flamboyant denunciations of the follies of laissez-faire, delivered from right stage as well as left, coincide with desperate efforts to reboot some reformed version of the same system, by socializing financial (rather than social) risk, by attempting to pep up credit markets and consumer demand, by reimposing debt conditionalities on developing countries, by tamping down "protectionist" sentiments and talk of new entitlements, by facilitating the market disciplining of unionized segments of the workforce in order to "save" overproducing industries like automobiles, and so on.

Bright lines of various kinds, drawn between a neoliberal past and various forms of new realism in the turbulent present, may indeed be found in the public statements of financial managers and political leaders, but their actions often reveal much stronger threads of continuity. And while the Republican right in the USA has taken to issuing hysterical accusations of "socialism" at each and every moment of intervention, the Obama Administration proceeds with what might best be characterized as pragmatic determination. If this is some kind of new New Deal, it lacks both a name and a clearly defined (social) purpose. As Greg Albo sees the situation:

> The initial policy efforts of governments have been an attempt
> to reconstruct the existing policy regime and political relations,
> despite the severity of the recession limiting the possibility of doing

so ... The economic turmoil has produced, however, an ideological crisis of neoliberalism: the free market ideology that has been virtually uncontested at the level of political power for almost two decades is now totally discredited ... What remains of neoliberalism, it needs to be underlined [however], is its political embeddedness in state structures, policy instruments and the political field of social forces (Albo 2009:121).

To speak of neoliberalism "in crisis", needless to say, presupposes an understanding of the character of this elusively dispersed yet deeply embedded form of social rule. A singular, monolithic, and unified neoliberalism might indeed be prone to a correspondingly "total" crisis. But if, as we have argued elsewhere,[4] a dynamic conception of neoliberal*ization* is to be favored over static notions of neoliberal*ism*— defining a prevailing pattern of regulatory restructuring, driven by a family of open-ended social processes and associated with polymorphic forms and outcomes—then it follows that crises and contradictions will often impinge on particular social spaces, regulatory networks, sectoral fields, local formations, and so on, rather than necessarily reverberate through the unevenly developed complex as a whole. Moreover, neoliberalism's proven capacities in the (downward and outward) displacement and (forward) rescheduling of risks and crisis tendencies mean that its associated regulatory landscapes are especially dynamic. Because, in this conception, "neoliberalism" does not exist as a unified and static structure, as an equilibrating system, or as an end-state condition, it is correspondingly less likely to *fail* in a totalizing moment of collapse. In this sense, the historical analogy between the institutionally centralized and monological regime of state socialism seems peculiarly inapt.

Turning to our second reservation about the Berlin Wall metaphor, one clearly needs to consider the relationship between the social formation in crisis and those actually existing alternatives positioned, as it were, on the other side of the wall. On the occasion of the collapse of state socialism, of course, the dominant presence on the other side of the wall was hardly benign; it was an aggressively expansive strain of free-market capitalism, disproportionately shaped by the Anglo-American "model", as more "coordinated" forms of Japanese and German capitalism began to falter (Albert 1991; Peck and Theodore 2007). Within months, countries of the former Soviet bloc were overrun not only by a new breed of postsocialist entrepreneurs, but also by a small army of policy advisers, macroeconomic engineers, management consultants, and shock therapists, working in conjunction with newly empowered elite cadres to propel an irreversible "transition" to capitalism (see Gowan 1996; Toporowski 2005). The installation of what some would characterize as "designer capitalism" (see Offe 1996, 1997; Stark 1992) never occurred on a tabula rasa, of course, but it did take place in the context of a radical delegitimation of the old order and the routing of large sections of the ruling elite. While this fatal rupture of the preexisting social order effectively created an ideological vacuum, the manner in which this vacuum was filled was shaped by the balance of geopolitical power in the "external" capitalist world; by the strategic promotion of favored institutional and ideological designs, particularly those carrying the imprimatur of the multilateral banks, powerful donor nations, and their various epistemic communities; and, not least, by a generative "transition imaginary", the coordinates of which were established by idealized visions of the Golden past and the Golden West.

> Eastern Europe's market for policy ideas, suddenly opened in 1989, was swiftly captured by an Anglo-American product with a liberal brand name. This policy equivalent of fast food erected barriers to other new entrants and established a virtual monopoly of advice in most target states in the region. While some critics view it as having as much connection with West European liberalism as a Big Mac has with boeuf bourguignon, it has made up for any deficiency by superb advertising and aggressive salesmanship (Gowan 1996:3).

If the transition politics of the early 1990s conformed to a partially self-fulfilling vision of free-market teleology, entrained on a utopian end point, unattainable yet at the same time socially galvanizing, the radical contrasts with the turbulent present are immediately apparent. Orthodox economic hubris has certainly been challenged, while political pundits have become gripped by quite new uncertainties. Far from driving forward towards a utopian end point—the self-regulating market society—the crisis managers of today conspicuously lack any kind of destination imaginary or narrative, beyond the apologia of growth restoration . . . at any cost. True, there is a visceral sense of the sociospatial "origin" of the crisis—the failure of the US credit markets and their geographical representation in the form of "Wall Street"— but there is dissensus, bordering on paralysis, around the question of the destination, and even the direction, of reform/transformation efforts. The crisis managers seem effectively to be flying blind, and occasionally will confess as much.

There is certainly little evidence today of the kinds of transition imaginaries that were such a powerful force in the period of postsocialist reconstruction. The dominant objective of crisis management efforts at the present time would seem to be, firstly, the stabilization of credit markets as a means, secondly, of restoring orderly accumulation and economic growth. (Ironically, the "complexity" of this task is apparently such that it can only be safely handled by the same elite of financial technocrats and bandits that brought us the crisis in the first place.) Political rhetoric aside, how much of a break from neoliberal practice does this entail? In public discourse, there is a somewhat inchoate understanding that the way out of the crisis will involve "more regulation", and perhaps more "active" state roles, but there are few clearly articulated visions of the (alternative) form that such a regulatory compromise should take. None of these halting movements, of course, need necessarily take us "beyond" neoliberalism, which was nothing if not a politics of growth, and which never eschewed *all* forms of state intervention. Mainstream assessments effectively imply that all that is required, to borrow an apt stock-market metaphor, is a correction—a correction in (financial) regulation—in order to bring about running repairs to the regime of financialized capitalism.

More telling historical parallels might arguably be found, not in the postsocialist politics of the early 1990s, but in the third way project that took shape later in that decade, which was based on a vaguely defined path *away from* spurned alternatives, instead of a clearly articulated destination (see Giddens 1998, 2000). So far, the *Realpolitik* of postneoliberalism looks more like a crisis-driven "fourth way", a harder-edged form of the revisionist accommodations and centrist triangulations fashioned by the likes of Blair, Clinton and Schröder during the 1990s. If this strikes some as vacuous, it is arguably the case that an even more profound social-regulatory vacuum lies *outside and beyond* this reformist space—with powerfully articulated, genuinely progressive *alternatives* to neoliberalism. In light of these silences, could another crisis-driven makeover of neoliberalism be in the cards? The absence of a robust ideological counterweight to neoliberalism certainly raises this prospect, as indeed do the urgent efforts of dominant state and class forces to bring about some kind of reformist restoration. Notwithstanding the evident frailties and limits of these efforts, they will no doubt continue along their frenetic course; that is, until they encounter countervailing forces of equivalent magnitude. As Colin Leys (1990:127) once remarked, in the context of the debate around the last gasps of Thatcherism, "for an ideology to be hegemonic, it is not necessary that it be loved. It is merely necessary that it have no serious rival".

This brings us to our third reservation with the Berlin Wall metaphor, that it calls to mind an image of an impermeable barrier between neoliberalism and its "others". The notion of neoliberalism somehow standing separate from other social formations and political projects seriously misconstrues both the character of neoliberalism and the nature of its advance. In ways that echo the idealized rendering of the self-regulating market, to which neoliberal ideologies defer, neoliberalism has not, does not, and cannot describe an autonomous, self-sustaining socioeconomic system, endowed with an equilibrating logic of reproduction. (For this reason, ideal-typical formulations of "the neoliberal state" are questionable as a matter of principle.) Rather, neoliberal*ization* should be conceived as an hegemonic *restructuring ethos*, as a dominant pattern of (incomplete and contradictory) regulatory transformation, and not as a fully coherent system or typological state form. As such, it *necessarily* operates among its others, in environments of multiplex, heterogeneous, and contradictory governance. More than this, neoliberalism invariably exists in an essentially parasitical relationship with those extant social formations with which it has an antagonistic relationship, such as state socialism, social democracy, or neoconservative authoritarianism. To be sure, projects of neoliberalization tend to be associated with a certain cluster of recurring features, tendential characteristics, and family resemblances—among which we would enumerate a structural orientation to export-oriented, financialized capital; deep antipathies to social collectivities and sociospatial redistribution; and open-ended commitments to market-like governance systems, non-bureaucratic modes of regulation, privatization, and corporate expansion—but these are always, inescapably, forged and revealed in context-specific ways. There are more than contingent differences, then, between neoliberalism as a restructuring ethos, defined in abstract terms, and the actually existing reform programs found in, say, Sweden, South Africa, or Chile. And there is no paradigmatic ground zero (Peck 2004).

It follows that the relationship between neoliberalization and contentious or oppositional politics is anything but singular, symmetrical, or sequential (see Leitner, Peck and Sheppard 2007b). First of all, neoliberalism itself is a form of contentious politics, conceived and operationalized in an antagonistic relationship to various (local) others, such as specific forms of the developmental or Keynesian state. Furthermore, the long history of social struggles and institutional transformations that have marked neoliberalism's uneven ascendancy, consolidation, and crisis-driven adaption—including those around privatization, public austerity measures, and welfare retrenchment—clearly cannot be assigned harmlessly to the past. They have shaped, and continue to shape, the form and trajectory of neoliberalism, which has never proceeded unopposed and which has never exhibited the purity in practice that it claimed in rhetoric. Uneven processes of neoliberalization therefore constitute a complex legacy, far beyond the monochromatic binary of neoliberalism versus resistance, and encompassing everything from the crushing defeat of progressive forces to complicity and cooptation. Over the course of some three decades, neoliberal restructuring imperatives have themselves been profoundly shaped by this long history of regulatory struggles and boundary disputes, and in the process they have become even more deeply interdigitated with other sources of social and institutional power. Consequently, "the project" of neoliberalization can only be understood as a politically (re)constructed, nonlinear, and indeed mongrel phenomenon. There is no crisp and clean divide between its "inside" and its "outside"; there is no iron curtain between neoliberalism and its others.

For these reasons, it was not evasive of David Harvey to state, in response to the question of whether the current crisis marks the death of neoliberalism, that "it depends what you mean by neo-liberalism" (Harvey 2009:1). If one were to represent the strategic core of the project in terms of the state-assisted mobilization of financialized forms of accumulation, coupled with a rolling program of regressive class redistribution and social repression, then the current crisis looks more like a qualitative transformation than a terminal event or reversal. Neoliberalism's intellectual project may be practically dead, but, as a mode of crisis-driven governance, it could be entering its zombie phase (Peck forthcoming; Wacquant forthcoming), animated by technocratic forms of muscle memory, deep instincts of self-preservation, and spasmodic bursts of social violence. Understanding the gyrations and mutations of actually existing neoliberalism, and positioning these projects within social fields and ideological landscapes that include a range of hybrid formations, orthogonal initiatives, and oppositional counter projects, need not be an exercise in detached observation or analytical fatalism. Rather, it can open up debate around the short- to medium-term threats of various forms of neoliberal resuscitation and reconstitution, and the terrains over which alternative projects might be prosecuted. Of course, the horizons, modalities, and registers of contentious politics will exceed this calculus (Hart 2008; Leitner et al 2007a), so this is but one way to explore opportunities and threats lurking in the present conjuncture.

Crisis, Theory

"Neoliberalism's transformation from a marginalized set of intellectual convictions into a full-blown hegemonic force", Mudge (2008:709) writes, "began with economic crisis". More than this, as an historically specific, fungible, contradictory, and unstable process of market-driven sociospatial transformation, neoliberalization has been repeatedly and cumulatively *remade* through crises. Even during the first half-life of neoliberalism—when it existed largely as an ideational project, almost completely detached from state power—it represented a form of crisis theory (Peck 2008). The *neo*liberalism of the late 1940s, the 1950s, and the 1960s was an amalgam of free-market utopianism on the one hand, and a pointed, strategic critique of the prevailing Keynesian order on the other. This project later achieved traction in the structural dislocations and macroregulatory failures of the 1970s—the crisis moment that it had long anticipated and which it was *designed* to exploit. In this sense, neoliberalism was both conceived and born as a crisis theory.

In the wake of the Reagan–Thatcher ascendancy, as neoliberalism mutated into a series of state projects, recurrent crises and regulatory failures would continue, in effect, to animate the lurching, uneven advance of transnational neoliberalization. Indeed, crises might be considered to be a primary "engine" of neoliberalism's transformation as a regulatory project, since (historically and geographically, socially and institutionally) *specific* crises of Keynesian welfarism and developmentalism established the socioinstitutional stakes and the fields of action for the first rounds of regulatory struggles, during the project's roll-back phase, while crises and contradictions of neoliberalism's own making have since shaped cumulative rounds of roll-out, reconstruction, and reaction (Brenner and Theodore 2002a; Peck and Tickell 2002).

The legacies of these tawdry, crisis-driven historical geographies of neoliberalism remain starkly present in the current conjuncture. They underscore the claim that the uneven development of neoliberalism is contextually genetic rather than simply contingent (Brenner et al 2010), that neoliberalism is a reactionary credo in more than just a pejorative sense (Peck 2008). It follows that programs of neoliberal restructuring are substantially absorbed not only with the (always-incomplete) task of dismantling inherited institutional forms, but also with the open-ended challenges of managing the attendant economic consequences, social fallout, and political counteractions. Neoliberal strategies are deeply and indelibly shaped by diverse acts of institutional dissolution, but this destructive moment is more than just a "brush-clearing" phase; it is actually integral to the origins, dynamics, and logics of neoliberalization. Each and every actually existing neoliberalism carries the residues, therefore, of past regulatory struggles, which recursively shape political capacities and orientations, and future pathways of neoliberal restructuring. Perversely, programs of neoliberal restructuring are in many ways sustained by repeated regulatory failure; typically, they "progress" through a roiling dynamic of experimentation, overreach, and crisis-driven adjustment.

There are far-reaching consequences for the spatiality and sustainability of neoliberalism, in and beyond the current conjuncture. Neoliberalism has not and does not pulsate out from a single control center or heartland; it has always been *relationally* constituted across multiple sites and spaces of "co-formation". What is more, in light of neoliberalism's contradictory and crisis-animated "evolution", this process of relational constitution is a continuing one; it has entailed the cumulative *deepening* of neoliberalization tendencies, as regulatory trajectories have become increasingly interdependent, as transnational and cross-scalar policy learning has intensified, and as the rules of the game of regime competition have themselves been neoliberalized (Peck and Theodore 2007; Tickell and Peck 2003).

To invoke the "uneven development of neoliberalism" is not, then, simply to call attention to some kind of post facto geographical variation, or to a pattern of spatial deviations from a dominant, hegemonic or pure model (Brenner, Peck and Theodore forthcoming). It is, instead, a means of characterizing neoliberalism as an institutionally polycentric and multiply embedded form of market rule. This is not a story of some fully formed, coherently functioning, "regime-like" state of neoliberal*ism*, progressively expanding to encompass global regulatory space. Rather, processes of neoliberalization operate, articulate, and interpenetrate unevenly across places, territories, and scales. The uneven development of neoliberalization is therefore not a temporary condition, a product of its "incomplete" institutionalization or a reflection of partial hegemony. Neoliberalization (re)makes uneven development.

Neoliberalism's "new constitutionalism" (Gill 1998), was never a monocentric order, even if its consequences included the progressive "locking in" of certain mechanisms of market rule, the deepening of financialization and capital mobility, and the extension of various forms of commodification. In the process, coercive and competitive forms of policy transfer (cf Simmons et al 2008) became interpenetrated, remaking not only "local" regulatory formations but the macroinstitutional rule regimes within which these are recursively embedded. Regime competition and regulatory adaptation are not externally determined under these conditions, but underlying forces of "dull compulsion" effectively channel regulatory restructuring strategies along broadly neoliberal pathways—variously reinforced by hierarchical pressures from strong states and multilateral institutions; lubricated by networks of experts, practitioners, and advocates; and reproduced through the adaptive behaviors of social agents and institutions. Nevertheless, this could never produce simple convergence: institutional polymorphism and endemic regulatory failure, even under conditions of deep neoliberalization, remain stubborn facts of life.

Establishing "market rule" was never a matter of imposing, from above, a singular regulatory template. It has been about learning by doing (and by failing) within an evolving framework of market-oriented reform parameters and strategic objectives. If neoliberalism began life as a series of loosely interconnected projects of radical, market-oriented reform, each embedded within an antithetical social settlement, it has since been absorbed in the endless task of reconstructing these settlements. In the process, various "local" projects of neoliberal transformation have become increasingly interpenetrated and mutually referential (Tickell and Peck 2003), their ever-more intensive interaction progressively remaking regimes of macroinstiutional rule across plurinational scales and through transnational networks. Neoliberalism is no longer, if it ever was, an "internal" characteristic of certain social formations or state projects; it has since shaped the operating environment, the rules of engagement, the *relationality*, of these formations and projects themselves. In Jessop's (2000) terms, it has achieved the status of *ecological* dominance. This is what we have described as a shift from disarticulated to deep neoliberalization—from the uneven development of neoliberalization to the neoliberalization of regulatory uneven development itself (Brenner et al 2010).

It hardly needs to be pointed out that this is a far cry from neoliberalism's preferred forms of self-characterization and self-justification. In both the doxa and the dogma of neoliberalism, market solutions are peddled as universal cures. Channeling the *Grundrisse*, Altvater (2009:80) has observed that "the 'annihilation of time by space and space by time' . . . is inscribed into the neoliberal belief system [which] takes no notice of the specific characteristics of time and history". The excesses of "deregulated" financial capitalism surely represent one of the more grossly misguided attempts to realize this starkly utopian vision of disembedded market development, the inevitable overreach of which causes Altvater (2009:75) to contemplate "the last days of neoliberalism", while cautioning that postneoliberalism should not be elided with postcapitalism. The first condition may be a necessary prerequisite for the second, but in the current historical conjuncture it certainly will not be sufficient. And if neoliberal finance capitalism is not a singular, coherent, and logical system, but a contradictory and unevenly developed regime, bound together by a reworked package of market ideologies, hyper-rationalist truth claims, competitive pressures, and institutional practices, then its transcendence may not take the form of a big bang-style implosion.

Beyond Neoliberalism

If the experience of G20 meetings in the Spring of 2009 is anything to go by, neoliberal finance capitalism may go out with a whimper, if indeed it is going out at all. Here, rhetorical repudiations of market fundamentalism awkwardly coexisted with faltering explorations of various forms of "re-regulation". An unstable accord seems to have been forged, among the crisis managers of the G20, around the imperative to restart growth, to reflate slumping economies, and to restore faith (an apt word, in the circumstances) in global credit markets. The elite consensus is that, in order to staunch the deepening global recession, some combination of fiscal stimulus and judicious re-regulation is urgently needed. There is a shared desire, to coin a favorite Obama Administration phrase, to somehow hit the reset button.

Is this really the dawning of a postneoliberal era, in which the tyranny of market rule is vanquished through the rediscovery of multilateral cooperation and supranational regulation? It is tempting to conclude that neoliberalism's end arrived, quite appropriately, in the form of its very own short, sharp shock—of overdetermined financial crisis—and that what now beckons is a more humane, postneoliberal political order, governed by fundamentally different tenets and interests. Neoliberalism, we might reflect, was powerful enough to unleash financialized capitalism, but not powerful enough to save this destructively creative system from itself. Perhaps a double movement-style reflex toward more regulated markets is under way? Again, much turns on how the inherited neoliberal order is viewed in the rearview mirror. While this project may have traveled under the name of the free market, only with a deeply Polanyian sense of irony could it be said that this entailed a rerun of laissez faire; the *new* road to free markets having been "[re]opened . . . by an enormous increase in continuous, centrally organized and controlled interventionism" (Polanyi 1944:140–141). The twentieth century version of the free-market credo may have been a mobilizing ideological vision, a "strong discourse" aligned with major sources of political-economic power (Bourdieu and Wacquant 2001), but it was never a practically achievable socioeconomic destination, nor was it an accurate description of the realities of neoliberal governance. "Full" neoliberalization was never achieved because it could *never* have been achieved. And it never entailed an "absentee" state, but various kinds of reconstructed and reoriented states, dedicated to the ongoing tasks of market making and market-guided regulatory restructuring.

In this light, it is at the very least questionable that the hastily conceived plans—in treasury ministries around the world and at the G20 summits—to "bring the state back in" represent an emergent form of "financial socialism" (Sennett 2008), entailing "a step beyond the neoliberal mind-map" (Altvater 2009:79). Again, to paraphrase David Harvey, it really does depend what you mean by neoliberalism. The kind of neoliberal *Realpolitik* that has, for decades, fashioned a coexistence with selective corporate welfare, with the public absorption of private risk, with periodic bailouts of financial and credit markets, and with a succession of state author(iz)ed projects of "deregulation", can surely learn to live with the occasional violation of textbook principle—in the interest of getting the markets moving again, of course. Recent experience of rolling bank bailouts and publicly funded reflations of credit markets do not mark such a major break with neoliberal practice as some have been claiming, while the return of debt financing—along with loan conditionalities—threatens to recreate the circumstances in which multilateral banks "shoved the Washington Consensus down the throats of low- and middle-income countries" (Hailu 2009:1).[5] However, the very public exposure of what were previously obfuscated or clandestine acts of hypocrisy and incompetence may yield (political) consequences of its own. The seeds of an indeterminate legitimation crisis may indeed have been planted.

All of this begs the question of what it will take truly to escape the "neoliberal mind-map". On their own, crisis conditions will never be enough, not least because the tools of neoliberal governance were forged in, and for, precisely such conditions, and because the project of market rule has been periodically rejuvenated and restructured through crises. This said, the challenges posed by a genuinely global crisis are of a qualitatively different order from the succession of local (or local*ized*) crises that neoliberalism has confronted since the 1980s. The present crisis is clearly placing considerable pressure on the neoliberal operating system itself. At the same time, the world that this system has wrought—of globally integrated, heavily privatized, trade exposed, deeply financialized, and socially segregated capitalism—is clearly far more profoundly entrenched than any particular facet of neoliberal governance. Realistic near-term threats, such as a protracted overaccumulation crisis, some kind of global lock-in of public-sector austerity, renewed pressure for micro-neoliberal strategies, endemic failure in multilateral coordination, a widespread debt crisis, and a relegitimatation of neoliberal centrism under the Obama Administration, have led Bond (2009:194), among others, to issue a stern caution against "illusory postneoliberal hubris". Crisis-plus-governance failure may also be insufficient, then, to secure a transition to a progressive variant of postneoliberalism.

Should such an hegemonic transition occur, it may well take the form, as some have been arguing from a Latin American perspective (Brand and Sekler 2009b; Sader 2009; Sekler 2009), of an extended war of position, rather than a big bang. It is here that the uneven development of neoliberalism makes a difference, because while this may reduce the likelihood of a unified, ruptural collapse, it does open up the possibility of a *multi-front* war of position, waged across a differentiated terrain and through a range of contextually specific, conjunctural struggles. Following this logic, and recognizing the *constructed* nature of neoliberal capitalism (cf Block 2000; Peck 2005), leads Sekler (2009:62–63) to conclude that, "Just as neoliberalism cannot be regarded as a monolithic block, but as (re)constituted in different contexts, postneoliberalism or the respective *counter-hegemony* has to be considered 'under construction' . . . [through] many postneoliberalisms". This raises the prospect of a form of neoliberal transcendence grounded not only in strategic opposition to axiomatic neoliberal positions (regarding, for instance, financialization, deregulation, labor flexibililization, privatization, and trade liberalization), but also in a comprehensive and principled rejection of the neoliberal development imaginary, based on market universalism, one-size-fits-all policymaking, and global integration via commodification. The (re)mobilization, recognition, and valuation of multiple, *local* forms of development, rooted in local cultures, values, and movements—what might be called the progressively variegated economy—would indeed represent a radical break with neoliberal universalism (see Piore 2009). And just as Latin America was the "laboratory for neoliberal experiments par excellence" (Sader 2009:171), it is perhaps fitting that this region should also have become one of the principal proving grounds for alternative forms of socioeconomic politics (Kennedy and Tilly 2008; Brand and Sekler 2009b).

While Latin American experiences can and should spur the postneoliberal imagination, the region's lessons are also sobering ones. Here, audacious forms of neoliberalized accumulation by dispossession inadvertently prepared the ground for widespread social mobilization and radical resistance politics. And in the decade or so that followed, electoral realignments in Venezuela, Brazil, Argentina, Bolivia, Chile and elsewhere consolidated progressive gains, as a period of hegemonic dispute gave way to region-wide hegemonic instability (Sader 2009). Moving purposefully in the direction of postneoliberal forms of governance has, however, been a challenge, even for the region's largest economies. Global financial flows, trading regimes, and investment policies continue to be guided by logics of short-term, price competition—in the context of global overaccumulation—while progressive forms of multilateral coordination can only be negotiated in the long shadows of imperial and neoimperial power (Drake 2006). As Sader (2009:176) notes:

> the deregulation fostered by neoliberal policies favoured the hegemony of financial capital in its speculative mode. In order to instate a different model, it would be necessary to introduce new forms of economic regulation, which would be very difficult, even in the current crisis, once deregulation has a foothold. It could not come from a single country, no matter what its importance, because others would benefit from the flow of capital rejected in this country. At the same time, it would be hard to come to a large-scale international agreement, due to the different interests of the biggest powers and international corporations.

Whereas neoliberalism may have exposed the limits of financial capitalism, it has also undermined the strategic and organizational resources required for its transcendence. In Sader's (2009) eyes, the root of the problem for progressive forces is what he characterizes as a "gulf" between the evident failures of neoliberalized capitalism and the potential of postneoliberal movements, forces, and interests. The short- and medium-term prospects for such forms of alternative politics will surely be structured (and to some extent constrained) by the neoliberalized terrains on which they must be prosecuted. This is not simply a matter of contending with (residual) neoliberal power centers, in economics ministries, in international financial institutions, in think tanks, in the media, and in much of the corporate sector. Perhaps more intractably, it must also entail overcoming the profound reconstitution of cross-national, interlocal, and cross-scalar *relations* through various forms of market rule, which facilitate the reproduction of neoliberalized logics of action, institutional routines, and political projects—both through the dull compulsion of competitive pressures and through the harsh imperatives of regulatory downloading.

The long-run consequences of the current crisis may indeed include an intensification of these hostile conditions, logics, forces, and relations, such that some modalities of neoliberal rule are reconstituted almost by default. If the untidy arc of the neoliberal ascendancy was characterized, more or less successively, by a root-and-branch challenge to faltering Keynesian hegemonies, by conservative vanguardism and stridency, and by centralist accommodation and technocratic normalization, it may indeed be about to enter a post-programmatic or "living dead" phase, in which residual neoliberal impulses are sustained not by intellectual and moral leadership, or even by hegemonic force, but by underlying macroeconomic and macroinstitutional conditions— including excess capacity and overaccumulation at the world scale, enforced public austerity and global indebtedness, and growth-chasing, beggar-thy-neighbor modes of governance. In such a climate, the transformative potential of progressive, postneoliberal alternatives— for all their social, ecological, and indeed economic urgency—may be preemptively constrained, if not neutralized. It will continue to be imperative, therefore, to push for radical transformations in interlocal and international regulatory relations, the liminal zones in which residual neoliberalisms lurk, through every channel available, including the nation state. New spaces must be carved out not only for a global ethics of responsibility, but also for sustainable forms of sociospatial redistribution—anathema to neoliberalism—which can ultimately only be secured *between* places, through a reconstitution of sociospatial *relations* (see Massey 1994; 2007). This is not simply to say that progressive localisms can only be secured, in the long term, through complementary "top-down" interventions, but to suggest that the effective propagation of such alternatives, while a prerequisite for postneoliberalism proper, will ultimately require a transformative shift in inherited macroinstitutional rules of the game—neoliberalism's last hiding place as a "living dead" ideology? Without this, the potential of progressive postneoliberal projects will continue to be frustrated by the dead hand of market rule.

Acknowledgements

Thanks to Eric Sheppard, Loic Wacquant, Kevin Ward, and to *Antipode*'s referees, for comments on this essay, responsibility for which remains our own, and to Nik Heynen for this forbearance.

Endnotes

[1] Data on academic articles are from the ISI's *Web of Knowledge*. *New York Times* articles are retrieved from ProQuest Historical Newspapers and LEXIS/NEXIS. Similar, historically consistent measures for countries in the structurally adjusted South, and/or for Spanish language publications, are more difficult to come by, but would be expected to reveal a somewhat earlier onset of critical and popular concerns with neoliberalism, dating to the debt crises of the 1980s (see Fourcade-Gourinchas and Babb 2002; Nef and Robles 2000).
[2] See also Aguilar and Herod (2006), Brenner and Theodore (2002b), England and Ward (2007) and Laurie and Bondi (2005).
[3] See, especially, Arrighi (2007), Brenner (2002), Duménil and Lévy (2004), Foster and Magdoff (2009), Tabb (2008) and Wallerstein (2008).
[4] See Brenner and Theodore (2002a), and Peck and Tickell (2002); for elaborations of these arguments, see Brenner (2004), Brenner et al (2010), Peck (2004), and Peck et al (2009).
[5] During 2008, no less than 224 different conditionalities were placed on multilateral bank loans to some 15 countries, enforcing less-than post-Washington Consensus policy positions like fiscal reform, financial liberalization, privatization, trade liberalization, exchange rate adjustments, and price liberalization (Hailu 2009). As per the established operating procedure, the toughest reforms were imposed on the poorest countries.

References

Aguilar L L M and Herod A (eds) (2006) *The Dirty Work of Neoliberalism*. Oxford: Blackwell
Albert M (1991) *Capitalisme contre capitalisme*. Paris: Le Sevil
Albo G (2009) The crisis of neoliberalism and the impasse of the union movement. *Development Dialogue* 51:119–131
Altvater E (2009) Postneoliberalism or postcapitalism? The failure of neoliberalism in the financial market crisis. *Development Dialogue* 51:73–86
Arrighi G (2007) *Adam Smith in Beijing*. London: Verso
Barnett C (2005) The consolation of "neoliberalism". *Geoforum* 36(1):7–12
Block F (2000) Deconstructing capitalism as a system. *Rethinking Marxism* 12(3):83–98
Bond P (2009) Realistic postneoliberalism—a view from South Africa. *Development Dialogue* 51:193–211
Bourdieu P and Wacquant L (2001) NewLiberalSpeak: notes on the new planetary vulgate. *Radical Philosophy* 105:2–5
Brand U and Sekler N (2009a) Postneoliberalism: catch-all word or valuable analytical and political concept? *Development Dialogue* 51:5–13
Brand U and Sekler N (2009b) Struggling between autonomy and institutional transformations:social movements in Latin America and the move towards post-neoliberalism. In L Macdonald and A Ruckert (eds) *Post-neoliberalism in the Americas* (pp 54–70). New York: Palgrave
Brenner N (2004) *New state spaces*. Oxford: Oxford University Press
Brenner N, Peck J and Theodore N (2010) Variegated neoliberalization: Geographies, modalities, pathways. *Global Networks* 10(2):1–41

Brenner N and Theodore N (2002a) Cities and the geographies of "actually existing neoliberalism". *Antipode* 33(3):349–379

Brenner N and Theodore N (eds) (2002b) *Spaces of Neoliberalism*. Oxford: Blackwell

Brenner R (2002) *The Boom and the Bubble*. London: Verso

Clarke J (2008) Living with/in and without neo-liberalism. *Focaal* 51(1):135–147

Drake P W (2006) The hegemony of U.S. economic doctrines in Latin America. In E Hershberg and F Rosen (eds) *Latin America after Neoliberalism* (pp 26–48). New York: New Press

Duménil G and Lévy D (2004) *Capital Resurgent: Roots of the Neoliberal Revolution*. Cambridge, MA: Harvard University Press

England K and Ward K (eds) (2007) *Neoliberalization*. Oxford: Blackwell

Erlanger S (2008) Sarkozy stresses global financial overhaul. *New York Times* 26 September:C9

Foster J B and Magdoff H (2009) *The Great Financial Crisis*. New York: Monthly Review Press

Fourcade-Gourinchas M and Babb S (2002) The rebirth of the liberal creed: paths to neoliberalism in four countries. *American Journal of Sociology* 108(3):533–579

Gibson-Graham J-K (2008) Diverse economies: Performative practices for "other worlds". *Progress in Human Geography* 32(5):613–632

Giddens A (1998) *The Third Way: The Renewal of Social Democracy*. Cambridge: Polity

Giddens A (2000) *The Third Way and its Critics*. Cambridge: Polity

Gill S (1998) New constitutionalism, democratisation and global political economy. *Pacifica Review* 10:23–38

Gowan P (1996) Neo-liberal theory and practice for Eastern Europe. *New Left Review* 216:3–60

Gowan P (2009) Crisis in the heartland: Consequences of the new Wall Street system. *New Left Review* 55:5–29

Gusenbauer A (2008) La Strada on Wall Street. *Project Syndicate Commentary* October, http://www.project-syndicate.org Accessed 15 January 2009

Hailu D (2009) Is the Washington consensus dead? *One Pager* 82. Brasilia: International Policy Centre for Inclusive Growth

Hardt M and Negri A (2000) *Empire*. Cambridge, MA: Harvard University Press

Hart G (2008) The provocations of neoliberalism: Contesting the nation and liberation after Apartheid. *Antipode* 40(4):678–705

Harvey D (2005) *A Brief History of Neoliberalism*. Oxford: Oxford University Press

Harvey D (2009) The crisis and the consolidation of class power: is this *really* the end of neoliberalism? *Counterpunch* 13–15 March, http://www.counterpunch.org/harvey03132009.html Accessed 15 March 2009

Hobsbawm E (2008) Is the intellectual opinion of capitalism changing? *Today* program, BBC Radio 4, 20 October, www.news.bbc.co.uk/today/hi/today/newsid_7677000/7677683.stm Accessed 20 October 2008

Jessop B (1992) Fordism and post-Fordism: A critical reformulation. In M Storper and A J Scott (eds) *Pathways to Industrialization and Regional Development* (pp 46–69). New York: Routledge

Jessop B (2000) The crisis of the national spatio-temporal fix and the ecological dominance of globalizing capitalism. *International Journal of Urban and Regional Research* 24(2):323–360

Kennedy M and Tilly C (2008) Making sense of Latin America's "third left". *New Politics* 11(4):11–16

Klein N (2007) *Shock Doctrine: The Rise of Disaster Capitalism*. New York: Metropolitan Books

Klein N (2008) Wall Street crisis should be for neoliberalism what fall of Berlin Wall was for communism. Lecture at the University of Chicago, http://www.stwr.org Accessed 4 January 2009

Laurie N and Bondi L (eds) (2005) *Working the Spaces of Neoliberalism*. Oxford: Blackwell

Leitner H, Sheppard E S, Sziarto K and Maranganti A (2007a) Contesting urban futures: Decentering neoliberalism. In H Leitner, J Peck and E S Sheppard (eds) *Contesting Neoliberalism: Urban Frontiers* (pp 1–25). New York: Guilford

Leitner H, Peck J and Sheppard E S (2007b) Squaring up to neoliberalism. In H Leitner, J Peck and E S Sheppard (eds) *Contesting Neoliberalism: Urban Frontiers* (pp 311–327). New York: Guilford

Leys C (1990) Still a question of hegemony. *New Left Review* 181:119–128

Macdonald L and Ruckert A (eds) (2009) *Post-neoliberalism in the Americas*. New York: Palgrave

Massey D (1994) *Space, Place and Gender*. Minneapolis: University of Minnesota Press

Massey D (2007) *World City*. Cambridge: Polity

Mirowski P and Plehwe D (2009) *The Road from Mont Pelerin: The Making of the Neoliberal Thought Collective*. Cambridge, MA: Harvard University Press

Mudge S L (2008) What is neo-liberalism? *Socio-Economic Review* 6(4):703–731

Nef J and Robles W (2000) Globalization, neoliberalism, and the state of underdevelopment in the new periphery. In R L Harris and M J Seid (eds) *Globalization and Neoliberalism in the Developing Countries* (pp 27–48). Leiden: Brill

Offe C (1996) Designing institutions in East European transitions. In R E Goodin (ed) *The Theory of Institutional Design* (pp 199–226). Cambridge: Cambridge University Press

Offe C (1997) *Varieties of Transition: The East European and East German Experience*. Cambridge, MA: MIT Press

Ong A (2006) *Neoliberalism as Exception*. Durham, NC: Duke University Press

Ong A (2007) Neoliberalism as a mobile technology. *Transactions of the Institute of British Geographers* 32(1):3–8

Peck J (2004) Geography and public policy: Constructions of neoliberalism. *Progress in Human Geography* 28(3):392–405

Peck J (2005) Economic sociologies in space. *Economic Geography* 81(2):129–176

Peck J (2008) Remaking laissez-faire. *Progress in Human Geography* 32(1):3–43

Peck J (forthcoming) Zombie neoliberalism and the ambidextrous state. *Theoretical Criminology* 13

Peck J and Theodore N (2007) Variegated capitalism. *Progress in Human Geography* 31(6):731–772

Peck J, Theodore N and Brenner N (2009) Neoliberal urbanism: Models, moments, mutations. *SAIS Review* 29(1):49–66

Peck J and Tickell A (1994) Searching for a new institutional fix: The after-Fordist crisis and global–local disorder. In A Amin (ed) *Post-Fordism* (pp 280–315). Oxford: Blackwell

Peck J and Tickell A (2002) Neoliberalizing space. *Antipode* 34(3):380–404

Piore M J (2009) Second thoughts: On economics, sociology, neoliberalism, Polanyi's double movement and intellectual vacuums. *Socio-Economic Review* 7(1):161–175

Polanyi K (1944) *The Great Transformation*. Boston: Beacon Press

Przeworski A (1991) *Democracy and the Market*. Cambridge: Cambridge University Press

Sader E (2009) Postneoliberalism in Latin America. *Development Dialogue* 51:171–179

Sekler N (2009) Postneoliberalism from a counter-hegemonic perspective. *Development Dialogue* 51:59–71

Sennett R (2008) Expand state ownership to save jobs. *Financial Times* 1 October:11

Simmons B A, Dobbin F and Garrett G (2008) Introduction:the diffusion of liberalization. In B A Simmons, F Dobbin and G Garrett (eds) *The Global Diffusion of Markets and Democracy* (pp 1–63). New York: Cambridge University Press

Stark D (1992) Path dependence and privatization strategies in East Central Europe. *East European Politics and Societies* 6(1):17–54

Stiglitz J E (2008) The end of neo-liberalism? *Project Syndicate Commentary* July, http://www.project-syndicate.org Accessed 20 December 2008

Tabb W K (2008) Four crises in the contemporary world system. *Monthly Review* October:43–59

Tickell A and Peck J (2003) Making global rules: Globalization or neoliberalization? In J Peck and H W-c Yeung (eds) *Remaking the Global Economy* (pp 163–181). London: Sage

Toporowski J (2005) *Theories of Financial Disturbance*. Cheltenham: Edward Elgar

Turner R (2008) *Neo-liberal Ideology*. Edinburgh: Edinburgh University Press

Wacquant L (forthcoming) Crafting the neoliberal state: Workfare, prisonfare and social insecurity. *Theoretical Criminology* 13(3)

Wallerstein I (2003) Cancun: The collapse of the neo-liberal offensive. *Commentary* 122. Fernand Braudel Center, Binghamton University

Wallerstein I (2008) The demise of neoliberal globalization. *MRZine* February, http://www.mrzine.monthlyreview.org Accessed 4 January 2009

Wallerstein I (2009) The politics of economic disaster. *Commentary* 251, Fernand Braudel Center, Binghamton University

Wang H (2003) *China's New Order*. Cambridge, MA: Harvard University Press

WIN Magazine (2009) Capitalism's burning house: Interview with John Bellamy Foster. *MRZine* January, www.mrzine.monthlyreview.org Accessed 1 July 2009

Wu F (2009) China's neoliberal urban transformation. Mimeo, School of City and Regional Planning, Cardiff University

D/developments after the Meltdown

Gillian Hart

University of California, Berkeley, CA, USA
University of KwaZulu-Natal, Durban, South Africa;
hart@berkeley.edu

Abstract: Part of what makes the current conjuncture so extraordinary is the coincidence of the massive economic meltdown with the implosion of the neoconservative Project for a New American Century, and the reappearance of US liberal internationalism in the guise of "smart power" defined in terms of Diplomacy, Development, and Defence. This essay engages these challenges through a framework that distinguishes between "Development" as a post-war international project that emerged in the context of decolonization and the Cold War, and capitalist development as a dynamic and highly uneven process of creation and destruction. Closely attentive to what Gramsci calls "the relations of force at various levels", my task in this essay is to suggest how the instabilities and constant redefinitions of official discourses and practices of Development since the 1940s shed light on the conditions in which we now find ourselves.

Keywords: development, capitalist crisis, US hegemony, militarism, Gramsci, Polanyi

Introduction

> It may be ruled out that immediate economic crises of themselves produce fundamental historical events; they can simply create a terrain more favourable to the dissemination of certain modes of thought, and certain ways of posing and resolving the entire subsequent development of national life... The specific question of economic hardship or well-being as a cause of new historical realities is a partial aspect of the question of the relations of force, at various levels (Gramsci 1971:184–185).

Appearing before the US Senate Intelligence Committee on 12 February 2009, Director of National Intelligence Dennis Blair announced that "The primary near-term security concern of the United States is the global economic crisis and its geopolitical implications" (Blair 2009:2). While noting that most of the demonstrations (thus far) have been in Europe and the former Soviet Union, Blair's Threat Assessment report underscores the economic and political vulnerability of many African and Latin American countries, along with the growing influence of China in these regions which is "boosting Chinese economic and diplomatic influence... and generating questions about Beijing's

Antipode Vol. 41 No. S1 2009 ISSN 0066-4812, pp 117–141
doi: 10.1111/j.1467-8330.2009.00719.x

Source: Zapiro, *Mail & Guardian*, 11 June 2009 (reproduced with permission from Jonathan Shapiro)

long-term intention in the developing world—potentially as an alternative development model" (Blair 2009:20). These new security priorities acquire additional significance in light of Hillary Clinton's definition of the key elements of "smart power"—Diplomacy, Development, and Defence.

Blair also calls attention to the growing critique of US stewardship of the global economy and international financial structure, pointing out that "The widely held perception that excesses in US financial markets and inadequate regulation were responsible has increased criticism about free market policies, which may make it difficult to achieve long-time US objectives, such as the opening of national capital markets and increasing domestic demand in Asia" (Blair 2009:3). It was of course the Reaganites' move to prise open national capital markets in the context of the debt crisis in the early 1980s that helped to siphon massive resources from parts of the global South into Wall Street, and inflict the agony of "adjustment" on poor residents of countries hit by financial crises (Gowan 1999, 2009).

In the context of the meltdown a vigorous debate is taking shape around the question of whether we now find ourselves in a postneoliberal era, and if so how to characterize it.[1] It seems to me that this debate is misplaced. Rather than an ideal-type (or, for that matter, yet another iteration of post-ist critique) the imperative is for analyses that can illuminate the shifting relations of force in the present conjuncture—precisely because, as Gramsci points out in the epigram at the start of this essay, political dynamics can't be read off economic crises. The most important point about any concrete analysis of the relations of force, he goes on to observe, is that "such analyses cannot and must not be ends in themselves (unless the intention is merely to write a chapter of past history), but acquire significance only if they serve to justify a particular practical activity, or initiative of the will" (Gramsci 1971:185). In short, *how* one writes a history of the present—or of the present conjuncture—carries significant political stakes.

With that in mind, my task in this essay it to situate the present conjuncture in relation to a series of key turning points since the 1940s, of necessity in extremely broad brush strokes. Building on and extending earlier work, I suggest a framework for thinking about these moments of crisis and redefinition that distinguishes between "big D" and "little d" development.[2] "Big D" Development I define as the multiply scaled projects of intervention in the "Third World" that emerged in the context of decolonization struggles and the Cold War. "Little d" development refers to the development of capitalism as geographically uneven but spatially interconnected processes of creation and destruction, dialectically interconnected with discourses and practices of Development.

It is important to differentiate this framework from the distinction often drawn between development as an immanent process and as intentional practice (see for example Arndt 1981). In *Doctrines of Development* (1996), the most deeply historicized analysis along these lines, Cowen and Shenton contend that development in the sense of intentional intervention was present at the very birth of industrial capitalism to contain the depredations wrought by development understood as immanent process. They also maintain that "the idea of the intentional practice of development was not an invention of the post-1945 international order"; rather, "it had been invented to deal with the problem of social disorder in nineteenth-century Europe through trusteeship" (Cowen and Shenton 1996:60).

Instead of an immanent process distinct from intervention, "little d" development refers to the simultaneously creative and destructive tendencies inherent in the workings of global capitalism that require and call forth ongoing intervention.[3] A partial but important inspiration is Karl Polanyi's (2001 [1944]) account of capitalism's double movement, about which Cowen and Shenton are silent. In addition to insisting that "the road to the free market was opened and kept open by an enormous increase in continuous, centrally organized and controlled interventionism" (2001:146), Polanyi maintained that the unleashing of markets for labor, land/nature, and money wreaks profound havoc and generates countertendencies and demands for social protection. Far from the countermovement representing some sort of "external" intervention in an inexorable unfolding teleology, these opposing tendencies are contained *within* capitalism. By the same token, the conditions for global capital accumulation must be actively created and constantly reworked. The conception of "little d" development with which I am working brings Polanyi's conception of the double movement together with Gramsci's insistence on attention to "relations of force at various levels" within an explicitly spatialized frame of understanding that owes a great deal to Lefebvre's (1991 [1974]) relational conceptions of the production of space.

Also in contradistinction to Cowen and Shenton, I insist that interventions and claims made in the name of "big D" Development in the post-1945 period cannot be reduced to a historically continuous model of trusteeship. While such continuities are undoubtedly important, I agree with Corbridge (1997) that Cowen and Shenton's relentless focus on continuity obscures more than it illuminates. What I am calling "big D" Development was deeply entangled in the end of colonial empires and the rise of new forms of US hegemony in the context of the Cold War. My task is to suggest how instabilities and constant redefinitions of official discourses and practices of Development since the 1940s shed light on the current conjuncture.

Polanyi is relevant here as a theorist of imperialism as well as capitalism's double movement. One of the many contributions of Giovanni Arrighi's extraordinary book *Adam Smith in Beijing: Lineages of the Twenty-First Century* (2007), along with Silver and Arrighi (2003), is a critical elaboration and extension of Polanyi's theory of imperialism along Gramscian lines to highlight the distinctive geopolitical and economic reconfigurations of finance capital, industrialism, and militarism that marked the *belles époques* of British and US hegemony a century apart, as well as their limits. As I argue more fully in a companion piece to this essay (Hart, 2009), there are some significant complementarities between Arrighi and Silver's approach and my conjunctural analysis of post-war D/developments.

Periodizing Post-war D/developments

The modern constructive [colonial] policy advocates State intervention in promoting development . . . *Laissez-faire* is dead, but economic forces still remain active, everywhere, unceasingly. When a colonial power adopts a constructive policy with a view to enhancing welfare, it must first repair the ill-effects of economic forces in the past, and then bring them under control so as to prevent further damage (Furnivall 1948:313).

In his remarkably Polanyian analysis of British and Dutch colonial policy and practice since the nineteenth century, Furnivall shows how periods of economic liberalism were invariably followed by more "protective" forms of interventionism to contain the destructive fallout. A Fabian and former colonial officer in Burma, Furnivall was writing in the period immediately prior to Burma's declaration of independence in 1948. The "modern constructive policy" to which he refers was embodied in the Colonial Development and Welfare Act of 1940. Unlike earlier colonial grants that were limited to capital expenditure to facilitate colonial extraction, the 1940 Act focused on "development in the widest sense, and it also permitted grants for recurrent expenditure on certain services, such as agriculture, education, health and housing; beyond this it provided an additional £500,000 for colonial research" (Furnivall 1948:314). While critical of the destruction wrought by colonialism and supportive of "moderate" nationalism, Furnivall asserted that "like the time-expired convict, a people that has known subjection is in need of after-care" (p 468).[4] At the same time, he acknowledged "the rude challenge to western dominion in the tropics . . . [and] the general growth of discontent and unrest" (p 2) as forces driving the "modern constructive policy" of Development.

Writing from a very different perspective, historian Fred Cooper also locates the origins of Development in the imperial crisis of the late 1930s and 1940s, brought on by a series of militant strikes and boycotts in the West Indies and different regions of Africa, as well as national liberation movements all over the colonial world. He shows how Development "did not simply spring from the brow of colonial leaders, but was to a significant extent thrust upon them, by the collective action of workers located within hundreds of local contexts as much as in an imperial economy" (Cooper 1997:85). In the post-World War II period, Development became a means by which Britain and France sought to hang on to their African colonies. They did so in part through efforts to consolidate and manage an urban African working class. Yet colonial ambitions to create a docile class of urban citizens were thwarted by nationalist leaders, trade unionists and other anti-colonial movements, who deployed precisely these seemingly a-cultural discourses of Development in order to stake claims and demands. Beyond illuminating African decolonization struggles, Cooper's intervention underscores how Development can operate as much as a discourse of entitlement as a discourse of control.

Proponents of the "post-Development" critique that emerged in the 1990s tell a significantly different origin story. For them, the birth of Development can be timed quite precisely: "We propose to call the age of development that particular historical period which began on 20 January 1949, when Harry S. Truman for the first time declared, in his inauguration speech, the Southern hemisphere as 'underdeveloped areas'" (Sachs 1992:2; see also Escobar 1995:3). From the perspective of post-Development, Truman's promise of an enlightened "West" bringing

Journal compilation © 2009 Editorial Board of *Antipode*.

progress to a benighted "Rest" inaugurated Development as a discursive formation through which the "Third World" came to be defined as backward, and in need of intervention and guidance along the path to modernity. Clearly the Cold War and Truman's Point IV are crucial elements of post-war Development. Through the Truman doctrine, as Craig and Porter (2006:47) point out, "security fears powerfully linked 'independent' national development to active multilateralism, in ways that the US Congress would fund". Yet there are clear limits to understandings of Development cast in terms of a power/knowledge system originating in the West that seamlessly produces subjects who define themselves as backward and underdeveloped.

More generally, I suggest, Development is most usefully understood in terms of the exercise of power in multiple, interconnected arenas, inseparably linked with the socially and spatially uneven dynamics of capitalist development. Part of what is useful about this sort of framing is its capacity to illuminate key turning points in official discourses and practices of Development since the late 1940s. It provides the basis, in other words, for a conjunctural analysis of shifts in the relationships between "big D" and "little d" development that can very broadly be periodized as follows:

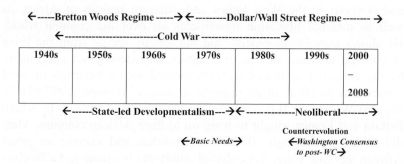

In the discussion that follows, I focus on two key turning points and the connections between them: the shift in the early 1970s from the Bretton Woods system of fixed but adjustable exchange rates to what Peter Gowan (1999) calls the Dollar/Wall Street Regime, along with the rise of novel forms of finance capital and a new phase of American imperialism; and (b) the shift in the early 1980s from the post-World War II era of state-led Developmentalism to the neoliberal counterrevolution in the context of the debt crisis, along with the vastly increased powers of the World Bank and International Monetary Fund to impose loan conditionalities in much of Latin America, Africa, and parts of Asia.

While my main focus will be on the era of neoliberalism, it is important at least to touch on the multiple instabilities and pressures that emerged over the course of state-led, neo-Keynesian Developmentalism and forced a redefinition of official discourses and practices in terms of "Basic Needs" in the early 1970s. They included the limits of import substitution industrialisation (ISI); the neglect of peasant agriculture through much of the 1960s associated with the disposal of US grain surpluses; and the breakdown of the post-war international food order at the end of that decade.[5] Of great importance as well are the Vietnam War, and the rise of anti-systemic movements (Arrighi, Hopkins and Wallerstein 1989)—including what Watts (2001) calls Fanonite post-colonial movements:

> By the 1960s the nationalist wardrobe looked worn and threadbare. A broad swath of Latin American and African regimes had descended rapidly into military dictatorship, and the first generation of political elites—whether Sukarno in Indonesia, Nasser in Egypt or Nkrumah in Ghana—were quick to abandon any serious commitment to popular democracy. From this conjuncture emerged a veritable pot pourri of guerilla impulses—there were at least 30 major guerilla wars during the 1950s and 1960s!—student-led democratic movements, worker and union struggles, and nascent "culturalisms" seen in the rise of the Muslim brotherhoods and aggressive ethnic communalism for whom corrupt state apparatuses, and a questionable record of nation-building, provided the fuel for their political aspirations. Whatever their obvious ideological and tactical differences, Maoist militants in Peru, middle-class students in Mexico City, Naxalite organizers in India and Muslim reformists in Cairo all shared a radical disaffection from the postcolonial state and the decrepit political cronyism of peripheral capitalism (Watts 2001:172).

These pressures are central to grasping the redefinition of Development, exemplified by McNamara's accession to the presidency of the World Bank in 1968. No doubt Bob's efforts to expiate his guilt for war crimes in Vietnam played into the new emphasis on poverty, inequality, and unemployment, but it was the conjunctural crisis that created the conditions for the shift. The intellectual ethos of Basic Needs hinged on the neopopulist claim that small-scale forms of production are relatively more efficient, and on the inversion of earlier dualisms. In place of notions that growth of the "advanced" sector would drain the swamp of surplus labor lurking in the "backward" sector, the "informal" sector came to embody all the virtues lacking in its clunky, inefficient counterpart. The simultaneous discovery of hard-working women and small peasants contributed to the mix, as did the widespread availability of Green Revolution foodgrains technologies that seemed to promise a quick solution to the world food crisis as well as redistributive forms of production.

While discourses and policies of Basic Needs in general fell far short of their stated aim of poverty alleviation, they were accompanied by massive resource flows. Between 1970 and 1980, according to Wood (1986:83), total flows of financial resources to "less developed countries" burgeoned from around $17 billion to $85 billion. Over the same period, loans grew from 79% of total resource flows to 91.4%. The most dramatic increase was in commercial bank lending and portfolio investment, which rose from $777 million in 1970 to nearly $18 billion in 1980. According to Wood (1986:130), medium- and long-term public debt shot up from $75.1 billion in 1970 to $634.4 billion in 1983. It was the so-called Volcker shock (1979–1982)—when the US Federal Reserve base rate rose from an average of 8% in 1978 to over 19% in 1982—that ushered in the debt crisis and vastly changed roles of the World Bank and IMF in Latin America, Africa, and parts of Asia.

From Bretton Woods to the Dollar-Wall Street Regime

The passage from the collapse of the Bretton Woods system of fixed but adjustable exchange rates in August 1971 to the onset of the debt crisis in the early 1980s is a tale typically told in the following terms. First, the Nixon administration's ending dollar convertibility and the devaluation of the dollar represented a defeat for a weakened American capitalism, battered on the one hand by competitive pressures associated with the economic ascendance of Germany and Japan and, on the other, by the quagmire in Vietnam and the rise of oppositional movements in the USA and beyond. Second, while the devaluation of the dollar created the conditions for the OPEC oil price rise, the escalation of oil prices in 1973 was carried out by the Gulf states as part of an anti-Israel and anti-US policy connected to the Yom Kippur wars. Third, the flood of petrodollars pouring into commercial banks created the economic incentive for massive loans to Third World governments during the 1970s that paved the way for the debt crisis. This narrative is often linked to a related set of claims about the collapse of the Bretton Woods system presaging the decline if not the disappearance of the nation state, and the slide into a chaotic non-system driven by inexorable technological and market forces. These are precisely the ingredients of what I have elsewhere called the "impact model" of globalization (Hart 2002b).

In *The Global Gamble* (1999), Peter Gowan offers a revisionist interpretation that carries extremely important implications for grasping the current conjuncture. First, he contests the widely held view that the ending of dollar convertibility represented the decline of US hegemonic power. Instead, Gowan maintains that "the Nixon administration was determined to break out of a set of institutionalized arrangements which limited US dominance in international monetary politics in order to establish a new regime which would give it monocratic power over international monetary affairs" (1999:19). He concedes that US capital was indeed being challenged by its capitalist rivals in product markets at the time in the context of generalized overaccumulation, but argues that "the breakup of the Bretton Woods system was part of a strategy for restoring the dominance of US capitals through turning the international monetary system into a dollar-standard regime" (1999:19).[6]

Gowan also maintains that the Nixon administration exercised direct influence on the OPEC oil price rise—initially with the intention of whacking Germany and Japan, and subsequently insisting that petrodollars be recycled through commercial banks:

> The Nixon administration's second step was to try to ensure that international financial relations should be taken out of the control of state central banks and should be increasingly centred upon private financial operators. It sought to achieve this goal through exploiting US control over international oil supplies. Yet as we now know, the oil price rises were the result of US influence on the oil states and they were arranged in part as an exercise in economic statecraft directed against America's "allies" in Western Europe and Japan. And another dimension of the Nixon administration's policy on oil price rises was to give a new role, through them, to the US private banks in international financial relations (Gowan 1999:21).[7]

As early as 1972, the Nixon administration planned for US private banks to recycle petrodollars to non-oil-producing states; other governments wanted petrodollars recycled through the IMF—but the US rejected this (Gowan 1999). At the same time, Gowan points out that US banks were hesitant to lend to Third World governments, and had to be provided with incentives and insurance. These included the abolition of capital controls in 1974, scrapping the ceiling on bank loans to a single borrower, repositioning the IMF to structure bailout arrangements that shifted the risk of such loans to the populations of borrowing countries, and the prising open of capital markets. While ensuring the banks would not lose, these arrangements have also meant that financial crises in the South provoked capital flight of private wealth holders that ended up strengthening Wall Street.[8]

In other words, the recycling of petrodollars through the private banking system to Third World governments was not simply the product of disembodied market forces.[9] Instead it was a key element of the re-engineering of international monetary and financial arrangements that undergird what David Harvey calls "the new imperialism."[10] A related and crucially important point is that what has come to be called neoliberal globalization emerges from this analysis *not* as a set of inexorable technological and market forces increasingly divorced from state-political controls, but as the product of deliberate power ploys that could have gone in other directions.

The shift from the Bretton Woods Regime to the Dollar/Wall Street Regime in the 1970s coincided with the defeat of the US in Vietnam— and, as Mahmood Mamdani (2004) has shown, with the shift in the center of gravity of the Cold War from Southeast Asia to Southern Africa, Central Asia, and Central America, along with a US decision to harness, or even to cultivate, terrorism in the struggle against regimes it considered pro-Soviet. In other words, the 1970s represented a moment of major reconfigurations of US military engagements with the global South as well as of finance capital.

In the wake of the debt crisis that erupted in 1982, Asian, African, Latin American, and Middle Eastern countries became sharply bifurcated according to "how well the state concerned coped with the volatile and often savage dynamics of the new Dollar/Wall Street Regime" (Gowan 1999:48). Those countries that had taken the borrowing course became entrapped by debt, and hauled through the stabilization (IMF) and structural adjustment (World Bank) wringer. In many Latin American countries, the 1980s became known as the "lost decade". For many in Africa, the 1980s were the start of an ongoing nightmare with average incomes plummeting 30% in real terms between 1980 and 1988 (Ghai 1991). A number of East Asian countries, in contrast, were able to avoid the debt trap. The reasons for these divergent trajectories are subject to intense debate. In the early phases of the neoliberal counterrevolution, key figures in the World Bank invoked rapid East Asian growth as incontrovertible evidence of the superiority of "the market" over "the state" (see for example Balassa 1981; Kreuger 1981). This interpretation came under fire from a number of academics who invoked Chalmers Johnson's (1982) notion of the "developmental state" to assert the powerful role of the state in East Asian accumulation.[11] It was in the context of growing tension between the USA and Japan over the deregulation of financial markets that the battle over the interpretation of East Asian "miracles" moved into top gear, culminating in the World Bank's publication of *The East Asian Miracle* in 1993. Funded by Japan, this awkward, heavily vetted text conceded to state intervention in East Asian economies, but held firmly to a "market-friendly" interpretation. Robert Wade's (1996) fascinating account of the production of this text illuminates how key figures within the Bank sought to fend off the Japanese challenge to neoliberal orthodoxy, and the larger configurations of power within which this challenge unfolded. The story of *The East Asian Miracle*, he argues, shows the determining force of US values and interests in the functioning of the Bank. Yet this influence does not simply reflect direct pressure from US government officials. It operates primarily through the Bank's reliance on world financial markets and "the self-reinforcing congruence between the values of the owners and managers of financial capital and those of the US" (Wade 1996:35).

Any effort to grasp the present meltdown must pay close attention to how the shift to the Dollar/Wall Street Regime and the US-sponsored neoliberal counter-revolution have played out through interconnections between the US and different regions of the global South over the past 30 years. The rapid rise of East Asia and more recently China have fed escalating US demand for cheap industrial products and credit, feeding in turn into the largest debt overhang the world has ever known. At the same time, the prising open of capital markets in much of Africa and Latin America, parts of Asia and the former Soviet Bloc has produced a massive re-routing of surplus capital to the USA. Rather than just a one-sided plunder, Gowan (2002:139) points out, the opening up of capital markets has had real appeal to the propertied classes in these countries, enabling them to transfer their assets to Wall Street and other financial centers and live as rentiers rather than risking their wealth in local investment. At the same time, of course, this process has been riddled with tensions and contradictions—and it is to some of these contradictions and their interconnections that we now turn.

The Laboratory of Neoliberalism

The neo-liberal ideological wave that inundated the United States following the election of Ronald Reagan, and Great Britain under the Thatcher government . . . began in Chile in 1974 not simply as a set of economic measures, but rather as a broad, revolutionary ideology . . . In the context of violent change in political power structures, it was used by the new military rulers as the requisite substance for radical transformation of the state (Valdés 1995:5).

When the CIA-sponsored military coup headed by Augusto Pinochet overthrew socialist president Salvador Allende's government on 11 September 1973, a group of 50–100 Chilean economists trained at the University of Chicago since the late 1950s were waiting in the wings. Funded by US government representatives in Chile who sought to combat "socialist ideology", the so-called Chicago boys were the product of close connections between conservative forces in Chile and key figures in the Department of Economics at the University of Chicago (Valdés 1995:49). By 1975, the Chicago boys had launched what was then the most radical free market strategy anywhere in the world.

At the height of Keynesian influence in the post-war period, the University of Chicago became a bastion within whose walls neoliberal tenets were forged. In *Capitalism and Freedom* (1982:vi), Friedman and Friedman recalled how, in the 1950s, "Those of us who were deeply concerned about the danger to freedom and prosperity from the growth of government, from the triumph of the welfare state and Keynesian ideas, were a small beleagured minority regarded as eccentrics by the great majority of our fellow intellectuals". At the same time his colleague Harry Johnson spoke of "the small band of the initiate" who "kept alive the understanding of the fundamental truth through the dark ages of Keynesian despotism" (cited by Valdés 1995:60). Key Chicagoans also participated in the Mont Pelerin Society, an exclusive band of brothers (and apparently one sister) established in 1947 by Freidrich von Hayek, Keynes' right-wing rival since the 1930s who moved to the University of Chicago in 1952. Its purpose, articulated by Hayek in no uncertain terms, was to "win the battle of ideas". The Mont Pelerin Society, in turn, spawned a plethora of conservative think tanks with global reach (see also Cockett 1994; Desai 1994; Peck 2008). In his glowing history of the Society, R.M. Hartwell deploys military metaphors to describe how, at the height of the Keynesian onslaught, the Society "saved the flag" and "renewed the attack" (Hartwell 1995:203).

While the discrediting of Keynesianism in the 1970s was of course bound up with broader economic crises, the Chilean coup provided the opportunity for a frontal assault on both Keynesian and Development economics. The Chicago boys received direct and active backup support from their mentors: "Key figures like Milton Friedman, Hayek himself, and Arnold Harberger, a Chicago economist married to a Chilean who was the spiritual godfather of many of the Chicago Boys, appeared in Chile, often to throw their weight behind their proteges at crucial moments" (O'Brien and Roddick 1983:57).[12] Thus, at precisely the moment that global financial arrangements were in the process of being reconfigured, Chile provided the testing grounds upon which neoliberal economic doctrines gained traction—and from which they were picked up and used in other parts of the world. When the debt crisis hit in the early 1980s, IMF and World Bank economists made extensive use of the Chilean "success"—along with the twisted interpretation of East Asian "miracles" mentioned earlier—to set in place the harsh stabilization and structural adjustment policies of the 1980s in many other parts of Latin America and Africa.

In his compelling analysis of the connections between Chile and New Zealand, Len Richards observes that:

> Neoliberalism arrived in New Zealand, like Chile, as the result of a "calculated bid" to implant it, but it arrived at its destination via the Trojan Horse of the 1983–90 Labour Government rather than at the point of a gun. The role of the Labour Party was crucial. The implementation of policies that attacked the very mechanisms of class compromise in New Zealand would probably have required . . . some form of dictatorship if not carried out by what is putatively the working class's "own" political party (Richards 2003:130).

The Chilean experiment also played directly into the rise of Thatcherism and Reaganism. Following their Chilean "victory", key Chicagoans exercised their influence on Reaganism through their insertion into channels of connection between capital and the state. Dezalay and Garth (2002:81) describe how the "core of the economic brain trust that in 1981 would introduce the nation to Reagonomics" had met regularly at the Bechtel Corporation since the 1970s. The meetings were convened by the CEO of Bechtel George Schultz, former professor at the University of Chicago business school, who went on to become secretary of the treasury in the Ford administration, and secretary of state under Reagan. Schultz's "brain trust" included Friedman, his fellow Chicago economist George Stigler, and Walter Wriston of Citibank—the leading recycler of petrodollars to the Third World in the 1970s and a key architect of the IMF bailout arrangements that saved the banks, and ushered in programs of stabilization (IMF) and structural adjustment (World Bank) over huge swathes of Africa and Latin America.

In short, neoliberal forms of capitalism did not simply arise in the "core" and spread from there to the "periphery". Instead they are more usefully seen as the products of power-laden practices and processes of spatial *interconnection*. These processes also underscore how the installation of neoliberal forms of capitalism articulates with the political structure of the state, the balance of political forces, and forms of class and non-class struggle in ways that are historically and geographically specific, *as well as* spatially interconnected.

While Chile was the laboratory for neoliberal economic policies, it was also an important locus in the emergence of the international human rights movement in the mid-1970s that gathered force over the 1980s. Dezalay and Garth (2002) provide a compelling account of how, reacting to revelations of the role of the CIA in the fall of Allende, a group of activist members of Congress and US academics sought "to put the country on the side of the angels, by using human rights as the touchstone of US foreign policy" (Dezalay and Garth 2002:129). They show how the human rights movement took shape through interconnected "palace wars" in the USA and key Latin American countries, and contributed to the move away from military regimes in Argentina, Brazil, and Chile. This new transnational orthodoxy of power encompassed *both* neoliberal economics *and* liberal human rights. Hence, for example, the observation by Dominguez that "Chilean democracy accomplished what Pinochet's Chicago Boys never could in an authoritarian context: it bound the nation's future to the market by means of a nation's consent" (cited by Dezalay and Garth 2002:177). At the same time, as a number of observers have pointed out, the authoritarian resonances of the Pinochet era remained powerfully evident in relations between capital and labor.[13]

The human rights movement also helped to propel the massive burgeoning of NGOs all over the world in the 1980s, many of which took upon themselves the mantle of "global civil society", helping to implement neoliberal reforms while also managing some of the destructive fallout. Craig and Porter (2006:61) report that by 1988 the rapidly growing number of NGOs provided approximately US$5.5 billion in financing, compared with the World Bank's US$4 billion, going on to note that "After a long courtship, World Bank financing of NGOs jumped by more than 300 percent in 1989." The intertwining of neoliberal economic policies with liberal discourses of democracy and human rights in the 1980s are crucial to grasping the conjuncture in the early 1990s when Fukuyama and others celebrated the global convergence on market capitalism and liberal democracy.

Renovating Neoliberalism?

Elsewhere (Hart 2001, 2002a) I have traced some key processes through which the market orthodoxy that seemed so firmly entrenched in the early 1990s gave way to far more overtly interventionist moves to contain disruptive tendencies, with multilateral and bilateral aid agencies actively reasserting and extending their mission of trusteeship in the name of Development, good governance, participation, social capital, and so forth. At the risk of oversimplifying, these disruptive forces include the so-called IMF bread riots in many parts of Africa and Latin America in the 1980s that were subjected to harsh stabilization and structural adjustment measures; myriad environmental movements fighting against the destruction of nature; struggles unleashed by the privatization of water and other basic services; the rise of militant land movements such as the *Movimento Sem Terra* in Brazil; the disruptions that accompanied the Asian financial crisis, and of course the anti-capitalist/anti-globalization movements that burst onto the international stage in Seattle in 1999. In addition, as Paul Lubeck (2000), Michael Watts (2003), and others have suggested, the rise of Political Islam understood as an "anti-systemic movement" is intimately linked with the implosion of the secular nationalist Development project.[14] These dynamics go a long way towards explaining the paradox to which Henry Bernstein calls attention:

> Freeing the market to carry out the tasks of economic growth for which it is deemed uniquely suited rapidly escalated into an extraordinarily ambitious, or grandiose project of social engineering ... [T]he terrain of development discourse and the range of aid-funded interventions have become ever more inclusive to encompass the reshaping, or transformation, of political and social (and, by implication, cultural) as well as economic institutions and practices (Bernstein 2005:116).

   This reincarnation of what Furnivall (1948) might call a "modern constructive policy" of Development differs in some important ways from the Basic Needs thrust of the 1970s. Whereas the rhetorical focus of the latter was on the relative efficiency of small-scale forms of production, what Mohan and Stokke (2000) call "revisionist neoliberalism" is marked by a convergence on "the local" as both more efficient and more democratic. The turn to "the local" has gone hand in hand with the invocation of "civil society" understood—in good liberal fashion—as a distinctively separate sphere from "the market" and "the state", and a key site for the production of social capital. While the World Bank in alliance with NGOs (and increasingly with philanthropic organizations like the Gates Foundation) have been on the forefront of expertise and knowledge production, these "third way" shifts have emanated from multiple sources and sites in the global North and South that are often deeply interconnected with one another.

   In seeking to grapple with these shifts, a number of us have turned to Polanyi (2001 [1944]) whose account of capitalism's double movement seems to be unfolding before our very eyes.[15] Yet, while Polanyi's insights are indispensable, his analysis is also limited by what Burawoy (2003) identifies as his Durkheimian conception of society.[16] Among other problems, this has enabled abstracted (and dare I say disembedded) readings of Polanyi that hamstring our capacity to grapple with the current conjuncture. In one common interpretation, Polanyi has served as the handle for a mechanistic hydraulic model in which "top-down" neoliberalism automatically calls forth "bottom-up" resistance. Yet, as Burawoy (2003:240) points out, this "optimistic" reading of Polanyi is made possible by his inadequate conception of society.

   Others deploy Polanyi to maintain that what he called "enlightened reactionaries" have successfully engaged in conservative projects of social containment.

   Reading Polanyi through Regulation theory, Porter and Craig (2004), for example, argue that a range of such reactionaries—which can include functionaries in international financial institutions, central governments, NGOs, "ordinary left voting constituents", and so on—rally to mitigate the social disruptions of market-led liberalization: "Each in various ways contests and regulates the market orientation, giving it a human face or policy limit" (Porter and Craig 2004:391). Far from challenging the neoliberal capitalist global order, they maintain, this re-embedding movement serves to reinforce the agents of global capitalism. At least for the time being, it represents a "triumph of the technical and consensual over the political and contested . . . since it offers many avenues to deflect and redirect politically alert critique or grassroots activism"; accordingly, "the poor are left very much within local framings, where their vulnerabilities, lacks and needs are apparent, but where they must seize on opportunities to participate in structures of national and global competitiveness" (Porter and Craig 2004:411–415).

An alternative—although complementary—view is that neoliberalism (especially in its revisionist form) often works as a seductive cultural project. In this view, which draws heavily on Nikolas Rose's (1999) neo-Foucauldian conception of neoliberal (or advanced liberal) governmentality, neoliberalism represents a *new modality* of government predicated on interventions to extend an "enterprise model" and market logic to all forms of conduct. In addition, this process of "responsibilization" often goes hand in hand with new or intensified invocations of "community" as a sector "whose vectors and forces can be mobilized, enrolled, deployed in novel programmes and techniques which encourage and harness active practices of self-management and identity construction, of personal ethics and collective allegiances" (Rose 1999:176).

While describing what are undoubtedly important dimensions of official projects, Regulationist and neo-Foucauldian accounts are severely limited by their reliance on ideal types. Neither attends to struggle, acquiescence, negotiation, and contestation as active constitutive forces in multiple, interconnected arenas.[17] By the same token, neither can come to grips with the slippages, openings, and contradictions that are crucial to any effort to grapple with possibilities for more far-reaching social change. The limits of both formulations— either singly or in combination—emerge with great clarity from Nancy Postero's brilliant book *Now We are Citizens* (2007) on what she calls neoliberal multiculturalism in Bolivia. This richly detailed historical ethnography based on her extended engagements with Guaraní Indian residents of Bella Flor, a peri-urban community on the outskirts of Santa Cruz, turns around the Law of Popular Participation (LPP). Implemented in the mid 1990s in response to increasingly confrontational marches, strikes, and mass mobilizations in many regions of Bolivia, the LPP redirected a substantial proportion of public spending from national to municipal governments, and recognized indigenous groups as legitimate participants. The intent was "to pass some of the responsibility for governing onto the citizens themselves, make the population more governable, and soften the costs of painful economic policies" (Postero 2007:161).

Postero shows how, while the LPP initially acted as a palliative, new forms of activism emerged as a consequence of Guaraní participants' contradictory engagements with the institutions and practices of the LPP. On the one hand they were subjected to "new techniques of the self", with technocratic NGOs promoting "a bureaucratic, professional indigenousness" in combination with transparency, efficiency, and rational participation (2007:186). Yet Guaranís' participation in these new forms of local government also brought them face to face with ongoing racism and massive corruption by political elites, whose positions were strengthened by the LPP. At the same time LPP reforms fell far short of addressing material deprivation and wrenching processes of urbanization and social disintegration on the edges of an expanding city. Emphasizing that neoliberal rationalities of rule were only part of the conditions in which Guaranís found themselves, Postero points out that:

> focusing on the acquiescence and the internalization of the logic of responsibilization can obscure the other equally strong forces and discourses at work. The discourse and rationalities of neoliberalism are powerful, but so are the ongoing discourses of race and class as well as long-term patterns of state–civil society opposition. While one discourse may create Bolivian neoliberal subjects responsible for their own governing, the other reminds those subjects that they are lazy Indians. One creates a citizen expecting to benefit from the state's resources, and the other empowers the traditional *patrones* (masters) to continue their control. (Postero 2007:187)

Now We are Citizens makes three important sets of contributions that extend well beyond Bella Flor. First, it enables powerful new understandings of the Bolivian revolution that brought Morales and the *Moviemento al Socialismo* (MAS) to power in 2005. Postero argues that the October 2003 gas war—a decisive moment in this revolution—demonstrated in part how both the inclusions and the exclusions of the LPP and other reforms "enabled citizens, particularly indigenous citizens, to act against the continuing limitations of state-sponsored multiculturalism and the costs of neoliberal economic policy" (2007:220). She emphasizes that this was not simply an "Indian uprising", but the coming together or articulation of multiple grievances which gave rise to a new Bolivian public "that presented the state with demands based on experiences of race and class discrimination . . . raising its demands in the language of citizenship, rights, and democracy" (2007:5).

Second, especially when read in conjunction with Mark Goodale's *Dilemmas of Modernity: Bolivian Encounters with Law and Liberalism* (2009), Postero's work illustrates the limits of neo-Foucauldian and Regulationist analyses of neoliberalism, as well as the relational and processual understandings made possible by critical ethnography. Together they enable us to grasp the historically and geographically specific forces that fed into the Bolivian revolution, while also reflecting on its wider interconnections, reverberations, and implications.[18]

Finally, recent Bolivian history serves as a reminder that poor populations in large regions of the global South have for several decades been subject to the agonies of economic contraction now convulsing Europe and the USA. At the same time, it exemplifies the contradictions that have accompanied the ascent of rapacious forms of finance capital backed by the military might of the USA; the transformation of the IMF into a public insurance organization for financial operators and speculators in the ongoing financial blow-outs; and arrangements that have forced poor populations in many parts of the South to shoulder the burden of adjustment while at the same time enabling property-owning classes in these countries to transfer their assets to Wall Street and other destinations. What is so significant about Bolivia is how palliative measures designed to contain popular discontent fed into a far more radical project of social change. Bolivian experience is also of great significance when situated in relation to diverse but interconnected forces at play in other parts of the world. While crises of capitalism hold out progressive possibilities, they also carry significant dangers—including the rise of new forms of fascism, racism, and xenophobia. In concluding, let me suggest how the sort of conjunctural analysis of D/development outlined in this essay might speak to some key challenges thrown up by the conditions in which we now find ourselves.

Some Challenges of the Conjuncture

> The world is a unit, whether one likes it or not, and . . . all countries, when they remain in certain structural conditions, will pass through certain "crises" (Gramsci 1995:220–221).

In the epigram at the start of this essay, Gramsci warns against reading politics off economic crises. There is now a huge body of analysis and debate on the economic dynamics responsible for the meltdown, but far less attention to "the relations of force at various levels". Gramsci used this phrase to refer to reciprocally interconnected economic and political relations that are linked in turn with what he calls the relations of military forces, both technical and "politico-military" (1971:175–185). In addition—and directly connected to his emphasis on militarism— Gramsci insisted that analysis of relations of force cannot be limited to the national level, but must focus on how "international relations intertwine with internal relations of nation states, creating new, unique and historically concrete combinations" (1971:182); and that "this relation between international forces and national forces is further complicated by the existence within every State of several structurally diverse territorial sectors, with diverse relations of force at all levels" (1971:182).

Over the past 30 years "new, unique, and historically concrete combinations" have indeed taken shape that far exceed what could have been imagined in the late 1970s. Instead of what was widely seen at the time as the collapse of US hegemony, we have witnessed a fundamental reconfiguration in relations between the US and different regions of Asia, Africa, Latin America and the Middle East that have simultaneously strengthened and undermined US economic and political dominance. Intense debates are underway over whether US global hegemony is now in terminal crisis—and whether the ascent of China (and India) is opening the way for a reversal of power relations between the global North and South, and the emergence of an alternative to capitalism as we have known it.[19] In one of his final essays, co-authored with Lu Zhang, Giovanni Arrighi argued that the backfiring of the neoliberal counterrevolution has created conditions favorable to the emergence of a new Bandung—a claim that is provoking intense debate, especially among those who assert the emergence of an "empire of capital" that cuts across any North–South divide. Yet it is also important to recall that Arrighi insisted that the future is wide open, and that any alternative will be crucially shaped by what he called anti-systemic movements of protest and self-protection.[20]

Of great importance in grappling with these questions and debates in present conjuncture is the coincidence of the economic meltdown with the implosion of the neoconservative Project for a New American Century, and the reappearance of US liberal internationalism in the guise of "smart power". First articulated by Suzanne Nossel in *Foreign Affairs* in 2004 as an attack on the Bush administration, "Smart Power" asserts the imperative for a liberal internationalist strategy to reclaim and refurbish tattered US hegemony, as well as insisting that military power and humanitarian endeavors can be mutually reinforcing. In her confirmation hearings, as we saw earlier, Hillary Clinton emphasized Development along with Diplomacy and Defence as key elements of the Obama administration's vision of smart power.[21] The reappearance of Development in US foreign policy discourse hand in hand with militarism is central to Dennis Blair's redefinition of "security" in his *Annual Threat Assessment* (2009), which focuses on efforts to maintain US financial and political dominance in relation to Chinese incursions into Africa and Latin America. Also of significance is a revival of US military strategy towards Vietnam-era counterinsurgency in Central Asia as well as "ungoverned" spaces in Africa: "The recent establishment of the US Africa Command (Africom) and the growing presence of Special Operations forces in places like Mali, Chad and Somalia hint at what might be in store" (Klare 2009:4).[22] In short, Development forms a key element in the latest round of liberal internationalism, inextricably linked with US militarism and deeply implicated in politico-economic relations between China and the USA.

A central theme in this essay has been that Development is not just about the domination of the Rest by the West. Rather, it emerged from the crisis of imperialism in the late 1930s as part of an effort to deal with challenges from below, signaling in effect the impending end of colonial empires. In the immediate post-World War II era, French and British Development projects aimed at holding on to African colonies overlapped with those emerging from new forms of heavily militarized US hegemony, Pax Americana, and the Cold War. Since the 1950s, official discourses and practices of Development have undergone constant redefinition, under pressure from anti-systemic movements along with the contradictions thrown up by global capital accumulation and geopolitical force fields. Born out of anti-colonial movements, appropriated by multiple social forces, and intertwined with the vagaries of capitalism and imperialism, projects of Development have always been shot through with tensions and contradictions—and these are likely to multiply and amplify in the conditions in which we now find ourselves.

A central challenge of the present conjuncture is grasping how these tensions and contradictions are being produced in practice—and how they hold open the possibility for something different to emerge. If it is in concrete, everyday practice that these tensions are produced, then it is in practice that we must look for them. This is precisely the importance of critical ethnography combined with what I have called relational comparision (Hart 2002; 2006b). Far more than just an empirical method, critical ethnography is a means for advancing from the abstract to the concrete, in the sense of concrete concepts that are adequate to the concrete in history.

In this essay I have drawn heavily on work in Bolivia both because recent Bolivian history embodies the possibilities of social change, and because this work exemplifies what seems to me the promises of critical ethnographic practice. As in many other parts of the world, (neo)liberal ideologies, policies, and forms of rule in Bolivia have been deeply entwined with interconnected historical geographies of racialized dispossession. Postero's (2007) ethnography illuminates far more than just a neoliberal rationality of rule or conservative re-embedding strategy operating in the idiom of Development. Neoliberal projects helped create conditions in which histories, memories, and meanings of specifically racialized forms of dispossession erupted in the present, crystalizing around struggles over the control of natural resources. Working in another region of Bolivia, Goodale (2009) shows how marginalized campesinos appropriate and vernacularize expectations of modernity. In so doing, he argues, they do not simply become conscripts of the very episteme that would apparently liberate them. Instead, they combine "the grandeur of human rights discourse with indigenist imagery from selected moments in Bolivian history, gestures toward redistributive modes of production, and direct democracy" (2009: 170).

In short, these Bolivian studies are significant both for the light they shed on one of the most remarkable ruptures of the neoliberal era, and in illustrating the capacity of critical ethnographies to come to grips with the contradictory dynamics that hold open possibilities for social change. They also show how these possibilities rest crucially on specific but interconnected historical geographies as well as on how memories and meanings of the past are reconfigured in the present in and through everyday situated practices. Precisely because politics can't be read off economic structures and crises, such specificities and interconnections will be crucial to any effort to produce a different politics, and to forge alliances across registers of difference.

Acknowledgements

Thanks to Jean Lave and David Szanton for endless patience and wise counsel, and to Noel Castree, Jenny Greenburg, Keith Hart (no relation!), Nancy Postero and two anonymous reviewers for constructive suggestions.

Endnotes

[1] See for example McDonald and Ruckert (2009) and a recent issue of *Development Dialogue* (no. 51, 2009) entitled "Postneoliberalism: A beginning debate".

[2] Hart (2001; 2002a; 2004). This essay also incorporates part of Hart (2006a).

[3] It seems to me that Cowen and Shenton deploy a rather narrow conception of immanent development that operates at a very high level of abstraction, in part to underscore Marx's sharp critiques of both the utopian socialists and List. For a useful discussion of Marx's conception of immanence in terms that are deeply critical of a teleological interpretation, see Gramsci (1971:399–402, 449–452).

[4] See Pham (2005) for a fascinating account of Furnivall's ambivalent views on colonization and Burmese independence.

[5] For an interesting take on import substitution industrialisation, see Maxfield and Nolt (1990). Friedmann (1982) provide an extremely useful analysis of the global structure of foodgrain production and distribution, and its breakdown in the late 1960s and early 1970s.

[6] He notes, for example, that "The August 1971 decision to 'close the gold window' meant that the US was no longer subject to the discipline of having to try to maintain a fixed par value of the dollar against gold or anything else; it could let the dollar move as the US Treasury wished and pointed towards the removal of gold from international monetary affairs. It thus moved the world economy on to a pure dollar standard" (Gowan 1999:19–20).

[7] The denomination of oil in terms of dollars is, of course, one of the key reasons why the US has been able to run huge deficits with the rest of the world.

[8] For example, during the debt crisis of the early 1980s, the capital outflow from Argentina, Mexico, and Venezuela has been estimated at $58.8 billion (Gowan 1999:35).

[9] While borrowing from Wall Street was both easy and economically rational in the conditions of the 1970s, borrowing governments failed to grasp that the entire macroeconomic framework could be transformed by "*political decisions about the dollar price and interest rates of the US government transmitted through the world economy by the DWSR [Dollar Wall Street Regime]*" (Gowan 1999:48; italics in original).

[10] Indeed Harvey draws directly on Gowan in his analysis of how the shift from the Bretton Woods regime to the Wall Street/US Treasury/IMF regime has served as a "formidable instrument of economic statecraft to drive forward both the globalization process and the associated neoliberal domestic transformations" (Harvey 2003:129). In

a forthcoming essay I discuss more fully some important distinctions between Harvey's new imperialism and Arrighi's (2007) analysis of US hegemony.
[11] They include Amsden (1989), Castells (1992), Evans (1995) and Wade (1990). Yet the construction of East Asian debates in terms of "states versus markets" fails to recognize how East Asian strategies "are based on an explanatory framework which analyses national patterns and processes within a global context, and a nationalist normative framework which seeks national economic development through rapid industrialization" (Gore 1996:78).
[12] Harberger was a key figure in the discrediting of Development economics. As a junior faculty member in the Department of Economics at Boston University in the early 1980s, I observed the dismantling of Development economics at first hand.
[13] See for example the collection edited by Winn (2004).
[14] Elements include what Watts calls the "decrepit rentier capitalism" associated with the oil boom; the petro-bust of the mid 1980s that brought IMF/World Bank-led austerity and neoliberal reforms crashing down on a number of Middle Eastern and West Asian states; and the complex geopolitics of the region:"The historical confluence of these powerful forces—all saturated with an American presence in the form of oil companies, global regulatory institutions, foreign investment, and military commitments—crippled, one might say destroyed, a secular nationalist project that was, in any case, of shallow provenance" (Watts 2003:8).
[15] For example, Hart (2001, 2002a, 2004), Jessop (2002), Peck and Tickell (2002).
[16] Thus Burawoy draws on Gramsci to complement Polanyi, while others turn to Weber or neo-Gramscian Regulation theory.
[17] For an illuminating discussion of the uses and limits of concepts of governmentality, see Li (2007). Despite their protestations to the contrary, Rose, O'Malley and Valverde (2006:92) concede that the tripartite division of liberalism, welfarism and advanced liberalism has tended to become formalized into a typology and chronology in which explanation entails placing every program, technology, and strategy under this general covering law.
[18] As I argue more fully in a forthcoming paper, they also compel us to pay serious attention to questions of liberalism not only in Bolivia, but also more generally.
[19] Much of this debate has been shaped by the work of Giovanni Arrighi (2007, 2009), whose theorizing on imperialism and hegemony I discuss more fully in a forthcoming *festschrift* in his honor.
[20] See the postscript to the second edition of *The Long Twentieth Century* published in 2009.
[21] Jenny Greenburg, whose PhD project focuses on the relations between Development and militarism, has pointed out that tendencies in this direction were evident in the late Bush era.
[22] Initiated by the Bush administration in 2007, Africom was opposed by a number of African governments. For a discussion of how the Obama administration is promoting Africom, see Volman and Minter (2009).

References

Amsden A (1989) *Asia's Next Giant: South Korea and Late Industrialization*. New York: Oxford University Press
Arndt H (1981) Economic development: A semantic history. *Economic Development and Cultural Change* 29:457–466
Arrighi G (2007) *Adam Smith in Beijing: Lineages of the Twenty-First Century*. London: Verso

Arrighi G (2009) Postscript to the Second Edition of *The Long Twentieth Century*. London: Verso

Arrighi G and Zhang L (forthcoming) Beyond the Washington Consensus: A new Bandung. In J Shefner and P Fernandez-kelly (eds) *Globlization and Beyond: New Examinations of Global Power and Its Alternatives*. University Park: Penn State University Press

Arrighi G, Hopkins T and Wallerstein I (1989) *Antisystemic Movements*. London: Verso

Balassa B A (1981) *The Newly Industrializing Countries in the World Economy*. New York: Pergamon Press

Bernstein H (2005) Development studies and the Marxists. In U Kothari (ed) *A Radical History of Development Studies: Individuals, Institutions and Ideologies* (pp 111–137). London: Zed Books

Blair D (2009) *Annual Threat Assessment of the Intelligence Community for the Senate Select Committee on Intelligence*, http://www.dni.testimonies/20090212_testimony.pdf Accessed 14 February 2009

Burawoy M (2003) For a sociological Marxism: The complementary convergence of Antonio Gramsci and Karl Polanyi. *Politics and Society* 31:193–261

Castells M (1992) Four Asian tigers with a dragon head: A comparative analysis of the state, economy and society in the Asian Pacific Rim. In R Appelbaum and J Henderson (eds) *States and development in the Asian Pacific Rim* (pp 33–70). New Park, CA: Sage

Cockett R (1994) *Thinking the Unthinkable: Think-Tanks and the Economic Counter-Revolution 1931–1983*. London: Harper Collins

Cooper F (1997) Modernizing bureaucrats, backward Africans, and the development concept. In F Cooper and R Packard (eds.) *International Development and the Social Sciences: Essays on the History and Politics of Knowledge* (pp 64–92). Berkeley: University of California Press

Corbridge S (1997) Review of *Doctrines of Development*. *Antipode* 29:218–220

Cowen M and Shenton R W (1996) *Doctrines of Development*. London and New York: Routledge

Craig D and Porter D (2006) *Development Beyond Neoliberalism? Governance, Poverty Reduction & Political Economy*. London: Routledge

Desai R (1994) Second hand dealers in ideas: Think tanks and Thatcherite hegemony. *New Left Review* 203:27–64

Dezalay Y and Garth B (2002) *The Internationalization of Palace Wars: Lawyers, Economists, and the Contest to Transform Latin American States*. Chicago: University of Chicago Press

Escobar A (1995) *Encountering Development : The Making and Unmaking of the Third World*. Princeton, NJ: Princeton University Press

Evans P (1995) *Embedded Autonomy: States and Industrial Transformation*. Princeton, NJ: Princeton University Press

Friedman M and Friedman R D (1982) *Capitalism and Freedom*. Chicago: University of Chicago Press

Friedmann H (1982) The political economy of food: The rise and fall of the postwar international food order. *American Journal of Sociology* 88:248–286

Furnivall J S (1948) *Colonial Policy and Practice: A Comparative Study of Burma and Netherlands India*. Cambridge: Cambridge University Press

Ghai D (1991) *The IMF and the South*. Geneva: United Nations Research Institute for Social Development

Goodale M (2009) *Dilemmas of Modernity: Bolivian Encounters with Law and Liberalism*. Stanford: Stanford University Press

Gore C (1996) Methodological nationalism and the misunderstanding of East Asian industrialization. *European Journal of Development Research* 8:77–122

Gowan P (1999) *The Global Gamble: Washington's Faustian Bid for World Dominance*, London and New York: Verso

Gowan P (2002) After America? *New Left Review* 13:136–145

Gowan P (2009) Crisis in the heartland: Consequences of the new Wall Street system. *New Left Review* 55:5–29

Gramsci A (1971) *Selections from the Prison Notebooks*. London: Lawrence & Wishart

Gramsci A (1995) *Further Selections from the Prison Notebooks*. Minneapolis: University of Minnesota Press

Hart G (2001) Development debates in the 1990s: Culs de sac and promising paths. *Progress in Human Geography* 25:605–614

Hart G (2002a) Development/s beyond neoliberalism? Power, culture, political economy. *Progress in Human Geography* 26:812–822

Hart G (2002b) *Disabling Globalization: Places of Power in Post-Apartheid South Africa*. Berkeley: University of California Press

Hart G (2004) Geography and development: Critical ethnographies. *Progress in Human Geography* 28:91–100

Hart G (2006a) Post-apartheid developments in historical and comparative perspective. In V Padayachee (editor) *The Development Decade? Economic and Social Change in South Africa 1994–2004* (pp 13–32). Pretoria: HSRC Press

Hart G (2006b) Denaturalizing dispossession: Critical ethnography in the age of resurgent imperialism. *Antipode* 38:977–1004

Hart G (2009) Forging connections: Giovanni Arrighi's conception of the world. Paper prepared for a conference on The Dynamics of the Global Crisis, Antisystemic Movements and New Models of Hegemony in honor of Giovanni Arrighi. Museo Nacional Centro de Arte Reina Sofía, Madrid, 25–29 May

Hartwell R M (1995) *History of the Mont Pelerin Society*. Indianapolis: Liberty Fund

Harvey D (2003) *The New Imperialism*. Oxford: New York, Oxford University Press

Jessop B (2002) Liberalism, neoliberalism and urban governance: A state theoretical perspective. *Antipode* 34:452–472

Johnson C (1982) *MITI and the Japanese Miracle: The Growth of Industrial Policy, 1925–75*. Stanford, CA: Stanford University Press

Klare M (2009) The Gates revolution. *The Nation* 4 May:3–4

Krueger A (1981) Loans to assist the transition to outward-Looking policies. *The World Economy* 4:271–282

Lefebvre H (1991 [1974]) *The Production of Space*. Oxford: Blackwell

Li T M (2007) *The Will to Improve: Governmentality, Development and the Practice of Politics*. Durham: Duke University Press

Lubeck P (2000) The Islamic revival: Antimonies of Islamic movements under globalization. In R Cohen and S Rai (eds) *Global Social Movements* (pp 146–164). London: Athlone

Mamdani M (2004) *Good Muslim, Bad Muslim: America, the Cold War and the Roots of Terror*. New York: Pantheon

Maxfield S and Nolt J (1990) Protectionism and the Internationalization of Capital: US sponsorship of import substitution industrialization in the Philippines, Turkey, and Argentina. *International Studies Quarterly* 34:49–81

McDonald L and Ruckert A (2009) *Postneoliberalism in the Americas*. Houndmills, Basingstoke, Hampshire: Palgrave McMillan

Mohan G and Stokke K (2000) Participatory development and empowerment: The dangers of localism. *Third World Quarterly* 21:247–268

Nossel S (2004) Smart power. *Foreign Affairs* 83:131–142

O'Brien P J and Roddick J (1983) *Chile, the Pinochet Decade: The Rise and Fall of the Chicago Boys*. London: Latin American Bureau

Peck J (2008) Remaking *laissez faire*. *Progress in Human Geography* 32:3–43
Peck J and Tickell A (2002) Neoliberalizing space. *Antipode* 34:380–404
Pham J (2005) J. S. Furnivall and Fabianism: Reinterpreting the "plural society" in Burma. *Modern Asian Studies* 39:321–348
Polanyi K (2001 [1944]) *The Great Transformation* (2001 edition). Boston, MA: Beacon Press
Porter D and Craig D (2004) The third way in the third world: Poverty reduction and social inclusion in the rise of "inclusive liberalism". *Review of International Political Economy* 11:387–423
Postero N (2007) *Now we are Citizens: Indigenous Politics in Postmulticultural Bolivia*. Stanford: Stanford University Press
Richards L (2003) Class struggle and travelling theory: From the Chile experience to the New Zealand experiment. *New Zealand Sociology* 18:115–134
Rose N (1999) *The Powers of Freedom*. Cambridge: Cambridge University Press
Rose N, O'Malley P and Valverde M (2006) Governmentality. *Annual Review of Law and Social Science* 2:83–104
Sachs W (ed) (1992) *The Development Dictionary: A Guide to Knowledge as Power*. London: Zed Books
Silver B and Arrighi G (2003) Polanyi's "double movement": The *Belle Epoques* of British and US Hegemony compared. *Politics and Society* 31:439–451
Valdés J G (1995) *Pinochet's Economists: The Chicago School in Chile*. Cambridge: Cambridge University Press
Volman D and Minter W (2009) Making peace or fueling war in Africa. *Foreign Policy in Focus* 13 March, http://www.fpif.org Accessed 15 May 2009
Wade R (1990) *Governing the Market: Economic Theory and the Role of Government in East Asian Industrialization*. Princeton: Princeton University Press
Wade R (1996) Japan, the World Bank, and the art of paradigm maintenance: The East Asian Miracle in Political Perspective. *New Left Review* 217:3–36
Watts M (2001) 1968 and all that. *Progress in Human Geography* 25:157–188
Watts M (2003) Development and governmentality. *Singapore Journal of Tropical Geography* 24:6–34
Winn P (2004) (ed) *Victims of the Chilean Miracle: Workers and Neoliberalism in the Pinochet Era, 1973–2002*. Durham: Duke University Press
Wood R (1986) *From Marshall Plan to Debt Crisis: Foreign Aid and Development Choices in the World Economy*. Berkeley: University of California Press
Zapiro (2009) *Mail & Guardian* 11 June

Is the Globalization Consensus Dead?

Robert Wade

Development Studies Institute, London School of Economics
and Political Science, London, UK;
r.wade@lse.ac.uk

Abstract: The development economist Dani Rodrik recently declared that "the globalization consensus is dead". The claim has momentus implications, because this consensus has steered economic policy around the world for the past quarter century. It emanates from the heartland of neoclassical economics, and defines the central tasks of the Washington-based organizations which claim to speak for the world. This essay answers two main questions. First, is Rodrik's claim true, and by what measures of "consensus"? Second, to the extent that the consensus has substantially weakened, is the state returning to the heart of economic life, as Karl Polanyi might have predicted? The answers? First, the globalization consensus about desirable economic policy has weakened, though it is far from "dead". Second, the western state is returning to the heart of economic life in response to the current global economic crisis, but will retreat soon after national economies recover—because unless the crisis becomes a second Great Depression, the norms of more free markets and more global economic integration will be politically challenged only at the margins. New rules of finance may be introduced, but with enough loopholes that by 2015 Wall Street and the City will operate in much the same way as in the recent pre-crisis past.

Keywords: globalization consensus, Washington consensus, financial crisis, income distribution, poverty, catch-up growth, pension funds

If we want things to stay as they are, things will have to change (Lampedusa, *The Leopard*).

This being a book intended to mark the 40th birthday of the journal *Antipode*, I should begin with a disclaimer. I have never identified myself as a "radical", for the reason contained in Robert Frost's warning against youthful idealism, "I never dared to be radical when young, for fear it would make me conservative when old". At the same time, I find it difficult to avoid conferring approval and disapproval on social arrangements, and in that sense I admit to not being a good scholar, if "good scholar" means a person who is dispassionate and dispassionate means "conservative" (as in neoclassical economics' belief that markets are natural and therefore good and governments are artificial and therefore suspect).

My subject is the globalization consensus—the consensus which has provided the dominant economic narrative for the past three decades, since the early days of the Reagan and Thatcher governments. It says, in a nutshell, that national economies with more liberalization of trade and finance, higher market integration across borders, easier hostile

Antipode Vol. 41 No. S1 2009 ISSN 0066-4812, pp 142–165
doi: 10.1111/j.1467-8330.2009.00720.x

takeovers of corporations, and a narrower economic role of the state experience higher economic growth, less poverty, higher social mobility and less inequality than those with less, other things being equal. The normative conclusion is that market liberalization, increasing economic integration across borders, and the exit of the state from trying to steer the composition of economic activity is the right direction of policy reform everywhere. More specifically, the claim is that since about 1980 governments around the world have undertaken trade and financial liberalization, and the outcomes have been broadly as predicted. Developing countries' incomes have grown faster than developed countries' incomes, poverty rates have fallen, and inequality on a world scale—between countries and between individuals regardless of country—has fallen (though not within most countries). The correlation between the two big trends provides strong empirical support for the underlying "efficient markets hypothesis" and "comparative advantage theory"—the combination of arguments which says that unhindered competition, as distinct from regulation, is the best way to discipline market behaviour, because markets, including financial markets, are flexible, reach equilibrium by themselves and clear continuously, most of the time; and that this unhindered competition, on a world scale, shunts economies into their areas of appropriate specialization, in which their production is as high in value terms as it can be. Multilateral organizations like the World Bank and the International Monetary Fund (IMF) are right to try to inject these principles into the policy regimes of their borrowing countries, including into the functioning of the public sector (for example, in the form of "new public management").

This narrative has proved remarkably resilient, able to absorb other arguments—like the importance of "institutions" for setting the incentive framework of economic activity—while protecting an inner core of propositions in support of trade and financial liberalization and against "protectionism" and other kinds of "interventionism". So protected has this inner core been, it might be described as "the deep slumber of a decided opinion", in John Stuart Mill's phrase.

But the financial crisis that began in the summer of 2007 in the USA has shaken this deep slumber. Conservative media are sounding the alarm bell about the new wave of government regulation of business and the economy and the backlash against laissez faire sweeping the USA in the wake of the credit crunch. This new context raises two main questions:

First, is the globalization consensus dead, as the development economist Dani Rodrik recently asserted, citing qualifications to the consensus made by the likes of Paul Samuelson, Paul Krugman, Alan Blinder, Martin Wolf, and Larry Summers? (Rodrik 2008). My short answer is that the globalization consensus has been weakening. There is less certainty than there used to be, partly because of growing awareness of the flimsiness of much of the empirical evidence adduced in support of the globalization consensus. Eventually, facts kick, or in Galbraith's words, "the conventional wisdom" gives way not so much to new ideas as to "the massive onslaught of circumstances with which [it] cannot contend" (Galbraith 1999:17).

Second, is a more intrusive state staging a comeback at the free market's expense, emulating the governmental response to the economic crisis of the 1930s? If "yes", it would be consistent with Karl Polanyi's "double movement" of capitalism, in which a period of market deregulation generates such volatility and suffering as to prompt a political reaction to "embed" markets in social controls. So the second question can be rephrased: are we in the early period of the second leg of Polanyi's double movement?

My short answer is that the state is making a comeback in finance, and even in some of the productive sectors, but its comeback will be limited because firstly neoliberal norms and institutions have been hard-wired into economies around the world in the past several decades, and secondly an alternative set of principles has not emerged as the core of a new consensus, leaving free market principles and international economic integration as the default position, *faute de mieux*. Political parties which call themselves center-left, like the British Labour Party, remain deeply committed to globalization and neoliberalism as the right direction of travel, not least because they depend on media and financial support from private economic interests deeply committed to these policies and their justifying ideas. Their more interventionist responses to the current crisis are ad hoc and driven by desperation.

A lawyer known as a Wall Street eminence grise recently assured an audience that the future of Wall Street would be much the same as its recent past. As he explained, "I am far from convinced there was something inherently wrong with the system" (Krugman 2009). Already Wall Street insiders are taking the mildness of Treasury and Fed policy towards Wall Street as a sign that they will soon be able to resume business as usual. If Wall Street is not reformed, neither will the City of London be. And if Wall Street and the City are not reined in, the value priorities of acquisitive individualism—which sanction the belief that the pursuit of self-interest within social rules is the best route to maximizing the public interest and that the optimal degree of economic openness is the maximal degree—will be little changed.

The Globalization Consensus

Surveys of economists' opinions show that western economists in general, American economists especially, from at least the early 1980s onwards, have shown a strong consensus on both positive and normative propositions about economic openness and its effects—and specifically, consensus on the desirability of free trade policy for all countries, developed and developing, and the desirability of floating exchange rates and more or less free capital mobility.

For example, a survey of economists in five industrial countries around 1980 (America and four continental European countries) presented them with about 30 positive and normative propositions about the economy, and asked them to "agree", "agree with qualifications", "disagree". Overall, they agreed most with the proposition, "Tariffs and import controls lower economic welfare". Fifty-five percent of them said "agree", more than for any other proposition. Of the Americans, 79% said "agree". Of the French at the other end, only 27% said "agree". In general, American economists showed high consensus on microeconomic propositions about openness, privatization, and the like, and less consensus on propositions about macroeconomic stability (because by 1980 Keynesian propositions were coming under stronger attack from Friedman-style monetarism). The continental European economists in 1980 were somewhat less wedded to free market propositions than the Americans, the French least of all. Later surveys of American economists, one in 1990, another in 2000, showed continuing high consensus around positive and normative propositions about openness (see Frey et al 1984; Fuller and Geide-Stevenson 2003). For example, about the same high proportion of economists said "agree" to the above proposition about tariffs and import controls in 2000 as in 1980.

Around 1990 John Williamson crystallized out the consensus he encountered among development economists in Washington (where he lived) and in Latin America (where he often visited, his wife being Brazilian), and called it the Washington Consensus. The Washington Consensus embraced the sorts of microeconomic propositions about openness and privatization that the 1980 survey showed American economists strongly agreed with. Later Williamson said he should have named it the Universal Convergence—to make clear, first, that he was referring to a direction of policy movement rather than a single package, and second, that not only Washington-based or Washington-oriented economists agreed to it, but practically all economists with proper training around the world.

The Washington Consensus, or globalization consensus, or neoliberal consensus—these phrases are used interchangeably—was transmitted into policies and institutions around the world not only through graduate education in economics but also through the conditions on access to resources.

For example, the World Bank and the IMF hard-wired tough liberalizing and privatizing conditionality on their World Bank and IMF loans to developing countries. In 1996–97, the IMF targeted Ethiopia—of all poor countries, of no interest to international investors—and twisted the government's arm to make it open its capital account and to establish a Treasury bill market, partly to signal to the rest of sub-Saharan Africa that *everyone* should move towards financial liberalization (Wade 2001).

Starting in the 1990s the World Bank adopted a Country Policy and Institutional Assessment (CPIA) formula by which borrowing countries were scored—by Bank staff and other experts—according to the "pro-developmental" impact of their policies and institutions. The score counted heavily in the allocation of International Development Association loans for the Bank's low-income borrowing countries, and also affected Bank lending to middle-income countries. The scoring criteria for the economic dimensions reflect the Washington Consensus. For example, a country could get the top score on its trade regime only if it had a virtually free trade regime—with maximum tariff under 15%, a low average tariff, and no export subsidies or taxes.

Also in the 1990s the Bank adopted a "global pension policy" which encouraged developing countries to switch from pay-as-you-go (PAYG) systems—current taxpayers pay current pensions—to a pension fund system, in which individuals pay contributions to a fund of their choice while working and at retirement receive a pension related to the performance of the fund's investments (Orenstein 2005). The Bank was especially keen on this switch as part of a larger strategy to build a particular type of capitalism in developing countries: an Anglo-American type, with the capital market as the pivot. Individuals would pay into one or other of the funds. Governments would privatize state-owned enterprises and float the shares on the national stock market. The funds would invest in both foreign shares and local shares—so the supply of shares of newly privatized companies would be matched by a demand for shares coming from the pension funds. A virtuous circle. The Bank even pushed for mandatory, defined contribution pension funds in countries like Kazakhstan, which had hardly any trained accountants and where each of the dominant clans established their own fund, which the clan leaders proceeded to treat as their personal income (Hoffmann et al 2001).

It is worth noting that the formation of the globalization consensus was achieved without the word "globalization". The word itself began to buzz—began to be used as the *leitmotif* of the present era—as recently as the second half of the 1990s. In August 2000 the Harvard University Library contained 271 books whose title included the word "globaliz/sation", of which only five were published before 1990 and 85% dated from the latter half of the 1990s. Five years later, in 2005, the number of books in the library with globaliz/sation in the title was almost 10 times larger, at 2500.

By 2004, "globalization" was buzzing loudly, and in that year Martin Wolf, doyen of *The Financial Times*, published a globalization manifesto called *Why Globalization Works*. Wolf argued, first, that the world's people had the opportunity to make huge advances in material wellbeing by pushing on with economic integration between states, a process which, he said, had barely begun.

> The failure of our world is not that there is too much globalization, but that there is too little. The potential for greater economic integration is barely tapped. We need more global markets, if we want to raise the living standards of the poor of the world (Wolf 2004:4).

Indeed, he held up the United States as the model for the world—a globalized world where national governments have no more influence on transactions across their borders or on domestic political economy arrangements than do the governments of the states of the USA.

Wolf argued, second, that this opportunity for huge advances in material wellbeing was under threat by "anti-globalists". In the face of this threat:

> Social democrats, classical liberals and democratic conservatives should unite to preserve and improve the liberal economy against *the enemies mustering both outside and inside the gates*. That is the central argument of this book (Wolf 2004:4, emphasis added).

Questioning the Globalization Consensus

In terms of what American economists think, the comparison between their answers to propositions about liberalization and openness in the surveys of 1980, 1990, and 2000, on the one hand, and the survey to come in 2010, on the other, will allow us to gauge the extent to which the globalization consensus has weakened. My prediction is that the comparison will reveal a substantial weakening, for several reasons.

The Financial Crisis

Nothing so disturbs the deep slumber of a decided opinion than a sharp crisis which damages the material wellbeing of politicians, officials, and intellectuals and which seems to have arisen out of the arrangements endorsed by the deep slumber. The current financial crisis is doing just that.

The great wave of financial deregulation going on around the world from the 1970s was justified by the philosophy of Milton Friedman and his Chicago School colleagues. They formulated it in the form of the "efficient market hypothesis", which, as noted, says that unhindered competition, as distinct from regulation, is the best way to discipline financial market behaviour, because financial markets are flexible, reach equilibrium by themselves, clear continuously, and price risk and return correctly. The implication is that competitive asset markets cannot become substantially over- or undervalued in relation to "fundamentals". Any proposed policy intervention to curb asset price booms is dismissed, from this perspective, as "financial repression", an automatic negative.

These arguments came increasingly to prevail after the breakdown of the Bretton Woods arrangements in the early 1970s, and the world moved to an optimal financial model with three pillars of responsibility: central banks keep inflation at a low level using short-term interest rates; regulators ensure that individual financial firms act prudently; and capital markets determine asset prices and investment allocation on their own, without "government intervention".

The current financial crisis is the first time this architectural division of responsibility has come into serious question. All three pillars have malfunctioned at once. Indeed, the crisis provides a natural test of the efficient markets hypothesis.

The USA underwent a major financial liberalization in the 1990s—not a de jure liberalization but a de facto liberalization, as barely regulated entities in the shadow banking system, such as mortgage brokers, came to play a much larger role in the financial system. In particular, the sub-prime mortgage market was the least regulated part of the American mortgage market and was celebrated as such by many economists, including Alan Greenspan, chair of the US central bank. Thanks to practically no regulation, they said, the sub-prime mortgage market generated lots of financial innovation, which was not only a good in itself but also had the added benefit of enabling poor Americans to buy their own homes and become stakeholders in the American dream.

We now see the effects of the de facto liberalization differently. Wall Street's and the shadow banking system's loose and negligent lending into the sub-prime market was an important driver of what has become a global economic crisis. Their behaviour was caused by the combination of lack of regulatory oversight, cheap credit from the central bank, and a corporate governance system that rewarded management and mortgage brokers for maximizing the quantity of loans regardless of prudence (Palley 2008; Wade 2008a). "Securitization" techniques based on ICT technology allowed managers to disguise risky assets as safe assets and sell them on around the world to buyers who understood little about the contents of the asset-backed securities, and then to book the income on sale—to the benefit of their end-of-year bonuses.

As Martin Wolf put it, ruefully:

> What is happening in credit markets today is a huge blow to the credibility of the Anglo-Saxon model of transactions-orientated financial capitalism (Wolf 2007).

Paul Volker, the former chair of the US central bank, put it still more sharply:

> The bright new financial system, with all its talented participants, with all its rich rewards, has failed the test of the marketplace (quoted in Chakrabortty 2008).

Re-regulation is in the air. Some mainstream voices are even calling for the re-introduction of measures like the *Glass-Steagall Act*, the Depression-era regulation which separated US deposit-taking commercial banks from investment banks and securities traders, repealed in 1999. Globalization champions like Alan Greenspan are deeply alarmed. "The world must repel calls to contain competitive markets", he declared in *The Financial Times* (5 Aug 2008).

Weaknesses in the Globalization Evidence

In short, many analysts and policymakers who had earlier accepted the arguments for the deregulated financial model have come to question their faith, thanks to the US financial crisis. This questioning of the model of deregulated finance encourages a more sceptical stance towards other evidence advanced in support of the wider globalization story.

It turns out that when subjected to critical scrutiny much of this evidence falls apart, and one marvels at the strength of the "confirmation bias" operating within the economics profession which has allowed economists to get away with advancing flimsy claims for so long. Here I illustrate the weakness of three familiar kinds of pro-globalization evidence.

The Catch-up Growth Story

First, the positive correlation between (a) the trend towards trade and financial policy liberalization beginning on a world scale around 1980, and (b) the trend towards catch-up of average incomes in developing countries to the average of developed countries; and the claim that (a) has driven (b) (see also Wade 2008b).

Figure 1 shows the average income of several regions, measured in purchasing power parity (PPP) dollars, as a fraction of that of the average of the North or First World, from 1950 to 2001. The broad trend towards divergence is clear. Asia is the exception. Even after the increase of the past two decades the Asian average remains (2001) at about equal to the average of the South. So Figure 1 shows a mix of strong divergence in several regions and convergence from a low level in Asia. It is not consistent with the argument that a general process of globalization has driven a general process of catch-up growth.

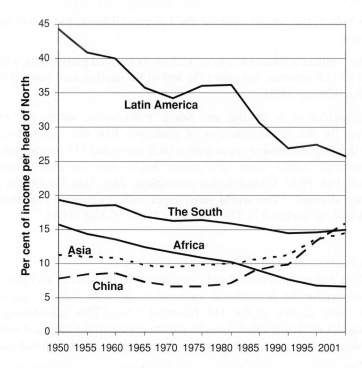

Figure 1: Income per head (PPP$) as percentage of North (source: produced by, and reproduced here with the permission of, Bob Sutcliffe using data from Maddison 2003)

Figure 2 shows a more aggregate version of the same measure: the ratio of Third World to First World average income from 1960 to 2007 (PPP dollars). It excludes "transitional" countries. Taking the line which includes China, we see a strong and robust trend towards catch-up starting in the late 1980s and continuing till today—consistent with the globalization story. However, note that even after the 20-year period of catch-up the Third World PPP average income was still less than 20% of the First World average (Freeman forthcoming).

The other trend line in Figure 2 shows Third World to First World income excluding China. This line shows no catch-up. On the contrary, the line falls after 1980 to the end of the 1980s, then flattens out or falls a bit up to 2004, and only then does it increase to 2007—reaching 15% of First World income (as distinct from 18% when China is included). This line tells a story of divergence, not catch-up.

In short, no China, no overall catch-up. If the empirical validity of the globalization story depends on one country, China, the empirical validity of the globalization story is in doubt. All the more so if the policy regime of that one country fails in many ways to correspond with the "globalization" policy regime. China's policy regime is too heavily managed to score well by globalization or Washington Consensus

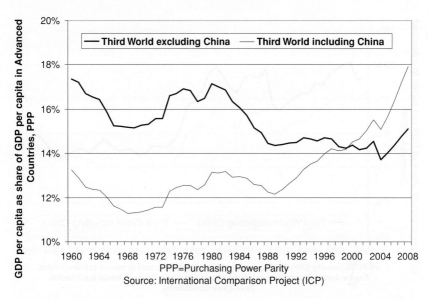

Figure 2: World inequality using PPP (low = less equal) (source: Freeman 2009, reproduced with permission)

criteria, as distinct from the policy regimes of, say, Mexico or Haiti, which score much better by these criteria.

Moreover, when incomes are compared at market exchange rates (MERs), it makes no difference whether China is included or excluded: the globalization catch-up story does not work, period. Figure 3 shows the ratio of Third World to First World income from 1960 to 2007, in MER, including and excluding China. The globalization story is not confirmed by either line—we see no catch-up growth after the onset of trade and financial liberalization in the 1980s. Instead we see a dramatic falling behind through the 1980s as the ratio fell from 8–10% to 4–5%, followed by flattening out in the 1990s and early 2000s, followed by a small uptick after 2004. According to the latest evidence, the ratio of Third World to First World incomes (at MER) in 2007 was well below the level reached in 1980.

Clearly, the between-country distribution of MER income has become much more unequal since 1980, and has only in the past few years begun to become less unequal thanks to the commodity boom of the 2000s— not, as the globalization story says, since the onset of trade and financial liberalization.

In short, the empirical validity of the globalization catch-up story, which posits a positive correlation between (a) trade and financial liberalization at the world scale and (b) catch-up growth in the Third World, depends entirely on the use of PPP exchange rates and the

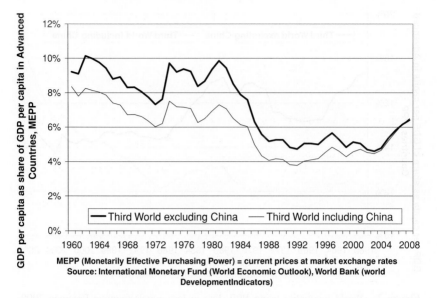

Figure 3: World inequality (low = less equal) (source: Freeman 2009, reproduced with permission)

inclusion of one country, China (in the sense that if this one country is excluded, even the PPP results are reversed).

Since the answer to the question of what is happening to world income distribution depends heavily on whether income is measured in PPP dollars or MER dollars, there is a further question of which measure is preferable. There is no general answer. Questions about the relative material wellbeing of people in different countries are, in principle, better answered with PPP incomes. Questions about the relative purchasing power of residents of different countries over goods and services produced in other countries—including questions about the capacity of developing countries to repay debts, to import capital and intermediate goods, to participate in international organizations and international treaties, and the incentive on people in one country to migrate to another—are, in principle, better answered with MER incomes—which is one main reason why sociologists generally use MER incomes for international comparisons.

Yet economists typically insist that only PPP incomes should be used, as though the only question of interest is relative material wellbeing. In an earlier essay I argued that MER incomes are more appropriate for some questions, PPP incomes are in principle more appropriate for others. A reviewer commented:

> The idea of using market exchange rates to calculate international inequality is unbelievably stupid, and it is amazing that it still makes

an appearance here. The UN had a commission of enquiry on this, which concluded unambiguously that using market exchange rates was wrong (quoted in Wade 2004a).

Economists who take this line routinely overlook fundamental weaknesses of the PPP statistics while stressing the weaknesses of the MER statistics. To cite just one weakness of the PPP figures, they are based on surveys of the prices of *consumer* goods and services; they exclude the prices of capital goods and intermediate goods from the calculation of purchasing power. Yet a survey of prices of capital goods in a set of developed and developing countries found that, on average, the price of capital goods relative to the price of consumer goods was just over 100% in developed countries, and over 200% in developing countries—in other words, the relative price of investment goods was twice as high as the price of consumption goods in developing countries (Freeman forthcoming). Much the same would probably apply to the price of intermediate goods.

The price of capital goods and intermediate goods is a critical factor in industrialization and productivity growth. The purchasing power of developing countries' currencies over these critical inputs is much less than their purchasing power over consumer goods. By excluding capital goods and intermediates from the items counted in the survey of prices for PPP calculations, the PPP numbers exaggerate developing countries' development, and underplay the handicaps facing their industrialization. They also, of course, make the world economy look as though it is performing much better than it looks when incomes are expressed in MER terms, with a stronger purchasing power catch-up momentum than really exists.

Economists who say that only the PPP numbers should be used are probably afflicted by confirmation bias. As Alan Freeman says, "PPP statistics . . . make globalization look good. They also make the World Bank and the IMF look good" (Freeman forthcoming).

But in 2007 the World Bank announced major revisions to its current PPP income series—which must be among the biggest ever revisions to an international economics statistical series. Based on a new international price survey conducted in 2005 the Bank lowered China and India's PPP GDPs by almost 40%. Some non-World Bank analysts say that the new GDP figures translate into a tripling of China's extreme poverty headcount from 100 million to 300 million, and a doubling of India's extreme poverty headcount from 400 million to 800 million, though the World Bank calculates the increases in the poverty headcounts as substantially smaller but still significant (Chen and Ravallion 2008).[1]

On the face of it, the revision is a blow to some of the claims of the globalization story. It seems to reinforce what other evidence suggests, that developing countries are in general much poorer than was thought, and that the gap between them and the developed countries is much greater. Perhaps (though more contentiously) the new figures also give stronger support to the argument that the basic direction of the world economy is towards income *divergence* between rich and poor countries, with China and some other parts of Asia as exceptions. But the question arises of whether the new PPP figures can be given more credence than the former ones.

At least in the case of China, the answer is not clear. First, China's PPP GDP and poverty headcount prior to the latest estimates were based on no direct price survey, because the Chinese government refused to undertake a price survey in line with the methodology of the International Price Comparison (IPC) project (the project which produces the PPP numbers), ever since the first such survey in 1980. The Chinese PPP numbers, from the beginning, were based on econometric regressions from other countries' prices supplemented by ad hoc bits of direct knowledge about prices; not quite "finger in the wind", but not far off. Second, when the Chinese government agreed for the first time to undertake a price survey in line with the ICP methodology in 2005 it sampled prices in only 11 cities, giving a strong urban bias; and it interpreted the instruction in the methodology handbook to sample "internationally comparable goods and services" to mean to select goods sold in department stores.[2] No wonder the resulting price level "in China" came out much higher than had been previously calculated, and so the purchasing power of China's renmimbi GDP over real goods and services came out much lower. But it is not clear how much more confidence one can have in the new results than in the old figures. Which, given the weight of China in world trends, is a serious problem of knowledge.

The Falling Poverty Story

A second type of evidence adduced by globalization champions is the trend in the poverty headcount—the number of people in the world at large, or in specific regions or countries who live on an income of less than, say, $1 a day measured in PPP dollars. $1 a day is commonly referred to as the "extreme" poverty line, and $2 a day as the "ordinary" poverty line. The World Bank's extreme poverty headcount shows that in 1981, 1.5 billion people lived in extreme poverty, and in 2001, 1.1 billion, a fall of 400 million people. The proportion of world population living in extreme poverty was almost halved, from 33% in 1981 to 18% in 2001 (Wade 2008a).

The figures for the extreme poverty headcount have been widely advertised, especially by the World Bank, as confirmation that "globalization works", since the dramatic fall in the extreme poverty headcount goes with the global shift to trade and financial liberalization.

Not incidentally, the poverty figures also confirm that the World Bank has been doing a good job in fighting world poverty.

But there are at least two problems. First, the fall in the extreme poverty headcount depends entirely on China. If China is taken out, the extreme poverty headcount increases (though the *proportion* of the world-minus-China's population in extreme poverty still falls). Second, if we use the $2 a day "ordinary" poverty line, then even with China included, the number in ordinary poverty *increased* between 1981 and 2001 (Wade 2008a).

The Trade-growth Story

A third kind of commonly used evidence is concerned with trade: econometric evidence of the relationship between trade and economic growth. A typical example is the left-hand side of Figure 4, which shows the correlation between the share of trade in GDP and growth in GDP, for a large number of countries. The positive correlation is commonly taken to imply that as the share of trade in GDP increases, the growth rate increases. Globalization champions have extended this result to suggest that *trade policy liberalization* raises growth, on the assumption that higher levels of trade in GDP result from more liberal trade policy. Hence, trade liberalization leads, by assumption, to increases in trade/GDP, which, by evidence, leads to higher growth (Rodriguez 2008a).

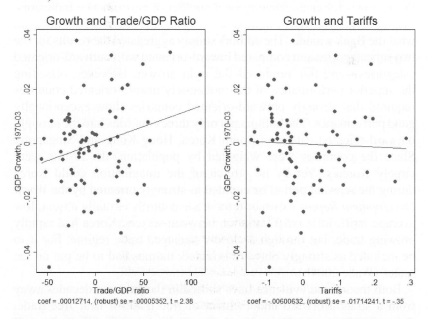

Figure 4: Growth, trade, and trade liberalization (source: Rodriguez 2008b, Copyright © 2008 by M.E. Sharpe, Inc. Reprinted with permission. All rights reserved. Not for reproduction)

© 2009 The Author
Journal compilation © 2009 Editorial Board of *Antipode*.

Of the many problems with this argument, one is that it relies on a *linear* regression. The choice of a linear regression builds in the assumption that the effect of increasing the value of the independent variable (in this case, trade share) will be the same for all countries, regardless of the initial value of that variable and of other variables that might affect the result; so the effect on growth of a 10% increase in trade share is *assumed* to be the same regardless of whether the increase is from an initial trade share of 5% or 30%, and regardless of whether the country is a primary-resource exporter or a manufacturing exporter.

Worse, the argument fudges the distinction between policy instruments and "outcomes", by *assuming* a positive correlation between trade share and tariffs and import controls. When we correlate tariffs as the independent variable against growth as the dependent variable, we find no relationship between growth and tariffs. See the right-hand side of Figure 4. Needless to say, the globalization champions do not emphasize the right-hand side of Figure 4. More confirmation bias.

The World Bank knows all about confirmation bias. For example, the authors of its *World Development Report 1987* set out to show that "outward-oriented" economies had better performance than "inward-oriented" ones. They classified developing countries on a scale with four categories: "strongly" and "moderately" inward oriented, and "moderately" and "strongly" outward oriented. They then calculated the averages for each category on a number of performance indicators. The moderately inward-oriented category had the best results—not at all what the Bank wanted. The authors simply aggregated the results for the two subcategories and compared inward-oriented with outward-oriented categories—and this produced the right answer. However, offsetting the superior performance of the moderately inward-oriented countries required that strongly outward-oriented countries show exceptionally good performance. The authors put only three countries into the strongly outward-oriented category: South Korea, Hong Kong and Singapore. Since the countries were weighted by population, the results were largely Korea's. Yet by no stretch of the imagination could Korea during the relevant period be counted as strongly oriented by the *World Development Report*'s own criteria: trade controls virtually absent, low average tariff, little tariff variation between sectors. Korea had rapidly growing trade, but through a closely managed trade regime. For it to be included as strongly outward oriented, thumbs had to be put on the scales (Wade 2004b).

Both theory and evidence have shifted in the past two decades away from a straightforward endorsement of free trade or near free trade. Among trade cognoscenti today, the proposition that "Tariffs and import controls lower economic welfare" would command less agreement than among general economists (Wade 2009). But "the international development community" has hardly moderated its commitment to largely free trade.

Conclusion

The acceptance of hypotheses, including by more or less dis-interested scientists, is always underdetermined by the evidence. Nevertheless, for those who like to believe that we can both confer approval and disapproval in accordance with prior values and allow evidence to constrain our conclusions, it is a shock to discover how thin is the evidence commonly accepted in support of the globalization argument. Give it one or two nudges and a lot of it falls down. It looks as though the globalization champions have been indulging in policy-based evidence-making under the banner of evidence-based policymaking. I predict that the weaknesses of the evidence will—given how the current global financial crisis has disturbed the deep slumber of a decided opinion— feed through into a significantly higher proportion of "disagree" answers to pro-globalization propositions in the survey of American economists due for 2010.

The Second Leg of Polanyi's Double Movement?

Let us accept that the globalization consensus among economists has indeed weakened. Does this mean that the age of Milton Friedman is drawing to a close? By 2010, or 2015, will we see a significant change in the direction of travel of financial policy away from ever more liberalization, mirroring the change of direction that occurred in the several years after 1933? For example, will the IMF explicitly recognize the legitimacy of capital controls as normal instruments of economic management? Will the World Bank push PAYG pension systems, as distinct from pension funds? Will national central banks become more proactive in curbing asset booms, on grounds that if they have to clean up after boom turns to bust they should have authority and instruments to curb the boom? Will we see a bigger component of public ownership or at least public guarantees in Anglo-American-type banking systems, creating more of a "mixed economy" in banking and finance?

If we extrapolate from current trends—governments are throwing every conventional and unconventional policy they can think of at the gathering crisis—then the answer is clearly yes. But extrapolation beyond the recovery from the crisis would be unwise.[3]

The Shock Behind the New Deal

The first reason for being sceptical is that the current crisis is unlikely to be anywhere near as damaging for any major economy as the Great Depression was for the USA—where output fell by a third between 1929 and 1933 and unemployment rose to 25%. (It looks as though Japan in the first half of 2009 may be contracting at an even faster rate than any country during the Great Depression rate.) Had the US shock during the Great Depression been of significantly less magnitude, progressive New Deal reformers would not have overcome the intense resistance of US business, especially finance, to things like the *Glass-Steagall Act* and the creation of the Securities and Exchange Commission (to supervise investment banks). Since the 1980s US finance has become much more entrenched in the political process than it was and its resistance more difficult to overcome—a point I come back to shortly. Provided inter-state cooperation on liberal economic rules does not break down in the way that it did in the 1920s—paving the way for the Great Depression—the current shock will not be big enough to seriously qualify liberal norms once the recovery occurs, at least in the West.

The Aftermath of the East Asian Crisis

The second reason comes from the aftermath of the East Asian crisis in 1997–1998. After it became clear that the East Asian crisis would be contained to the periphery of the world economy, the initial talk about the need for a "new international financial architecture" fell away. The consensus settled around the argument that the East Asian crisis occurred because East Asian firms and governments had misled western investors, as in the words of a World Bank paper about the East Asian crisis, published in 2001:

> The findings suggest that these [crisis-affected] countries did not follow International Accounting Standards and that this likely triggered the financial crisis. Users of the accounting information were *misled* and were not able to take precautions in a timely fashion (Vishwanath and Kaufman 2001: 44, quoted in Wade 2007).

This line of explanation, of course, keeps the efficient markets hypothesis intact—and its implication that financial markets are best left largely to regulate themselves (always provided information is of good quality and symmetrically available to all participants).

The response to the East Asian crisis, then, was to create a number of talk-shops, like the Financial Stability Forum and the G20, and to formulate many "standards of best practice" in such domains as banks' risk-assessment models, corporate governance, financial accounting, and data dissemination. The IMF was given a stronger role in monitoring countries' compliance with the standards and in drawing national authorities' attention to areas of concern. It was assumed that "the markets" would provide the compliance mechanism: the IMF's assessments of compliance would, directly or indirectly, inform investment decisions of financial actors, who would reward countries with higher levels of compliance and punish those with lower levels, thereby inducing governments to undertake various reforms to bring their country more closely in line with the standards of best practice. I call this the "standards-surveillance-compliance" (SSC) system (Lukaskas and Livera-Batiz 2001; Wade 2007).

The intention behind the SSC system was, first, to improve the quality of information in financial markets; second, to undercut momentum towards additional national constraints on the behaviour of financial firms (eg constraints of the Glass-Steagall kind); third, to undercut momentum towards stronger international or supranational regulation; and fourth, to fortify the Anglo-American model of capital-market-based capitalism as the "best practice" type of capitalism. In a sense, the SSC system which was put in place after the East Asian crisis constituted a shift from the Washington Consensus' emphasis on "liberalizing the market" to what we could call a Post-Washington Consensus emphasis on "standardizing the market" around the norms of Anglo-American capitalism (Vestergaard 2009).

The irony, of course, is that after all the effort to formulate standards of best practice in the wake of the East Asian crisis—so as to improve the quality of information and standardize national political economies around the Anglo-American model—the current debt crisis is partly the result of the sheer opacity of Anglo-American financial markets, opacity generated by the incentives in the "originate and distribute" model of banking that swept all before it over the 1990s (Wade 2008a).

Financialization has Gone too far Towards the Complex and the Global

A third reason for doubting that there will be much more than a short-term second leg of the Polanyi double movement is that finance in the OECD countries and in the governing bodies of the world economy has become "too big to challenge" other than at the margins—short of a second Great Depression. The process of financial dominance—which I call the "financialization of the economy" (FOE)—is measured quantitatively by ratios such as the total credit outstanding as a percentage of GDP in the USA, which doubled from 170% in 1981 to more than 350% in 2007. FOE is also measured institutionally by the way that other economic institutions, including corporations, households and pension funds have been reorganized in support of the capital market as the economy's pivotal institution (Dore 2000). Polanyi, not surprisingly, did not foresee how finance could become so dominant as to block the double movement.

The normative shift away from PAYG pension systems to pension funds, much encouraged by the World Bank and the IMF, is an important part of the larger process of financialization of the economy. So much is it taken for granted that PAYG systems are obsolete and the future lies with funded pensions that Merrill Lynch produced a report on "pension reform" with a league table that separates the laudable pension "reformers" from the laggards on the basis largely of the extent to which state involvement in support of the elderly has been reduced (Merrill Lynch 2001).

The shift is justified by the fact of rapid aging of the world's population, as though the fact of aging gives no alternative but to shift to pension funds and shrink the role of the state in providing for income in old age. However, the willingness to dismiss PAYG systems as obsolete and not seriously examine how they can be re-engineered to cope with population aging owes a lot to the objective of building a bigger constituency of support for the "globalization project" and of weakening coalitions that might support a national "opt-out" from neoliberalism.

The shift towards privately managed, defined contribution funds creates a large and growing constituency of people—relatively affluent, articulate, and influential people—with a direct stake in global financial markets and investment banks, because their savings flow into global markets through asset managers operating in secondary markets around the world rather than through banks. Hence this large and growing constituency has an interest in protecting the flows of capital income (including dividends) more than in protecting the flows of labour income (employment above all). Conversely, by shifting an important part of the economy from the state to the market, and by shrinking the pooling of risks across generations, the shift weakens the legitimacy of the state as the organ for implementing the norm of social solidarity; and social solidarity is a precondition for building coalitions that might push for something less than maximum openness to the international economy.

The switch from PAYG towards pension funds therefore helps to lock in place a set of national and global institutions that promote financialization of the economy. These institutions are celebrated in the name of efficiency, poverty reduction and even inequality reduction. But the coalitions behind them support them—and reward the analysts who support them—because of how markets, configured in this way, distribute income and wealth upwards, within nations and between nations. In the wake of the collapse of many of these funds in the current crisis there may be renewed attention to PAYG systems; but as stock markets recover the effort will again be to boost pension funds.

Globalization and Upwards Income Redistribution

Figure 5 is the key to understanding the inner imperative of the globalization project and why those whose voices count strongly support its central thrusts towards privatization, liberalization and deregulation. It shows that the share of income accruing to the top 1%, 0.1% and 0.01% of US income earners (including capital gains) peaked in 1929 at about 22.5%, then fell sharply through to about 1970, bottomed

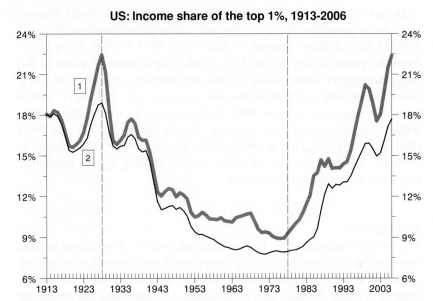

US: Income share of the top 1%, 1913-2006

• **[1]** = including realised capital gains; and **[2]** = excluding capital gains. 3-year moving averages. ***Source:*** Piketty and Sáez (2003; updated to 2006 in http://elsa.berkeley.edu/~saez/TabFig2006.xls). This is the source of all data on income distribution in the US below.

Figure 5: Share of top 0.01%, 0.1%, 1% in US household income (source: Palma 2009, reproduced with permission)

out at about 9%, and then after 1980, with "globalization" and the Reagan/Thatcher economic reforms, began to increase sharply, reaching the 1929 peak by 2006. Understandably, those at the very top of the US income distribution are very satisfied with the institutional arrangements that have yielded this result, and will seek to restore them as soon as possible, removing whatever state constraints have been introduced in the meantime (Dumenil and Levy 2004; Harvey 2005; Palma 2009).

Moreover, the same "neoliberal" institutions have yielded a very low rate of social mobility in Anglo-American type economies (relative to continental European economies), which gives those at the top assurance that their children and grandchildren will be similarly privileged. This too is a desirable outcome of the neoliberal framework and its supporting ideology, from the point of view of the rich. Note the irony: the USA and the UK, where market reforms have been taken the furthest in the name of improving opportunities for all, have the lowest rates of intergenerational social mobility. Canada, Germany, and the Nordic economies, with what *The Economist* likes to scorn as their "nanny states", all have substantially higher rates of intergenerational mobility (Blandon, Gregg and Machin 2005).

On a world scale, very few states in the post-Second World War era have risen permanently in the income scale (substantially raised the ratio of their average income to that of the First World). Even better from the point of view of the First World, the number of states in the income category immediately below the category of First World in a four-fold income categorization—the category of "challenger" states whose average incomes put them within reach of First World income within a generation or two—actually shrank between 1978 and 2000 (Milanovic 2005).[4] This is another plus for an ideology that claims to enhance opportunities for all while largely shoring up the economic oligarchy of the western countries.

Conclusion

The current financial crisis has cast a cloud over the deregulated market model in financial markets; and it also prompts more attention to existing evidence which runs against the claims of the globalization argument. How this feeds through into economists' opinions and the operating procedures of development organizations remains to be seen. Two key indicators to watch out for are, first, the 2010 survey of American economists' opinions, and second, the World Bank's Country Policy and Institutional Assessment (the scoring system that currently gives built-in support to the Washington Consensus or globalization consensus).

As suggested, a lot of the evidence adduced in support of the globalization argument is remarkably weak, and its acceptance is testimony to the power of "confirmation bias" in the context of neoliberal ideology. In particular, I have suggested that between-country income distribution, by plausible measures, has become more unequal during the globalization era. Divergence dominates convergence, especially when China is excluded. Catch-up is not the dominant process—which has far-reaching implications for global governance, rivalries between states, migration, and the rise of messianic leaders.

However, even as the globalization consensus weakens among economists and even as governments "intervene" much more in finance, we can be fairly confident that additional constraints on the behaviour of financial actors will apply only until the current crisis is clearly over, if at all. Financial interests in the major states remain too strong; their free market ideology has been too hard-wired into the DNA of western economic thinking for them to be permanently displaced from their previous position of pre-eminence in setting the policy paradigm. The shift from PAYG to pension funds illustrates just one of several deep institutional changes in capitalism through which the coalitions in support of capital markets and free capital movement have been boosted. Even at the time of writing (May 2009), after repeated tax payer bailouts of US banks running into several hundred billions of dollars, the government has provided the funds with few conditions, little by way of tax payer benefits when the banks strengthen, and with scrupulous avoidance of the "n" word ("nationalization").

On the other hand, the continuing dominance of finance and the resulting erosion of norms of social solidarity runs into conflict with two tectonic shifts of our era. The first is the economic rise of some populous and/or energy-rich developing countries, notably the BRICs (Brazil, Russia, India, China), to the point where they cannot be excluded from the top table of global economic governance. Since they all have a much bigger role of government in the economy than do most of the OECD countries, they may bring different preferences to the table, less favourable to free markets. The second is climate change, where increasingly powerful coalitions are urging the need for government regulation to protect forests, increase the efficiency of energy use, and mandate approaches such as clean coal technologies.

These two shifts are certain, and they may qualify the continued dominance of finance. A third shift is less clear, but could qualify the continued dominance of finance even more.

"It can be argued", to put no finer point on it, that the current crisis—together with its "precursor" crisis, the dot.com collapse of 2000—is not the collapse of an "ordinary" bubble but the collapse of a technology-driven bubble of the kind that since the Industrial Revolution has tended to occur about half way through the diffusion of a family of transformative technologies. The argument in a nutshell is that in the first two to four decades of the technology surge finance capital is in the driving seat, and shapes state policy in line with its drive for maximum flexibility as it forces the new profit-making paradigm into new sectors—hence finance capital wants minimal state-imposed restrictions.[5] At a certain point, this "installation" process leads to a major bubble in the rush to apply the technology, followed by collapse. The power of finance capital is weakened by enough to bring back an alliance between the state and production capital, which sponsors the second, "deployment" phase of the surge. Production capital is dominant, oligopoly flourishes, social protections are strengthened, the market is "embedded" in regulations through the political process. The reason is that production capital, being less flexible than finance capital, needs stably expanding markets. During this second phase the transformative technologies penetrate far and wide and the social benefits are spread more equally than in the first phase. In this perspective, the current crisis—running from 2000, with an interregnum between 2003 and 2007—marks the mid point of the diffusion of the information, computer and telecommunication (ICT) technology paradigm. If so, there may be a period of two to four decades to come in which production capital is dominant and the role of the state changes to promote the different needs of production capital.

However, the tidal movement described by this mechanism may be blocked by things like the rise of new major state powers, and rising inequality within most countries, which combine to hinder concerted corrective action on many problems, including both climate change and new rules of political economy. The tensions between global finance wanting a restoration of its pre-crisis freedoms as soon as it is rescued by taxpayers, and national populations wanting protection against economic crises and climate change will be central to the trajectory of the next several decades, and even to the survival of human civilization as we know it. The great question is, where is the Left in all this? Progressives have had next to no voice in the policymaking process, and are effectively "missing in action".[6]

Endnotes

[1] The tripling and doubling of China and India's extreme poverty headcount is suggested in Keidel (2007), but disputed by Chen and Ravallion (2008).

[2] From a World Bank expert on China's statistics, who requested anonymity.

[3] Even the technical language itself is an obstacle to a more central role of the state. "Financial repression" is the standard phrase to describe any government "intervention" in financial markets which "distorts" prices away from their "true" equilibrium. Any such intervention faces knee-jerk opposition on the basis that anything labelled "repression" must be bad.

[4] The challenger category is defined as per capita PPP income equal to two thirds or more of the per capita income of the poorest state of Western Europe/North America/Oceania (Greece in 2000) (see also Wade 2008b).

[5] Here I draw on arguments developed by Carlota Perez (2002, 2004).

[6] Another reason for scepticism about a new long-lasting phase of financial re-regulation is that economic conservatives have a ready explanation for the crisis that sets their minds at rest: just as Friedman blamed the Federal Reserve for causing the Great Depression, present-day conservatives are blaming too much regulation, too much "government intervention". The government's implicit guarantee to Fannie Mae and Freddie Mac, the giant mortgage financing companies, distorted the market by giving them subsidized finance, which enabled them to pump up the housing bubble (see Palley 2008).

References

Blandon J, Gregg P and Machin S (2005) Intergenerational mobility in Europe and North America. *Centre for Economic Performance, LSE*, http://cep.lse.ac.uk/about/news/IntergenerationalMobility.pdf Accessed 17 July 2009

Chakrabortty A (2008) Capitalism lies in shambles, and the left has gone awol. *The Guardian* 7 August

Chen S and Ravallion M (2008) China is poorer than we thought, but no less successful in the fight against poverty. Working Paper 4621, Development Research Group, World Bank.

Dore R (2000) *Stock Market Capitalism v Welfare Capitalism*. Oxford: Oxford University Press

Dumenil G and Levy D (2004) *Capital Resurgent*. Cambridge: Harvard University Press

Freeman A (forthcoming) The poverty of statistics. *Third World Quarterly*

Frey B, Pommerehne W, Schneider F and Gilbert G (1984) Consensus and dissensus among economists: An empirical inquiry. *American Economic Review* 74:986–994

Fuller D and Geide-Stevenson D (2003) Consensus among economists: Revisited. *Journal of Economic Education* Fall:369–387

Galbraith J K (1999) *The Affluent Society*. London: Penguin

Harvey D (2005) *A Brief History of Neoliberalism*. Oxford: Oxford University Press

Hoffmann L, Bofinger P, Flassbech H and Steinherr A (2001) *Kazakstan 1993–2000: Independent Advisors and the IMF*. New York: Physica-Verlag

Keidel A (2007) The limits of a smaller, poorer China. *Financial Times* 13 November

Krugman P (2009) Stressing the positive. *International Herald Tribune* 9–10 May

Lukaskas A and Livera-Batiz F (eds) (2001) *The Political Economy of the East Asian Crisis and its Aftermath*. Cheltenham: Edward Elgar

Maddison A (2003) *The World Economy: Historical Statistics*. Paris: OECD.

Merrill Lynch (2001) Progress report: European pension reforms, pension barometer for Europe. *Global Securities Research and Economics Group* 17 January

Milanovic B (2005) *Worlds Apart*. Princeton: Princeton University Press

Orenstein M (2005) The new pension reform as global policy. *Global Social Policy* 5(2):175–202

Palley T (2008) *Scapegoating Regulation*, http://www.thomaspalley.com Accessed 17 July 2009

Palma G (2009) The revenge of the market on the rentiers: How neo-liberal reports on the end of history turned out to be premature. *Cambridge Journal of Economics* 33(4):829–869

Palma J G (forthcoming) The revenge of the market on the rentiers. *Cambridge Journal of Economics*

Perez C (2002) *Technological Revolutions and Financial Capital: The Dynamics of Bubbles and Golden Ages*. Cheltenham: Edward Elgar

Perez C (2004) Finance and technical change: A long-term view. CERF Working Paper 14, Cambridge University, http://www-cfap.jbs.cam.ac.uk/publications/files/WP14%20-%20Perez.pdf Accessed 17 July 2009

Rodriguez F (2008a) Questions about growth regressions. *Challenge* July/August

Rodriguez F (2008b) What can we really learn from growth regressions? *Challenge* 51(4):55–69

Rodrik D (2008) The death of the globalization consensus. *Policy Innovations* 30 July

Vestergaard J (2009) *Discipline in the Global Economy? International Finance and the End of Liberalism*. London: Routledge

Vishwanath T and Kaufman D (2001) Towards transparency: New approaches and their application to financial markets. *World Bank Research Observer* 16(1):41–57

Wade R (2001) Capital and revenge: The IMF and Ethiopia. *Challenge* September/October:67–75

Wade R (2004a) Is globalization reducing poverty and inequality? *World Development* 32(4):567–589

Wade R (2004b) *Governing the Market*. Princeton: Princeton University Press

Wade R (2007) A new financial architecture? *New Left Review* July/August:113–129

Wade R (2008a) The first-world debt crisis of 2007–2010. *Challenge*, July/August

Wade R (2008b) Globalization, poverty, inequality, resentment and imperialism. In J Ravenhill (ed) *Global Political Economy* (pp 373–409). Oxford: Oxford University Press

Wade R (2009) Trade liberalization and economic growth: "Does trade liberalization contribute to economic prosperity?" No. In A Haas, J Hird and B McBratney (eds) *Controversies in Globalization* (pp 19–38). Washington DC: Congressional Quarterly Press

Wolf M (2004) *Why Globalization Works*. London: Yale University Press

Wolf M (2007) These are historic moments for the world economy. *Financial Times* 12 December

The Uses of Neoliberalism

James Ferguson

Department of Anthropology, Stanford University;
jgfergus@stanford.edu

Abstract: The term "neoliberalism" has come to be used in a wide variety of partly overlapping and partly contradictory ways. This essay seeks to clarify some of the analytical and political work that the term does in its different usages. It then goes on to suggest that making an analytical distinction between neoliberal "arts of government" and the class-based ideological "project" of neoliberalism can allow us to identify some surprising (and perhaps hopeful) new forms of politics that illustrate how fundamentally polyvalent neoliberal mechanisms of government can be. A range of empirical examples are discussed, mostly coming from my recent work on social policy and anti-poverty politics in southern Africa.

Keywords: neoliberalism, governmentality, South Africa, basic income, poverty

In thinking about the rapidly expanding literature on neoliberalism, I am struck by how much of the critical scholarship on topic arrives in the end at the very same conclusion—a conclusion that might be expressed in its simplest form as: "neoliberalism is bad for poor and working people, therefore we must oppose it." It is not that I disagree with this conclusion. On the contrary. But I sometimes wonder why I should bother to read one after another extended scholarly analysis only to reach, again and again, such an unsurprising conclusion.

This problem in recent progressive scholarship strikes me as related to a parallel problem in progressive politics more broadly. For over the last couple of decades, what we call "the Left" has come to be organized, in large part, around a project of resisting and refusing harmful new developments in the world. This is understandable, since so many new developments have indeed been highly objectionable. But it has left us with a politics largely defined by negation and disdain, and centered on what I will call "the antis." Anti-globalization, anti-neoliberalism, anti-privatization, anti-imperialism, anti-Bush, perhaps even anti-capitalism—but always "anti", not "pro". This is good enough, perhaps, if one's political goal is simply to denounce "the system" and to decry its current tendencies. And, indeed, some seem satisfied with such a politics. In my own disciplines of anthropology and African Studies, for instance, studies of state and development tend, with depressing predictability, to conclude (in tones of righteous indignation) that the rich are benefiting and the poor are getting screwed. The powerless, it seems, are getting the short end of the stick. This is not exactly a

Antipode Vol. 41 No. S1 2009 ISSN 0066-4812, pp 166–184
doi: 10.1111/j.1467-8330.2009.00721.x

surprising finding, of course (isn't it precisely because they *are* on the losing end of things that we call them "powerless" in the first place?). Yet this sort of work styles itself as "critique", and imagines itself to be very "political".

But what if politics is really not about expressing indignation or denouncing the powerful? What if it is, instead, about getting what you want? Then we progressives must ask: what do we want? This is a quite different question (and a far more difficult question) than: what are we against? *What do we want?* Such a question brings us very quickly to the question of government. Denunciatory analyses often treat government as the simple expression of power or domination— the implication apparently being that it is politically objectionable that people should be governed at all. But any realistic sort of progressive politics that would seek a serious answer to the question "what do we want?" will have to involve an exploration of the contemporary possibilities for developing genuinely progressive arts of government.

In his 1979 lectures on neoliberalism (2008), Michel Foucault famously spoke of the "absence of a socialist art of government", and the historic failure of the left to develop an "autonomous governmentality" comparable to liberalism. Stated as starkly as this, the point is no doubt debatable. Various forms of democratic socialism and social democracy (including but not limited to the German case treated in the lectures) may perhaps leave us with a richer trove of governmental arts than Foucault's very schematic account acknowledged, and the diverse histories of "unhappy symbiosis" of socialism with liberalism that he referred to parenthetically (2008:94n) may well have a greater originality than his analysis allowed. But what seems less open to dispute is that any program for governing from the left today faces an obstacle that we could describe (in Foucaultian terms) as a failure to develop new arts of government adequate to the challenges of our time. New progressive approaches to the problem of government are necessary, it now seems clear, because neither the governmental mechanisms, nor the political strategies of mobilization, that the left came to rely upon in the twentieth century (and which characterized, in different ways, both socialist and social democratic or "welfare state" regimes) are capable of getting the sort of traction that they once did. There are at least two reasons for this that are relevant both to my broader argument here, and to the particular topic of social assistance that I will address in the latter part of this article.

The first reason is the increasing prominence (especially in the region of my own special interest, Africa, but not only there) of urban masses who are not, and are not likely to become, formal wage laborers. Such people (variously, and inadequately, described as "the informal sector", "the lumpen", "the youth", and so on) now constitute the majority of the population in many African cities, and a very substantial proportion in much of the rest of the world, as Mike Davis (2007) has recently pointed out in his usual alarmist style. The twentieth-century social democracies, on the other hand (and still more so the state socialist regimes), were built on the putatively universal figure of "the worker". The Keynesian welfare state, as we know, was founded on a pact between capital and organized labor, and the domain we have come to know as "the social" was constructed on the foundation of the able-bodied worker. Indeed, the list of those requiring "social" intervention (the elderly, the infirm, the child, the disabled, the dependent reproductive woman) sketches a kind of photographic negative of the figure of the wage-earning man. Today, however, the question of social assistance is transformed in societies where young, able-bodied men look in vain for work, and are as much in need of assistance as everyone else. A compact between capital and labor, meanwhile, even were it politically possible, risks leaving out most of the population. New approaches to distribution, and new approaches to the question of social assistance, will need to be based on a fundamental rethinking that gives a new prominence to those hard-to-categorize urban improvisers who have for so long been relegated to the margins both of society, and of social analysis.

The second challenge to progressive thought and politics that I would like to identify is the rise of what we might call transnational forms of government, and particularly of the philanthropic funding of what we used to call "the social". Much has been written about the governmental role played by international organizations like the IMF and the World Bank. But the last couple of decades have also seen an explosion in de facto government carried out by an extraordinary swarm of NGOs, voluntary organizations, and private foundations. The Gates Foundation in Mozambique, to take just one example,[1] is carrying out a wide range of projects (in health, hygiene, education, sanitation, etc) that looks something like the twentieth century "social" of the social welfare state. But there is obviously a very different relation to the nation-state here, and to the national political arena. Social policy and nation-state are, to a very significant degree, decoupled, and we are only beginning to find ways to think about this.

More generally, technical prescriptions for "making poverty history" often seem almost irrelevant because they presume the central actors to be states—and certain sorts of states at that: well-financed, bureaucratically capable, poverty-fighting states that resemble nothing so much as twentieth century European welfare states. Couldn't the Democratic Republic of the Congo solve all its problems, reformers seems to say, if only its government would start to behave like that of Sweden? Well, maybe so, but it's the sort of ahistorical and asociological formulation that is worse than useless. Yet what happens when states of the imagined, poverty-fighting kind are simply not present? How can poverty policy be effective where states are (as the political scientists, rather misleadingly, say) "weak", or even actively anti-developmental? Where financial capacity is tiny and needs are enormous? What happens when the key implementers of poverty policy are not national states at all, but transnational NGOs, or private transnational foundations? What would count as progressive politics here?

One response here—understandable in the wake of the neoliberal restructuring of recent decades—is to call for the reinstating of old-style developmental states, effectively undoing the neoliberal transformations of the 1980s and 1990s and going back to the 1970s. I am skeptical that this is an adequate response—partly because the supposedly developmental states I know from the 1970s in Africa were pretty awful, and partly because I doubt that you can run history backward (as if you could just hit the rewind button and try again). The world has changed, and simply re-asserting Third World sovereignty will not get us very far in dealing with a fundamentally reconfigured politico-spatial world order. Imperialism is undoubtedly alive and well. But I don't think we have a good analysis of, say, the Gates Foundation, or the Soros Foundation, if we see them simply as the imperial tools of the global rich, undermining the sovereignty of African governments. It is much more complicated than that—and perhaps also more hopeful. Can we find ways of thinking creatively about the progressive possibilities (and not only the reactionary dangers) of this new terrain of transnational organization of funds, energies, and affect? Can we imagine new "arts of government" that might take advantage of (rather than simply denouncing or resisting) recent transformations in the spatial organization of government and social assistance?

Most broadly, can we engage with these new configurations of governmental power in a way that goes beyond the politics of denunciation, the politics of the "anti"? Can we develop new ways of thinking through the problem of government that are genuinely progressive, but that don't take for granted the absolute solidity or centrality of those two figures of twentieth-century left common sense: the worker and the nation-state?

It is here that we have to look more carefully at the "arts of government" that have so radically reconfigured the world in the last few decades, and I think we have to come up with something more interesting to say about them than just that we're against them. With respect to poverty and social policy, for instance (my particular interest here), it is simply not the case (as is often suggested) that neoliberal government ignores poverty, or leaves it to "the market". (Later in this essay, I will discuss a range of welfare-like interventions and social payments that coexist with—and may, in fact, be necessary complements to— neoliberal economic models.) At the same time, there is sometimes room (in part because of the political spaces opened up by "democracy" as the characteristic mode of legitimation of neoliberal regimes) for social movements and pro-poor organizations to have some real influence on matters of "social policy". (Hence my current interest in the "Basic Income Grant" (BIG) campaign in South Africa, which I'll discuss in a moment.) To understand the political possibilities and dangers that such emergent phenomena contain, we will surely need empirical research on the actual political processes at work. But beyond this, there is a palpable need for conceptual work, for new and better ways of thinking about practices of government and how they might be linked in new ways to the aspirations and demands of the economically and socially marginalized people who constitute the majority of the population in much of the world.

It is in this spirit, then, that I want to consider what I am calling "the uses of neoliberalism". I begin with a consideration of "uses" in the literal sense of semantic usage, as the wide variation in the way the term is used forces some clarification before we can begin to ask some new questions that might bring to light the surprising affinity of some aspects of what we call "neoliberalism" with certain forms of progressive politics.

As even a cursory inspection reveals, there is huge variation in the way the word, "neoliberalism" is used in contemporary scholarship. In perhaps the strictest sense, neoliberalism refers to a macroeconomic doctrine (and is, in this sense, a true "-ism"). The key elements of the doctrine are variously described, but always include a valorization of private enterprise and suspicion of the state, along with what is sometimes called "free-market fetishism" and the advocacy of tariff elimination, currency deregulation, and the deployment of "enterprise models" that would allow the state itself to be "run like a business". (See Peck 2008 for an illuminating review of the rise and dissemination of this doctrine.)

A related usage would have "neoliberalism" refer to a regime of policies and practices associated with or claiming fealty to the doctrine referenced above. Such a regime of practice is obviously different from the doctrine itself. Indeed, as David Harvey (2005) has argued, this divergence is, in fact, necessary, since neoliberal doctrine, if applied consistently, implies a world that could never, in fact, exist (which leads Harvey to term it "utopian"). Rather than purely applying the utopian neoliberal doctrine, Harvey points out that dominant groups around the world have used neoliberal arguments to carry out what is in fact a class project. "Neoliberalism", in this sense, has become the name for a set of highly interested public policies that have vastly enriched the holders of capital, while leading to increasing inequality, insecurity, loss of public services, and a general deterioration of quality of life for the poor and working classes.

But the policies of neoliberal states have often diverged from neoliberal doctrine for other reasons as well—reasons which have less to do with straightforward power grabs by the rich than with the contingencies of democratic politics. This no doubt helps to account for the otherwise paradoxical fact that a number of regimes pursuing undoubtedly neoliberal macroeconomic policies have also seen substantial recent rises in social spending (examples include India, Brazil, and South Africa, among others). Neoliberal policy is thus much more complicated than a reading of neoliberal doctrine might suggest.

Finally, it is perhaps worth mentioning, if only schematically, some other common uses of the term. One is as a sloppy synonym for capitalism itself, or as a kind of shorthand for the world economy and its inequalities. In much current anthropological usage, "neoliberalism" appears in this way, as a kind of abstract causal force that comes in from outside (much as "the world system" was reckoned to do at an earlier theoretical moment) to decimate local livelihoods. Another, more interesting, usage sees "neoliberalism" as the name of a broad, global cultural formation characteristic of a new era of "millennial capitalism"—a kind of global meta-culture, characteristic of our newly de-regulated, insecure, and speculative times (eg Comaroff and Comaroff 2000). And finally, "neoliberalism" can be indexed to a sort of "rationality" in the Foucauldian sense, linked less to economic dogmas or class projects than to specific mechanisms of government, and recognizable modes of creating subjects. (I will have more to say about this last usage shortly.)

It is, then, possible to identify many quite distinct referents for the same widely used term. This has some obvious dangers, of course. There is plainly a danger of simple confusion, since the meaning of the term can slip in the course of an argument being passed from author to reader (or, indeed, even in the course of an argument made by a single author). There is also another danger, only slightly less obvious, which is that such an all-encompassing entity can easily come to appear as a kind of gigantic, all-powerful first cause (as categories like "Modernity" or "Capitalism" have done before it)—that malevolent force that causes everything else to happen. This yields empty analysis (since to say that all our problems are caused by "neoliberalism" is really not to say much), and may also lead to an ineffectual politics—since all one can do with such a gigantic, malevolent "thing" as "neoliberalism" conceived in this way is to denounce it. (And *that*, the evidence suggests, doesn't seem to do much good).

One response would be to stop using the word altogether. This is indeed very tempting. If the word is so ambiguous, perhaps we should just be careful to be more specific, and use less all-encompassing terms. When the term "neoliberalism" is used as imprecisely as it is in many texts, one is tempted to pencil one's objections in the margins as one might in reading a student essay: "What do you mean by 'neoliberalism' here? Do you mean the liberalization of trade policies? Then say so! Do you mean techniques of government that work through the creation of responsibilized citizen-subjects? Then say *that*! The two don't necessarily go together. Say what you mean, and don't presume that they are all united in some giant package called 'neoliberalism'." Such insistence on specificity and precision would undoubtedly improve the analytical clarity of many of our discussions.

But there is also some utility in words that bring together more than one meaning. As long as we can avoid the mistake of simply confusing the different meanings, the word can be an occasion for reflecting on how the rather different things to which it refers may be related. In particular, I would like to use this confusing, conflating word as an occasion for thinking about the relation between the following two things:

First, we may consider the new governmental rationalities that emerged through the Thatcher–Reagan assaults on the North Atlantic, post-war welfare state. Key here was the deployment of market mechanisms and "enterprise" models to reform government, restructure the state, and pioneer new modes of government and subjectification. (See, eg, Barry, Osborne and Rose 1996; Rose 1999; Cruikshank 1999; Miller and Rose 2008.) There is a clear analysis in this literature of what it is that distinguishes "neoliberalism" from liberalism. Liberalism, in this account, was always about finding the right balance between two spheres understood as properly distinct, if always related: state and market, public and private, the realm of the king and the proper domain of the merchant. Neoliberalism, in contrast, puts governmental mechanisms developed in the private sphere to work within the state itself, so that even core functions of the state are either subcontracted out to private providers, or run (as the saying has it) "like a business". The question of what should be public and what private becomes blurred, as the state itself increasingly organizes itself around "profit centers", "enterprise models", and so on. Rather than shifting the line between state and market, then, neoliberalism in this account involved the deployment of new, market-based techniques of government within the terrain of the state itself. At the same time, new constructions of "active" and "responsible" citizens and communities are deployed to produce governmental results that do not depend on direct state intervention. The "responsibilized" citizen comes to operate as a miniature firm, responding to incentives, rationally assessing risks, and prudently choosing from among different courses of action.

Against this understanding of the neoliberal, consider what we might call neoliberalism in the African sense. Here, neoliberalism has meant first of all the policy measures that were forced on African states in the 1980s by banks and international lending agencies, under the name of "structural adjustment". Reforms focused on removing tariffs, deregulating currency markets, and removing the state from production and distribution (via dismantling of state marketing boards and parastatals). This did involve privatization, and an ideological celebration of markets. But the development of new technologies of government, responsibilized prudential subjects, and so on (all the things that Nikolas Rose and other "Anglo-Foucauldians" tend to emphasize) was very limited. Neoliberalism here was (in these terms) not very "neo" at all. It was, in fact, largely a matter of old-style laissez-faire liberalism in the service of imperial capital. And it had disastrous and wildly unpopular results (especially, the selling off of precious state assets to foreign firms at fire-sale prices, massive deindustrialization, and increased unemployment). Across much of the continent, it has raised the specter of a kind of recolonization. The result is that "neoliberalism" in Africa refers to a quite fundamentally different situation than it does in Western Europe and North America. The hasty and uncritical application of ideas of neoliberalism-as-rationality to Africa is thus clearly a mistake, based on a simple confusion (an art of government versus a crude battering open of Third World markets).

But bringing these two different referents together can be more interesting, if we don't just equate them, but instead reflect on the conceptual themes they share (broadly, a technical reliance on market mechanisms coupled with an ideological valorization of "private enterprise" and a suspicion of the state), and use such a reflection to ask if the new "arts of government" developed within First World neoliberalism might take on new life in other contexts, in the process opening up new political possibilities.

Can we on the left do what the right has, in recent decades, done so successfully, that is, to develop new modes and mechanisms of government? And (perhaps more provocatively) are the neoliberal "arts of government" that have transformed the way that states work in so many places around the world inherently and necessarily conservative, or can they be put to different uses? To ask such questions requires us to be willing at least to imagine the possibility of a truly progressive politics that would also draw on governmental mechanisms that we have become used to terming "neoliberal".

I have been led to these questions by my current interest in anti-poverty programs in southern Africa that seek to provide cash support for incomes, and thus (in theory) harness markets to the task of meeting the needs of the poor. This is happening in several African countries, but also in a great many other postcolonial states—from Brazil and Venezuela to Mexico and Bangladesh—where leftist and rightist regimes alike have seen fit to introduce policies that transfer cash directly into the hands of the poor. (See Fiszbein and Schady 2009; Standing 2008 [2007] for reviews.) The South African Basic Income Grant campaign is the example I will explore here. The proposal, which I will discuss in some detail shortly, is to deal with a crisis of persistent poverty by providing an unconditional minimum monthly payment to all. The argument goes like this: markets aren't working for poor people because they're too poor to participate in them; government programs aren't working because the state is inefficient. So, provide income support directly, in the form of cash, and then say to the poor: "you are now empowered to solve your own problems in the way you see best". In contrast to older forms of "welfare" assistance, the claim is that such grants rely on poor people's own ability to solve their own problems, without imposing the policing, paternalism, and surveillance of the traditional welfare state. More broadly, similar new lines of thought are calling for an increased role for direct cash transfers in many forms of social and humanitarian policy (eg famine relief, which will be briefly discussed shortly). The reasoning here often includes recognizably neoliberal elements, including the valorization of market efficiency, individual choice, and autonomy; themes of entrepreneurship; and skepticism about the state as a service provider. But the politics are avowedly (and, I think, on balance, genuinely) "pro-poor" (as the phrase has it). "Pro-poor" and neoliberal—it is the strangeness of this conjunction that is of interest here. For the sorts of new progressive initiatives I have in mind seem to involve not just opposing "the neoliberal project", but appropriating key elements of neoliberal reasoning for different ends. We can't think about this (or even acknowledge its possibility) if we continue to treat "neoliberal" simply as a synonym for "evil". Instead, I suggest (and this is a deliberate provocation) that some innovative (and possible effective) forms of new politics in these times may be showing us how fundamentally polyvalent the neoliberal arts of government can be.

Let me emphasize that to say that certain political initiatives and programs borrow from the neoliberal bag of tricks doesn't mean that these political projects are in league with the ideological project of neoliberalism (in David Harvey's sense)—only that they appropriate certain characteristic neoliberal "moves" (and I think of these discursive and programmatic moves as analogous to the moves one might make in a game). These moves are recognizable enough to look "neoliberal", but they can, I suggest, be used for quite different purposes than that term usually implies. In this connection, one might think of statistical techniques for calculating the probabilities of workplace injuries. These were originally developed in the nineteenth century by large employers to control costs (Ewald 1986), but they eventually became the technical basis for social insurance, and ultimately for the welfare state (which brought unprecedented gains to the working class across much of the world). Techniques, that is to say, can "migrate" across strategic camps, and devices of government that were invented to serve one purpose have often enough ended up, though history's irony, being harnessed to another. Might we see a similar re-appropriation of "market" techniques of government (which were, like workplace statistics, undoubtedly conservative in their original uses) for different, and more progressive sorts of ends? Maybe not—one should remain genuinely open-minded about this—but it is perhaps worth at least considering. Let me present two empirical examples from southern Africa as a way of making this proposition perhaps a bit more plausible.

Basic Income

My principal example is the basic income grant (BIG) campaign in South Africa. For historical reasons, South Africa came to democratic independence in 1994 with a quite well developed system of social grants and pensions (which I am not able to describe here for reasons of space). In recent years, as neoliberal restructuring has led to widening inequality and very high rates of unemployment, these social grants have substantially expanded, and have been instrumental in holding together what might otherwise be an explosive situation (a fact of which the ANC government appears to be acutely aware). But planners have been bothered by the patchy and arbitrary spread of the coverage, and the inefficiency and cost of administering a host of cumbersome and bureaucratic targeted programs.

It is in this context that proposals emerged for a far-reaching new comprehensive system of income support, anchored by a BIG to be paid to all South Africans (Department of Social Development 2002). The idea of a BIG was first put forward by the labor union federation, COSATU, in 1998, and it acquired new legitimacy when it was embraced in 2002 by a government-appointed committee (the Taylor Committee) charged with recommending measures for the rationalization of the system of social assistance (see Barchiesi 2007; Department of Social Development 2002; Ferguson 2007; Tilton 2005). The proposal has been advocated from 2001 onward by a formal coalition of church groups and labor, the BIG Coalition).[2]

The proposal was for a modest payment of about R100 (at that time, about $16) per person per month, to be paid to all South Africans, irrespective of age or income. Advocates insist that a universal system of direct payments is by far the most efficient way to direct assistance to all poor South Africans. Means testing, in their view, would not be necessary; better off South Africans would also receive the grant, but the funds they received (and then some) would be recuperated through the tax system. Economic analyses prepared by BIG advocates (eg Standing and Samson 2003) argue that the measure could be funded through increases in either the income tax or the VAT, as well as by savings created by rationalizing the existing system of pensions. The idea of a BIG has been supported by church groups, NGOs, and the powerful Congress of South African Trade Unions (COSATU); and a watered down version has even been endorsed by the main (and historically white) opposition party, the Democratic Alliance. The ruling

ANC, however, has thus far rejected the plan, though it does enjoy support from at least some key players within the party (including the Minster for Social Development, Dr Zola Skweyiya).

The BIG campaign is significant not only as an interesting and potentially progressive policy proposal, but also as an illustration of some new ways of thinking about questions of poverty and welfare that bring neoliberal themes to bear on the question of social assistance in ways that are very different from those we have become accustomed to in the last few decades. I begin by acknowledging that the arguments for a basic income grant in South Africa have been many sided and complex, and they are not reducible to a single logic or rationality (neoliberal or otherwise). Older languages of social democracy and solidarity continue to have significant currency, and a reading of pro-BIG documents shows that traditional welfare-state arguments are regularly deployed. These include themes of social solidarity and moral obligation; the advantages of social cohesion and dangers of class war; Keynesian arguments about stimulating demand; and labor-rights arguments about giving workers the security to say no to dangerous and demeaning work.[3] Yet these lines of argument lie side by side with others, which are markedly different from social democratic reasoning, and surprisingly similar to the neoliberal rationality that we more usually associate with anti-welfare discourses. The intermingling of these different themes speaks to the complex political struggles around the BIG, which have been discussed by others (eg Mattisonn and Seekings 2003; Barchiesi 2007). My interest here, though, is not in analyzing these politics, but in identifying some surprising ways in which certain discursive "moves" that we can readily identify as neoliberal are being put to work in the service of apparently pro-poor and pro-welfare political arguments. To make this process visible, it is useful to pull some of these neoliberal "moves" out of the broader mix of BIG arguments so that we can see the work that they are doing. (Note that the following is a highly condensed summary. For a more detailed analysis that includes citations of specific texts, see Ferguson 2007.)

One of the most important themes in arguments in favor of a BIG is the idea of "investment in human capital". A BIG, supporters say, would enable poor South Africans to increase their spending on such things as nutrition, education, and health care. And this, advocates insist, should be understood as an "investment" in a kind of "capital". Such "investment", they insist, will bring handsome returns, in the form of productivity gains. The poor individual is in this way conceived, in classic neoliberal fashion, as a kind of micro-enterprise, earning a rate of return on invested capital.

More surprising is the way that pro-BIG arguments neatly reverse the usual right-wing arguments against social payments by insisting that basic income can be justified precisely as a way of *combating* "dependency". The existing "safety net", the BIG promoters argue, relies on very destructive forms of dependency, since any economically productive poor person is surrounded by relatives and other dependents who must be supported. This is destructive, in economic terms, because it constitutes an effective "tax" on the productivity of the poor. The worker whose wages are soaked up by dependents in this way suffers from both a disincentive to work, and a drag on his or her ability to build up human capital. The "dependency" of absolute poverty in this way hurts productivity, and also makes it hard for workers to be economically active, to search for better jobs, etc. The passivity associated with this predicament, moreover, inhibits entrepreneurship and "risk-taking behaviors". Providing basic income security for all, it is claimed, will enable the poor to behave as proper neoliberal subjects (ie as entrepreneurs and risk takers); the status quo prevents it, and promotes "dependency". In this way, the BIG would provide not a "safety net" (the circus image of old-style welfare as protection against hazard) but a "springboard"—a facilitator of risky (but presumably empowering) neoliberal flight.

Equally striking is the way that basic income arguments appropriate neoliberal critiques of welfare paternalism and put them in the service of a pro-welfare argument. Echoing the old Margaret Thatcher complaint about the "nanny state" that tries to run everybody's life in the name of the needs of "society", BIG advocates point out that South Africa's *existing* social assistance system makes moralizing judgments about "the undeserving poor", and requires (at great expense) the surveillance and normalization of grant recipients, who are publicly labeled as such, and thus potentially stigmatized. In contrast to all this, the BIG would be paid to everyone; citizens would access their funds (in the ideal scheme) by simply swiping their national identity cards at at automatic cash dispenser. They would not need the government to tell them how to spend the funds. They would use them (like good rational actors) in the way they saw best. There would be no "nanny state": no policing of conduct, no stigmatizing labels, no social workers coming into homes—and no costly bureaucracy to sort out who does or doesn't qualify. Grant recipients, in this vision, appear as sensible people who know their problems and predicaments better than any bureaucrat could. The state, meanwhile, appears as both omnipresent and minimal—universally engaged (as a kind of direct provider for each and every citizen) and maximally disengaged (taking no real interest in shaping the conduct of those under its care, who are seen as knowing their own needs better than the state does).

Finally, the most radical shift from traditional social democracy visible in the arguments for a BIG is the explicit rejection of formal employment as the "normal" frame of reference for social policy (let alone as an entitlement to which all have rights). The 2002 Taylor

Committee Report projected that, even with strong economic growth, formal sector employment in South Africa was not likely to expand at the sort of rate that would be necessary for anything close to full employment (a prediction that recent developments have certainly borne out). On the contrary, it forecast that developing countries like South Africa were likely, over the long term, to see an inexorable shift *away from* (and not toward) formal employment. According to the report:

> In developing countries, where stable full-time waged formal sector labour was never the norm, it is increasingly unlikely that it will become the norm (Department of Social Development 2002:38).

> The reality is that in the developing world formal sector employment may never become the norm that it is in Europe (ibid 2002:154).

The need for assistance, then, is not about being "between jobs" or correcting for dips in the business cycle; it is part of a world in which many, or even most, people, for the foreseeable future, will lack formal sector employment. Social assistance is here radically decoupled from expectations of employment, and, indeed, from "insurance" rationality altogether. Instead, the Taylor Committee Report re-understands the condition of unemployment not as a hazard, but as the normal condition.

Yet unemployment, in this understanding, need not imply idleness or a lack of productivity. On the contrary, in a world where livelihoods in the "informal economy" will become increasingly important, small expenditures on minimum income support (like the BIG) can have big payoffs in enabling and enhancing economic action in that domain. Social payments, in this optic, are most significant not as temporary substitutes for employment, but as a way of promoting greater productivity, enterprise, and risk-taking in the "informal" domain within which more and more South Africans are expected to make their living.

I hope to have identified some recognizably neoliberal motifs here. But I hope it is also clear that this is not the neoliberalism we love to hate, the so-called "neoliberal project" identified by Harvey (2005). It's something else—a set of much harder to place arguments that link markets, enterprise, welfare, and social payments in a novel way. It leaves us neither with something to hate, nor something to love, but rather something to ponder. I will return to the question of the perils and promise of the BIG in the conclusion to this article, but for the moment, let us try to hold in our minds the apparently paradoxical idea that a major policy initiative might be, all at once, "pro-poor", redistributive, and neoliberal.

Food Aid and Cash Transfers

It may be helpful to briefly discuss one additional example, to help suggest something I am increasingly convinced is the case: that the BIG campaign is part of a much wider, worldwide shift in thinking about poverty and social and humanitarian assistance. The example I have in mind is the increasingly influential argument that hunger is best dealt with by boosting the purchasing power of those at risk, rather than by distributing in-kind food aid.

The current international food aid system is based on the subsidized overproduction of agricultural crops (especially grain) in rich countries like the USA. Food aid programs then take this surplus grain and transport it to places (largely in Africa) where it is distributed to people who are at risk of hunger due to drought, natural disasters, political violence, or other sorts of humanitarian emergency. Critics like Amartya Sen have long noted the (largely unintended) negative impacts of such policies, which tend to depress producer prices for local farmers, while damaging local institutions for producing and distributing food crops. Once food aid has arrived, local food production may never recover. Too often, what was supposed to be a "temporary" crisis becomes a long-term decline in food self-sufficiency (see, eg Sen 1983; Dreze and Sen 1991).

As an alternative, Sen's followers have pushed for cash payments to be made directly to those at risk of food deficit (either via employment guarantees, or through direct cash transfers). People with money in their pockets, these advocates point out, usually don't starve. And cash support allows famine victims to preserve or restore productive assets (eg livestock) in ways that simply supplying a certain number of calories does not. What is more, the economic chain of events that is set in motion by boosting purchasing power not only avoids the destructive effects of food aid, but creates a virtuous cycle, in which market forces lead to increased capacity for local production and distribution. A number of pilot projects have been launched putting these principles into practice in recent years. Among the best known is the Cash for Relief Programme in Ethiopia, which used cash payments to enable households that had been hit by crop failure to rebuild their assets and regenerate their livelihoods, and not only to eat (USAID/OFDA 2004). Another widely discussed project has been the Kalomo Social Cash Transfer Scheme in Zambia. Here, too, cash took the place of food aid, with the result that recipients were able to meet non-nutritional as well as nutritional needs, including education, transportation, and health care (Schubert and Goldberg 2004). An impressive range of similar projects are reviewed in Standing (2008 [2007]) and Farrington and Slater (2006). (See also the review of the potential for cash transfers in "unstable situations" that was recently done by Harvey and Holmes (2007) for the UK Department for International Development.)

The arguments made by the increasingly numerous promoters of such programs are in many ways similar to those made on behalf of the South African BIG. Dispensing cash, they insist, is in the first place more efficient and less expensive than other sorts of assistance, and often requires less infrastructure and institutional capacity. In any case, they argue, why should bureaucrats decide on behalf of recipients what their needs are? Cash transfers provide hungry people with the flexibility to access a broad range of goods and services available on the market to meet their needs. And poor people, in this conception, are good judges of how to do that—using money to go to the clinic this month, to pay school fees for a child the next, to buy a bag of maize meal the next, and so on. Rather than wasting the money on frivolous expenditure, advocates insist, recipients generally apply their scant cash resources very rationally, and even make canny small investments. As one PowerPoint presentation on the Kalomo project put it: "The 'grannies' turned out to be excellent economists!"

Top-down, state-planned attempts to directly meet nutritional needs through trucking in food, in this view, are bound to be clumsy, inefficient, and wasteful. Cash transfers, on the other hand, put more decision-making power in the hands of those who know their predicament best—the hunger afflicted—and empower them to use the flexibility and efficiency of markets to help solve their own problems. Unlike direct food aid, cash transfers can have a catalytic effect on many other income-gaining activities, thereby contributing powerfully to the "multiple livelihood strategies" that are so important in keeping the poorest households afloat.

Such arguments recall Jane Guyer's (1989) groundbreaking work on feeding African cities. Consider, Guyer suggests, how food ends up finding its way to consumers' plates in the vast megacities of West Africa such as Lagos. The logistical task of moving thousands of tons of food each day from thousands of local producers to millions of urban consumers would be beyond the organizational capacity of any state (to say nothing of the less-than-exemplary Nigerian one). Here, market mechanisms, drawing on the power of vast self-organizing networks, are very powerful, and very efficient. Such forms of organization must appear especially attractive where states lack capacity (and let us remember how many progressive dreams in Africa have crashed on the rocks of low state capacity).

Why should relying on this sort of mechanism be inherently right-wing, or suspect in the eyes of progressives? The answer is, of course, not far to find: markets serve only those with purchasing power. Market-based solutions are thus likely to be true "solutions" only for the better-off, whose needs are so effectively catered to by markets. But the food aid example shows a way of redirecting markets toward the poor, by intervening not to restrict the market, but to boost purchasing power. I have become convinced that (at least in the case of food aid) this is probably good public policy. Is it also neoliberal? Perhaps that is not the right question. Perhaps we should rather ask: are there specific sorts of social policy that might draw on characteristic neoliberal "moves" (like using markets to deliver services) that would also be genuinely progressive? That seems like a question worth asking, even if we are at this point not fully ready to answer it.

Let me be clear that none of the examples discussed here are (in my view) unequivocally good (or unequivocally bad, for that matter). Instead, they leave us feeling uneasy, unsure of our moorings. They leave us less with strong opinions than with the sense that we need to think about them a bit more. They do not permit the simple denunciations (Aha! Neoliberalism!) that have become so familiar a part of the politics of the "anti-", even as they clearly require us to turn a thoughtfully critical and skeptical eye toward their dangers and ambiguities.

I also want to emphasize as clearly as possible that none of these examples is a matter of "leaving it to the market". All require major non-market interventions (either by states or by state-like entities such as foundations or international agencies), and all are premised on the principle that public policy must play a major redistributive role. But they are interventions that create a situation where markets can arguably serve progressive ends, in ways that may require us to revise some of our prejudices that automatically associate market mechanisms with the interests of the well-to-do.

The Point is to Change It!

If we are seeking, as this special issue of *Antipode* aspires to do, to link our critical analyses to the world of grounded political struggle—not only to interpret the world in various ways, but also to change it—then there is much to be said for focusing, as I have here, on mundane, real-world debates around policy and politics, even if doing so inevitably puts us on the compromised and reformist terrain of the possible, rather than the seductive high ground of revolutionary ideals and utopian desires. But I would also insist that there is more at stake in the examples I have discussed here than simply a slightly better way to ameliorate the miseries of the chronically poor, or a technically superior method for relieving the suffering of famine victims.

My point in discussing the South African BIG campaign, for instance, is not really to argue for its implementation. There is much in the campaign that is appealing, to be sure. But one can just as easily identify a series of worries that would bring the whole proposal into doubt. Does not, for instance, the decoupling of the question of assistance from the issue of labor, and the associated valorization of the "informal", help provide a kind of alibi for the failures of the South African regime to pursue policies that would do more to create jobs? Would not the creation of a basic income benefit tied to national citizenship simply exacerbate the vicious xenophobia that already divides the South African poor, in a context where many of the poorest are not citizens, and would thus not be eligible for the BIG? Perhaps even more fundamentally, is the idea of basic income really capable of commanding the mass support that alone could make it a central pillar of a new approach to distribution? The record to date gives powerful reasons to doubt it. So far, the technocrats' dreams of relieving poverty through efficient cash transfers have attracted little support from actual poor people, who seem to find that vision a bit pale and washed out, compared with the vivid (if vague) populist promises of jobs and personalistic social inclusion long offered by the ANC patronage machine, and lately personified by Jacob Zuma (Ferguson forthcoming).

My real interest in the policy proposals discussed here, in fact, has little to do with the narrow policy questions to which they seek to provide answers. For what is most significant, for my purposes, is not whether or not these are good policies, but the way that they illustrate a process through which specific governmental devices and modes of reasoning that we have become used to associating with a very particular (and conservative) political agenda ("neoliberalism") may be in the process of being peeled away from that agenda, and put to very different uses. Any progressive who takes seriously the challenge I pointed to at the start of this essay, the challenge of developing new progressive arts of government, ought to find this turn of events of considerable interest.

As Steven Collier (2005) has recently pointed out, it is important to question the assumption that there is, or must be, a neat or automatic fit between a hegemonic "neoliberal" political-economic project (however that might be characterized), on the one hand, and specific "neoliberal" techniques, on the other. Close attention to particular techniques (such as the use of quantitative calculation, free choice, and price driven by supply and demand) in particular settings (in Collier's case, fiscal and budgetary reform in post-Soviet Russia) shows that the relationship between the technical and the political-economic "is much more polymorphous and unstable than is assumed in much critical geographical work", and that neoliberal technical mechanisms are in fact "deployed in relation to diverse political projects and social norms" (2005:2).

As I suggested in referencing the role of statistics and techniques for pooling risk in the creation of social democratic welfare states, social technologies need not have any essential or eternal loyalty to the political formations within which they were first developed. Insurance rationality at the end of the nineteenth century had no essential vocation to provide security and solidarity to the working class; it was turned to that purpose (in some substantial measure) because it was available, in the right place at the right time, to be appropriated for that use. Specific ways of solving or posing governmental problems, specific institutional and intellectual mechanisms, can be combined in an almost infinite variety of ways, to accomplish different social ends. With social, as with any other sort of technology, it is not the machines or the mechanisms that decide what they will be used to do.

Foucault (2008:94) concluded his discussion of socialist government-ality by insisting that the answers to the Left's governmental problems require not yet another search through our sacred texts, but a process of conceptual and institutional innovation. "[I]f there is a really socialist governmentality, then it is not hidden within socialism and its texts. It cannot be deduced from them. It must be invented". But invention in the domain of governmental technique is rarely something worked up out of whole cloth. More often, it involves a kind of bricolage (Lévi-Strauss 1966), a piecing together of something new out of scavenged parts originally intended for some other purpose. As we pursue such a process of improvisatory invention, we might begin by making an inventory of the parts available for such tinkering, keeping all the while an open mind about how different mechanisms might be put to work, and what kinds of purposes they might serve. If we can go beyond seeing in "neoliberalism" an evil essence or an automatic unity, and instead learn to see a field of specific governmental techniques, we may be surprised to find that some of them can be repurposed, and put to work in the service of political projects very different from those usually associated with that word. If so, we may find that the cabinet of governmental arts available to us is a bit less bare than first appeared, and that some rather useful little mechanisms may be nearer to hand than we thought.

Endnotes

[1] I refer here to the remarkable PhD research now being carried out by Ramah McKay (Department of Anthropology, Stanford University).

[2] Barchiesi (2007) gives a detailed and illuminating account of the origins of the BIG campaign and the Taylor Committee report.

[3] As Barchiesi (2007) noted, some more conservative formulations of the BIG campaign have also made the contrary argument, that it would help move unemployed people into very low wage jobs. He also points out another important theme that I do not explore here: the implicit or explicit moralism of much of the discussion around "the social question" in South Africa.

References

Barchiesi F (2007) South African debates on the Basic Income Grant: Wage labour and the post-apartheid social policy. *Journal of Southern African Studies* 33(3):561–575

Barry A, Osborne T and Rose N (eds.) (1996) *Foucault and Political Reason: Liberalism, Neo-liberalism and Rationalities of Government.* Chicago: University of Chicago Press

Collier S (2005) *The Spatial Forms and Social Norms of "Actually Existing Neoliberalism": Toward a Substantive Analytics.* International Affairs Working Paper. New York: New School University

Comaroff J and Comaroff J (2000) Millennial capitalism: First thoughts on a second coming. *Public Culture* 12(2):291–343

Cruikshank B (1999) *The Will to Empower: Democratic Citizens and Other Subject.* Ithaca: Cornell University Press

Davis M (2007) *Planet of Slums.* New York: Verso

Department of Social Development (2002) *Transforming the Present—Protecting the Future: Report of the Committee of Inquiry into a Comprehensive System of Social Security for South Africa.* Pretoria: Government Printer

Dreze J and Sen A (1991) *Hunger and Public Action.* New York: Oxford University Press

Ewald F (1986) *L'etat Providence.* Paris: Bernard Grasset

Farrington J and Slater R (2006) Cash transfers: Panacea for poverty reduction or money down the drain? *Development Policy Review* 24(5):499–511

Ferguson J (2007) Formalities of poverty: Thinking about social assistance in neoliberal South Africa. *African Studies Review* 50(2):71–86

Ferguson J (forthcoming) Declarations of dependence: Labor, personhood, and welfare in South Africa

Fiszbein A and Schady N (2009) *Conditional Cash Transfers: Reducing Present and Future Poverty.* Washington DC: The World Bank

Foucault M (2008) *The Birth of Biopolitics: Lectures at the College de France, 1978–1979.* Translated by Graham Burchell. New York: Palgrave MacMillan

Guyer J (ed) (1989) *Feeding African Cities: Studies in Regional Social History.* Manchester: Manchester University Press

Harvey D (2005) *A Brief History of Neoliberalism.* New York: Oxford University Press

Harvey P and Holmes R (2007) *The Potential for Joint Programmes for Long-term Cash Transfers in Unstable Situations: A Report Commissioned by the Fragile States Team and the Equity and Rights Team of the UK Department for International Development.* London: Humanitarian Policy Group, Overseas Development Institute

Lévi-Strauss C (1966) *The Savage Mind.* Chicago: University of Chicago Press

Mattisonn H and Seekings J (2003) The politics of a basic income grant in South Africa, 1996–2002. In G Standing and M Samson (eds) *A Basic Income Grant for South Africa* (pp 56–76). Cape Town: University of Cape Town Press

Miller P and Rose N (2008) *Governing the Present.* Malden, Massachusetts: Polity Press

Peck J (2008) Remaking laissez-faire. *Progress in Human Geography* 32(1):3–43

Rose N (1999) *Powers of Freedom: Reframing Political Thought.* New York: Cambridge University Press

Schubert B and Goldberg J (2004) *The Pilot Social Cash Transfer Scheme: Zambia.* Lusaka: GTZ (Deutsche Gesellschaft für Technische Zusammenarbeit)

Sen A (1983) *Poverty and Famines: An Essay on Entitlement and Deprivation.* New York: Oxford University Press

Standing G (2008 [2007]) *How Cash Transfers Boost Work and Economic Security.* DESA Working Paper No. 50. New York: United Nations Department of Economic and Social Affairs

Standing G and Samson M (eds) (2003) *A Basic Income Grant for South Africa.* Cape Town: University of Cape Town Press

Tilton D (2005) *BIG Fact Sheet #1*, http://www.big.org.za/index.php?option=articles&task=viewarticle&artid=5 Accessed 11 September 2005

USAID/OFDA (2004) *Evaluation of OFDA Cash for Relief Intervention in Ethiopia.* Prepared by Robert H. Brandstetter. Washington DC: United States Agency for International Development (USAID)

Crisis, Continuity and Change: Neoliberalism, the Left and the Future of Capitalism

Noel Castree

School of Environment and Development,
Manchester University, Manchester, UK;
noel.castree@man.ac.uk

Abstract: This essay's point of departure is the coincident economic and environmental "crises" of our time. I locate both in the dynamics of capital accumulation on a world-scale, drawing on the ideas of Marx, Karl Polanyi and James O'Connor. I ask whether the recent profusion of "crisis talk" in the public domain presents an opportunity for progressive new ideas to take hold now that "neoliberalism" has seemingly been de-legitimated. My answer is that a "post-neoliberal" future is probably a long way off. I make my case in two stages and at two geographical scales. First, I examine the British social formation as currently constituted and explain why even a leading neoliberal state is failing to reform its ways. Second, I then scale-up from the domestic level to international affairs. I examine cross-border emissions trading— arguably *the* policy tool for mitigating the very real prospects of significant climate change this century. The overall conclusion is this: even though the "first" and "second" contradictions of capital have manifested themselves together and at a global level, there are currently few prospects for systemic reform (never mind revolution) led by a new, twenty-first century "red-green" Left.

Keywords: economic crisis, environmental crisis, social formation, emissions trading, climate change, Britain, the EU

A crisis consists precisely in the fact that the old is dying and the new cannot be born; in this interregnum, a great variety of morbid symptoms appear (A. Gramsci 1971:276).

The world can and has been changed by those for whom the ideal and the real are dynamically contiguous (W. James 1956:42).

Introduction

Gramsci's famous dictum, formulated in a prison cell on the eve of the Great Depression, remains instructive almost 80 years later—or so I want to argue. To say that we live in remarkable times is not only a cliché but an understatement. Talk of "crisis" has, in the space of three short years, become commonplace at all points of the compass. But unlike the 1930s, the idea of crisis has not one but two world-historical referents. Beginning in August 2007, the butterfly effect caused by the "credit crunch"—which within a year led to a virtual meltdown of

Antipode Vol. 41 No. S1 2009 ISSN 0066-4812, pp 185–213
doi: 10.1111/j.1467-8330.2009.00722.x

the global financial system and plunged the so-called "real economy" into an ongoing recession—has been coincident with a long overdue recognition that climate change is a clear and present danger. As the Marxist theorist James O'Connor (1998) would have it, the "first" and "second" contradictions of capitalism have at last manifested themselves simultaneously and on a planetary scale. After 30 years of neoliberal political economy, and an even longer period of materials-intensive capital accumulation, "red" and "green" Leftists have together been vindicated. The questions on so many people's lips are these: not just "what comes après le deluge?", but also "who gets to decide?"

To my mind, the Left should not get its hopes up—at least not yet. It's sad to say, but only the most wild-eyed optimist could believe that the two perceived crises of our time are harbingers of a better future. Taking two cases—one national scale, one international—I want to argue that Gramsci was right. The "old" may be dying, but it's far from dead. The essay comprises four parts. I begin in the heat of the moment, by describing how and why the idea of two concurrent worldwide "crises" became commonplace in a surprisingly short space of time (2007–2009). Following this, I take a theoretical detour intended to explain why these crises have arisen, and how they might play out. Marx, Karl Polanyi and James O'Connor are my guides. Focusing on Britain as an illustrative case, I then explain why the present moment is not, regrettably, a propitious one for left-wing change-makers. My point is to show that even in neoliberalism's heartlands, in the thick of a financial crisis, there is only weak impetus for change. After this examination of how crisis is playing-out at the scale of one notable nation state, I delve into the world of international emissions trading philosophy and practice—with a particular focus on the European Union's still young scheme. I suggest that the myriad practical failures of this and other market approaches to greenhouse gas mitigation belie the abstract logic of "free market environmentalism". Even so, these approaches will be with us for many years to come in all probability. A short conclusion looks to a future hopefully free of those "morbid symptoms" that Gramsci described just after the Great Crash of 1929. It's a future that will, I fear, be very hard to make. If William James were writing today, he probably would not bet on the Left making its ideals flesh any time soon. Not for the first time, some optimism of the will is required—quite a lot, in fact.

The Making of a Double Whammy: Crises Perceived and Real

As Scott Prudham rightly observes, "There is no crisis without someone to call it one" (2005:21).[1] Until recently, talk of global crisis was a minority sport exclusive to societal "outsiders"—the preserve of extreme environmentalists, humanitarians or die-hard socialists. But by mid-2008 it seemed to become widespread—something scarcely predictable even two years before. Why did all this crisis talk suddenly enter the mainstream? The reasons are several, but not hard to seek. Their coming together at a single moment in the early twenty-first century must be considered a conjunctural accident—something of an historical fluke, notwithstanding their common connections to processes of capital accumulation (about which more in the next section).

New Ecological Anxieties

On the environmental side, it seems to me that three things have been important. Two have been slow-burning, the third a catalyst whose dramatic effect would've been impossible without the first and second. To begin with, the environmental movement—which both internationalised and professionalised itself from the mid-1970s onwards—has persistently pointed to the deleterious effects of modern, highly industrialised forms of production and transportation, along with mass consumption. True, its messages—which were so loud and clear during the decade when the solidities of post-war Keynesianism (or "embedded liberalism") melted into air—became victims of a "green backlash" during the 1980s and the early 1990s. But the movement has nonetheless remained visible and principled over the last 30 years, even as some of its most famous organisations (such as Greenpeace) have traded a share of their radicalism for respectability. At the same time—and secondly—this movement's influence partly explains why environmental issues started to be routinely placed on intergovernmental agendas, even during years when—as with Margaret Thatcher's opening of the North Sea oil fields—domestic politics paid environmental issues little mind. The United Nations provided an essential institutional forum here.

Without the persistent campaigning of the environmental movement this last 35 years, or the existence of a longstanding institutional infrastructure for intergovernmental action on shared environmental problems, I doubt the third reason for the recent emergence of crisis talk could have had its dramatic effect. I'm referring to the temporal juxtaposition of the Stern Review (2006) on the economics of climate change, and the fourth assessment report of the IPCC (allied with the results of a subsequent scientific meeting in Copenhagen in March 2009)[2]. The Stern report, commissioned by the British Treasury, was championed by Tony Blair (then still British premier) and Gordon Brown. It quickly managed to insinuate its message about the costs of global warming into the various established intergovernmental fora (eg G7, G8, G20 and Davos meetings), and its lead author was a respected political economic insider who'd worked at the World Bank. Within days of its publication *The Economist* devoted a whole issue to the subject and the reputable newspapers editorialised frantically. A few months later the fourth IPCC report appeared, rendering the science on which the Stern review is based already obsolete. This report is now the most authoritative and credible thing that politicians, publics and businesses worldwide have to determine the likely degree of future climate change—even as IPCC scientists acknowledge that its findings now need to be revised upwards in light of new evidence. It predicts an average global temperature rise of as much as 4°C by the end of the century. Without drastic action to reduce greenhouse gas emissions, it seems that anthropogenic environmental change will be as profound as it is unintended.[3]

Even the USA, under Barak Obama, has seen fit to reverse its longstanding refusal to be a signatory to the Kyoto Protocol. The historic, if far from satisfactory, Waxman-Markey climate change bill[4] was passed into US law in June 2009 and constitutes a vital precondition for meaningful American participation in efforts to mitigate global greenhouse gas emissions. The next challenge will be getting China, now the world's largest atmospheric polluter, on board. At the time of writing (September 2009) the outcome of the crucial Copenhagen meeting of the Kyoto parties is not yet known.

Political Economic Turmoil

So much for environmental matters. What of economic affairs? Here the reasons for a recent outbreak of crisis talk are, of course, far easier to discern. The sheer suddenness and severity of what has happened to the global economy this last two and a half years caught policymakers and the corporate sector completely by surprise.[5] First, there was the unanticipated firestorm within the world's financial sector, centred on Wall Street and the City. The collapse of Lehman Brothers took the drama to new heights, but was only one of several jaw-dropping incidents. Second, there were on the on-the-hoof, all-hands-to-the-pump economic measures taken to rescue the financial sector by central bankers and finance ministers. Recapitalisations, serial interest rate cuts, new short-term borrowing facilities, currency revaluations, extra guarantees on depositors' savings, insurance guarantees against bank write-downs, historically low interest rates, and even printing money (euphemised as "quantitative easing"): any and all weapons from the arsenals of fiscal and monetary policy have been deployed. The interventions are ongoing. The monetary sums involved are eye-wateringly large, and tax payers now find themselves propping up institutions whose reckless behaviour has cost many their jobs and hard-earned savings. In the case of Iceland, three large banks have brought the country to its knees: the debts are so large they will probably necessitate years of austerity, blighting the life chances of one or even two generations.

Inevitably, given the virtual dominance of finance over productive capital this last 30 years, the domino effect of the "credit crunch" spilled over into the "real economy". The USA and Britain are worst affected, which is no surprise given how important the finance sector has become in both countries. But they're hardly alone. We're in the midst of a synchronised recession that could turn into a full-blown depression reminiscent of the 1930s.[6] Countries highly dependent on exports for revenue—such as China and Japan—have seen a sharp drop-off in demand for their goods; very poor countries dependent on overseas aid are seeing aid budgets contract, in large part because the G8 nations calculate them as a percentage of (now declining) GDP; migrant remittances have contracted considerably as legal and illegal overseas workers lose their jobs and return home; borrowing to fund existing or new productive activities is increasingly difficult because most lending institutions are now risk averse; and, all the while, many countries are saddled with huge debts (including Britain and the USA), the servicing of which is not only increasingly difficult but also reduces their room for economic manoeuvre moving forward.[7]

Theorising Crisis, Continuity and Systemic Change

I now want to stand back from the details of the present malaise and suggest how and why the conjoined crises of our time have arisen. But before this theoretical detour, I think it's important to set the extraordinary period in which we're living in some sort of historical context.

Historicising the Present

For all their uniqueness and high drama, the events of the last 3 years are simply the latest manifestation of some rather enduring (and remarkably durable) processes. In the case of the "credit crunch" and its fall-out, we need to situate the current period in the context of previous economic crisis events. I'm thinking here of the Asian economic meltdown of the late 1990s; the collapse of the hedge fund Long Term Capital Management in 1998; the spectacular demise of Barings Bank (which, quite apart from Nick Leeson's recklessness, was an early illustration of the new high-risk culture infecting global banking); the bursting of the dot.com bubble, "solved" by Greenspan decreasing interest rates; and the Argentinian economic calamity of the early noughties.[8] To my mind these events should all be considered part of a long period in which neoliberal policymakers have been seeking to manage, with partial success, the chronic over-accumulation tendencies of the capitalist mode of production. In many ways, the global economic crisis of the early

© 2009 The Author
Journal compilation © 2009 Editorial Board of *Antipode*.

1970s has not gone away: it has simply been serially rechannelled and diverted, entraining ever more peoples and territories.[9]

On the environmental side of things, we need to take an even longer-term perspective. While the global economic growth experienced during the years of the "Washington consensus" has undoubtedly increased the likelihood of severe environmental change, it is not the only culprit. True, it has been the period of China's "dirty industrialisation": still communist in name, the reality is that the People's Republic is now a fully capitalist economy with a colossal (and growing) ecological footprint. In the West, this has been the era of the Hummer, the SUV, budget airlines, private jets, the two-car/new car family, home improvement, growing food miles, and debt-fuelled mass consumption.[10] But the rather dire predictions of the latest IPCC report reflect the impacts not just of recent economic growth, but of more than a century of materials-intensive capital accumulation.[11]

With these points in mind, let me quickly summarise and connect the key insights of Marx, Karl Polanyi and James O'Connor. I claim absolutely no originality here—many others on the Left have looked to them to make sense of our times, including some of the contributors to this volume. Joined together, their ideas offer us some powerful insights into the causes and likely consequences of the political economic and ecological maladies of this "crisis" moment. (Readers all too familiar with this trio's principal ideas may want to skip ahead to the next section.)

Marx, Finance Capital and Over-accumulation Crises

The editors of Britain's only remaining liberal-left broadsheet recently noted that this "is a moment Karl Marx would have relished" (*The Guardian* 2008:32). How true. Marx's late writings as a political economist mark him out as a crisis theorist. Because capitalism is growth orientated, predicated on inter-firm competition and given to perpetual technological changes in process and product, it faces a constant value-realisation problem. Marx showed that one of capitalism's several peculiarities is that economic value is denominated in temporal terms as the difference between "necessary" and "surplus" labour. A further, related peculiarity is that while living labour is the source of all value in capitalism, it is "rational" for individual capitalists to enhance productivity levels and capture surplus value by replacing wage workers with technology, assembly lines and all the paraphernalia of computerised commodity production. Marxists have long glossed this as the contradiction between "the forces and relations of production". As effective demand fails to match the supply of capital looking for profitable returns, various incomplete "solutions" suggest themselves. One is to expand the frontiers of capitalism and export surpluses abroad. But in the long run, Marx argued, over-accumulation crises are unavoidable. The question is not so much "will they happen?" and more "when, how and with what consequences?"

The "neoliberal era" (my scare quotes indicate an awareness that neoliberal policies have had a complex and uneven historical-geography this last three decades) began in the crisis conditions of the 1970s. It has been marked not only by economic "globalisation" but also "the financialization of everything", backed by powerful ruling parties who captured the state apparatus at the end of the post-war boom (Harvey 2005:33). Why has finance capital become so dominant, resulting in a political economic crisis in which monetary surpluses have played a pivotal role?[12]

According to David Harvey (2005:27–31), the "deregulation" of global finance (which began 30 years ago on Wall Street) was a direct response to the generalised economic downturn of the early 1970s. A combination of surplus funds (especially "petrodollars" accumulated by OPEC states) and declining rates of profitability in the core capitalist states (in part because organised labour was so strong) forced ruling elites into a desperate search for new investment opportunities. Trading on their historic advantage as financial centres, New York and London became central to a new geography of liquidity and investment. As part of a wider neoliberal program of "free market" capitalism, these and other centres set about moving huge sums of money into developing countries, emerging markets and the former communist bloc (and they also led to a deep restructuring and deindustrialisation of the core capitalist economies). The removal of previous regulatory constraints— like the 1933 *Glass-Steagall Act* in the USA—was designed not only to secure the financial dominance of Wall Street, the City and other established (if lesser) financial centres. It was also intended to set the engine of accumulation on a new and preferably stable footing by directing surplus funds into hitherto restricted or inaccessible territories and ventures—hopefully for a healthy profit.

There's no doubt that global, "deregulated" finance capital has been central to whatever economic successes can be claimed for the neoliberal era. But the limits of its achievements are all too evident today. Robert Pollin (2003) and Robert Brenner (2006) have shown that average rates of GDP growth since the mid-1970s compare unfavourably with those achieved during the post-war boom. While some countries, like China, have enjoyed sustained growth, even prior to the summer of 2007 the overall global picture for the "real economy" was one of growing surpluses chasing ever riskier investment and market opportunities— this in an era where working people's share of wealth was not, in aggregate, growing. The preconditions for "casino capitalism" in the financial sector have been in place for some time. To be sure, the proximate causes of the current economic crisis cannot be gainsaid (eg "light touch" regulation). But, in Marxian terms, these are surface manifestations of the structural contradictions besetting capitalism in its neoliberal form. As John Bellamy Foster and Harry Magdoff (2009) show in *The Great Financial Crisis*, it's not the financialisation of the world economy that explains the sluggish growth of recent decades; rather, it is the sluggish growth and the lack of investment opportunities for productive capital (in a context where labour's share of overall wealth has been checked) that explains why finance capital has, after 30 years of relative success, caused the engine of accumulation to stall.

Polanyi and the Double Movement

Marx's ideas remain relevant, even though they were shaped by the particularities of "liberal capitalism". So too does the thinking of economic historian Karl Polanyi, judging by the ready use that radical commentators have made of his most famous book in recent years. A close student of Marx's writings, Polanyi's argument in *The Great Transformation* (1944) repeats but also usefully supplements the former's political economic teachings. Four Polanyian insights about the long period of liberal capitalism speak to the current crisis of neoliberalism. First, *The Great Transformation* made use of the important idea of a "pseudo-" or "fictitious commodity". This is any commodity whose social, cultural and/or ecological value *exceeds* the market value placed upon it within a capitalist system.[13] Such commodities are thus characterised by "doubleness" or "duality": they inhabit a world both within and beyond "the market". Second, this connects to the notion of "embeddedness"—the idea that a capitalist economy must exist in a more-than-capitalist world. This is a world of social, cultural, economic, political and biophysical diversity that confronts capitalist economies as both opportunities and barriers: "outsides" that can be made profitable given the right conditions but whose non-commodification may also be necessary to capitalism's survival.

Third, Polanyi coined the term "the double movement" to describe a situation where attempts to expand the reach and depth of capitalist commodification are met by more-or-less vocal (even violent) forms of resistance. The "self-protection" of society from the excesses of "unregulated" capitalism—such as low wages, a minimal public sector, unchecked environmental externalities and asset bubbles—can take various forms. However, the double movement need not be read as a prediction—borne out by past history—of the likely fate of neoliberalism. For Polanyi's fourth key insight was that a "market economy" can extend itself quite far so long as what he called a "market society" can be engineered and suitably regulated. A market society is one where individuals and communities are somehow encouraged to "live with" the fairly stark forms of creative destruction that are the hallmark of capitalism in its "free market" form. It entails a moral economy created as a mirror image of *laissez faire* economics—or, if power-through-consent is not enough, it entails coercion by the state. This means that Polanyi was ultimately far less sanguine than Marx often was about the possibility for crises (of capital, the state, working people, of resource availability, and/within civil society) leading to planned structural change or strong reform.

James O'Connor and the Second Contradiction of Capitalism

Though not a theorist of neoliberalism per se, James O'Connor— perhaps the most intellectually influential "ecoMarxist" of the last 20 years—has something to say about the perceived "environmental crisis" that's coincident with the political economic problems of our time. He is not only a student of the late Marx; he has also taken a good deal of inspiration from Polanyi.

In his book *Natural Causes* (1998) and a series of programmatic journal essays, O'Connor has coined the terms "the second contradiction", "the conditions of production" and "under-production crises". The first captures O'Connor's belief that self-generated environmental problems can be every bit as consequential for the future trajectory of capitalism as classic overaccumulation problems. By conditions of production O'Connor refers to all those phenomena upon which capitalism *depends* for its existence but which, either absolutely or relatively, it is *unable to produce by itself*.[14] His central contention is that capitalism has a tendency to "underproduce" its conditions of production, though in practice not necessarily to the same degree worldwide nor across all production conditions simultaneously.[15] This is a thoroughly Marxist argument because "underproduction" results from the fact that the biophysical world is but a means to the end of realising an ecologically indifferent form of "value", one measured in specifically capitalist terms as abstract, temporally denominated labour.[16]

Routine problems of "underproduction" not only affect capitalist enterprises. They can also become problems for society at large because resource scarcity and environmental degradation pose the wider question of who has access, or suffers the consequences, when particular elements of the biophysical world are enclosed or altered by processes of capital accumulation. If that world is, for capitalists, merely a vehicle for making money, for diverse other stakeholders it is variously a source of spiritual meaning, aesthetic pleasure, subsistence use-values, recreational endeavour and so on. When "underproduction" problems are especially acute, O'Connor argues that they can become "crises"—again, not only for those firms whose previous indifference to "environmental externalities" had underpinned their profits; they can also be crises for elements of the wider society, possibly obliging state bodies to step-in to defuse or address the pressing problems in question. Nicholas Stern has famously said that global warming is the greatest externality ever produced by modern markets. In O'Connor's view it's better understood as the most profound of several environmental problems caused by capitalism's "second contradiction".[17]

Prior to the current moment, O'Connor speculated that the "second" and "first" contradictions might at some point be global and concurrent rather than contained and unsynchronised (1998:176–177). His work has also pointed to the organic connections between classical forms of opposition to capitalist political economy—for instance, trade union organising—and the more recent oppositional movements to be found in civil society. It is no surprise, he has argued, that concerns about such things as poverty, working conditions and unemployment might peak at the same time as concerns about resource scarcity and pollution. The challenge is to connect "red" and "green" politics so that they become more than the sum of their separate parts. If this challenge can be met, any "double crisis" might be a moment of double opportunity for progressives.

From Theory to Reality: Neoliberalization, Social Formation and the Barriers to Change

Having brought the insights of Marx, Polanyi and O'Connor together, let me now focus them on the immediate future in this and the following section. If their insights possess any programmatic relevance, then one might reasonably expect, if not revolution, then a major bout of reform to the global capitalist system. The global *alter-mondial* movement is currently in no position to effect worldwide radical change. Its bark remains loud at keynote meetings (like the London G20 of 2009), but its bite is weak. The best-case scenario in the short term is a widespread shift towards moderately post-neoliberal policies, using established political mechanisms—especially so in those countries who've embraced neoliberal ideas most strongly. After all, their political leaders and business elites have had to make a very public *volte face* since the sub-prime defaults began in the USA. Out of several possible cases, I want to focus first on the place where I live and work: Britain. As a core (if no longer world-leading) capitalist state that has long championed the neoliberal approach, developments in Britain ought to tell us something about the likely future governance of global capitalism. That "something", as will become even more evident in the next section, should worry progressives greatly.

Reasons to be Cheerful?

In late 2007, one British current affairs analyst was already predicting "the end of the free market consensus" (Milne 2007:33). Two years on, there are—seemingly—reasons to concur. I have already described the outbreak of "crisis talk", something that has occurred as much in Britain as it has anywhere else—not least because of the City's centrality to the national economy, and the efforts of several high-profile insiders (like Stern and former Chief Scientific Adviser Sir David King) to keep climate change near the top of the domestic agenda. Notwithstanding some public support for the far right—notably, Nick Griffin's National Party—there is evidently also potential for a turn to the left. This potential lies not so much within New Labour, as outside the party system altogether (with the signal exception of the British Green Party, led by Caroline Lucas). Well beyond the political mainstream, a plethora of radical environmental and anarchist groups (going back to the anti-road, anti-GMO, and anti-capitalist protests of the 1990s) remain active and visible.[18] This much was obvious at the important March 2009 meeting of the G20 in London, where Climate Camp activists were especially prominent. Likewise, Britain's most outspoken public intellectual—the author and campaign journalist George Monbiot—continues to get a hearing for his radical ideas in the quality press, in book stores, and on TV and radio.[19]

Nearer the mainstream, the trade union movement still has some leaders who find the New Labour version of progressive politics too insipid by far (such as Trades Union Congress leader Brendan Barber). Then there's Neal Lawson's extra-parliamentary Compass movement, a big-tent coalition that manages to bring together a plethora of charitable, social justice and environmental groups to press for an end to neoliberal policies. Its unofficial parliamentary representative is Labour MP John Cruddas. It was an affiliate of Compass, the New Economics Foundation, which published an ambitious and aspirational Green New Deal plan for Britain's future in early 2009. This ideas-rich plan sets out a vision for a more equitable and low-carbon British economy and society for the twenty-first century, and has been widely circulated and discussed within the country's left-intelligentsia—most of which, today, exists in universities, think tanks and independent organisations like the Fabian Society. Importantly, much of the current discussion identifies "capitalism" as the major problem, not simply its "neoliberal version" nor finance capital in particular.[20]

In short, there are plenty of individuals, groups and organisations in Britain who see the sense in reforming capitalism in a way that synergises aspirations for greater social equality and opportunity with ambitions for a less materials-intensive form of growth. The British Left, today a largely non-parliamentary entity separate from party politics, is far less intellectually one-eyed and "labourist" than it was during its last heyday, the early 1970s. It is possessed of ideas and energy. For the most part, it does not contemplate the end of capitalism. But it does seek a dramatic reconfiguration of the capitalist system and recognises the urgency of the task. But can it seize the moment? Alas, I suggest not.

The Causes of Morbidity

Creating a new political economic and social order requires well-placed people of action, a popular base of support, and a fund of good concepts and messages—this much I suggested earlier. On the latter score, I have argued that the British Left suffers no shortage of ideas in whose image a post-neoliberal future could be forged—or, to be more precise, that moderate portion of the left (like Compass) capable of connecting to sections of the wider public given the right circumstances. The problems, as I see them, lie in the weak practical (not intellectual) capacities of the British non-parliamentary left, and the lack of a sufficiently visible and influential grassroots constituency able to guarantee the national hegemony of progressive ideas.

First, the question of the popular base. On the face of it, the British people have good reason to be furious with their political and business leaders. It's not just the suddenness, speed and severity of the present economic crisis. It is also the fact the under New Labour, social inequality has increased sharply in Britain—notwithstanding the several measures it has introduced to tackle child poverty, low pay and old-age poverty (Mount 2004; Wilkinson and Pickett 2009).[21] Relatedly, twenty-first century Britain has more prisoners, more mental illness, more homelessness, greater levels of substance abuse, more alcoholism, more teenage pregnancies, more anti-social behaviour, more relationship breakdown, and more household indebtedness than it did a generation ago—all this even after 15 years of uninterrupted economic growth prior to mid 2007. Levels of social mobility remain stubbornly low, even according to the government's own investigations.[22] In David Harvey's (2005:31) terms, drawing on the evidence assembled by Dumenil and Levy (2004), the neoliberal period has seen the "restoration of class power" in Britain (as it has in many other countries worldwide).[23]

On top of this, the many people concerned about environmental issues know New Labour's record to be very poor. The country remains highly fossil-fuel dependent, has a weak renewable energy base (despite the enormous potential for wind and wave power) and remains vulnerable to oil and gas price fluctuations in international markets. A rhetoric of environmental radicalism going back to Blair's last days as premier is belied by a lack of meaningful action: the recent, momentous decision to okay a new runway at Heathrow Airport indicates as much. Far from being "hollowed out", the British state has shown just how powerful it can be when it comes to containing the financial wildlife. This makes New Labour's poor environmental record appear all the more unforgivable.

Why, despite all this, has there been no groundswell of opposition to the current order? The answer, I suggest, partly lies in the creative and destructive aspects of Britain's neoliberalisation since the early 1980s. On the destructive side, the defeat of the trades union movement along with an evisceration of Britain's manufacturing base long ago removed two pillars of post-war social solidarity and moral concern. On the creative side, the ethic of individual "freedom" and "rights" has bitten deep, especially among the young, who have no memory of pre-Thatcher Britain at all. Social commentator Polly Toynbee (2007:41) is right that "British life is [still] riven by class", but the fact is that Brits don't recognise it by-and-large. A recent Joseph Rowntree Foundation survey discovered that the average person thinks that high pay is earned-cum-deserved through hard work, and that long-term unemployment, drug taking and other indices of "underclass" status result from failings of the individual or their family (Ashley, 2009).

This sort of thinking has been underpinned by years of easy credit (now at an end). High levels of personal and household borrowing have allowed millions to go on a consumer binge, creating an illusion of personal wealth that's concealed the real income inequalities documented by Dumenil and Levy (2004), among others.[24] Easy credit has also sustained a culture of individual acquisitiveness (Lawson 2009). Successive surveys reveal that most Brits think they are "middle class" and—until recently at least—faring well. This, in part, reflects the doubling of the number of university graduates since 1995. Even now, one senses that most ordinary Brits think that the good times could return soon, not realising that the country has years of belt-tightening ahead of it. These are not the intellectual conditions in which popular protest can flourish. On top of this, New Labour has succeeded in rendering the "social welfare democracy" version of capitalism out-of-bounds politically. The Liberal Democratic Party flirts with elements of this model, but the party lacks mass support. For years, political "common sense" has been to combine "free market" economics with highly targeted redistributive policies aimed at "deserving groups" in need of special help. While it's true that huge public investment has gone into modernising the National Health Service and schools, the formal introduction of "consumer choice" in both domains has weakened the sense that they are collective goods rather than ones geared to meeting individual wishes and desires.

Economic change has also attenuated any strong sense of social solidarity within, or on behalf of, the least well-off members of British society. The move to a service- and finance-sector-dominated economy in which small and medium-sized firms have proliferated has fragmented any collective sense of worker experience. So too has a widespread shift towards flexible and temporary labour practices at the bottom end of the job market. Large-scale immigration, involving people from every part of the world, has also put barriers in the way of social solidarity. A much diminished trade union movement has sought to protect immigrants' rights and to organise them—but it's proven to be a real challenge. Britain's long history of being a racist rather than a liberal cosmopolitan country was made manifest in the ethnic riots in the north of England several years ago. White working class Brits do not necessarily see themselves in class terms, in contrast to a previous generation. They are as likely to take a nationalist "us–them" attitude towards first, second and third-generation immigrants as they are to make common cause with them on the grounds of class inequality. Meanwhile, many middle class Britons have only encountered working class migrants when eating or drinking out. Likewise, New Labour's demonisation of certain white working class people (eg "lager louts", "ASBO kids"[25]) has eroded some of the empathy middle class liberals might otherwise possess.

On the environmental side of things, even as the level of concern has risen, many Brits have chosen to act out their politics in the marketplace: somehow, buying organic food or Fair Trade coffee is seen as more effective than voting for the British Green Party or joining Greenpeace UK. More generally, the seductions of consumption during the late 1990s and the noughties have inured many people to the environmental damage of their spending habits. Easy money, low inflation and a flood of cheap imports (especially from China) have tested the resolve of even the most environmentally conscience members of the British public. In any case, aside from some notable flood events, occasional water shortages and some hikes in petrol prices, most Britons over the last 30 years have not been directly affected by resource and environmental problems. These problems have seemed remote, even as the press and broadcasters report the realities of global warming in ever-more alarming terms. This is because Britain, like all wealthy countries today, successfully off-shores the worst ecological effects of its commodity consumption: these effects are felt most keenly in the sites of commodity production (the Far East, the former Eastern Bloc and Latin America).

Second, the evident lack of grassroots support for even a fairly mild turn to the left is allied with the lack of an effective infrastructure for changing the terms of political debate. I have already mentioned the trade union movement, whose reach into the national population remains fairly limited. I have also mentioned the Labour Party, whose relationship with the unions has been arms-length for many years and whose considerable apparatus remains dedicated to the "third way" policies of neoliberalism-with-a-human-face. But there are some other things to mention. Under New Labour, a multitude of charitable, voluntary and third sector bodies have arguably been more visible than they were during the 1970s and 1980s. This represents a creeping "responsibilisation" of civil society and the need to fill holes left by the 30-year switch from a "cradle-to-grave" to an "enabling" state apparatus.

Organisations like Shelter, Oxfam, The Big Issue, and Greenpeace are now familiar components of the national scene and are highly professionalized. While some of these issue-based organisations are ostensibly non-partisan, many are overtly political. They work hard to attract members and donations, and have benefited from the upturn in voluntary giving in Britain since the mid 1990s.[26] To the extent that there's a substantial portion of the population who are left of New Labour, these people have often lent their support to organisations like Friends of the Earth or the Stop The War coalition of 2001. This has divided and diffused the voices of those leftists who dissent from the policies promoted by Blair and now Brown. Though there are some large, well-run, left-leaning organisations in Britain, they rarely pool their resources or share their networks. The result is a dissenting community divided by issue focus and institutional affiliation. New Labour defector James Purnell puts it thus: "the [British] left has become balkanized into small groups, based on small differences" (2009:26).[27]

Only the British Green Party offers a joined-up, broad-based alternative that is left of New Labour. As a political party it has learnt to connect the social equality agenda with the environmental agenda. However, it has a relatively small membership and competes for influence with environmental organisations in the NGO sector. In addition, its social justice commitments are not widely recognised (many think it's still exclusively a single issue outfit) and it must reckon with the trades unions when it comes to garnering the left-worker vote. The Greens aside, the sort of intellectual and infrastructural umbrella that the Compass group is aiming for is to be strongly welcomed. But it's battling against over 20 years of division within the non-New Labour left. A plurality of think tanks, NGOs, NSMs and charities does not make a movement. What's ultimately needed is a new political party that can harness the energy and resources of those who run and support the various organisations referred to above. But this will be a really tall order.

Finally, some peculiarities of British politics and society present further impediments to any leftist attempt to make this double-crisis moment one of opportunity. These peculiarities have been well documented, and it's a moot point whether or not they're a direct result of neoliberal thought and policy. First, executive decision-making has become increasingly immune to public scrutiny or pressure. Gordon Brown presides over a highly centralised and hierarchical state apparatus. His recent promises to devolve authority are an open admission that the pendulum has swung much too far.[28] The decision by the Blair government to invade Iraq, in the teeth of intense public and parliamentary opposition, demonstrated well the post-Thatcher drift towards a less democratic and consultative form of government. Arguably, one reason that anarchists and DIY activists have so often resorted to direct action since the mid-1990s is because of the strong perception that politicians no longer listen. Second, the British electorate seem increasingly less interested in politics. In recent years, there has been a steady decline in voter turnouts for local, European and even national elections. At the same time, there has been a sharp decline in membership of all three big political parties, and no notable rise in the membership of smaller parties, like the Greens. One can speculate why. Finally, the "first past the post" nature of British national elections makes it impossible for election results to reflect voters' true preferences. A government with a large majority can govern with well under half the popular vote. Only a handful of swing voters determine election results, and only a minority of local constituencies ultimately matter. This is precisely why Labour and the Conservatives do not want proportional representation to replace the existing system.

The Future of Global Climate Change Governance: Why "Weak Markets" Will Persist

This account of the British social formation is, of course, little more than a rough sketch.[29] But it is, I hope, plausible enough to sustain my major point: yes, Marx and O'Connor can help us understand why we're currently experiencing not one but two global crises; but Polanyi had a point when he said that the reform of *laissez faire* capitalism need not be radical. A social order does not crumble over night—unless there's a revolution led by well-organized dissidents, preferably with popular support. Even when "crisis talk" becomes mainstream, it's as likely to result in the application of palliatives rather than root-and-branch reform.[30] Having illustrated this point with reference to Britain—a country whose previous embrace of neoliberalism one might now expect to be much less intimate, but is not—I want to scale-up to the international level in this penultimate section.

This is the level at which so much of what matters to us all is being, and will be, decided. To break the extended monetary chain that connects a mortgage payment default in Detroit to a sharp drop in Malaysian or Mexican exports 12 months later we need a new global financial architecture.[31] To tackle climate change, and related issues of energy supply and security, we need effective international cooperation. This much is obvious. What interests me is the precise content and detail of current and likely future transnational accords. We don't yet know how global finance will be re-regulated or how the roles of the World Bank and IMF might change moving forward. But we *can* say something about how global climate change is likely to be addressed in the short-to-medium-term future. Here, it seems to me, a business-friendly market approach will remain alive and kicking: the die is already cast. Why is the international community—with the USA and China at the helm as the world's largest polluters—placing its faith firmly in a market in environmental bads? Isn't *limiting* markets, rather than championing them, supposed to be the new catch-cry of this crisis period? I will briefly describe and evaluate international emissions trading to date (focusing on the European Union scheme), before proposing some answers to these questions.

International Pollution Trading Schemes

"Climate change", writes Scott Barrett, "is arguably the greatest collective action problem the world has ever faced" (2008:257). It is a "tragedy of capital accumulation" based on nature's pseudo-commodity status—or, in more conventional terms, a "tragedy of the environmental commons" arising from "missing markets". In recognition of this, a large number of new agreements, policies and pledges relating to greenhouse gas (GHG) emissions, improved energy efficiency, "clean" energy supplies, and the protection (or enhancement) of natural sinks have been formulated in recent years. Some of these are sub-national or national-scale initiatives, but ultimately they are all referenced to the global scale—for the simple reason that the unfolding problem of climate change will respect no political boundaries. The Kyoto Protocol is an explicit recognition of the need for international action, and it's certainly "the most significant instrument within global climate policy" (Hepburn 2007:378).[32] Its long-term ambition is to stabilise parts per million CO2 equivalent concentrations at 450–500 by the century's end.[33] The centrepiece of the Protocol is the creation of a global market in GHG emissions through so-called "cap and trade".[34] This policy approach is favoured over global pollution taxes, global green subsidies or global green standards. "Excess" pollution (ie that beyond a politically determined level informed by the IPCC) is priced, with the price determined by an exchange between "over-polluters" and those in a position to offset above-cap emissions. This is the essence of Kyoto's three so-called "flexible mechanisms", namely: emissions allowance trading between registered polluters; the Clean Development Mechanism (CDM, which encourages offset trade between rich Annex 1 countries and developing countries not bound by emissions caps); and Joint Implementation (JI, which permits investment and participation by high-polluting Annex 1 industries in mitigation projects in transition economies, such as those in eastern Europe). Together, these mechanisms are intended to deliver "effectiveness" (ie real decreases in GHG emissions), "efficiency" (ie least-cost solutions for individual polluters) and "equity" (through cash and technology transfers from the rich world to the rest).

Both within and apart from Kyoto, a number of regional, national and international emissions trading schemes have come on-stream in recent years.[35] By far the most significant—both practically and symbolically—is the new European Union Emissions Trading Scheme (EU-ETS). It has been rightly described as a "flagship . . .scheme" (Nye and Owens 2008:2), "a showcase . . . scheme" (Worthington 2008), and "a prototype for a global emissions-trading regime" (Helm 2008:212). In effect, it's Europe's version of Kyoto, not least because a so-called "linking directive" permits the involvement of registered polluters in non-European CDM and JI projects.[36] The EU accounts for around 20% of global GDP and produces a similar percentage of world GHG emissions. The ETS covers around 11,500 pollution sources in over 25 countries and is a "bubble agreement", meaning that national allowances vary such that the burden of emissions reduction is shared unevenly (in reflection of different national circumstances). Nation states propose levels of "permitted pollution" and the European Commission then negotiates around these levels before allocating permits. The pilot period ran from 2004 to 2007, with the first "proper" period of the EU-ETS now midway through (it runs 2008–2012, to coincide with the first Kyoto commitment period).[37] By 2006 the scheme comprised 67% of the global carbon market by volume, and 81% by value (Hepburn 2007:380). It remains the most important example of carbon trading in the world, and the lessons learnt to date will undoubtedly shape the fine detail of the wider Kyoto scheme during its second compliance period (2012 onwards).

The Record so Far

The ETS is one of several "market-based instruments" associated with the approach to environmental regulation sometimes called "free market environmentalism". In the words of one advocate, it is "orders of magnitude more significant in terms of its scope, ambition and likely impact, than any other application of environmental economics I can think of " (Convery, 2009:121). The ETS is a large and complicated entity that has taken tremendous effort to create and sustain. The underlying logic is well known. Market failure is identified as the cause of pollution and this is "corrected" by internalising costs so that pollution is eventually eliminated. Rising costs, so the theory goes, makes pollution increasingly uneconomic and simultaneously creates market incentives for cleaner technologies to come on-stream (Pigou 1920; Coase 1960; Dales 1968). The state is central to the creation of such managed markets; they do not arise "spontaneously", and it's precisely the problem of "market failure" that the ETS and similar schemes seek to address.

The theory has some validity—judging by the success of America's cap-and-trade scheme for sulphur dioxide in the 1990s, and several "trade quota" schemes applied to over-exploited fisheries. However, during its pilot phase the EU-ETS did not perform at all well: so far, it's been a notably "weak market". In the scheme's current phase, it's unlikely that significant emissions reductions will be achieved (Betz, Rogge and Schleich 2006). There is, thus far, an enormous gap between environmental rhetoric and reality in the EU. In 2008 the European Commission, seeking to take a global lead on climate change, announced a 20-20-20 plan (by 2020 the aim is to have 20% of Europe's energy needs met by renewables, a 20% reduction in energy consumption, and a 20% reduction on current emissions levels).[38] This "triple-20" plan acknowledges the alarming evidence contained in successive IPCC reports. But if the ETS is to contribute meaningfully to achieving the plan's targets, then its several serious problems will need to be addressed very urgently.

So what are the problems in question? They're well documented, and far too numerous to list or explore in detail. I'll highlight just a few:

- A loose emissions cap: the overall, aggregate emissions level has been set too high, meaning only marginal aggregate reductions are called for.
- Permits issued at no cost to polluters: this means that costs attach to pollution only if and when a polluter exceeded their emissions allowance.
- Grandfathering: polluters with historically large emissions have been given generous emissions allowances, minimising the costs of any pollution beyond permitted levels and, in fact, encouraging pollution so that these levels continue to be set high.
- Over-allocation of emissions permits: the post-2007 economic crisis exposed "over capacity" in the carbon credit market, as numerous polluters ended up with permits to sell.
- Unstable carbon prices and carbon price crashes: the above three factors have conspired not only to keep the carbon price low, but also to create two crashes in the price (in May 2006 and late 2008). This has badly affected the viability of CDM and JI projects outside the EU.
- "Hot air" windfalls for polluters: polluters with "excess permits" have sold them for large sums—even in a depressed pollution market—yet without having to make any real reductions in their emissions.
- Low fines for offenders: those polluters who may fail to pay for "over-polluting" by purchasing carbon credits currently face small fines that hardly act as a deterrent.
- Aviation and shipping emissions left outside ETS, as well as those of other significant polluters: the scheme only covers 30% equivalent of all GHG emissions in the EU (Betz, Rogge and Schleich 2006: 362).

- Extrinsic drivers: the current recession in Europe plus cheaper gas
  and oil prices have together reduced GHG emissions, but have also
  deflated the carbon price, making "over-pollution" unduly cheap.
  This exemplifies the fact that the ETS, like all emissions trading
  schemes, cannot control factors that decisively affect the polluter
  pays market.

In light of all this, it's no wonder that the EU's scheme has been described
sardonically as the "all too flexible ETS" (*The Guardian* 2007:28). Even
Lord Browne, former chief executive of British Petroleum, is no fan:
he delivered a withering assessment of its future potential in a keynote
speech in March 2009.

Emissions Trading: Why Do Weak Markets Persist?

How one chooses to explain the poor record of EU-ETS profoundly
affects whether and how one regards it as salvageable. Insiders have
described the scheme's several problems as inevitable features of
institutional learning (eg Betz and Sato 2006). Though some of these
problems are necessarily beyond policymakers' control (such as the
oil price), it's argued that most can be fixed through ingenuity and
negotiation (eg more permits will be auctioned after 2012). Other
commentators worry that challenges of complexity and scale will make
these problems recurrent and intractable, no matter how clever the policy
fixes are (Gardiner 2004). Neither perspective is entirely wrong. But,
equally, both are incomplete until a third, essential perspective on the
source of the EU-ETS's problems is added to the mix. This perspective
sees these problems as manifestations of a problematic business-friendly
approach on the part of EU states. In short, it sees the EU-ETS as far
too neoliberal.

It is neoliberal *not* in the sense that it's a market-based approach. The
sheer existence of a market in something does not make that something
"neoliberal".[39] Instead, the EU-ETS is neoliberal in the sense that the
pollution market currently favours the big, carbon-intensive industries
that have sustained the European economy through that boom period
which ended in 2007.[40] The "freedom" of these industries to pollute at
the expense of the global environment and the global public is currently
upheld by EU legislators. The latter shy away from what Polanyi called
"the freedom that proper regulation creates" (1944:256).[41] Even after the
disastrous pilot phase, the changes made for the current implementation
period (2008–2012) are limp. For instance, five GHGs remain outside
the scheme, as do aviation and shipping; grandfathering is still the
practice, and the EU cap is only marginally tighter than before. The
scheme's problems are thus more ones of regulatory failure (ie regulatory
capture by big capital) rather than problems of the market mechanism

per se: a more aggressively managed ETS *could* produce results of a certain kind. European heads of state, as a collective, are simply unwilling to place undue pressure on their energy utilities, steel makers, cement factories, oil companies, airlines and the like. Only a Pollyanna could believe that the ETS will make a real contribution to the EU's triple-20 plan.

Why and how have EU politicians permitted such a self-evidently weak tool to be offered as a model for global attempts to address the real threat posed by runaway GHG emissions? Whatever the historic differences between Anglo-Saxon capitalism and "social Europe", the ETS demonstrates adherence to a common neoliberal line. So what's going on? I should say immediately that it's not enough to attribute politicians soft-soaping on the ETS rules to the current recession. We need to look elsewhere and longer term for an explanation.[42] First, creating a new pollution market inevitably opened the door for polluters to lobby regulators; after all, the polluters were now to be market participants. Given the economic clout of the polluters in question— for instance, energy firms like E.ON—it's no surprise that the ears of ministers and regulators have been constantly bent. But "trade leakage" was also a card that industry lobbyists played, citing "unfair competition" if a tight pollution cap added unduly to their production costs relative to overseas rivals. Second, unlike the financial sector— which, in the EU, only possesses strategic economic importance in Britain and Germany—the polluters covered by the ETS are all central to the economic welfare of member states, albeit to varying degrees. Under Donald Tusk's and Silvio Berlusconi's respective leadership, Poland and Italy demonstrate this fact in spades. Third, the historic lack of adequate state support given to the renewable energy sector—where the barriers to market entry can be extremely high—means that this sector lacks the lobbying power to shift government policy onto a low-carbon trajectory. Recent arguments that immediate investment in "clean tech" industries could spark a new Kondratieff wave for Europe have so far fallen on deaf ears—if not intellectually, then practically. Fourth, most Europeans are not even aware that the ETS exists. Aside from efforts by the usual green activists and a few newspaper editors, the scheme has not been negatively politicised in the public domain, meaning that there's been little or no grassroots pressure on EU policymakers to beef it up. Finally, the usual short-termism of politicians has posed a barrier to the long-term vision required if a switch to a low-carbon future is not to be endlessly deferred. European voters would rebel in large numbers if their leaders allowed steep increases in energy prices in the name of a scheme designed to tackle a future problem—one more likely to affect not them but unborn generations. Such rebellion is economically rational (especially for those on low incomes), but it also reflects the failure of European politicians—in power and opposition—to create a

popular bloc persuaded of the need to decarbonise society in the common
interest.

All of this speaks to the enduring power of carbon capitalism and
carbon capitalists in the EU. As Oscar Reyes of Carbon Trade Watch
puts it, "The ETS has bowed to corporate self-interest at every stage of
its design and implementation . . ." (quoted in Macalister 2009:23). The
structural causes underpinning the ETS's so far weak pollution market
pose formidable barriers to a more progressive climate change policy.
The lock-in is vice-like, and binds European governments, national
publics and carbon-intensive industries into a status quo relationship.
Some disagree and say it's too early to pass judgement. Optimists
suggest that a switch to a low-carbon economy *can* be made using
the ETS, with the scheme's early phases acting as a Trojan horse that
progressively commits big polluting firms to the triple-20 plan and
beyond.[43] I wouldn't want to bet on this, however. It will take something
remarkable to get EU leaders to set European capitalism on a new, low-
carbon path before 2050, never mind 2020. In the meantime, ambitious
targets will continue to be set, and they'll be consistently honoured in
the breach. The same will apply to the wider Kyoto scheme.[44]

Conclusion

This essay had two major objectives. It sought to describe and explain
the temporal coincidence of political economic and environmental
crises less than a decade into the twenty-first century; and it offered
some reasons for a seeming paradox, taking both a national level and
international scale example—the paradox of crisis conditions leading
to more of the same rather than a sharp turn away from the neoliberal
path. The hopeful lessons of Marx's, Polanyi's and O'Connor's work
will not (yet) be borne out: "strong reform", never mind something
more radical, is still a long way off. What we call "neoliberalism" in
the singular is, in reality, a variegated and uneven global formation
constituted differentially at a range of scales. Its existence and multiple
incarnations are overdetermined. Even so, I've suggested that this fact
does not necessarily render neoliberal policies vulnerable, even at a time
of perceived "crisis". If my analysis has any validity, then it calls to mind
Gramsci's judgement that the "morbid symptoms" of an existing order
unwilling to die may persist for some considerable time.

When might these symptoms disappear? Answers to this question
are likely to be as reliable as a long-range weather forecast. Naomi
Klein (2009:30), sensing the folly of detailed prophecy, offers some
general speculations. Reflecting, as I have done, on the coincident
political economic and ecological crisis, she argues that "Capitalism can
survive this [double] crisis. But the world can't survive another capitalist
comeback". I agree entirely with the first part of this statement, but not

necessarily the second. Capitalism will morph and adapt as it has always done: the operating hardware will remain intact, even as the all important details will alter quite profoundly. But at what cost? Leftists have not just to hope for, but work vigorously towards, a future that can set capitalism on a path of much greater social and environmental justice. The legacy of neoliberal capitalism constitutes a sickness that can be cured sooner rather than later: but the Left, in its national and international forms, must do a lot more to administer the necessary medicine. An essential, if not sufficient, condition is to occupy the political space vacated by established political parties that claim to be on the left. Until then, the Left's case will remain marginal to public life worldwide.

Acknowledgements

Thanks to Jason Beery for research assistance, and to Andrew Baldwin, Nik Heynen and Melissa Wright for reactions.

Endnotes

[1] James O'Connor—whose work on capitalism and nature I will summarise later in this essay—has offered a formal treatment of this proposition in his book *The Meaning of Crisis* (1987). Habermas's (1976) influential book *Legitimation Crisis* also provides a way of avoiding economism in crisis theory while nonetheless acknowledging the decisive role that capital accumulation plays. I should acknowledge that at the level of both perception and actuality, "crisis" is always experienced differently by different sections of society: it has a relative dimension that's ineluctable.

[2] I should also note a new federal government report in the USA, fronted by Barak Obama's science advisor John Holdren, which some believe will act as a "game changer" in US politics and business. It conveys the same sense of urgency communicated in the fourth IPCC report. See "*Global Climate Change Impacts in the United States*", http://www.globalchange.gov/publications/reports/scientific-assessments/us-impacts

[3] Established by the United Nations Environmental Program and the World Meteorological Organisation in 1988, the IPCC is a remarkable outfit. Over two decades it has created a highly inclusive—and surprisingly consensual—scientific peer community that is at once large and international. This is why its assessment reports are so hard to ignore, notwithstanding the attempts—now pretty much discredited—of the climate change sceptics. The IPCC's receipt (along with Al Gore) of a Nobel Peace Prize in 2007 was a highly public, and symbolically important, acknowledgement of the Panel's signal contribution to human understanding. The first three reports had made a clear and persistent case for concerted global action to reduce the level of greenhouse gas emissions (a case the Stern review took very seriously). But it seems to me that the fourth report has really hit home. Soon after its publication the UN Security Council discussed climate change for the first time ever (in April 2007).

[4] Otherwise known as the *American Clean Energy and Security Act*.

[5] I wouldn't, however, have surprised US economist Hyman Minsky (1919–1996). His "financial instability hypothesis" has receive resounding verification of late, leading members of the Western financial commentariat to call this a "Minsky moment". See Minsky (1982).

[6] In the UK chief Treasury minister Alistair Darling's words, it's "the sharpest . . . global downturn for generations" (2009:31). This is why he and Gordon Brown have repeatedly pressed their G8 and European Union counterparts to take strong, coordinated counter-cyclical action, despite understandable fears about inflation and unsustainable levels of

public borrowing. Reaching back even further in time than the 1930s, we often forget that the capitalist countries of the late Victorian era suffered a long period of acute economic instability between 1873 and 1896.

[7] As if this were not enough, it's all occurring against a background of volatile energy and food prices, the spiking of which exacerbates current economic woes for the many countries highly dependent on imported oil, gas and staple foods.

[8] We might also add the Enron accounting scandal, which—like the Barings Bank collapse—was symptomatic of a business culture in which finance professionals routinely took high risks with other people's money and rewarded themselves richly—by legal means or otherwise.

[9] I note, for example, that back in 1985 David Harvey was expressing real worries about the ongoing economic problems that had first manifested themselves globally during the early 1970s. His feeling was that economic crisis was by no means a thing of the previous decade (Harvey 1985). As Greenspan (2007) noted even prior to the current meltdown, the neoliberal years had amounted to an "age of turbulence"—a view shared by Marxisant economic historian Robert Brenner (2006). But compared to the economic shocks of the 1990s and early noughties, what's special about the economic problems of today is they have heavily impacted all the core capitalist countries (unlike the Asian and Argentinian crises); and they are synchronised between a large number of national economies in both the developed and developing worlds. They are the most generalised and acute of the many economic shocks experienced over the last three decades.

[10] And, of course, the umbilical connection between China's growth—so too that of many East Asian economies—and the growth of many Western economies is to be found in international trade and credit transfers. The new "tiger economies", plus a resurgent Japan, have allowed Western countries to run trade deficits, budget deficits and leveraged spending programmes in order to maintain overseas demand for their manufacturing goods.

[11] Which ever "variety of capitalism" one wishes to consider, past or present, Anglo-Saxon or otherwise, the conclusion is the same: since the early nineteenth century, economic growth has entailed the ceaseless destruction and (re)production of the biophysical world. It is because of this long history of resource extraction, transformation and disposal that we are now in what Nobel laureate Paul Crutzen calls "the anthropocene". The many challenging environmental problems on the horizon have been a very long time in the making.

[12] Though Marx's writings on finance and the capitalist state remained unsystematised, it's perfectly possible to narrate the current "crisis of neoliberalism"—with all its particularities—in fundamentally Marxian terms. I'll elaborate very briefly in the rest of this sub-section, since others have already covered this ground in some detail. See, for example, Panitch and Konings (2009).

[13] Polanyi identified labour (workers, their dependents and the unemployed), land (nature and environment) and money among his list of fictitious commodities. This is because neither human beings, nor the biophysical world, nor money exist exclusively to meet the demands of capital accumulation. Even so, they are deeply affected by and implicated in its logics and rhythms.

[14] This is a version of the fictitious commodity and embeddedness arguments, but it is given a systematic spin by O'Connor. He identifies "environmental conditions" (biophysical resources, be they economically productive, indirectly productive or ambient), "personal conditions" (all those things necessary to self-reproduce a living person, like housing) and "communal conditions" (all those shared amenities and assets that people rely upon for social and biological reproduction, like roads, public transport, schools, the legal system etc). O'Connor's materialism here is arguably more plausible than Neil Smith's (1984), whose "production of nature" idea can be read—perhaps wrongly—as overly Promethean and inattentive to the obstacles that "nature" places

in the way of capital accumulation. I have in years past favoured Smith's metaphor of "production" because it refuses the nature–society dualism that arguably provides the epistemological underpinning of O'Connor's thinking (Castree 2000). I would still approve of Smith's refusal, but with the rider that the differing "materialities" of the "social" and "non-social" are somehow respected (see the first half of Castree 1995).

[15] For instance, if we take environmental conditions, it is clear that firms rely upon naturally occurring resources and spaces for a range of things, notably: raw materials for immediate production and a range of built environments that support such production; energy supplies; spaces to make, move, sell, service and consume commodities (factories, airports, road systems, shopping malls etc); and zones into which to expel wastes generated by commodity producers, distributors, sellers, servicers and consumers. In all these roles and capacities, the biophysical world has a materiality that capitalist production cannot ultimately master or control. For example, raw material deposits become exhausted; insufficient space may be available in the right places for new infrastructure projects; and environmental sinks may become polluted and harm a range of constituencies.

[16] This ecological indifference underpins the idea that modern capitalism has created a "metabolic rift" between humanity and the biophysical world. John Bellamy Foster has promoted this idea vigorously, drawing on Marx.

[17] Note that, as a Marxist, O'Connor has little time for "natural limits" arguments. Instead, resource scarcity is, for him, socially produced.

[18] *Antipode* coeditor Paul Chatterton, I should note, was one of a group of environmental campaigners who sabotaged a train delivering coal to the Drax power station in 2008. Their 2009 trial resulted in prosecution and a fine, but also some positive reporting in the news media.

[19] Monbiot is a columnist in *The Guardian* newspaper, author of best-sellers like *Heat: How to Stop the Planet Burning* (2006) and appears frequently on news programmes.

[20] This problem identification even extends to the heartlands of corporate thinking. For instance, in early 2009 the *Financial Times* of London organised a series of major essays on the theme "The future of capitalism".

[21] Robert Frank (2007) has documented a similar trend in the USA since the Reagan years; see also Jacob Hacker's (2006) *The Great Risk Shift*.

[22] For instance, a recent report fronted by senior New Labour politician Alan Milburn tells a story of class inequality reproducing itself more acutely than any time since before the Second World War. See "Unleashing aspiration" (2009) at http://www.cabinetoffice.gov.uk/media/227102/fair-access.pdf

[23] The most graphic evidence of this is the quantum leap in the number of millionaires and billionaires residing in the country—most of them based in London, where their spending has grossly inflated housing prices to the detriment of ordinary people. The gap between average and top salaries is now a yawning one: a business elite earns more in a lunchtime than most Britons do in a lifetime. As one of New Labour's architects, Peter Mandelson, (in)famously said in 1998, "We are intensely relaxed about people becoming filthy rich". (His words were not uttered on record, but have been oft-quoted since). This sentiment summarises the ethos of post-Thatcher Britain. The ethos lives on. In the financial sector, where so much of the wealth has been concentrated, the departing chief executives of Britain's troubled banks received huge salary and pension "goodbyes"— perversely, they were "compensated" for steering the ships they'd captained onto the rocks. A disbelieving public looked on askance.

[24] See also Sutcliffe (2004). Harvey (2005) neatly describes this as neoliberal *ideology* masking neoliberal *realities*.

[25] ASBOs are anti-social behaviour orders, legal instruments created by New Labour to address the symptoms (but not causes) of (mostly teenage) bad behaviour by a minority

of individuals—ones typically living in very low income neighbourhoods in British cities and towns.

[26] On several occasions over the last decade the National Council for Voluntary Organisations has reported an increase in the level of personal giving and also a move from "spontaneous" to "planned" giving among the British population.

[27] In his new role at the left-leaning think tank Demos, Purnell has launched an Open Left project, asking a simple but contested question: what does it mean to be on the Left today?

[28] For the second time in his brief premiership, Brown talked in May 2009 of constitutional reform aimed at greater democratisation of politics. This followed sharp internal criticism of his controlling style of leadership by fellow MPs. The paradox of New Labour's approach to democracy is that the centralisation of power has gone hand-in-hand with things like devolution of power to Scotland and Wales.

[29] It is really a gloss of arguments presented at length in a new book edited by Pat Devine et al (2009) entitled *Feelbad Britain*. I have a chapter in this volume.

[30] In none of the leading capitalist states is there civil unrest, widespread protest or an emergent grassroots movement relating to one or both of the current crises. The possible exceptions are: China, where internal dissent and disorder is far more common than the outside world believes, but where news reporting is patchy and typically biased towards state agendas; and South Africa, where in July 2009 major public protests were made by workers feeling the pinch of recession. Regardless, we might say that we're at the end of the beginning: the real consequences of both global recession and ongoing environmental change will only begin to become evident in the next 5–10 years. In the meantime, it's highly likely that many of the major policies, institutions and actors that currently dominate domestic and international affairs will remain in place—chastened, perhaps, but hardly on their death beds.

[31] And, clearly, things should not stop with finance capital. Global trade agreements are equally important.

[32] It creates a *mandatory* emissions market for signatories and is thus, legally, very different from the growing market in voluntary "off-setting".

[33] The "equivalence" qualifier reflects the fact that CO2 is only one of six major "greenhouse gases". This raises interesting technical questions about how one "converts" between the "warming potentials" of different gases in the absence of the ability to conduct a real-time atmospheric experiment on these gases' thermal effects.

[34] This was due, in large part, to the efforts of one Al Gore who, as Vice President, used the example of the domestic market in sulphur dioxide emissions in the USA to press for an international market in GCG emissions—even though the Clinton government then failed to ratify Kyoto.

[35] For instance, Britain had a domestic scheme between 2002 and 2007 and there have been other schemes in Denmark, New South Wales, northeastern USA and Holland.

[36] The EU initially resisted emissions trading as an approach, but relented from 1997 onwards because of pressure from the USA in the Kyoto accord discussions, and the fact that imposing pan-European environmental taxes is, because of EU rules, far more difficult than imposing a polluter-pays scheme. The fact that Europe leads the world in implementing Kyoto is no surprise: the sheer fact that the infrastructure of the EU exists gave the Union countries an institutional lead over other parts of the world in terms of enacting transnational cooperation.

[37] The outcome of the Kyoto protocol discussions in Copenhagen, in December 2009, will decisively affect the substance of the EU-ETS for the 2012–2016 period.

[38] The emissions reduction will go up to 30% if other major polluters outside the EU commit to Kyoto from 2012 onwards. Securing the agreement of EU member states for this triple-20 plan proved to be especially difficult, and was brokered by then EU President Nicolas Sarkozy.

[39] Markets in environmental goods and services are sometimes thought to be *intrinsically* bad by many on the left. This is a rather unthinking viewpoint since the real question is what specific form markets take in particular cases. Using markets to engineer change should also be seen in the context of other measures—in the present case, such things as taxes, subsidies, new performance standards for industry and consumers, etc. See Sayer (1995) for a wider argument about how to select targets for critique and then evaluate them. Larry Lohmann—a trenchant critic of pollution trading—might profit from reading Sayer's book. His critique of Kyoto (Lohmann 2005) would be far more persuasive if he separated out problems intrinsic to *this* Protocol and those likely to affect any feasible attempt to tackle global warming.

[40] The same, unsurprisingly, can be said of the new Waxman–Markey climate change bill in the USA.

[41] In this sense, the debate over whether prices or taxes are the best pollution abatement instrument (eg see Nordhaus 2007) is in part a red-herring. The real issue is whether the instrument in question reflects a political willingness to attack the power of carbon-intensive industries.

[42] In spirit, the following analysis hews close to that offered by Peter Newell and Matthew Paterson (1998) over a decade ago.

[43] A new EU directive has introduced some potentially important and positive changes into the detail of the ETS that constitute an improvement on the earlier phase of the Scheme. See Bailey and Maresh (2009) and Skjærseth and Wetterstad (2009).

[44] At this point in the process, and on pragmatic grounds, I would not argue for an abandonment of emissions trading schemes in the EU or for the Kyoto parties. The challenge is to regulate emissions much more aggressively using these schemes in conjunction with a raft of other domestic and international measures pertaining to land use, energy efficiency, carbon sequestration measures, and so on. Shrill polemics against carbon trading are easy to author (see, for instance, Frank 2009), but contribute little to helping us move forward.

References

Ashley J (2009) The battle for Labour's soul starts and ends with equality. *The Guardian* 6 July

Bailey I and Maresh S (2009) Scales and networks of neoliberal climate governance: the regulatory and territorial logics of the EU emissions trading system. *Global Environmental Politics* 9(2):101–123

Barrett S (2008) Climate treaties and the imperative of enforcement. *Oxford Review of Economic Policy* 24(2):211–238

Betz R and Sato M (2006) Emissions trading: lessons learnt from the 1st phase of the EU ETS and prospects for the 2nd phase. *Climate Policy* 6:351–359

Betz R, Rogge K and Schleich J (2006) EU emissions trading: an early analysis of national allocation plans for 2008–12. *Climate Policy* 6:361–394

Brenner R (2006) *The Economics of Global Turbulence*. London: Verso

Castree N (1995) The nature of produced nature. *Antipode* 27(1):12–49

Castree N (2000) Marxism and the production of nature. *Capital and Class* 76:5–32

Coase R (1960) The problem of social cost. *Journal of Law & Economics* 3(1):1–44

Convery F (2009) The emerging literature on emissions trading in Europe. *Review of Environmental Economics and Policy* 3(1):121–137

Dales J (1968) *Pollution, Property and Prices*. Toronto: University of Toronto Press

Darling A (2009) Only a global fix will do. *The Guardian* 10 March

Devine P, Purdy D and Pearmain A (eds) (2009) *Feelbad Britain*. London: Lawrence & Wishart

Dumenil G and Levy D (2004) *Capital Resurgent*. Cambridge: Harvard University Press

Foster J B and Magdoff F (2009) *The Great Financial Crisis*. New York: Monthly Review Press

Frank C (2009) The bankruptcy of capitalist solutions to the climate crisis. *Capitalism, Nature, Socialism* 20(2):32–43

Frank R (2007) *Falling Behind*. Berkeley: University of California Press

Gardiner S (2004) The global warming tragedy and the dangerous illusion of the Kyoto Protocol. *Ethics and International Affairs* 18(2):23–39

Greenspan A (2007) *The Age of Turbulence: Adventures in a New World*. New York: Penguin

Habermas J (1976) *Legitimation Crisis*. Boston: Beacon

Hacker J (2006) *The Great Risk Shift*. Oxford: Oxford University Press

Harvey D (1985) The geopolitics of capitalism. In D Gregory and J Urry (eds) *Social Relations and Spatial Structures* (pp 128–163). London: Macmillan

Harvey D (2005) *A Brief History of Neoliberalism*. Oxford: Oxford University Press

Helm D (2008) Climate change policy: Why has so little been achieved? *Oxford Review of Economic Policy* 24(2):211–238

Hepburn C (2007) Carbon trading: A review of the Kyoto mechanisms. *Annual Review of Environment and Resources* 32:375–393

Klein N (2009) What might the world look like if the bailout works? *The Guardian* 31 July

Lawson N (2009) *Consumed*. Harmondsworth: Penguin

Lohmann L (2005) Marketing and making carbon dumps. *Science as Culture* 14(3):203–235

Macalister T (2009) Polluters cash in on carbon trading. *The Guardian* 28 January

Milne S (2007) This crisis spells the end of the free market consensus. *The Guardian* 13 December

Minsky H (1982) The financial instability hypothesis. In C Kindleberger and J-P Laffargue (eds) *Financial Crises* (pp 1–39). Cambridge: Cambridge University Press

Monbiot G (2006) *Heat: How to Stop the Planet Burning*. Harmondsworth: Penguin

Mount F (2004) *Mind the Gap*. London: Short Books

New Economics Foundation (2009) *A Green New Deal*, http://www.neweconomics. org/gen/greennewdealneededforuk210708.aspx Accessed 5 July 2009

Newell P and Paterson M (1998) A climate for business: Global warming, the state and capital. *Review of International Political Economy* 5(4):679–703

Nordhaus W (2007) To tax or not to tax? Alternative approaches to slowing global warming. *Review of Economics and Policy* 1(1):26–44

Nye M and Owens S (2008) Creating the UK emission trading scheme. *European Environment* 18(1):1–15

O'Connor J (1987) *The Meaning of Crisis*. Oxford: Blackwell

O'Connor J (1998) *Natural Causes*. New York: Guilford

Panitch L and Konings M (2009) Myths of neoliberal deregulation. *New Left Review* 57 May-June 67–83

Pigou A (1920) *The Economics of Welfare*. London: Macmillan

Polanyi K (1944) *The Great Transformation*. Boston: Beacon

Pollin R (2003) *Contours of Descent*. London: Verso

Prudham S (2005) *Knock on Wood*. New York: Routledge

Purnell J (2009) New Labour became too much of a sect. *The Guardian* 20 July

Sayer A (1995) *Radical Political Economy*. Oxford: Blackwell

Skjærseth J and Wettestad J (2009) The origin, evolution and consequences of the EU emissions trading system. *Global Environmental Politics* 9(2):101–123

Smith N (1984) *Uneven Development*. Oxford: Blackwell

Sutcliffe B (2004) World inequality and globalization. *Oxford Review of Economic Policy* 20(1):15–37

The Guardian (2007) Coming clean on going green. 13 August

The Guardian (2008) Maelstrom in the markets. 16 September

Toynbee P (2007) We need to start a social revolution by truly putting children first. *The Guardian* 19 October

Wilkinson R and Pickett K (2009) *The Spirit Level: Why More Equal Societies Almost Always Do Better*. London: Allen Lane

Worthington B (2008) It takes more to stop the climate change juggernaut. *The Guardian* 13 December

Money Games: Currencies and Power in the Contemporary World Economy

John Agnew

Department of Geography, UCLA, Los Angeles CA, USA;
jagnew@geog.ucla.edu

Abstract: A well-known cliché has it that "money makes the world go round" Certainly, monetary arrangements, specifically exchange-rate mechanisms, can serve to show the degree to which markets and states intersect to direct the workings of the world economy. It is common to assume that the singular model over recent decades has been a neoliberal one based on independent floating exchange rates. I challenge this assumption by showing that a number of different combinations of money and power have operated in the recent past, creating a number of distinctive "money games". Only one of these, the globalist/transnational, is facing a particularly severe crisis. The others, what I term the classic/territorial, integrative/shared, and imperialist/substitute provide available alternatives. The recent history, geographical features, and future prospects of the various money games are the main concerns of the essay. The analysis welcomes the recent financial crisis as providing an opportunity to further pluralize political-economic visions beyond the perceived dominant one-size-fits-all neoliberal ideology of the globalist regime.

Keywords: money games, exchange rates, power

Much discussion of the world economy by radical geographers is currently still posed in terms of either US hegemony or US Empire. Yet, many states and other actors in world politics are already part of global political-economic arrangements of one sort or another that point beyond such limited options. In fact, the world economy as a whole has never been entirely anchored to that of the USA. This has been particularly true of the world monetary system since the 1980s. But we have become used to thinking of the world economy as centered on the USA and of the spread since the 1980s of a neoliberal globalization that has enshrined so-called Anglo-American capitalism as the global standard of economic practice. Even within the US domain of systematic influence, however, those parts of the world most immediately tied to the US economy and with the least institutional independence from it, change is also in the air. The floating monetary exchange rates at the heart of the US-dominated global financial system since the 1970s have now transmitted the contradictions of a US economy increasingly in hock to the rest of the world back home (Bulard 2008; Wade 2008).[1] In this context, the possibility that the USA can be the singular source of any new and, at least, potentially *global* system, as it was in 1944

Antipode Vol. 41 No. S1 2009 ISSN 0066-4812, pp 214–238
doi: 10.1111/j.1467-8330.2009.00723.x

with the Bretton Woods system and after 1971 with the liberalized floating system, is very unlikely. A major shift in global power towards global creditor countries with managed currencies, such as China, is under way. They will be central to any resolution. At the same time, however, there will continue to be more than one money game—or system of monetary relations governing states and firms—in play. At least in the interim, there is little likelihood of a single new dominant power center. The world economy is already based on more than one model of monetary/economic power. This essay aims to describe these models, how they arose, and what is possibly entailed for them by the current global financial crisis.

Although the global financial implosion of 2008 has seen the resurgence of massive government economic intervention in the USA, the UK and elsewhere in the face of dramatic meltdown in the financial markets, the likelihood of a complete economic retreat behind state borders looks unlikely. If the Anglo-American model of global capitalism seems in deep trouble at this time, this does not in itself signify the imminent collapse of globalization on the whole. A major part of the Anglo-American model has been the spread worldwide of the financing of that popular capitalism associated with Reaganism and Thatcherism in the USA and UK, respectively, but with older roots in each country's distinctive sociology of a burgeoning "middle class" and dreadful encounter with the Great Depression (leading to dramatic expansion of homeownership and other mass consumption) without in recent years the necessary growth in median personal incomes to underwrite it.[2] Borrowing abroad to fund American and British credit card and homeownership debt (and that from all those other places which jumped on the same bandwagon: Iceland, Hungary, etc) looks to be at an end. Of course, this model increasingly favored those bankers and brokers involved in massively recycling mortgages and other financial instruments more than those ordinary people now left with lost assets and depleted wealth. Geopolitically, what the financial crisis does suggest is that the continued US leadership of globalization, particularly the neoliberal form it has taken since the 1980s, has suffered a shock from which it will be difficult to recover. That leadership has rested to a significant degree on the use of the US currency as the dominant medium of world trade and investment. But that currency can only carry out that function as long as foreigners regard the US economy as a relatively stable and attractive destination for their investment and US agencies as reliable brokers of a range of different interests (Walter 2006). For some time these assumptions have been an open question. They are now totally problematic.

US-led *neoliberal* globalization since the 1970s, however, is only part of the story of the contemporary world economy. In my view, we have clearly overemphasized it. A variety of other modes of economic interaction and political regulation have also been at work alongside the trend towards neoliberal globalization.[3] These others are perhaps the ones to see rising fortunes in the context of the present political-economic conjuncture. In this essay I outline the four major types of political-economic regime I see at work in the world economy today. I then show how they work in terms of distinctive types of money game.[4] Finally, I suggest that the world economy is likely to see the strengthening of the least neoliberal regimes and associated games. I argue that some of these should be encouraged because of the intrinsic value of a world economy in which there is a diversity of modes of monetary operation rather than the one size fits all model of neoliberalism. Not only would this geographically limit the dangers of future worldwide bubble-bust patterns but also allows for greater political agency by governments and people around the world in the face of pressures to conform to a single hegemonic menu.[5] Rather than a single system of global monetary and financial regulation, therefore, presumably beholden to the tenets of the very Anglo-American capitalism that has brought us to this pass, what is needed is a system sensitive to local differences in levels of development and preferences for regulation with a minimal set of guidelines governing international spillovers. The fading of the USA as an enabler and enforcer of a singular neoliberal globalization, therefore, could have some very positive political-economic outcomes.

Geographies of Power in the World Economy

Scholars working from a range of theoretical perspectives have argued for the intimate connection between money and power in the modern world.[6] The tendency, however, has been to see the relationship largely in a coercive light and without much attention to its geographical mediation in distinctive ways. At best, center-periphery and similar binary conceptions of the world's geography have tended to dominate thinking. Thus, hard currencies are distinguished from soft and reserve and trading currencies are differentiated from ones largely restricted to exchange within national borders. It is more useful, in my view, to begin with a basic discussion of the nature of power before proceeding further.

Modern power, according to Michael Mann, has always had two aspects to it: despotic power and infrastructural power (Mann 1984). If the former refers to the power exerted by socio-economic elites that occupy political office, the latter refers to the power that accrues to the state as such from its delivery of infrastructural or public goods to populations. Much social science, both mainstream and radical, has tended to focus on one or the other rather than on both together. Historically, the rise in relative importance of infrastructural power, as elites have been forced through political struggles to become more responsive to their populations, led to a territorialization of political authority. Until recently, the technologies for providing public goods have had built-in territorial bias, not least relating to the capture of positive externalities. Increasingly, however, infrastructural power can be deployed across networks that, though sited in discrete locations, are not necessarily territorial in the externality fields that they produce. Thus, currencies, systems of measure, trading networks, educational provision, and welfare services need not be associated with exclusive membership in a conventional territorialized nation-state. New deployments of infrastructural power both deterritorialize existing states and reterritorialize membership around cities and hinterlands, regions, and continental-level political entities such as the European Union (Scott 1998). There is a simultaneous scaling up and scaling down of the relevant geographical fields of infrastructural power depending on the political economies of scale of different regulatory, productive, and redistributive public goods. Consequently, ". . . the more economies of scale of dominant goods and assets diverge from the structural scale of the national state—and the more those divergences feed back into each other in complex ways—then the more the authority, legitimacy, policymaking capacity, and policy-implementing effectiveness of the state will be eroded and undermined both within and without" (Cerny 1995:621). In the US case this is exacerbated by the difficulties of coordination of purpose and direction within a divided federal governmental system.

Around the world today the geographies of despotic and infrastructural power combine in distinctive ways. The two basic dimensions to a typology of state political-economic sovereignty (patterns of control and authority) are defined by the relative strength of central state authority (state despotic power) on one axis and its relative consolidation in state territoriality (state infrastructural power) on the other. The former involves judgment about the extent to which a state has acquired and maintains an effective and legitimate apparatus of rule. The latter refers to the degree to which provision of public goods and operation of markets is heavily state provided and regulated and bounded territorially. These dimensions define both the extent of state autonomy and the degree to which it is territorial in practice. Intersecting continua rather than discrete categories, four extreme cases can be identified nevertheless as ideal types for purposes of theoretical discussion and empirical analysis. These are relational in character, referring to how sovereignty is exercised effectively over time and space, rather than discrete territorial categories into which existing states can be neatly slotted.

The literature critical of hyper-globalist conceptions of globalization has tended to make a similar point from simple observation of the mosaic-like nature of globalization impacts and its own variegated

Table 1: Sovereignty regimes

		State territoriality	
		Consolidated	*Open*
Central state	*Stronger*	Classic	Globalist
authority	*Weaker*	Integrative	Imperialist

character. Thus, Helen Milner and Robert Keohane observe that "the impact of the world economy on countries that are open to its influence does not appear to be uniform" (1996:14). With respect to the character of globalization itself, Paul Hirst and Grahame Thompson and David Held et al, among others, note that it is not a singular process but a congeries of different cultural, political, and economic processes that have equally enmeshed and repulsed places into worldwide webs of connectivity in complex and fractured ways (Hirst and Thompson 1996; Held et al 1999).

The four ideal types of political-economic alignment I identify can be called "regimes", recognizing that any actual real-world case might not exactly conform to a particular regime but involve mixes of them (Table 1). By regime I mean a dominant calculus of political-economic organization relative to a given state or set of states. In this regard the term anchors power to states. But it does so in full acknowledgment of the role of other sources of power operating beyond the purview of the particular state in question. What I have in mind is the role of non-state actors both beyond state borders (firms, speculators, credit rating agencies, etc) and internal actors such as domestic businesses, unions, NGOs, political parties, and so on pursuing goals that include pushing for or against different regimes. Mann's "autonomous" state is not the only actor involved. This usage should be clearly distinguished from that which uses the term "regime" to refer only to explicit agreements between states in certain issue areas, although such agreements, to the degree that they involve sharing or pooling power, would also be covered by this conception of the term.

Of the four exemplary cases, the *classic* example is the one closest to the story frequently told about the Westphalian state, although even here there can be complications (for example, on Hong Kong and Taiwan for China). The sense is one of both despotic and infrastructural power still largely deployed within a bounded state territory (even if increasingly dependent on foreign direct investment and overseas markets for its exports) and a high degree of effective central state political authority. In broadly political-economic terms, the classical power–state nexus is also perhaps best thought of as akin to the doctrine of mercantilism in its totalizing of territorial borders and its emphasis on central state regulation of all transactions entering and leaving the state's home territory. Contemporary China is a good test case for how long such absolute sovereignty can survive pressures for divisibility and the need to establish the state's democratic legitimacy when increasingly open to the rest of the world. Internal pressures to allow increased political dissent over the economy, social inequality, and regional problems (such as Tibet) signify that this model is subject to serious domestic stresses and possible reformulation.

The second case resembles most a story that emphasizes hierarchy in world politics but with networked reach over space rather than direct territorial control. This *imperialist* regime is in all respects the exact opposite of the classic case. Not only is central state authority seriously in question because of external dependence and manipulation as well as corruption and chronic mismanagement; state territoriality is also subject to separatist threats, local insurgencies, and poor infrastructural integration. Infrastructural power is weak or non-existent and despotic power is often effectively in outside hands (including international institutions such as the IMF as well as distant but more powerful states). It is imperialist; if also reliant on the assent and cooperation of local elites, because the practice of sovereignty is tied ineluctably to the dependent political-economic status that many states endure in the regions, such as the Middle East, sub-Saharan Africa and parts of Latin America, where it prevails. Territorial incursions by a dominant external power, such as the USA in Central America and the Caribbean or in Iraq, may also bring with them largely coerced and permanent military bases.[7]

The other two cases are less familiar in relation to both conventional and critical perspectives on states and power. The third regime is the *integrative*, represented here by the European Union. In this case power has complexities relating to the co-existence between different levels or tiers of government and the distinctive functional areas that are represented differentially across the different levels, from EU-wide to the national-state and sub-national regional. But the territorial character of some of its infrastructural power is difficult to deny (consider the Common Agricultural Policy, for example), even if central state authority for both the entire EU and the member states is weaker than when each of the states was an independent entity. Quite clearly, many of the founding states of the Westphalian system have thrown in their lot with one another to create a larger and, as yet, politically unclassifiable entity that challenges existing state power in functionally complex and oftentimes non-territorialized ways (Hofmann 2008).

Finally, the fourth regime is the *globalist*. Perhaps the best current example of this is the power that has been exercised by the USA within and beyond its nominal national boundaries when it enrolls other states in its policies. Certainly, Britain in the nineteenth century also followed a version of this regime. But in both cases attempts have been made to recruit other states, by co-optation and assent as much as by coercion, into the regime. Indeed, globalization can be seen as the process (along with necessary technological and economic changes) of enrolling states and other actors in the globalist regime.[8] From this viewpoint, the globalist state relies on hegemony, in the sense of a mix of potential coercion and active consent, to bring others into line with its objectives. The revolution in information technologies and telecommunications has allied with the end of the Bretton Woods monetary system in the early 1970s to lower transaction costs in financial centers and spur the deregulation of financial markets to the extent that the networks connecting the various global financial centers (in New York, London, and Tokyo, in particular) are increasingly the collective center of the globalist regime. As a result, this regime relies more than any of the others on non-territorial mechanisms of power. It is under its auspices that markets have tended to challenge the authority of states through the privileged role of the world–city network as a system of authority and control. The world economy today is indeed truly global to a degree never seen before in its geographical scope; the pace of transactions between widely scattered places within it; and its hollowing out of simple territorial forms of political authority across a wide range of issue domains (economic, social, and political). And it has undoubtedly become so in the way it has because of the nature of US hegemony (Agnew 2005:chapters 4 and 6). That hegemony, however, has made itself increasingly redundant. The influence of capital is now mediated through global financial markets, the flow of trade within multinational firms, and the limited capacities of global regulatory institutions. Its benefits and costs now fall on all parts of the world. If they still fall unevenly, the unevenness is no longer simply on a country by country or bloc by bloc basis. Geographical variation in economic growth is increasingly local and regional within and across countries.

But it is not the global that is "new" in this globalization so much as that it represents a changing and expansive geographical logic to the world economy. In other words, it is not its "globality" that is new but, rather, its combination of global networks and localized territorial fragmentation emerging as a result of pressures from the USA and international institutions that the USA has dominated (such as the IMF) to follow the economic policies of the so-called Washington Consensus since the 1980s. Under the "previous" global, the world economy was structured largely (but never entirely) around territorial entities such as states, colonial empires, and geopolitical spheres of influence. The main novelty today is the increasing role in economic prosperity and underdevelopment of *cross-border flows* in relation to national states and to networks linking cities with one another and their hinterlands and the *increased differentiation* between localities and regions as a result of the spatial biases built into flow networks.

Rather than the "end" of geography, therefore, globalization entails its reformulation away from an economic mapping of the world in terms of state territories towards a more complex mosaic of states, regions, global city-regions, and localities differentially integrated into the global economy. There is a geopolitics of contemporary globalization, therefore, both with respect to its origins and with respect to its continuing operation. Culturally, the world is also increasingly "creolized" rather than simply Americanized (Pells 1997). This is not surprising given the increasing cultural heterogeneity of the USA itself and the need for businesses, be they American, European, or whatever, to adapt their products to different markets at home and abroad. Crucially, for the first time since the eighteenth century the "cradle of capitalism"— Western Europe and the USA—"has as much to fear from the rapidity of change as does the periphery" (Desai 2002:305). More specifically, the most important political change is the dramatic decline in the autonomy of many of the most powerful states in the face of the globalization of production, trade, technology, and communication.

Although US central state authority remains relatively strong (notwithstanding the problems of its republican constitutionalism in coping with its global role and the widely recognized inefficiencies of its various governments, both federal and local), its centrality to world politics catches it between two conflicting territorial impulses: one that presses towards a scattered imperium (as in Iraq) and one that pushes towards keeping the USA as an open territorial economy. The basis of its hegemony is a historical welcoming of immigrants and foreign investment and goods and encouraging of these tendencies elsewhere, but at the same time being increasingly subject to fiscal overextension as it endeavors to intervene globally yet also serve the demands of its population for, among other things, pensions and healthcare benefits. States other than the hegemonic one that enter into the globalist regime are not as likely to experience the tension because they can restrict their military expenditures and thus can benefit from it as long as they retain a relatively high degree of central state authority. In other words, open borders can be beneficial as long as states retain the potential capacity to close them down. Otherwise the danger is always that the globalist regime becomes imperialist for states other than the dominant one.

In no specific case can exactness of fit be expected between specific states and the classification of political-economic sovereignty regimes. Thus, the contemporary USA exhibits a classic territorial sovereignty at home while being the base for the globalist and an imperialist regime elsewhere. At the same time, while the European Union is an integrative regime internally it exhibits a mix of features of the globalist and classic regimes in relation to the rest of the world: globalist in relation to the

USA and classic, for example, in relation to Russia. Some European
states, for example France, also have an imperialist relationship to some
former African colonies but this one seems in decline. The classification
is a guide to understanding the variety of forms that political-economic
sovereignty can take, not a simple set of categories that each state slots
into neatly and completely.

Money and Power

Using the crucial example of currencies, which both materially serve
and symbolically represent state control and authority within the broader
political economy, the US has actively encouraged the use of the US
dollars in world trade and finance since the collapse of the Bretton Woods
system of exchange rates pegged to the US dollar in the early 1970s.
Initially designed by the Nixon Administration to make US exports
more competitive and to staunch the US balance-of-payments deficit,
the floating of the US dollar against other currencies has been a major
if unintended stimulus to globalization, both in facilitating trade and in
encouraging the explosion of global finance (Andrews 1994; Helleiner
1994).[9] There is little or no empirical evidence to suggest that any
one exchange rate arrangement is inherently better in a universal sense
than any other in producing such economic outcomes as higher average
growth, lower average inflation or lower output variability (Backus
2005). Exchange rate arrangements are transmission lines more than
energy-generating mechanisms within the world economy.

The political implications seem clearer. Although the US government,
for example, insofar as it can influence the Federal Reserve (the
US central bank), can still use its dollar to manipulate the world
economy to the benefit of its producers and consumers, there are real
limits to this when the USA depends on massive inflows of foreign-
originated investment, such a large proportion of the US dollars in
circulation circulate outside the territorial boundaries of the USA, and
other governments (such as China) peg their currencies closely to the
dollar and build up large reserves that they can use to maintain the
peg and thus keep the prices of their exports competitive in the US
domestic market. As a result the US dollar and other currencies of
wider circulation (such as the Euro and the Japanese yen) have slowly
eroded the independent monetary infrastructural power of both the states
in which their currencies circulate and themselves, to the extent that
they, and not just the bearers of less potent currencies, are now on
the receiving end of currency shocks from "outside". Global markets
increasingly determine the relative values of what are still nominally
national-state currencies when those currencies float freely against one
another. Indeed, the territorial "inside" and the "outside" of the state
are increasingly in question as to their material significance. Thus, in

a major area in which the USA has previously exercised economic hegemony there are increasing signs of hegemony—that of global currency markets—without a singular state hegemon that can *effectively* intercede in them.

Since the collapse of the Bretton Woods Agreement in the early 1970s no single worldwide exchange-rate arrangement has prevailed.[10] It is the exchange-rate mechanism which is central, when put together with associated institutional forms such as central bank independence and capital controls, to the ways in which currencies articulate with one another and thus to the extent to which any individual currency either monopolizes or extends its purview beyond a particular state territory. Since the 1980s a number of different exchange-rate models have prevailed with some countries switching between them while others have maintained a commitment to a single one over time. Typically, exchange-rate arrangements are classified into four or so categories: soft-pegged or relatively fixed exchange rates, with a foreign currency serving as the anchor but with government intervention to maintain the peg; independently floating, in which a currency is allowed to find its own exchange rate in open market trading (if with occasional intervention by single or several governments); managed floating, in which a government attempts to influence the exchange rate but without a predetermined rate path or target; and other arrangements, defined here as (1) a shared currency (with external floating), (2) a currency board, with a domestic currency fixed permanently (hard peg) against foreign exchange and fully backed by foreign assets thus eliminating government control, and (3) adoption of a foreign currency (such as the US dollar) as sole legal tender.[11]

In the 1980s soft-pegged arrangements were widespread with two thirds of all exchange rates set this way (Figure 1). This was probably a hangover from the Bretton Woods system of the post-war period in which all convertible currencies were pegged to the US dollar backed by gold. By the mid 1990s, however, a significant shift was afoot, with a huge expansion in the number of independently floating currencies at the expense of pegged and other arrangements. In the 1980s the spread of monetarist ideas among governments involved among other things the belief that governments should not actively intervene to direct their exchange rates. The most avid proponents of liberal globalization have been the biggest fans of floating currencies. The presumption is that floating currencies will better reflect the willingness of investors to "bet" on the value of a given currency as a judgment about the overall condition of its national economy. Free floating also has always involved the lifting of capital controls and the establishment of central bank independence, thus facilitating the "retreat of the state" mandated by a generous faith in the relative efficiency of market mechanisms. By 2004 a new pattern had emerged with a further retreat of soft-pegged currencies but with an

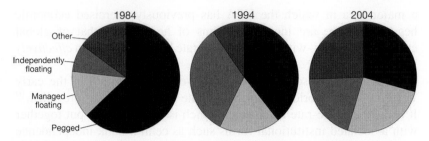

Figure 1: The distribution of exchange-rate arrangements in four broad categories: soft pegs, managed floats, independent floats, and other (including hard pegs such as currency boards and integrative currencies), 1984, 1994, 2004 (source: IMF 2004)

expansion of managed floating and other arrangements (mainly due to the arrival of the Euro as a shared currency in 1999) and a net waning of independent floats. Since 2004 the number of pegged rates and managed floats has increased further relative to independent floats. Even with a generally declining dollar (in free float) between 2006 and 2008, there was no rampant retreat from soft pegging (Chung and Garnham 2008). Some countries diversified their soft pegs from the US dollar to include the Euro but that was about all.

One interpretation might emphasize the relative eclipse of pegged arrangements over the 40 years since the demise of Bretton Woods, but another would stress a recurrent and dynamic pluralism of arrangements. The world of currencies does not seem to be on a single path simply away from pegged or towards a norm of independently floating currencies. This would be the either/or of state political-economic sovereignty converted to the realm of currencies. In fact, the picture painted in Figure 1 suggests that a variety of political-economic processes are at work, not simply a persisting territorial currency system mediated by an anchoring currency (or gold standard) versus a free-floating (and globalized) market capitalism. The actual experience of freely floating, particularly as manifest in the recurrent crises associated with "runs" on floating currencies that marked the Mexican monetary crisis of 1995, the Asian monetary crisis of 1997, and the Russian monetary crisis of 1998, seems to have had much to do with the pluralization of arrangements away from a single global norm. The period 1984–1994 was the high point of independent floating. Between 1994 and 2004 the number of independent floats contracted significantly in favor of managed floats and pegged arrangements of various sorts.

Some confusion is possible relative to my view of soft-pegged currencies as expressed above. From one viewpoint, pegged currencies represent a decision to subordinate the national currency to a foreign one and thus to give up monetary sovereignty (Lake 2007). It is then seen as merely a milder version of the hard peg of a currency board. The corollary is that under free floating a currency is freed from a hierarchical relationship to another currency. This thereby signifies "freedom" in monetary affairs. From my perspective, this argument is totally perverse. Pegging is in fact a way of trying to shield a currency from both markets and states other than the anchor and, when combined, as is typical, with capital controls and an absence of central bank independence, the best way of maintaining state control over a national currency. If the anchoring currency is a major trading partner or the one in which your state's exports are invoiced then so much the better. The general perception of governments seems to be that pegged (and managed) rates generate both more net policy autonomy and better exchange-rate stability. The danger of importing inflation from and having to follow the monetary policies of the anchor is seen as mitigated by all of these other advantages. The currency board and the substitution of a foreign currency are in fact the real candidates for monetary subordination to another state. Independent and managed floats represent, in various degrees, subordination to the markets. Now, whether soft-pegged exchange rates really do offer all the autonomy and stability that they are perceived to is something else again (Shambaugh 2004).

A tenet of contemporary open-economy macroeconomics, if not of that monetarism which always prefers floating exchange rates, is that there is in fact no "magic" to any exchange-rate arrangement. No single arrangement can guarantee capital mobility, a targeted exchange rate, and independent monetary policy at the same time. This is the so-called open-economy trilemma. Indeed, with increased worldwide trade and massive international investment, the trade off between exchange rate volatility and domestic price stability has become tougher than ever. According to some research, even when some states are officially committed to independent floating, in fact they really have "soft pegs" of some sort or another (Calvo and Reinhart 2002). Overall, however, the empirical evidence is that despite the difficulties of classifying exchange-rate arrangements, there is a wide range of such arrangements, official and actual, rather than dispersion around a central or median type (Reinhart and Rogoff 2004). From a political perspective it is the cross-mapping of dominant exchange-rate arrangements and sovereignty regimes that is of prime concern. This is reflected in the discussion that follows. What is the best exchange-rate arrangement from an economic perspective is not relevant to the present discussion.

There are four ways in which currencies tend to work with respect to any given national territory, paralleling the four sovereignty regimes. This in itself suggests that, at least for the geography of money, there is something useful theoretically about the fourfold schema of sovereignty regimes. The four currency processes are as follows:

1. The *territorial*, in which a national-state currency dominates a state territory and the population has restricted access to

currencies of wider circulation except through a pegged exchange rate controlled by central state authority; a managed float represents an intermediate case between this and reliance on a transnational currency.

2. The *transnational*, in which the currency issued by one state (invariably a powerful one) circulates widely among world financial centers, floats freely, is a standard (or reserve) currency in relation to which other currencies are denominated, and is a preferred currency for transacting global commerce.

3. The *shared*, in which a formal monetary alliance operates either through full monetary union (as with the Euro and the EU) or through an exchange-rate union among economic equals with an internal managed float and, in both cases, an external floating exchange rate.

4. The *substitute*, in which a transnational currency substitutes either officially or unofficially in all or many transactions for the nominal territorial currency of a given state. The substitute currency is particularly important as a store of wealth in local banks, hedge against inflation in the national currency, and medium of capital flight to foreign financial centers for local elites. Given the dominant economic role of the USA in some world regions this is usually a process of dollarization.

These processes map onto the four political-economic (sovereignty) regimes with the four cases taken from Table 1 (see Table 2). As noted earlier, however, there is no sense in which these various "solutions" are fixed for all time. Exchange-rate arrangements have been almost as volatile historically as floating exchange rates! They reflect decisions on the part of state and other influential actors based on socialized understandings of their "monetary interests" (Widmaier 2004:437). These understandings reflect, to one degree or another, views of state and market performance in relation to the different structural positions vis-à-vis the world economy that states and local actors find themselves in and the institutional and political characteristics of particular states. They also reflect judgments about the state's capacity to manage or direct a currency and its associated exchange-rate system. Thus, the

Table 2: Sovereignty regimes and currency processes (examples along the diagonal)

| | | Sovereignty regime | | | |
		Classic	Globalist	Integrative	Imperialist
Dominant	Territorial	China			
currency	Transnational		US + floaters		
process	Shared			EU	
	Substitute				Latin America

classic case can be seen as based on the Keynesian logic that states can mitigate market failures, the globalist represents a neo-classical approach that states should retreat and let markets work their magic, the imperialist stresses the classical monetary theory that state failure necessitates radical decoupling of domestic and monetary policies, and the integrative is a mix of Keynesian/inside and neo-classical/outside the grouping of states in question. Currency processes, therefore, are not the direct result of materialist pressures but are mediated by the perceptions and understandings of exchange rate mechanisms and other monetary policies governments and other actors bring to their material situations.

What is the worldwide distribution of the different combinations of sovereignty regime and currency process as defined in Table 2? In the contemporary world there are still examples of territorial currencies that reflect "classic" state sovereignty.[12] But the net trend of the past 40 years has been away from this singular regime toward the other ones. As of 2004, pegged rates were a shrinking part of the overall exchange-rate arrangements pie; although they have made something of a comeback latterly (Figure 1). Managed floats have everywhere emerged as a "balance" between the territorial and the transnational arrangements (Figure 2). In 2005 China finally made this move from soft peg to managed float. The 2004 world map of exchange-rate arrangements as classified by the IMF shows a wide variety of outcomes. In Asia managed floats prevail with China (at that time) as the main example of a soft-pegged currency. The Asian financial crisis of 1997

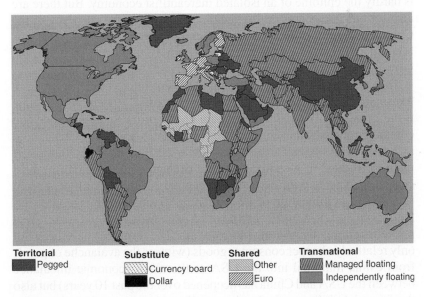

Territorial	Substitute	Shared	Transnational
Pegged	Currency board	Other	Managed floating
	Dollar	Euro	Independently floating

Figure 2: Mapping exchange rate arrangements by category (see text), 2004 (source: IMF 2004)

may have been a blessing in pointing to the limits of the IMF mandated policies and thus suggesting that governments had to create their own ways of protecting against both speculative runs on their currencies and the importation of more general economic shocks. Elsewhere, pegging is closely associated with oil-exporting countries (eg Saudi Arabia) and countries overtly jealous of their sovereignty in pursuit of different ethnicized and nationalist agendas (eg Ukraine, Malaysia, Syria). Independent floats prevail, unsurprisingly, in the most globalized countries including the Eurozone (the Euro floats externally).

One of the best examples of the closest to a classic/territorial regime today is perhaps China, whose currency, the renminbi (or yuan), was pegged against the US dollar until July 2005 and has been in a very carefully managed float since then, and whose economy is thereby insulated to a certain degree from monetary shocks emanating from the wider world economy. Nevertheless, given its overall dependence on manufactured exports for its economic growth and the fragility of its banking sector and capital markets, China is not without its own serious economic problems that owe much to its exposure to the world economy since its opening up in the late 1980s. It depends crucially on foreign investment and technology licensing to achieve its economic goals. It also critically has used its high rate of domestic savings to invest heavily in US Treasury bonds which in the absence of corresponding exports from the USA to repay the borrowing from China has resulted in an undervalued USA–China exchange rate and the US economic profligacy that led to the recent dramatic economic crash.[13] So, China is hardly the epitome of an isolated mercantilist economy. But there are also serious issues concerning the directing role in the economy of the Chinese Communist Party and the social (and ethno-regional) tensions accompanying the country's recent extremely rapid rate of economic growth.

The only contemporary example of an intersection between a transnational currency process and a "globalist" sovereignty regime is the USA. The US dollar is the main metric of transnational trade and commerce and the main currency that other states (including China) hold as a reserve. As a result, the US dollar is also the currency that is the main instrument of globalization. The exchange-rate mechanism most closely associated with the globalist regime is the free or independent float.[14] The combination of US dollar and floating exchange rates has long given the USA a privileged position from which it could acquire real resources simply by printing more dollars. The resources have been not only relatively cheaper consumer goods (witness the avalanche of goods from China imported into the USA as the macroeconomic imbalance between the USA and China has deepened over the past 10 years) but also the financial ability to deploy large military garrisons abroad without taxing its own population to do so. A diminished globalist regime under current conditions, therefore, would imply a further political rebalancing away from any singular hegemony.

The best current example of a shared currency is the Euro, associated as it is with the project of pan-European unification. It rapidly displaced the US dollar as the currency for denominating debt, issuing bonds, and pricing trade within the Eurozone after 1999.[15] Though there are others such as the CFA franc zone in West Africa and the ECCU currency board arrangement in the Caribbean. Historically, many national currencies such as the US dollar emerged out of the unification of more geographically variegated currency systems (Broz 1999).

Finally, to the extent that certain territorial currencies reflect the weakness of their national economies and are heavily dependent on foreign capital flows they are substituted for by the use of transnational currencies. Currently, the US dollar is the most important of the transnational currencies, either through informal or formal dollarization, and, more infrequently, through so-called currency boards or some variant thereof which insulate monetary decisions from domestic political pressures. In both cases any pretense at territorial monetary sovereignty is essentially sacrificed to dampen inflation, increase foreign investment, and reduce the proclivity for growth in government spending. Many Latin American countries have recently experienced this intersection between currency substitution and what I call the imperialist sovereignty regime even though relatively few countries have engaged in full-fledged or official dollarization (Ecuador and El Salvador).

How do the currency processes operate geographically relative to a given regime? The territorial and shared currency processes are the most evidently territorialized. But even they are hardly totally closed monetary spaces. They must co-exist with a transnational currency such as the US dollar that breaks down borders and challenges the hold of national currencies over a range of transactions, not the least by encouraging the development of currency markets at financial centers within their territories. This is an opening up of possibilities for the redistribution of political authority beyond capital cities whose central banks and finance ministries must now work to share power with other actors in the monetary realm. Of course, much of the monetary flow across territorial boundaries today tends to be between financial centers in the richest countries. Wall Street (in New York) and the City (in London) are the key places of authority with affiliates and collaborators scattered all over the world economy but with the densest presence in North American, European, and East Asian cities (Martin 1994; Thrift 1994). This is because most global flows are involved in "diversification finance", "intended to reduce risk through the fine-tuning of portfolios" (Taylor 2004:31). One hundred years ago a significant proportion of world capital flows moved from rich to poor countries in search of investment opportunities. Of course, much of this was within colonial currency blocs that used the same or closely pegged currencies (Helleiner 2002). That this is no longer the case globally, the net financial flow today is from poorer to richer countries, suggests that the use of substitute currencies is now more a question of subordinate state elites looking for a monetary port in an economic storm and of imbalances in the global system of production and consumption associated with the rise of China, than of hegemonic states actively looking to use currency as a mechanism of subordination. Imperialism today is not a simple facsimile of imperialism in the 1890s.[16] Yet, susceptibility to the demands of foreign capital provides a major incentive for some states and local actors to find shelter, however problematic, in the holding of a historically less volatile transnational currency such as the US dollar, as evidenced by the large domestic and foreign holdings of such currencies (in offshore and other "dollar salting" centers) by the nationals and governments of many countries, particularly in Africa, Latin America, and Eastern Europe.

Ways Forward?

In the current context of the implosion of Anglo-American neoliberal capitalism what are the most plausible scenarios for a new nexus between money and power as manifested in exchange-rate arrangements and ancillary activities as I have outlined them previously?

The current crisis is largely one of the globalist model and the floating exchange rate with which it is associated. The implications for the US dollar are particularly important. Even before the 2007–2008 financial implosion some countries with managed floats were already shifting away from singular US dollar pegs towards baskets of currencies. Partly this is a question of spreading risk to avoid tying one's currency too strongly to a single national currency, even one as widely held as the US dollar. But it also reflects the fact that the value of the US dollar has grown increasingly volatile reflecting both the predilection of recent US governments for monetary over fiscal policy and the increasing size of the US current account and federal government deficits which, in the absence of sufficient domestic saving, must be financed by foreign holders of US dollars. These holders are increasingly nervous about returns on their dollar holdings (*Reuters* 2008; Yardley and Bradsher 2008; *The Economist* 2008a).[17]

Although the US economy is itself now feeling the effect of these shifts, it has been smaller economies with floating currencies such as Iceland, Hungary, and New Zealand that have felt the brunt of the fall out of the collapse and near collapse of major US banks and investment funds in 2008. Indeed, high exposure to world trade plus exposure to currency fluctuations and exposure to dollar-denominated debt are the three main predictors of overall vulnerability and threat to national economic growth. Increased openness to the world economy as mandated by a floating exchange rate without capital controls, therefore, is increasingly in doubt as a national economic growth strategy. This calls into question the very foundations of the current globalist regime or at least of the Washington Consensus that has lain behind its expansion since the 1980s (Landler 2008).

In this context, the classic regime may beckon to some countries. China looks likely to weather the current crisis much better than many other countries (*The Economist* 2008b). From one viewpoint, the volatility of capital inward flows associated with the globalist regime encourages currency crises, external-debt defaults, and inflationary spikes. From another, it is not just the managed exchange rate but more particularly capital controls that limit the impact of potential external shocks (Reinhart and Reinhart 2008). Thus, although the neoliberal argument is invariably in favor of floating rates and against capital controls, recent experience suggests that the Chinese case with its managed float and limited capital controls will become highly instructive and encourage some countries, perhaps especially large countries with effective governments, to move in the Chinese direction: benefiting from the globalist regime but remaining institutionally on its margins.

Perhaps the Euro could replace the US dollar as the anchor of the globalist regime? This is certainly frequently touted as a possibility. Particularly now that the US financial system is both materially broken and ideologically in question, the dollar will follow. Yet, the US dollar has some continuing supports for its global role. One is simply inertia. The wide use of the dollar offers a degree of liquidity and acceptability that others cannot yet match. These so-called incumbency or network effects are reinforced by the political-security relationships that still shadow the floating zone such as those with Japan, Taiwan, and the Eurozone. Divesting dollar reserves creates a further dilemma. Even as China, in particular, loses an estimated 7–8% of its GDP per year (as of 2008) on its dollar reserves, selling those reserves would be catastrophic for China as well as the USA. Diversifying towards the Euro would make sense. But the Euro also has its problems. Even as it has taken a growing share of foreign exchange reserves at the expense of the dollar, internal economic divergence creates pressures for adjustment within the Eurozone as the Euro increases its value against the US dollar. More importantly, long-term differences in relative labor costs and industrial competitiveness between northern and southern Europe create problems for governments long used to using monetary rather than fiscal or labor market policy to resolve their economic problems. The Euro seems set to suffer for the heterogeneity of economies and still powerful and politically divergent national governments it serves (Eichengreen and Flandreau 2008; Plender 2008).

Yet the Eurozone is increasingly attractive, not least as a port in
the global financial storm, for adjacent countries. Notwithstanding the
challenges facing the Euro as a possible savior of the globalist regime,
therefore, its future as one of the bases for an integrative political-
economic regime seems even stronger than it was. Both Hungary and
Iceland have looked longingly towards the Eurozone as their currencies
have sunk within the free-floating globalist regime. The recent crisis
seems likely to encourage the enlargement of both the EU and the
Eurozone. Iceland is an interesting case in point. A small country with a
banking sector too large to be bailed out by its own government, Iceland's
experience suggests that much of non-Eurozone Europe, including
perhaps even much larger countries dependent on finance such as the
UK, is not economically viable when faced with the transmission of
shocks by their floating currencies. Membership in the Eurozone would
provide a common policy framework and shared protection against
speculative attacks. For Iceland it would also bring much lower interest
rates. The very fiscal and microeconomic heterogeneity that characterize
the current Eurozone, however, will probably work against any rapid
expansion in membership. There is enough variance as it is. But overall,
the current crisis looks likely to strengthen the Eurozone and similar
forms of integrative sovereignty that might be invented in the years
ahead (Münchau 2008; *The Economist* 2008c).[18]

The imperialist regime to the degree that it rests largely today on
dollarization, both formal and informal, looks increasingly troubled.
Even those countries formally dollarized, such as Ecuador, are pushing
in policy directions at odds with traditional US recipes for economic
growth and social welfare. As the US dollar loses some or all of its
luster as a shelter against inflation in local currencies and national
income-redistributive programs then the imperialist regime must go
into retreat. At the same time, those countries that are exporters of
major commodities, such as oil, industrial raw materials, and crucial
foodstuffs, are likely to see their currencies strengthen irrespective of
how pegged or managed they are. Net importers, particularly of oil and
foodstuffs, are likely to see the reverse. But as long as there is even a hint
that poorer countries do not benefit very much or at all from increasingly
flexible exchange rates, then it makes sense for them to move in the
direction of pegged rates and, thus, towards classic sovereignty (Husain
et al 2005). Of course, whether they can ever attain it depends on more
than just the type of exchange-rate arrangement in effect.

Conclusion
To the extent that there has been an era of American global dominance,
it now well may be coming to an end. But the recent world economy
has not been just about American power, as I hope I have shown. The

image of hegemonic epochs with dominant states heading up and down a metaphorical escalator leaves much to be desired in regard to both its historical grip and its geographical range. Using the idea of monetary power I have shown that rather than thinking in terms of just one or two models of world power it makes more sense to think in terms of at least four.

To the degree that any of us can see ahead, the globalist regime as created and enforced by the USA looks to be in trouble. The sustaining narrative of the past three decades about markets and governments has come to the end of its road.[19] Whether this will lead to a new similarly global but less neoliberal globalist regime is perhaps the biggest question of the moment. The USA itself seems humbled if not yet beyond internal repair. No likely replacements are as yet in evidence, notwithstanding claims that either the EU or China could serve such a role. Yet, many actors, including China, have a continuing stake in some sort of globalism. Geopolitically, everything seems more complex than a straightforward hegemonic succession. I see no likelihood of a single system soon replacing the plurality currently in place even as calls for singular "global" responses fall on increasingly deaf pluralistic ears.

This is a good thing. It opens up the possibilities for redesigning the world economy in ways that are more in tune with local desires. Referring to Karl Polanyi's idea of a "double movement" about market exchange and government intervention and designating the present as the second leg of this as a time of reaction against the excesses of the first, Robert Wade provides a conclusion compatible with mine when he writes that if the forthcoming period turns out to be one in "which consensus is largely absent, it may also provide space for a wider array of standards and institutions—economic and financial alternatives to the system-wide prescriptions of neoliberalism" (2008:21).[20]

Endnotes

[1] On the cultural character of the Anglo-American system of capitalism (views of competition, efficiency, etc), see d'Iribarne (1997).

[2] This is the so-called ownership or marketplace society. See, for example, Agnew (1981, 2005).

[3] See, for example, from a range of perspectives, Starr (2006), Stulz (2005), Armijo (2001), and Braga de Macedo et al (2001).

[4] By "game" I do not intend to suggest anything akin to the meaning of game in the "theory of games", only as a metaphor suggesting distinctive rules and strategies associated with different exchange-rate arrangements and their principal actors.

[5] From this perspective, I am sympathetic to the general view of Robin Blackburn (2008; 2009:135) when he writes: "A public-equity finance regime should have a democratic, regional, and devolved character, as well as nationally and globally determined constraints, norms and objectives. As someone once put it, socialism is not a monist practice".

[6] For example, for just two very distinctive arguments, compare, from the right, Ferguson (2001) with, from the left, Parboni (1985).

[7] The imperialist regime can take a variety of forms, only some of which deserve the territorial term "empire".

[8] Two authors as starkly divergent intellectually and politically as Carl Schmitt and Antonio Gramsci first noted the emergence of what Gramsci (1977:81) termed "Anglo-Saxon world hegemony" and what I am here terming the globalist regime. Their arguments came from very different theoretical premises and reflected very different sensibilities as to the consequences of globalism. On Schmitt see Rausch (2003), and on Gramsci see Morton (2007). I have developed a Gramscian argument about the origins and historical course of the contemporary globalist regime at length in Agnew (2005).

[9] An excellent review of the role of private finance in challenging state power is provided in Helleiner (1999).

[10] Benjamin Cohen (2006), makes a persuasive case for what he calls a worldwide "currency pyramid" in which currencies at the top make others, the majority below, pay for adjustment costs across all exchange-rate arrangements. Even after the collapse of the Bretton Woods Agreement which had semi-fixed exchange rates against the US dollar from 1944 until 1972 there was still an undeniable hierarchy among the world's currencies. Nevertheless, the way the hierarchy works is quite different for different exchange-rate arrangements and, in my view, cannot be reduced to a single worldwide process.

[11] There are two major problems with classifying exchange rates. The first is that they are really arranged along a continuum. The terms bear this out: fixed rate, hard peg, soft peg, managed float, free float. It is often hard to draw the line between the different categories. The second is that exchange rates correlate in complex ways with other monetary phenomena such as capital controls and how fiscal and monetary policies are coordinated.

[12] The freely floating currencies are the most integrated into the global economy with the most independently powerful financial centers where the US dollar serves as the most common metric of transactions. The countries with no independent currency obviously use substitute ones. The soft-pegged rates and, to a lesser extent, the managed floats signify those states in which state monetary authority (and other elements of authority) is relatively territorial. The countries with currency boards (hard pegs) are often either in macroeconomic crisis or in transition toward some other exchange-rate regime. "Network externalities", the snowball effect of surrounding countries operating with other systems, make these "intermediate" exchange-rate regimes inherently unstable with financial globalization and will push them towards shared currencies (as with central European countries awaiting admission to the Euro after joining the EU in 2004), substitute currencies (no independent currency) or, most likely of all in most cases under present conditions, towards free floating. In other words, 42 countries (plus the USA) could claim that they have the main features of "classic" monetary sovereignty. The US case is rather more complex than this. In most cases the retreat of central state authority is paralleled by an increasingly complex spatiality of currency flows and regulation.

[13] See, among other sources, Wolf (2009a) and Skidelsky (2009).

[14] In some of the macroeconomics literature "monetary sovereignty" is associated with an independently floating currency. Why giving up control over a currency to the markets should be seen this way perhaps reflects the classical and neoclassical sensibility that a currency should either "stand and deliver" or go to the wall. It certainly seems to have little or nothing to do with the reality of central state authority as indicated by different exchange-rate mechanisms. Perhaps because since the 1970s the US dollar is the floating currency that first comes to mind, all other floaters are assimilated to the one currency for which independently floating is not antithetical to monetary sovereignty. In the contemporary world it is soft-pegged currencies and, perhaps, heavily managed floats, as the closest mechanism to fixed rates, which signify the highest relative degree of central state authority in the monetary realm.

[15] See, for example, Hale and Spiegel (2008). On the history of the Euro more generally, see Marsh (2009) and Issing (2008).

[16] More specifically, there is now a much larger net financial transfer (including interest and profit payments) from so-called developing to developed countries than just a few years ago when there was a net flow in the other direction (from plus US$46 billion in 1995, to minus US$683 billion in 2006). Some of this trend does relate to debt financing but much more is due to the higher savings rates in countries such as China producing a counter flow as these savings are invested in stocks, bonds, and bank accounts in the USA as a result of US balance of payments and fiscal deficits produced, at least in part, by increased reliance on Chinese production for US consumption which is then financed by Chinese (and other) credits (UN 2007).

[17] Prior to the G20 Summit of 2 April 2009 on the global economic crisis, Zhou Xiaochuan, Governor of the People's Bank of China (China's central bank) proposed a rethinking of the global monetary system based on an enhanced version of the IMF's unit of account, the special drawing right or SDR (*Reform of the International Monetary System*, www.pbc.gov.cn/english—see also Bergsten 2009; *The Economist* 2009a). At the same time, China's government has entered into a variety of currency swaps with other countries to use the Chinese renminbi rather than the US dollar as the medium for trade (see, for example, Webber 2009).

[18] A persisting problem for the Eurozone is the lack of integration between monetary and fiscal polices, the former in the hands of the European Central Bank and the latter those of individual member governments. If in the years leading up to the introduction of the Euro there was striking convergence of long-term bond yields (a measure of overall economic integration) (Swanson 2008), in recent years there has been an increasing, and worrying, spread between German bond yields and those of Ireland, Italy and Greece, in particular, suggesting increased concern by investors about the viability of the latter economies in the absence of individual floating currencies with which to express their skepticism (*The Economist* 2009c).

[19] For a remarkably "Marxist" analysis of the current crisis from a seemingly unlikely source, see Wolf (2009b).

[20] See also, for a different if ultimately convergent view, Rodrik (2009).

References

Agnew J (1981) Homeownership and the capitalist social order. In M Dear and A Scott (eds) *Urbanization and Urban Planning in Capitalist Society* (pp 457–480). London: Methuen

Agnew J (2005) *Hegemony: The New Shape of Global Power*. Philadelphia: Temple University Press

Andrews D M (1994) Capital mobility and state autonomy: Towards a structural theory of international monetary relations. *International Studies Quarterly* 38:193–218

Armijo L E (2001) The political geography of world financial reform: Who wants what and why? *Global Governance* 7:379–396

Backus D K (2005) Comment on: 'Exchange rate regime durability and performance in developing versus advanced economies'. *Journal of Monetary Economics* 52:65–68

Bergsten F (2009) Beijing's currency idea needs to be taken seriously. *Financial Times* 9 April

Blackburn R (2008) The subprime crisis. *New Left Review* 50:50–106

Blackburn R (2009) Value theory and the Chinese worker. *New Left Review* 56:128–135

Braga de Macedo J, Cohen D and Reisen H (eds) (2001) *Don't Fix, Don't Float: The Exchange Rate in Emerging Markets, Transition Economies and Developing Countries*. Paris: OECD

Broz J L (1999) Origins of the Federal Reserve System: International incentives and the domestic free-rider problem. *International Organization* 53:39–70

Bulard M (2008) Financial realities after the dollar. *Le Monde Diplomatique* November

Calvo G A and Reinhart C M (2002) Fear of floating. *Quarterly Journal of Economics* 117:379–408

Cerny P G (1995) Globalization and the changing logic of collective action. *International Organization* 49:545–625

Chung J and Garnham P (2008) Plummeting dollar a big headache for pegged currencies. *Financial Times* 14 March

Cohen B J (2006) The macrofoundations of monetary power. In D M Andrews (ed) *International Monetary Power* (pp 35–61). Ithaca: Cornell University Press

Desai M (2002) *Marx's Revenge: The Resurgence of Capitalism and the Death of Statist Socialism*. London: Verso

d'Iribarne P (1997) A check to enlightened capitalism. In C Crouch and W Streeck (eds) *Political Economy of Modern Capitalism* (pp 161–172). London: Sage

Eichengreen B and Flandreau M (2008) The rise and fall of the dollar, or, when did the dollar replace sterling as the leading international currency? National Bureau of Economic Research, Working Paper 14154

Ferguson N (2001) *The Cash Nexus: Money and Power in the Modern World, 1700–2000*. New York: Basic Books

Gramsci A (1977) *Selections from the Political Writings, 1910–1920*. London: Lawrence and Wishart

Hale G and Spiegel M M (2008) The EMU effect on the currency denomination of international bonds. *Federal Reserve Bank of San Francisco Economic Letter* 26 September

Held D, McGrew A, Goldblatt D and Perraton J (1999) *Global Transformations: Politics, Economics and Culture*. Stanford: Stanford University Press

Helleiner E (1994) *States and the Reemergence of Global Finance: From Bretton Woods to the 1990s*. Ithaca: Cornell University Press

Helleiner E (1999) Sovereignty, territoriality and the globalization of finance. In D A Smith, Solinger D J and Topik S C (eds) *States and Sovereignty in the Global Economy* (pp 75–93). London: Routledge

Helleiner E (2002) The monetary dimensions of colonialism: Why did imperial powers create currency blocs? *Geopolitics* 7:5–30

Hirst P and Thompson G (1996) *Globalization in Question*. Cambridge: Polity

Hofmann H W (2008) Mapping the European administrative space. *West European Politics* 31:662–676

Husain A M, Mody A and Rogoff K S (2005) Exchange rate durability and performance in developing versus advanced economies. *Journal of Monetary Economics* 52: 35–62

IMF (2004) *Classification of Exchange-Rate Arrangements and Monetary Policy Frameworks*, http://www.imf.org/external/np/mfd/er/2004/eng/0604.htm Accessed 10 July 2009

Issing O (2008) *The Birth of the Euro*. Cambridge: Cambridge University Press

Lake D A (2007) Escape from the state of nature: Authority and hierarchy in world politics. *International Security* 32:65–66

Landler M (2008) West is in talks on credit to aid poorer nations. *New York Times* 24 October

Mann M (1984) The autonomous power of the state. *European Journal of Sociology* 25:185–213

Marsh D (2009) *The Euro: The Politics of the New Global Currency*. New Haven: Yale University Press

Martin R (1994) Stateless monies, global financial integration and national economic autonomy: The end of geography? In S Corbridge, R Martin and N Thrift (eds) *Money, Power, Space* (pp 253–278). Oxford: Blackwell

Milner H V and Keohane R O (1996) Internationalization and domestic politics. In R O Keohane and H V Milner (eds) *Internationalization and Domestic Politics* (pp 1–22). Cambridge: Cambridge University Press

Morton A D (2007) *Unravelling Gramsci: Hegemony and Passive Revolution in the Global Economy*. London: Pluto

Münchau W (2008) Now they see the benefits of the Eurozone. *Financial Times* 2 November

Parboni R (1985) *Il conflitto economico mondiale. Finanza e crisi internazionale*. Milan: Etas Libri

Pells R (1997) *Not Like Us: How Europeans have Loved, Hated, and Transformed American Culture since World War II*. New York: Basic Books

Plender J (2008) Don't assume the Euro will displace the dollar. *Financial Times* 24 September

Rausch W (2003) Human rights as geopolitics: Carl Schmitt and the legal forms of American supremacy. *Cultural Critique* 54:118–129

Reinhart C M and Reinhart V (2008) Capital flow bonanzas. National Bureau of Economic Research, Working Paper 14321

Reinhart C M and Rogoff K S (2004) The modern history of exchange rate arrangements: A reinterpretation. *Quarterly Journal of Economics* 119:1–48

Reuters (2008) China paper urges new currency order after 'financial tsunami'. 17 September

Rodrik D (2009) A 'Plan B' for global finance. *The Economist* 14 March

Scott A (1998) *Regions and the World Economy*. Oxford: Oxford University Press

Shambaugh J C (2004) The effect of fixed exchange rates on monetary policy. *Quarterly Journal of Economics* 119:301–352

Skidelsky R (2009) The world financial crisis and the American mission. *New York Review of Books* 16 July

Starr M A (2006) One world, one currency: Exploring the issues. *Contemporary Economic Policy* 24:618–633

Stulz R M (2005) The limits of financial globalization. *Journal of Finance* 60:1595–1638

Swanson E T (2008) Convergence of long-term bond yields in the Euro area. *Federal Reserve Bank of San Francisco Economic Letter* 21 November

Taylor A M (2004) Global finance: Past and present. *Finance and Development* March

The Economist (2008a) A taxonomy of trouble. 25 October

The Economist (2008b) China's economy: Domino or dynamo? 11 October

The Economist (2008c) No room in the Ark: The Euro may not be quite as safe a haven as enthusiasts are claiming. 15 November

The Economist (2009a) Handle with care: China suggests an end to the dollar era. 28 March

The Economist (2009b) High tensions. 7 February

Thrift N (1994) On the social and cultural determinants of international financial centres: The case of the City of London. In S Corbridge, R Martin and N Thrift (eds) *Money, Power, Space*. Oxford: Blackwell

UN (2007) *World Economic Situation and Prospects, 2007*. New York: UN Department of Economic and Social Affairs, www.un.org/esa/policy/wess2007files/wesp2007.pdf Accessed 17 June 2009

Wade R (2008) Financial regime change? *New Left Review* 53:5–21

Walter A (2006) Domestic sources of international monetary leadership. In D M Andrews (ed) *International Monetary Power* (pp 62–93). Ithaca: Cornell University Press

Webber J (2009) China and Argentina in currency swap. *Financial Times* 31 March

Widmaier W W (2004) The social construction of the "Impossible Trinity": The intersubjective bases of monetary cooperation. *International Studies Quarterly* 48: 433–453

Wolf M (2009a) *Fixing Global Finance*. Baltimore: Johns Hopkins University Press

Wolf M (2009b) Seeds of its own destruction. *Financial Times* 9 March

Yardley J and Bradsher K (2008) China, an engine of growth, faces a global slump. *New York Times* 23 October

Pre-Black Futures

Katharyne Mitchell

Department of Geography, University of Washington, Seattle, WA, USA;
kmitch@u.washington.edu

Abstract: In this essay I look at the contemporary production of surplus life in liberal democracies, and how it manifests a new type of sovereign spatial power. This power operates through the capacity to exile individuals and populations who are defined—in advance—as risk failures. I investigate further the ways that these pre-known risk failures are determined through historical and geographical processes of racial formation, arguing that certain kinds of bodies have become vessels for concepts of risk formed in anticipation of an inevitable future. This "inevitable future" involves the formation of populations, which I term *Pre-Black*, who are projected as outside of the enabling web of pastoral power. Moreover, as a consequence of this pre-failure, individuals and populations can be forcefully and, more importantly, "justifiably" removed from commonly held spaces and resources in a contemporary liberal form of sovereign dispossession.

Keywords: risk, future, Pre-Black, surplus, sovereign, dispossession

Future Risk and Surplus Life

"Murder," says Agatha.

Lying suspended in a pool of opaque blue water, Agatha has visions of the future, visions which are then relayed to the pre-crime unit of the Washington DC police force. After piecing these visions together into a coherent narrative, the head of the unit, John Anderton, leads his detectives to the scene of the pre-murder, and arrests the killer before the crime has been committed. Thus begins Steven Spielberg's film, *Minority Report*, a story about the future, and about the seductive pleasures and dangers of trying to control it.[1]

The film reflects contemporary anxieties about the future, and how to balance presumed sources of risk with those of security. With an increasing sense that society can preempt certain kinds of risks because of greater technologies of fore-knowledge, the temptation to take anticipatory action—action made *before* a crime or other problem occurs, is great. Zedner (2007:262) writes of this new zeitgeist: "In important respects we are on the cusp of a shift from a post- to a precrime society, a society in which the possibility of forestalling risks competes with and even takes precedence over responding to wrongs done."

Antipode Vol. 41 No. S1 2009 ISSN 0066-4812, pp 239–261
doi: 10.1111/j.1467-8330.2009.00724.x
© 2009 The Author
Journal compilation © 2009 Editorial Board of *Antipode*.

Most contemporary concerns about securitizing the future focus on anticipatory action in relation to the protection of a valued life, that is, a life that is considered to be worth saving. Progress in medical research, consumer safety, crime control, and other areas, enhances security and the quality of human life in numerous ways, generally engaging the willing consent of populations aided by the new protections. However, as Anderson (forthcoming) aptly observes, "some life may have to be abandoned, damaged or destroyed in order to protect, save or care for other forms of life". My interest in this essay is in this surplus life; that which might have to be "abandoned" in the process of securitizing valued life. I investigate in particular what the production and abandonment of this surplus life tells us about the inter-relationship of differing forms of power in contemporary liberal democracies (cf Cooper 2008).

The surplus life is outside of the ethopolitical order of individualized risk, and is often neglected in scholarly studies of new forms of pastoral power. In a sympathetic critique of Nikolas Rose, for example, Braun (2007) has noted how an exclusive focus on contemporary forms of bio-governmentality potentially obscures emergent forms of sovereign power. Moreover, both authors underplay the critical role of political economy in the emergence of new forms of sovereignty, for example the multiple ways in which populations seemingly located "outside" the pastoral web of risk and care are, in fact, economically integral to the constitution of those located on the "inside" (Rajan 2007).[2]

Further, many governmentality studies similarly neglect the crucial spatial dimension of regulation, and the ways that differing forms of power are constituted by and reflect differing forms of spatial organization. While discipline orders through enclosure, segmentation, and limitation, sovereignty and security operate with different spatial logics. Elden (2007:29) writes:

> Discipline seeks to regulate everything while security seeks to regulate as little as possible, but in order to enable: discipline is isolating, working on measures of segmentation, while security seeks to incorporate, and distribute more widely. But Foucault is not simply proposing a linear narrative from a society of sovereignty to a disciplinary society to a society of government (governmental management) ... Conceiving of these three "societies" not on a linear model, but rather as a space of political action allows us to inject historical and geographical specificity into Foucault's narrative. Different places and different times might be closer to one node or another ...[3]

In this essay I look at the contemporary production of surplus life, and how it manifests a new type of sovereign spatial power, one based not on the right to corporeal control over life and death, as Foucault (1977) so graphically depicted in *Discipline and Punish*, or on the reduction of bodies to bare life, as enumerated by Agamben (1998), but on the conceptual and physical banishment of whole populations. My concern here is threefold: to begin a preliminary investigation of the constitution of contemporary surplus populations; to introduce some of the ways in which contemporary forms of "abandonment, damage and destruction" in the USA can and have opened up new avenues for the accumulation of surplus value; and to examine how these highly spatial forms of contemporary sovereign power—the power to exile—are legitimated and made palatable for the "valued" members of liberal democracies through particular conceptions of future risk.

What If? and *When/Then* Visions of the Future

I begin with two different understandings of future risk and our relationship to it: these are *what if?* and *when/then* scenarios. According to the cultural theorists Elmer and Opel (2006), *what if?* settings involve attempts to predict the future by using known or controllable elements in the present and extrapolating forward. "Accurate" future predictions are more likely to occur the more contemporary data are available, and the more that current events, processes and people can be controlled. If data are unstable or abstract or variable, the less likely it is that one can accurately predict future relationships—such as voting patterns or consumer choices (see also de Goede 2008; Dillon 2007).

In *what if?* worlds of risk management, institutional norms involve monitoring and surveillance, polling and tracking, and the constant simulation of different futures in an effort to shape contemporary variables. In comparison, *when/then* relationships to risk look quite different. *When/then* scenarios envision an inevitable future—one that is not massaged and privileged, but rather that is already knowable in advance. This kind of relationship to risk incorporates an authoritarian attitude of sovereign right and knowledge, as well as a spirit of fatalism, a sense that certain events cannot be avoided; specific futures are pre-seen and pre-made and the only planning that needs to be done is around how authority figures can best handle or mitigate those necessary future events and moments.

When/then scenarios generally have an apocalyptic tone, an end of the world sense of futility, a rhetorical gaze backward. *When* Armageddon comes *then* we must be prepared for it. To give a contemporary example, Tom Ridge, the first Homeland Security director, said about future terrorist attacks in the USA, post September 11th, "It's not a question of if, but when."[4] Risk, in this scenario, is handled by *knowing* the future, and by producing the resources to deal with that future and take complete (sovereign) authority and responsibility for it.

Spielberg's film is initially set in a *when/then* world. The future is known: a murder will happen. As a consequence of this pre-knowledge, state agents, specifically the police, are authorized to act both precipitously and violently, literally flying down from the sky to descend on the pre-murderer, subsequently banishing him to a lifetime of cataleptic existence. Yet as the film progresses, it becomes increasingly clear that the future is *not* inevitable or foreseeable—as the protagonist learns to his great angst and eventual atonement. Through knowledge of the future, Anderton is able to change it, and the film thus highlights self-will and human agency, plus the possibility of a minority report or *dissent*: incompatible visions of the future among those presumed to know it best.

Although a typically heart-warming Spielberg resolution,[5] this narrative of redemption through self-will is less critical to understand than what actually happens in the protagonist's initial fall from grace. When Anderton loses his status of *pre-knower of future risk*, it's not just a fall from authority that he encounters; it's also a fall out of risk and into exile. It's a highly spatial fall.

To understand this fall from grace, it's important to establish the futuristic *what if?* and *when/then* scenarios not as separate epistemes of risk and security but rather as operating simultaneously on a complex field of political actions and relations. This political field is articulated with global financial systems in important ways. *What if?* financial scenarios, for example, involve attempts to control uncertainty and create profitable investment climates by regulating and predicting future risk using mechanisms of simulation (eg "disaster" and "eureka" scenarios), stress testing, and other forms of accounting and assessment (de Goede 2005, 2008).

Many studies have been conducted that illustrate the ways that these types of everyday technologies of financial risk assessment also enable (and constrain) individuals in perpetuating and increasing their own life chances as rational, risk-taking actors (Martin 2002; Rose 1999a). According to Rose (1999b), the freedom to engage in these types of entrepreneurial ventures and to succeed or fail depending on one's rational calculation of risk is one of the hallmarks of advanced liberalism. *What if* worlds of risk management can thus be directly associated with the notion of neoliberal governmentality, forms of social control which engage individual and group consent through entrepreneurial enablement and economic self-improvement, through both "making live" and living better (cf Foucault 2008).

What if? conceptions of the future correspond with the development of modern *homo economicus* and taken-for-granted assumptions about risk, including who can manage it, and who should be its object (Read 2009). In comparison with these *what if?* worlds of a (self) managed, benchmarked, and constantly simulated "logical" economic future, the shift to near total deregulation, frenzied, pyramidal speculation, and made-to-fail mortgage loans of the twenty-first century exemplifies a *when/then* approach to the future.[6] In this case, the future is known; it is a future of total collapse. But this is a future endlessly deferred, at least for some, and at least as far as the next paycheck or the next investor brought into the Ponzi world of monopoly money. For elite risk-takers there is simultaneously total risk and no risk because there is no viable economic future beyond each individual's or bank's inverted pyramid of derivative return. *When/then* conceptions of the economic future do not privilege an expected outcome through the governance of variables and behaviors; they guarantee a known (but endlessly deferred) future through the assumption of sovereign pre-knowledge.[7]

In many cases this pre-known future rests on the assumption of "abandonment, damage and destruction" as well as deferral. In the financial sphere, for example, the "valued" economic life is protected through the production of surplus economic life, that is, specific risk-related failures on the part of a subset of the population. In the mortgage market these are exemplified by the mortgages that were pre-known to end in default (risk failure), one of many types of subprime loans which helped to build up the unstable but highly profitable world of banking and corporate securitization in the heady days of the early twenty-first century (Ashton 2009; Crump et al 2008; Wyly forthcoming; Wyly et al 2009).

In other areas of future risk, the constitution of *pre-known* risk failure can take many forms, and may or may not be directly linked with the creation of surplus value in the speculative world of contemporary finance capitalism. For example, in the deportation of asylum seekers, and the long-term incarceration or banishment of drug users, sex offenders, and minority youth, we can also see the production and exile of "surplus" populations, who become permanently positioned outside of systems of credit, labor, health, justice, and other regulatory institutions of enablement and constraint (Pettit and Western 2004; Western and Beckett 1999). While the removal of some of these populations may lead to situations of economic profitability, especially through the potential of accumulation by dispossession, these are not necessary outcomes, but rather contingent possibilities, which must be investigated empirically.[8]

In a sense, these populations are located "outside" of the normalizing mechanisms associated with risk, yet are integral to its contemporary futurist constitution.[9] While risk "failure" has always been a part of risk-taking, I am interested in the ways in which failure is now judged and "known" ahead of its actual occurrence in real time. Further, in liberal democracies, how do specific individuals and populations become positioned as these pre-known risk failures and hence subject to constitution as surplus?

Who will fail? I argue that who is determined to fail is bound up with historical and spatial processes of racial formation. Those who are perceived as able to take advantage of *what if?* scenarios and control them to privilege a certain future outcome are or become "White". Those who are drafted into *when/then* scenarios in positions other than state authority, are or become "Black". White and Black function, in this case, as analytical antipodes with respect to the shifting definitions of risk and identity produced by dominant elites—not on the basis of the physical or cultural characteristics of a given population (see eg Anderson 1991).

Of course these positions are often changing. As the Irish and other early immigrants to the USA could "become White" and Chinese immigrants of the twentieth century could be "Whitened" or "Blackened" by virtue of their degree of monetary success, it is evident that there are constant movements in the co-construction of risk and race (Ignatiev 1996; Ong 1999; Roediger 2007). Those who fail to manage risk successfully can move from White to Black positions and vice versa. However, it is even more complicated than this. Because we are concerned with the future, where in the *when/then* scenario the future is already known and inevitable, then certain bodies can also become, what I term, "Pre-Black". Just as "pre-protesters" were arrested before the increasingly unpopular President George Bush's visits to many cities in 2007, bodies can become vessels for concepts of risk that are formed in anticipation of an inevitable future. This future involves the formation of Pre-Black populations who are pre-known as risk failures, and hence projected as outside of the enabling web of pastoral power— as surplus. Moreover, as a consequence of this pre-failure, individuals and populations can be forcefully and, more importantly, "justifiably" removed from commonly held spaces and resources in a contemporary liberal form of sovereign dispossession.

I argue further that over the past decade or so, many populations formerly defined and coded as "at-risk" have moved from situations of monitoring, surveillance and the self responsibilization of risk, in the *what if?* scenarios of neoliberal governmentality, to positions of banishment and a conceptual and physical location "outside" of risk. In *when/then* worlds of future risk management, the individuals and populations who are "pre-known" as failures, misfits, and terrorists, can be removed from social and physical space before a "crime" has even occurred. In *when/then* scenarios we thus see direct sovereign control through the actual removal (exile, banishment, disappearance, abandonment) of individuals and populations formed as Black in anticipation of a known future. Pre-Black individuals and populations are increasingly positioned as surplus.

How does this happen? Racialization processes are contingent, but never random in the sense that any body can become White or Black in any context. As Omi and Winant (1994) remind us, racial formations aren't formed in a vacuum; they operate through layered histories, spaces, and relationships that produce and reproduce common sense, "taken for granted" ways of comprehending the world (cf Pred 2000). The *when/then* futuristic status of Pre-Blackness is constructed through time and in space and it is tied to labor relations, discursive performances, visual cues, financial policies, cultural practices, political tactics, media representations and specific physical locations that are part of ongoing hegemonic processes (cf Hart 2007). In the rest of the essay I offer two disparate illustrations of these processes in the contemporary era, highlighting the ways that individuals and populations who were once positioned as at-risk are increasingly located as risk failures in the context of an already known and spatially secured future.

Risky Schools: From a Nation at Risk, to No Child Left Behind

In 1983, at the request of Ronald Reagan's Secretary of Education, a report was published by the National Commission on Excellence in Education. This report, entitled, *A Nation at Risk: The Imperative for Educational Reform,* condemned what the authors perceived as manifold problems in the system of public education, and initiated a rhetoric of public school failure that has remained deeply ingrained in American popular discourse to the present day (National Commission on Excellence in Education 1983; Rothstein 1993).

One of the main themes of the report was the USA's declining competitiveness with Asia, a problem which the authors linked directly to deep inadequacies and flaws in the educational system. According to the report, the poor quality of public education was endangering children and the nation itself, leading to a crisis situation, a "rising tide of mediocrity" which called for immediate intervention and reform:

> Our Nation is at risk. Our once unchallenged preeminence in commerce, industry, science, and technological innovation is being overtaken by competitors throughout the world ... The educational foundations of our society are presently being eroded by a rising tide of mediocrity that threatens our very future as a Nation and a people (National Commission on Excellence in Education 1983:7).

The report's authors extolled data that seemed to indicate declining SAT test scores, and drew on anecdotal evidence claiming serious problems in the culture of public schooling in the USA. Despite a follow-up study that showed the test score data were amalgamated incorrectly and in fact did not show serious long-term decline, the news of American students' educational inadequacies hit the mainstream media and became accepted dogma over the next years and decades (Rothstein 1998).

Among the many indicators of risk mentioned in the *Nation at Risk* account, one that stood out as causing particular alarm was the risk of illiteracy among minority youth (at 40%). Others included low achievement on standardized tests, and complaints by business and military leaders that they were having to spend too much money on remedial education and training programs for their new hires and recruits (National Commission on Excellence in Education 1983:10).

The recommendations of the commission for improving the current state of affairs included the following: the need for higher standards and greater standardization in curricula and tests; the need for federal intervention to provide leadership and fiscal support out of the presumed mess of current educational systems; the need for greater surveillance and monitoring of "at risk" children and their parents (the concept of children at educational risk emerges out of this document); and the need for parents to become more responsible for their child's learning. The report hailed parents thus:

> Your right to a proper education for your children carries a double responsibility. As surely as you are your child's first and most influential teacher, your child's ideas about education and its significance begin with you. You must be a *living* example of what you expect your children to honor and to emulate. Moreover, you bear a responsibility to participate actively in your child's education (National Commission on Excellence in Education 1983:29; italics in original).

A Nation at Risk thus both produced a concept of school failure, and simultaneously located it as the fault and responsibility of teachers and parents. It re-introduced the concept of bad parenting as contributing to school failure, alongside poor teaching and inadequate penalties for lack of progress, and thereby reduced attention to wider problems of poverty and inequity.[10] It also succeeded in disciplining poor and minority families (especially women) for their lack of the proper cultural capital necessary for their children to succeed. Alongside the implicit rebuke for parental insufficiencies, the report recommended a stronger interventionist role for the federal government in shaping education and especially the "at-risk" children and families who were bringing it down.

Lubeck and Garret (1990:327) write of the concept of at-risk children, which escalated after this report's publication:

> The concept of children at risk defines the nature of the social problem: certain children are unable (or, in the case of pre-schoolers, will be unable) to avail themselves of the opportunities that schools present. The problem of poor school performance resides not in social, political, economic, and educational institutions, but rather in the child, and, by extension, in the family.

As with many Reagan-era reforms, race was a strong subtext in the creation of the "at risk" child and family.[11] In the *Nation at Risk* report, for example:

> at-risk status was defined as a function of inadequate educational outcomes. Thus, the report provided a logic for assigning at-risk status to members of demographic groups whose educational outcomes were routinely judged inadequate. Consequently, when in ongoing studies of race and achievement racial groups were shown to have poor or depressed educational outcomes (relative to other racial groups), they were subsumed under the at-risk label ... (O'Connor, Hill and Robinson 2009:1).

As a result of this particular form of logic, at-risk status was and remains associated with minority groups, and is often unquestioningly accepted as an internalized trait of these populations.

A Nation at Risk marks the beginning of classic forms of governmentality in education. We can see the devolution of responsibility to the individual and the family and the constant admonitions for greater self control and competitive spirit; we can see the promotion of the educational "expert" to step in and provide necessary controls and interventions, most of which are aimed to help individuals and families understand their cultural failings and necessity for self-improvement; and, of course, in order for experts to measure success in these endeavors, we can see the call for standardization and benchmarking, combined with continual monitoring and surveillance. How much improvement has there been? One needs constant tests and scores to find out. Hence the schools must measure and simulate and predict in order to be sure of their degree of advancement, and in order to be held accountable for their successes and failures over the long term.

A Nation at Risk is among the many early *what if?* moments of risk control that were so intensely profitable in 1980s neoliberalism. It involved the production, identification and management of "at-risk" populations (in this case mostly poor, black children and women), and profited on it and on them in many different ways. In addition to a proliferation of educational aids, test-prep programs and training centers outside of the school system,[12] numerous for-profit charter schools and other educational corporations got a boost from increasing parental anxiety about the failures of both the public school system, as well as their own potential responsibility for the failings of their children.

High Stakes Testing

In comparison with this Reagan era discourse and mandates, the 2002 Act entitled *No Child Left Behind* (NCLB) manifests a different set of calculations around risk, profit, and control. Part of a wider movement often called "standards-based education", it initially attracted some progressive educators and politicians with the idea that setting high standards and establishing measurable goals for all students would improve individual outcomes in education, including for minority children.[13]

NCLB greatly increased the federal role in controlling and policing education vis-à-vis teacher training programs, curriculum design and testing, and most importantly, the allocation of funding. Like the reforms that were initiated following the publication of *A Nation at Risk*, NCLB advocated more standardized testing and other generalizable measures of assessment and accountability, but it also added a new element commonly known as high-stakes testing.

High-stakes testing refers to the increasingly harsh repercussions for those students and schools that do not perform well on standardized examinations. For example, students who do not pass specific tests, including required high-school exit exams in many states, are kept back a grade or not permitted to graduate. Further, if schools with significant numbers of "low-performing" students fail to show improvement in these test scores over time, they are denied federal funding in subsequent years. Since there was inadequate federal funding, if any, given to low-performing schools to help them improve initially, this highly punitive tactic to force compliance often produced the opposite effect of what progressive educators had hoped for initially; it often led to the failure or displacement of greater numbers of poor, minority, immigrant, and disabled children, the preemptive grade retention of low-performing children, the substitution away from low-stakes subjects such as social studies and music, and increasing suspension and expulsion rates nationwide for these same populations (Jacob 2005; Orfield, Losen and Wald 2004; Sternberg 2006).

High-stakes testing involves the possibility of total failure, along with direct retribution for that failure—the loss of institutional funding and teachers' jobs. The failure, moreover, is no longer considered to be primarily the concern of parents and children; it has also become the responsibility of the school and the teachers and staff and even the whole community neighborhood in which the school is situated. Determining and managing risk thus becomes the responsibility of local education systems, which must engage high-stakes risk on their own.

Some of the direct results of NCLB's high-stakes testing regime have included the firing or non-hiring of bilingual, often minority teachers considered unqualified under the new rules, the loss of courses, teachers and ideas not judged to be important for exam preparation (these include civics, art, music, geography, languages, science, and history, among others), and importantly, the rapid escalation in the numbers of children held back, suspended and expelled from public schools. The latter impact indicates the gradual exile of non-performing children from public school systems. These children are considered undesirable because of their poor performance on standard examinations or their presumed social misbehavior, and they are often not permitted to graduate, frequently suspended, or are shuffled from school to school until they end up dropping out altogether (Giroux 2004).

The rise in suspensions and expulsions is also attributable to the so-called zero tolerance regulations that have mushroomed in school districts around the country. "Zero tolerance" is a discourse and set of practices that refer to a harsh and highly punitive response to social misbehavior. Initially the term was used primarily in relation to drug enforcement, but it has become more widely known in recent years with respect to social control practices in schools and cities. In public school systems, the idea was originally advanced to punish students who brought firearms to school, but it quickly began to include any kind of "bad" behavior, including smoking, drug use, threats, and fighting. To counteract the threat of this misbehavior, schools often employed a greater police presence alongside the introduction of stricter rules and regulations. This increased police presence, combined with the new extraordinarily harsh punishments and limited flexibility for educators and administrators to provide any context for various school infractions, led to increasing numbers of student expulsions, suspensions and incarcerations, predominantly of poor youth of color (Casella 2003; Giroux 2001; Verdugo 2002).[14]

Evidence from research and advocacy groups indicate that expelled children are overwhelmingly from impoverished schools and school districts with high percentages of minority students, and that there are few avenues back from this particular form of exile (Carroll 2008). These are the institutional spaces that prefigure and constitute Blackness, and in this process of expulsion and banishment, it is possible to witness the formation of Pre-Black children through time. These children are constituted as low performers by virtue of their residence in particular kinds of impoverished school spaces, and these school spaces are then (re)produced as failing locations in a mutually constitutive process. With the introduction of high-stakes testing following the passage of the NCLB Act in 2002, their Pre-Black bodies are increasingly positioned outside of risk, as surplus, and they are essentially banished from the system, and eventually from society itself.

When the students fail. The future is known: the students will fail. Thus the school moves them from *what if?* scenarios of expert intervention and self-responsibilization to a place outside of risk—to exile. This *when/then* world of risk management manifests the politics of individual institutional survival.[15] As many education critics have noted, the discursive and material production of failure is one thread in a much larger conservative agenda of privatizing the assets and resources of public education (Burch 2006; Kohn 2004; Meier and Wood 2004;

Weiner 2005). With the ongoing discourse of public school failure, alongside the actual physical removal, through exile, of low-performing children, the promulgation of voucher programs and charter schools gets a decided boost. It is possible thus to see in NCLB a move from *what if?* future worlds to *when/then* scenarios of sovereign pre-knowledge and corporeal control, as well as a particularly transparent form of incipient accumulation through dispossession.

Risky Streets: From the Urban Underclass to Trespass Zoning

The idea of an urban underclass in the USA gained momentum with the publication of a *Time* article in 1977 entitled "The American underclass" (*Time Magazine* 1977). The piece was one of a number of cover stories in both *Time* and *Newsweek* during the post-war period through the 1990s, which focused on the issue of urban crime and linked it almost exclusively to black men (Barlow 1998). According to Barlow (1998) and Chambliss (1995), the issue of crime and lawlessness was not widely perceived as a major social problem until the mid 1960s, when conservative politicians and the news media successfully linked the concept of crime to racial unrest and civil rights struggles in the cities. The *Time* story of 1977 is notable for this exact type of conflation, which Barlow (1998:149) argues "cement(ed) the link between 'young black males' and crime forever" (see also Katz 1993).

In the article the authors evoked a specter of future risk and danger notable for both its strong language and its urban images of danger and decay.

> The barricades are seen only fleetingly by most middle-class Americans as they rush by in their cars or commuter trains—doors locked, windows closed, moving fast. But out there is a different world, a place of pock-marked streets, gutted tenements and broken hopes ... Behind its crumbling walls lives a large group of people who are more intractable, more socially alien and more hostile than almost anyone had imagined. They are the unreachables: the American underclass (*Time Magazine* 1977:1).

This intractable, alien, and hostile population was presented to *Times*-reading middle-class Americans as a dangerous inner city element that should be addressed through both stronger controls and incentives—such as employment, as well as through transforming an internalized culture of welfare dependency. The supposed welfarist mentality of this at-risk population was invoked repeatedly with anecdotes about women "turn(ing) illegitimate pregnancy into a virtual career" and quotes such as "If you keep giving people stuff, that's why they loot when the lights go out. Working is out of their minds. They think everything must be taken" (*Time Magazine* 1977:7).

The race of this underclass population was made explicit in many sections of the essay: "Though its members come from all races and live in many places, the underclass is made up mostly of impoverished urban blacks..." and the menacing aspect of this group was also evident in lines such as the following: "Rampaging members of the underclass carried out much of the orgy of looting and burning that swept New York's ghettos during the July blackout. They are responsible for most of the youth crime that has spread like an epidemic through the nation" (1977:2). Both alarmist and patronizing, the essay drew on earlier arguments by erstwhile liberals such as Daniel Moynihan (1981 [1965]), who wrote in 1965 about the cultural deficiencies of African American families, and by the anthropologist Oscar Lewis (1975 [1959]), who furthered arguments about the development of a value system and plethora of alienated and powerless feelings amongst the poor, a "culture of poverty", which hopelessly mired them in unchangingly bad conditions.

These ideas took root in urban policy rhetoric and programs during the Reagan era of the 1980s. Charles Murray's influential 1984 book, *Losing Ground*, appropriated the earlier liberal arguments about cultural entrapment to argue for stronger "expert" intervention in urban inner city areas in the form of corrective actions, policing, and law enforcement. For Murray and other conservative critics, urban blacks were at risk of anti-social behavior because of a permissive and lenient society which provided "incentives to fail" (Murray 1984:154). He believed that effective forms of deterrence waned in the 1960s because of an overly generous culture of remediation and welfare rather than punishment. For the conservatives of this era, arguments about inequity or a structural lack of opportunity deflected attention from the "real" problems of cultural and personal deficiencies and poor individual choices for advancement, employment, and regimes of personal self-fashioning.

The 1980s thus ushered in the era of responsibilization and criminalization of drug use, homelessness, and of poverty itself. In the *what if?* world of the urban underclass, inner city neighborhoods were (re)produced as sites at-risk for the development of a culture of urban poverty and a lack of residential responsibility among the populations who lived there.[16] As with the focus on at-risk schools, the notion of at-risk streets was deeply racialized, with specific neighborhoods and their inhabitants pathologized as culturally deficient and socially deviant (Barlow 1998). Problems were located in the individual rather than in wider structural forces, and profit on these individuals was possible from the resolution of those problems through welfare to work policies, and other "up by the bootstraps" types of programs and punishments, many of which continued through the 1990s (Peck 2001).

In addition to the profitable world of "expert" intervention in standard institutions of policing, social programs, and incarceration, the production of these at-risk streets and populations opened up numerous opportunities for speculative profit-making in cities through urban revitalization and real estate. Many urban scholars, for example, have demonstrated the connection between the invocation of fear, disorder and decay in certain New York neighborhoods and the subsequent "rehabilitation" and gentrification of these same districts, a process generally benefiting a limited number of elite investors and developers (Abu-Lughod 1995; Delaney 2001; Smith 2002). Similarly, the rise of the industrial prison apparatus, as Gilmore (2007) and Parenti (1999) have shown, produced the potential for soaking up excess capital and for profit-making in numerous other sites and venues.

  Losing Ground, and other popular and media texts of the 1980s era of neoliberal ideology and policy, helped to codify post-riot assumptions about risky Black streets and at-risk urban populations. The constant invocation of family and personal responsibility for neighborhoods aided in the conservative attack on welfare and other forms of socially oriented government intervention, and boosted the drive towards more punitive forms of urban social control. The production of "at-risk" streets and urban populations was racially coded in numerous ways, with the most predominant assumptions linking welfare to black women, and "raging" violence to black men. Both kinds of status were associated with personal failure, and the necessity for correction of this failure through greater expert supervision, monitoring, and law enforcement, as well as through the devolution of responsibility for neighborhood "improvement"—often through the call for greater democratic participation—to individuals and communities (Cruikshank 1999).

High-Stakes Trespassing
In contrast with the disciplining and governmentalizing production of at-risk urban populations through the discourse of the urban underclass, trespass zoning is a relatively new form of social control practice which effectively extends sovereign rights through spatial exclusion. Taking root mainly over the last decade, trespass ordinances of various kinds have become increasingly common across many American cities, and include parks exclusion laws, off-limits orders, drug exclusion zones, and generalized restrictions such as lying down in public spaces or sitting on the sidewalk (Beckett and Herbert 2009).

  Trespass zoning combines the principles of zoning with private property "no trespass" laws. While zoning has normally been used to denote acceptable usages of buildings and property within a specific area, trespass zoning includes the acceptable users of that property as well. Flanagan (2003:328) writes, "By identifying individuals, either by name or criminal pedigree, cities employ 'people-based zoning,' making the presence of such individuals in designated zones punishable as criminal trespass."

Many of these types of contemporary regulations permit law enforcement authorities to "trespass" previous offenders such as prostitutes or drug abusers from certain kinds of public spaces, including libraries, parks, schools, and social service agencies, for extended periods of time. According to Beckett and Herbert (2008:10), these admonishments can be sustained without evidence of current social misbehavior, and "there is no mechanism for appealing one's trespass admonishment". In some cases, "parks exclusion statutes authorize city officials to ban people who are alleged to have broken park rules from all city parks for up to a year".

Numerous municipalities have begun to employ these exclusions, often by designating "drug exclusion zones" or "prostitution free zones" where individuals who have been arrested for these types of offenses previously may no longer go. Reputedly liberal cities such as Seattle and Portland have been at the forefront of these kinds of exclusions by zoning, both adopting versions of these laws in the late 1990s. Other cities as diverse as Cincinnati, Tampa, Richmond and Knoxville have adopted similar ordinances, some focusing on trespass in public housing sites, others on city streets and parks (Goldstein 2003; Mitchell 2005). Flanagan (2003:329) writes approvingly of these types of ordinances: "To be apprehended, the excluded individual need not engage in criminal activity, nor even be suspected of it. Rather, it is the individual's mere presence in a particular area that offends."

The newly adapted trespass laws extend the rights of property owners and reduce those who rely on public spaces and institutions in two main ways: by including erstwhile public spaces as zones of potential exclusion, and by excluding people from these spaces over extended periods of time. While private property owners have always held the right to deny access to their *own* property to those considered objectionable, in a number of cities that right now extends to public spaces such as sidewalks or streets. Moreover, those who are "asked to leave a particular space" can be "banned from that space—which can be defined quite expansively—for extended periods of time" (Beckett and Herbert 2008:11). Often these banishments actually cover areas far greater than the initial space from which the individual was removed, possibly extending, for example, to *all* of the city's parks or public housing or metro stops.

These trespass ordinances and other civil statutes effectively banish individuals without due process and often before a crime has even been committed. People are spatially removed from certain public locations on the basis of sovereign pre-knowledge of crime and failure. This "knowledge" comes from the *status* of the person as previous miscreant:

drug user, homeless, prostitute, etc, as well as the associated space in which the person is located: back alley, park, loading dock.

The racialized component of trespass zoning is evident statistically. In Portland, for example, data released by the police bureau indicate that the city's drug and prostitution-free zones primarily exclude African Americans. The bureau's statistics, cited in the *Portland Mercury,* show that "between June 1 and October 31 of 2006, a total of 790 arrests were made in exclusion zones. Of those, 326—or 41 percent—were white, while 398—or 50 percent—were African American, despite the fact that African Americans make up only slightly more than 6 percent of the Portland population". Even more disturbing, of those arrested, 58.6% of the whites were given exclusions, whereas for African Americans, the exclusion rate was 100% (Moore and Davis 2007). These types of racial disparities are mirrored in Seattle's trespass exclusion statistics as well (Beckett and Herbert 2009).

What's crucial to observe here is that individuals can be exiled from numerous city spaces *before* they have done anything. Merely by having been accused of civil misbehavior in the past, and being in a specific space of personal exclusion, they are criminalized and at risk of incarceration or further exile should they return. As with the spaces of failing schools, marginalized (but often gentrifying) spaces and "deviant" populations interact and constitute each other in a mutually iterative process.

Similarly, as in the example of zero tolerance in the public schools, high-stakes trespassing is undergirded by zero tolerance approaches to social deviance. In cities such as New York, for example, these practices have involved a stronger police presence on the streets, the increased harassment of people of color, particularly African American men, and the massive incarceration of poor and homeless populations for minor social infractions.[17]

The rhetoric and practices of zero tolerance are among the many hegemonic processes which have helped to produce and codify risky streets and populations. Using computer-aided mapping and simulation programs such as Compstat, the police can profile specific areas of the city with high rates of crime and social infractions. As "risky" streets come into being as analytical objects, they can be monitored and surveyed both "at a distance" and also on the ground, through new geovisualization and other computer technologies and also through increased police presence and law enforcement on the streets.

The link to pre-known spaces of failure is crucial as it both constitutes Pre-Blackness (being in the wrong alley or park with the wrong kind of body), and it also provides the punishment—exile from those spaces. Through practices of evacuation and exemption such as these, the racialized populations of stigmatized streets and spaces are banished from society. They are both physically removed and effectively expelled from the rights and protections of citizenship through their loss of due process in law.

Again we can see Pre-Black formation by status and spatial location. And, as in previous eras, this formation potentially opens new channels for elite accumulation through dispossession. With specific populations banished from specific parts of the city, the opportunities for privatization, or various forms of public–private partnerships are greatly increased.[18]

Socially marginal, inner-city populations are located as outside of risk, as surplus. Whereas in previous decades, reputed cultural deficiencies positioned these populations and individuals as at-risk of failure, and liberals and conservatives alike promoted greater self-sufficiency and participatory practices in democracy and in the marketplace (with greater punishments for non-compliance advocated by conservatives), contemporary no-trespass ordinances and zones of exclusion mark both literal and metaphorical limits to the "conduct of conduct". In contemporary trespass admonishments, Pre-Black populations are positioned as pre-known failures. The removal of these groups in anticipation of future failure indicates the pre-emption of governmentalizing modes of consent, and an extension of sovereign power through time as well as across space.

Conclusion

What do we call this emergent form of regulation through exile, functioning not in lieu of, but alongside ongoing technologies of governmentality? Is this a form of direct, corporeal sovereignty based on the authority to control time as well as territory? A kind of power concerned with actual physical removal—the banishment of Pre-Black bodies—*before* a crime (risk failure) has even occurred? Is this exile made palatable in liberal regimes by *when/then* assumptions of sovereign pre-knowledge and a corresponding right to total authority?

In *what if?* scenarios, outcomes that are more predictable are more likely to realize a profit, and predictability is more likely to occur if contemporary variables are controlled and managed. The more predictable, privileged future is one where at-risk populations are both constrained and enabled, thus enhancing the likelihood of a certain kind of future, and at the same time facilitating the creation of value through the production of institutions of social constraint and productive enablement.

In *when/then* worlds we see the emergence of a different field of control, and a new assemblage of power. Financial risk is endlessly deferred for some, and unavailable for others, who are positioned outside of risk, yet integral to its constitution. The opportunity for profit to be made from exiled populations is also possible (although not functionally determined), but in new ways, potentially through accumulation by dispossession, or, in different parts of the world, through a different logic of "letting die" (Li 2009, this issue).

I end this essay with a return to *Minority Report*. The film is set in Washington DC in the year 2054. There are images of futuristic architecture and an antiseptic commercial city life, and the tone is white, hushed, and clinical. The theme of the movie is crime-fighting, and the city is one with a current demographic profile of a non-white majority, yet the issue of "race" is present only through its almost complete absence. The only non-white person in the entire film is the co-worker of John Anderton, who, interestingly, is one of four characters who eventually believes and helps him, a process which leads to his ultimate redemption.

Who are these four characters that enable the hero's atonement? They are the only three women in the film, and the only Black man. Who can restore John Anderton, the White man, a metonym for civilization itself, to wholeness, after the disastrous move to clinical silence and futuristic soul-destroying fatalism? Women and people of color, populations that, according to Haraway (1990), are chosen to perform this function because of their "primitive" status as entities both farther from science and closer to nature.

In the formation of children and urban populations outside of risk we can thus see the construction of Pre-Black populations as possible sites of accumulation through exile and dispossession; but in this film we can also see these populations as potential "reserve" sites of redemption and atonement. In the case that *when/then* futurist knowledge and apocalyptic thinking goes too far and threatens the wholeness of white men, there's a fall-back location, the return to the pure and untarnished individuals located outside of the corrupt game of entrepreneurial risk.

What do we need to do to avoid these dangerous futures? We need to investigate and speak of the racialization of risk in the everyday practices and codings that exist around us—past, present, and future. We need to see the intersections of governmentality, discipline, and sovereignty in multiple new and emergent forms in the spatial organizations of the contemporary era. And we need to embrace a theoretical analytic that enables us to work with both Foucault and Marx and their respective legacies: avoiding purist, functionalist, and reductionist arguments and positions, and remaining informed by concrete bodies and practices, in real times and places. Only then do we take the risk of imagining a different future.

Endnotes

[1] The film is based on a 1956 short story by Philip K. Dick.

[2] Matt Sparke, for example, studies the ways in which the highly profitable pharmaceutical industry has drafted populations in various locations in the global South,

into patient studies directly benefiting the individualized health risk managers of the global North. A political economy reading of this type, involving articulations of power in specific class interests, is rarely spelled out in most governmentality studies. See Sparke M and Ruddy L (nd) Bird flu biopolitics and the emergent geopolitics of global health. Manuscript under review. Cited with authors' permission.

[3] Elden is working with Foucault (2004) here.

[4] Quoted in Elmer and Opel (2006:481).

[5] See Weber (2005) for an interesting feminist critique of this familial resolution.

[6] See Martin (2007) for an insightful analysis of the (il)logic of twenty-first century speculative capitalism and its connection to a future and a war endlessly deferred. With respect to the rise of subprime mortgage loans, which were made in full knowledge that they would end in default, see Wyly (forthcoming) and Wyly et al (2009).

[7] The classic Ponzi scheme of the twenty-first century is exemplified in the Bernard Madoff case. Here the main perpetrator, Madoff himself, was well aware that his economic empire was built on fictitious capital, and that the entire edifice could continue only as long as new investors were brought into the scheme. Most of these investors, however, remained deliberately ignorant of how the Madoff investments were making such "unbelievable" returns on their money, choosing to rely on the sovereign authority of Madoff to "guarantee" a future of high investment return, well beyond what a rational *what if?* risk-taker would imagine as within the realm of economic possibility.

[8] In many instances, the social and spatial resources left behind by these dispossessed groups are accumulated by dominant "risk-taking" social groups. However, as Tania Li points out (this issue), in some cases accumulation does not immediately follow dispossession. In parts of the global South, for example, dispossessed populations are rendered as surplus and allowed to "let die", a process which involves a different form of future risk assessment and intervention.

[9] A position "outside of risk", as I use it here, does not refer to a location somehow unrelated to risk, but rather, through forming its conceptual outside, it is *integral* to risk's constitution. The hyper-speculative risk of advanced liberalism is a (self) confidence game that is buoyed and enabled by the knowledge of guaranteed failure . . . for others. Further, those populations and individuals increasingly falling outside of risk create new possibilities for dispossession and entrepreneurial risk-taking, some examples of which I illustrate below.

[10] Locating children's learning problems in deficient parenting and other social-psychological factors has a long history in American schooling. Prior to the concept of the "at-risk" child there was the culturally deprived child, the socially maladjusted child and the biologically inferior child, most of whom were the children of the poor and people of color. See Lubeck and Garret (1990).

[11] For some other examples see Paul Krugman (2007a). See also Krugman (2007b).

[12] Some examples: Kumon Math and Reading Centers, The Princeton Review, Kaplan Test Prep, ACT Test Prep, HELP Math for ELL, etc.

[13] For example, Massachusetts senator Ted Kennedy's support for NCLB was evident in his foreword to a 2006 special issue of the *Harvard Educational Review* on the legacy of the Act. See issue 76(4):1–3.

[14] Often the school infractions resulting in suspensions or total expulsions were as minor as shouting and pushing in line, or sharing medicated lemon drops.

[15] Elmer and Opel (2006) argue that the authoritarian impulse behind *when/then* futurist scenarios leads to the suppression of dissent and the rise of a politics of individualized survival.

[16] As with schooling, this narrative of cultural failure has a long history. In the progressive era, spatial and cultural deprivation was associated primarily with the working poor and immigrants. See Katz (1993) and Reed (1990).

[17] For national-level statistics on the increased incarceration rates of African Americans, see Gilmore (2007); for statistics on racial disparities in NYC marijuana arrests, see Golub, Johnson and Dunlap (2007); with respect to the disproportionate stopping and frisking of young men of color in both minority and predominantly white neighborhoods in New York City, see Rudovsky (2001).

[18] Exactly how or where this might take place, however, must be subject to empirical investigation.

References

Abu-Lughod J (1995) *From Urban Village to East Village: The Battle for New York's Lower East Side.* Oxford: Blackwell Publications

Agamben G (1998) *Homo Sacer: Sovereign Power and Bare Life.* Palo Alto: Stanford University Press

Anderson B (forthcoming) Preemption, precaution, preparedness: anticipatory action and the future. *Progress in Human Geography*

Anderson K (1991) *Vancouver's Chinatown: Racial Discourse in Canada 1875–1980.* Montreal: McGill-Queen's University Press

Ashton P (2009) An appetite for yield: the anatomy of the subprime mortgage crisis. *Environment & Planning A* 41(6):1420–41

Barlow M (1998) Race and the problem of crime in "Time" and "Newsweek" cover stories, 1946–1995. *Social Justice* 25(2):149–174

Beckett K and Herbert S (2008) Dealing with disorder: Social control in the post-industrial city. *Theoretical Criminology* 12(1):5–30

Beckett K and Herbert S (2009) *Banished: The New Social Control in Urban America.* Oxord: Oxford University Press

Braun B (2007) Biopolitics and the molecularization of life. *Cultural Geographies* 14:6–28

Burch P (2006) The new educational privatization: Educational contracting and high stakes accountability. *Teachers College Record* 108(12):2582–2610

Carroll M (2008) Educating expelled students after No Child Left Behind: Mending an incentive structure that discourages alternate education and reinstatement. *UCLA Law Review* 55(6):1909–1969

Casella R (2003) Zero tolerance policy in schools: Rationale, consequences, and alternatives. *Teachers College Record* 105(5):872–892

Chambliss W (1995) Crime control and ethnic minorities: legitimizing racial oppression by creating moral panics. In D Hawkins (ed) *Ethnicity, Race, and Crime* (pp 235–258). Albany: SUNY Press

Cooper M (2008) *Life as Surplus: Biotechnology and Capitalism in the Neoliberal Era.* Seattle: University of Washington Press

Cruikshank B (1999) *The Will to Empower: Democratic Citizens and other Subjects.* Ithaca: Cornell University Press

Crump J, Newman K, Belsky E, Ashton P, Kaplan D, Hammel D and Wyly E (2008) Cities destroyed (again) for cash: Forum on the US foreclosure crisis. *Urban Geography* 29(8):745–784

de Goede M (2005) *Virtue, Fortune and Faith: A Genealogy of Finance.* Minneapolis, MN: University of Minnesota Press

de Goede M (2008) Beyond risk. *Security Dialogue* 39(2–3):155–176

Delaney S (2001) *Times Square Red: Times Square Blue.* New York: New York University Press

Dillon M (2007) Governing through contingency. *Political Geography* 26(1):41–47

Elden S (2007) Rethinking governmentality. *Political Geography* 26(1):29–33

Elmer G and Opel A (2006) Surviving the inevitable future: Preemption in an age of faulty intelligence. *Cultural Studies* 20(4–5):477–492

Flanagan P (2003) Trespass-zoning: Ensuring neighborhoods a safer future by excluding those with a criminal past. *Notre Dame Law Review* 79:328–329

Foucault M (1977) *Discipline and Punish: The Birth of the Prison*. Alan Sheridan (trans). New York: Vintage Books

Foucault M (2004) *Sécurité, Territoire, Population: Cours au Collège de France 1977–1978*. Michel Senellart (ed). Paris: Seuil/Gallimard (pp 13–23 translated by G Burchell in *Political Geography* 2007, 26(1) as "Spaces of security: The example of the town. Lecture of 11th January 1978")–

Foucault M (2008) *The Birth of Biopolitics: Lectures at the College of France, 1978–1979*. Basingstoke: Palgrave Macmillan

Gilmore R (2007) *The Golden Gulag: Prisons, Surplus, Crisis and Opposition in Globalizing California Crossroads*. Berkeley: University of California Press

Giroux H (2001) Mis/education and zero tolerance: Disposable youth and the politics of domestic militarization. *boundary 2* 28(3):61–94

Giroux H (2004) *The Abandoned Generation: Democracy Beyond the Culture of Fear*. Basingstoke: Palgrave Macmillan

Goldstein E (2003) Kept out: Responding to public housing no-trespass policies. *Harvard Civil Rights-Civil Liberties Journal* 38:216–248

Golub A, Johnson B and Dunlap E (2007) The race/ethnicity disparity in misdemeanor marijuana arrests in New York City. *Criminology & Public Policy* 6(1):131–164

Haraway D (1990) *Primate Visions: Gender, Race and Nature in the World of Modern Science*. London: Routledge

Hart G (2007) Changing concepts of articulation: Political stakes in South Africa today. *Review of African Political Economy* 111:85–101

Ignatiev N (1996) *How the Irish Became White*. London: Routledge

Jacob B (2005) Accountability, incentives and behavior: The impact of high-stakes testing in the Chicago Public Schools. *Journal of Public Economics* 89(5–6):761–796

Katz M (1993) *The "Underclass" Debate: Views from History*. Princeton: Princeton University Press

Kohn A (2004) Test today, privatize tomorrow. *Phi Delta Kappan* April: 1–13

Krugman P (2007a) *The Conscience of a Liberal*. London: W W Norton and Company

Krugman P (2007b) Republicans and race. *New York Times* 19 November, http://www.nytimes.com/2007/11/19/opinion/19krugman.html Accessed 27 June 2009

Lewis O (1975 [1959]) *Five Families: Mexican Case Studies in the Culture of Poverty*. New York: Basic Books

Li T (2009) To make live or let die? Rural dispossession and the protection of surplus population. *Antipode* 41(6):

Lubeck S and Garret P (1990) The social construction of the "at-risk" child. *British Journal of Sociology of Education* 11(3):337–338

Martin R (2002) *Financialization of Daily Life*. Philadelphia: Temple University Press

Martin R (2007) *An Empire of Indifference: American War and the Financial Logic of Risk Management*. Durham: Duke University Press

Meier D and Wood G (2004) *Many Children Left Behind: How the No Child Left Behind Act is Damaging Our Children and Our Schools*. Boston: Beacon

Mitchell D (2005) Property rights, the first amendment, and judicial anti-urbanism: The strange case of Hicks v. Virginia. *Urban Geography* 26(7):565–586

Moore S and Davis M (2007) Black exclusion zones: Are drug-free zones targeting African Americans?" *Portland Mercury* 8 March, http://www.portlandmercury.com/portland/Content?oid=273589&category=22101 Accessed 6 July 2009

Moynihan D (1981 [1965]) *The Negro Family: The Case for National Action*. Santa Barbara: Greenwood

Murray C (1984) *Losing Ground: American Social Policy 1950–1980*. New York: Basic Books

National Commission on Excellence in Education (1983) *A Nation at Risk: The Imperative for Educational Reform*. Washington: Government Printing Office, http://www.mat.uc.pt/~emsa/PMEnsino/ANationatRisk.pdf Accessed 30 June 2009

O'Connor C, Hill L and Robinson S (2009) Who's at risk in school and what's race got to do with it? *Review of Research in Education* 33(1):1–34

Omi H and Winant M (1994) *Racial Formation in the United States: From the 1960s to the 1990s*. London: Routledge

Ong A (1999) *Flexible Citizenship: The Cultural Logics of Transnationality*. Durham: Duke University Press

Orfield G, Losen D and Wald L (2004) *Losing our Future: How Minority Youth are Being Left Behind by the Graduation Rate Crisis*. Cambridge: The Civil Rights Project at Harvard University

Parenti C (1999) *Lockdown America: Police and Prisons in the Age of Crisis*. London: Verso

Peck J (2001) *Workfare States*. New York: Guilford Press

Pettit B and Western B (2004) Mass imprisonment and the life course: Race and inequality in U.S. incarceration. *American Sociological Review* 69:151–169

Pred A (2000) *Even in Sweden: Racisms, Racialized Spaces, and the Popular Geographic Imagination*. Berkeley: University of California Press

Rajan K (2007) *Biocapital: The Constitution of Postgenomic Life*. Durham: Duke University Press

Read J (2009) A genealogy of homo-economicus: Neoliberalism and the production of subjectivity. *Foucault Studies* 6:25–36

Reed A (1990) The underclass as myth and symbol: The poverty of discourse about poverty. *Radical America* 24:21–40

Roediger D (2007) *The Wages of Whiteness*. London: Verso

Rose N (1999a) *Governing the Soul: The Shaping of the Private Self*. London: Free Association Books

Rose N (1999b) *Powers of Freedom*. Cambridge: Harvard University Press

Rothstein R (1993) The myth of public school failure. *American Prospect* 21 March, http://www.prospect.org/cs/articles?article=the_myth_of_public_school_failure Accessed 30 June 2009

Rothstein R (1998) *The Way We Were? Myths and Realities of America's Student Achievement*. New York: The Century Foundation

Rudovsky D (2001) Law enforcement by stereotypes and serendipity: Racial profiling and stops and searches without cause. *University of Pennsylvania Journal of Constitutional Law* 3(298):296–366

Smith N (2002) New urbanism: Gentrification as global urban strategy. In N Brenner and N Theodore (eds) *Spaces of Neoliberalism: Urban Restructuring in North America* (pp 427–450). Oxford: Blackwell

Sternberg B (2006) Real improvement for real students: Test smarter, serve better. *Harvard Educational Review* 76(4):557–563

Time Magazine (1977) The American underclass. *Time Magazine* 29 August, http://www.time.com/time/magazine/article/0,9171,915331,00.html Accessed 5 July 2009

Verdugo R (2002) Race-ethnicity, social class and zero-tolerance policies: The cultural and structural wars. *Education and Urban Society* 35(1):50–75

Weber C (2005) Securitising the unconscious: The Bush doctrine of preemption and Minority Report. *Geopolitics* 10(3):482–499

Weiner L (2005) Neoliberalism, unionism, and the future of public education. *New Politics* 10(2), http://www.wpunj.edu/newpcl/issue38/weiner38.htm (last accessed 27 October 2009)

Western B and Beckett K (1999) How unregulated is the U.S. labor market? The penal system as a labor market institution. *American Journal of Sociology* 104:1030–1060

Wyly E (forthcoming) The subprime state of race. In S J Smith (ed) *The Blackwell Companion to the Housing Wealth of Nations*. Oxford: Blackwell

Wyly E, Moos M, Hammel D and Kabahizi E (2009) Cartographies of race and class: Mapping the class monopoly rents of American subprime mortgage capital. *International Journal of Urban and Regional Research* 33(2):332–354

Zedner L (2007) Pre-crime and post criminology? *Theoretical Criminology* 11(2):261–281

The Shape of Capitalism to Come

Paul Cammack

Department of Politics and Philosophy, Manchester Metropolitan University,
Manchester, UK;
p.cammack@mmu.ac.uk

Abstract: The starting point for this paper is the observation that a reshaping of global capitalism is underway, centred on the rise of dynamic centres of accumulation in Asia. It is argued that a critical understanding of this process (supported without reservation by such organizations as the IMF, the OECD and the World Bank) requires a questioning of the imagined link between "capitalism" and the "West", and a recognition that the international organizations are committed to a universal project aimed at empowering capital and promoting competitiveness on a global scale. A case study is provided of the recently adopted plan for the creation of an ASEAN Economic Community as a "single market and productive space" by 2015. The regional context in which it is placed is contrasted with that of the European Union, and the need for further study of varieties of capitalism in emerging economies is noted.

Keywords: ASEAN, capitalism, competitiveness, neoliberalism, IMF, OECD, World Bank

Introduction

In August 2009, the London-based *Economist* (founded in 1843 by Scottish hat manufacturer James Wilson to campaign for free trade) reported that the gap between growth in emerging Asia and the G7 had never been wider: Asian production had turned up sharply in the second quarter while contraction continued in America and Europe, and Barclays Capital economist Peter Redward was forecasting average GDP growth of almost 5% over the year as a whole in emerging Asia, against a 3.5% drop across the G7 (*Economist* 2009a). A fortnight later it returned to the "astonishing rebound" this represented (*Economist* 2009b), upped the "growth gap" for 2009 to 9%, and dismissed the "green shoots" appearing in America as "nothing by comparison with the lush jungle sprouting in the East" (*Economist* 2009c). Picking up on the consensus of Western forecasters in 1998 and 2001, as well as earlier in 2009, that Asia's recovery would be slow, the weekly concluded that: "Westerners have always been too quick to pronounce the death of the Asian economic miracle" (2009c). It went on to downplay the dependence of the Asian tigers on exports to the USA (on the grounds that the increase in emerging Asia's trade surplus with the US between 2001 and 2006 contributed only 6% of its GDP growth), and predicted that in the context of rising labour supply and infrastructural investment in the region productivity should continue to rise. In contrast:

Antipode Vol. 41 No. S1 2009 ISSN 0066-4812, pp 262–280
doi: 10.1111/j.1467-8330.2009.00725.x

In America and many other rich countries . . . potential growth rates are likely to fall over the next decade as soaring government debt and hence higher taxes blunt incentives to work and invest, the lingering credit crunch dampens investment, and increased government regulation deters innovation. All this could reduce productivity growth at a time when labour forces in these countries will be growing more slowly or even shrinking (*Economist* 2009c).

The conclusion?

Emerging Asia as a whole might enjoy annual growth of 7–8 per cent over the next five years, at least three times the rate in the rich world. The sharp downturn in Asia late last year painfully proved that the region was not immune to America's downfall. But the speed and strength of its rebound, if sustained, show that it is not chained to Uncle Sam either. If anything, the crisis has reinforced the shift of economic power from the West to the East (*Economist* 2009c).

The *Economist* does not dwell much on the ugliness and inequality of Asian capitalism (in large part shared with capitalism everywhere), nor does it acknowledge the instability and ultimately insoluble contradictions to which it is subject. But it does pose a challenge for the radical and progressive critics of the contemporary global order whom I imagine as making up the bulk of the readership of *Antipode*. Firmly rooted as it is in a tradition of political economy that dates back to Smith (and, albeit with a crucial critical inflection, to Marx), it suggests that much contemporary critical commentary commits the double error of taking the power of the USA too seriously, and not taking the dynamism of capitalism seriously enough. I explore these issues in what follows— with a first cut rooted in classical political economy, and a second cut which turns to its critique.

First Cut 1: Looking Back

It is not fortuitous that the liberal *Economist* identifies labour supply and labour productivity as the key issues in evaluating the prospects for short- and medium-term growth in emerging Asia and the West respectively. Adam Smith, at the very beginning of *The Wealth of Nations*, identified the "annual labour of every nation" as "the fund which originally supplies it [directly or through trade] with all the necessaries and conveniences of life which it annually consumes", and suggested that the relationship between production and consumption would therefore be "regulated by two different circumstances; first, by the skill, dexterity, and judgement with which its labour is generally applied; and, secondly, by the proportion between the number of those who are employed in useful labour, and that of those who are not employed" (Smith 1999 [1776]:104). The key to abundance, Smith insisted, depended more on the first than the second. He therefore set himself to inquire into the causes of the "improvement in the productive powers of labour" that had brought about the contrast he observed between "miserably poor" nations on the one hand, and "civilized and thriving" nations on the other (p 105). The same focus on the proportion of the population in employment and the productivity of their labour is central to the thinking of New Labour in the UK (evidence that Gordon Brown's Kirkcaldy roots go deep), and to the Paris-based OECD, whose *Economic Surveys* and annual *Going for Growth* series, launched in 2005, have labour resource utilization and labour productivity as central themes (OECD 2005:15).

In the same vein, it is the difference in levels of labour input and (especially) productivity between the "East" and the "West" that the eminent economic historian Angus Maddison identifies as the source of divergent patterns of global growth from the eighteenth century onwards. Maddison's calculations of long-term growth rates in GDP by region present a telling and topical picture (Table 1). They show a trajectory in which the "West" (made up, note, of Japan as well as Western Europe and the "Western offshoots"—the USA, Canada, Australia and New Zealand) becomes the source of the majority of global production only late in the nineteenth century, and is close to losing that position by 2001.

As it happens, a "leading economic consultancy", the London-based Centre for Economics and Business Research, put out a press release on 2 June 2009, on the basis of an apparently rather different calculation relating to the USA, Canada and Europe (the £10,000 annual subscription deterred me from closer enquiry). Headed "Western world drops below 50% of world GDP this year", it also suggested that it would

Table 1: Levels of GDP: world and major regions, 1500–2001 (billion 1990 international dollars)

	1500	1820	1870	1913	1950	1973	2001
Western Europe	44.2	160.1	367.6	902.3	1396	4096	7550
Western offshoots	1.1	13.5	111.5	582.9	1635	4058	9156
Japan	7.7	20.7	25.4	71.7	161	1243	2625
The "West"	**53**	**194.4**	**504.5**	**1556.9**	**3193**	**9398**	**19331**
Asia (ex. Japan)	153.6	392.2	401.6	608.7	823	2623	11481
Latin America	7.3	15.0	27.5	119.9	416	1398	3087
Eastern Europe and former USSR	15.2	62.6	133.8	367.1	695	2064	2072
Africa	19.3	31.2	45.2	79.5	203	550	1222
The "rest"	**195.3**	**501.0**	**608.2**	**1175.2**	**2137**	**6626**	**17862**
World	**248.3**	**695.3**	**1112.7**	**2732.1**	**5330**	**16024**	**37194**
% West/World	**21.3**	**28.0**	**45.3**	**57.0**	**59.9**	**58.6**	**52.0**

Source: Maddison (2005:11).

fall to 45% by 2012 (Centre for Economics and Business Research 2009). It is certainly to the point to note that if Maddison's figures above are reworked to deduct Japan's production from the "West" and add it to the rest of Asia, with the production of Eastern Europe and the Russian Federation being credited to the West, the percentage of global production attributable to the "West" falls to only 50.5% in 2001. One way or another, the brief period of absolute "Western" ascendancy (which I like to think may date from 14 March 1883) can be assumed to be over.

The much shorter recent period of 40 years from 1969 to 2009, representing the lifespan of *Antipode*, also represents the phase of descent of the USA in the global economy. The writing was on the wall for the dollar as the world reserve currency throughout the 1960s, and only ad hoc arrangements with the European states and increasingly tough mandatory and voluntary capital controls in the USA itself staved off until 1971 the final breaking of the fixed link between the dollar and gold (Eichengreen 1996:ch 4). Purely for chronological neatness, the creation of Special Drawing Rights at the IMF in 1969 to supplement the role of the dollar as a reserve currency may be taken as marking a turning point. By the time that US trade entered into deficit in 1976, real wages for US workers had peaked and begun to decline. As Table 1 shows, GDP growth in Asia (ex Japan), outpaced that of the US-dominated "Western offshoots" sufficiently between 1950 and 1973 to reduce the gap between the two groups from a half to a third, then accelerated after 1973 to increase more than fourfold over the period, propelling Asia well ahead of the "Western offshoots", whose combined GDP did little more than double. The commonly quoted assertion that growth has been slower since 1973 than before is true for the West, and for the world as a whole. But Asia is the exception. Add to this the observation that the "world market" envisaged by Marx and Engels over a century and a half ago came into being only in the 1990s, and it is reasonable to suggest that far from it being the case that capitalism is a "Western" phenomenon, its "Western" phase, protracted though it seems from the point of view of the present, has merely coincided with its pre-history as a genuinely global form. If so, we may need to learn to think about capitalism without thinking first about the USA.

First Cut 2: Looking Forward

The argument made above in relation to the USA is just as strong in relation to Western Europe, whose larger continental economies in particular have been singled out by the OECD as laggards in the labour utilization and productivity stakes (OECD 2005:ch 1 and Table 1.1, p 24). In fact, the grim pursuit of global competitiveness in continental Europe dates back to the failure of Mitterand's 1981 socialist government and its capitulation in 1983 to the power of global finance capital. From it emerged what Abdelal (2007:ch 4) has called the "Paris Consensus" leading to the European Single Market and monetary union, pressed forward by Jacques Delors (Mitterand's Finance Minister and subsequent President of the European Commission), his *chef de cabinet*, Pascal Lamy (subsequently Director General of the WTO), and Michel Camdessus (Governor of the Banque de France under Mitterand, and subsequently Managing Director of the IMF). Following the mandating of freedom of movement for capital in 1988, the creation of the single market in 1992 and the introduction of the euro in 1999, the European Commission in 2000 launched the Lisbon Agenda (largely foreshadowed in the Delors White Paper on Competitiveness published in December 1993). Intended to make the EU the most competitive, knowledge-based economy in the world by 2010, and currently dubbed the Strategy for Jobs and Growth, it has limped along, suffering the indignity of a re-launch in 2005 after initially limited progress, and is far from achieving its objectives, as the logic of neoliberal reform meets resistance from entrenched welfare states and entitlements (Offe 2003). Given this record and the current crisis, the prospects for successful realization of the Agenda at any time in the near future, let alone by 2010, looks bleak.

In another respect, however, the European Union, like the OECD, has been much more successful—in exporting its models of integration and the promotion of competitiveness to the developing world/emerging economies. The pre-accession and accession processes that accompany enlargement are powerful, formal institutional processes through which liberal reforms are induced (Grabbe 2006), and as I have discussed elsewhere the EU energetically promotes competitiveness in Latin America, in conjunction with the UN's Economic Commission for Latin America and the Caribbean (Cammack 2007). In relation to the Asian context, the EU has recently claimed some credit for another development—the adoption of the ASEAN Charter, "an EU-inspired document that aims to make ASEAN a rules-based organisation" (EU 2009), and the commitment of the 10 members of ASEAN to the creation of a single market and productive space in the region by 2015.[1] Ironically, perhaps, the prospects for the ASEAN Economic Community look brighter than those of the EU, precisely because of the more robust state of capitalist development in the region.

The ASEAN Charter and Asian Integration

Following the adoption of the ASEAN Charter at the end of 2008, the 14th ASEAN Summit approved the Cha-am Hua Hin Declaration on 1 March 2009 and thereby the Roadmap for an ASEAN Community, to be implemented by 2015 (ASEAN 2009a:1–3). The Charter, intended as noted above to make ASEAN "a more rules-based, effective and people-oriented organisation", consisted of five elements: blueprints for the ASEAN Political-Security Community (APSC), the ASEAN Economic Community (AEC), and the ASEAN Socio-Cultural Community (ASCC), a Strategic Framework for the Initiative for ASEAN Integration (IAI), and a Work Plan to complete the process by 2015 (ASEAN 2009b:2–4). Two days earlier, on 27 February, ministers had signed the Agreement establishing the ASEAN–Australia–New Zealand Free Trade Area (AANZFTA); at the Summit itself agreements on investment and trade in goods and services within ASEAN itself were signed; and subsequent months saw investment agreements with Korea (June) and China (August), and a Trade in Goods agreement with India (August).

The ASEAN Economic Community Blueprint approved at the 14th Summit, aimed at the creation of a single market embracing the 10 member states, recalled in its preamble the adoption of ASEAN Vision 2020 at the Kuala Lumpur Summit in December 1997 (with its commitment to the creation of a "stable, prosperous and highly competitive region with equitable economic development, and reduced poverty and socio-economic disparities"), the Bali Summit decision of October 2003 to create the ASEAN Economic Community by 2020, the 2006 agreement of the ASEAN Economic Ministers to develop a *blueprint* for the Economic Community by 2015, and the decision taken in January 2007 (at the 12th ASEAN Summit) to "hasten the establishment of the ASEAN Economic Community by 2015 and to transform ASEAN into a region with free movement of goods, services, investment, skilled labour, and freer flow of capital" (ASEAN 2009a:21). It pledged to establish ASEAN as "a single market and production base making ASEAN more dynamic and competitive", and at the same time to "address the development divide", by accelerating the integration of Cambodia, Laos, Myanmar and Vietnam. And as foreshadowed two years earlier, the single ASEAN market and production base would comprise five core elements: "(i) free flow of goods; (ii) free flow of services (iii) free flow of investment; (iv) freer flow of capital; and (v) free flow of skilled labour" (p 22). In every one of these areas, the emphasis was upon improving the competitiveness of the region in the global economy. And the vision of an Economic Community in place by 2015 was buttressed by two complementary initiatives—"a scorecard to monitor the implementation of the blueprint (for first report in October 2009); and a communications plan to inform and engage all stakeholders in the AEC building exercise" (ASEAN 2009b:7).

The picture this presents should give pause for thought. The decision to move to a single market and pursue liberal principles of integration has come *despite* three successive crises in a decade—the "Asia" crisis, the collapse of the "dot-com boom", and the current crisis.

The response of the ASEAN 10 has not been to reject integration into the global economy, but to reinforce their common commitment to regional integration in pursuit of global competitiveness. The overall shape of the framework has close affinities with that of the EU (though crucially it lacks the EU's central supranational authority structure), and the design of the economic community is thoroughly in line with the current thinking of the Bretton Woods organizations, even down to the focus on *skilled* labour, and the cautious attitude to freedom of movement for capital. Indeed, the impetus behind it is celebrated in the latest *World Development Report* as "a special blend of regional integration against a backdrop of globalization" (World Bank 2009:113). But this does not make it an imposition on the part of the "West" or the international organizations, let alone of the USA. The European Union has no particular leverage in the region. None of the leading protagonists are dependent upon IMF support, and the evidence of WDR 2009 is that the Bank is taking lessons from Asia rather than the reverse. And while there are certainly governments among the ASEAN 10 that are close to the USA—the Philippines under Arroyo being the most conspicuous case—they are in a distinct minority. Malaysia in contrast has been notoriously hostile to external imposition; and the smaller economies of Vietnam and Laos—still like China under the rule of monolithic Communist parties—have taken a Chinese path of liberalization under tight party control which is the product of quite specific regional and national circumstances (Painter 2003; Gainsborough 2007, 2009; Kittikhoun 2009; Stuart-Fox 2005). Vietnam's liberalizing *doi moi* reforms ran ahead in some ways of those of China, and in Laos the adoption in the 1980s of the "New Economic Mechanisms" that spelled the end of socialism followed the recommendation of both Vietnamese and Soviet advisers (Stuart-Fox 2005:37–41). In 2007 Vietnam volunteered for a full-scale Investment Policy Review from the United Nations Conference on Trade and Development, once a bastion of national developmentalism but now an avid disseminator of integration and competitiveness (UNCTAD 2008). The Review (funded by the Government of Ireland) urged the Vietnamese Government to "consider a 'Doi Moi 2' in investment policy in order to allow companies to become more competitive, innovative, flexible and in tune with the needs of the people and the market", while devoting a whole chapter, at the request of the Vietnamese government, to attracting investment into the electricity sector (p 126). Indonesia, by far the largest economy in ASEAN, similarly put itself forward for an UNCTAD Peer Review on Competition Policy in July 2009 (UNCTAD 2009). Malaysia has preceded and outdone the EU and its Lisbon agenda in its embrace of competitiveness and the knowledge economy, targeting women in particular as appropriate subjects for this exercise (Elias 2009). The orientation of these regimes reflects national trajectories that have seen the outflanking or defeat of more radical class and developmental projects by enthusiastic proponents of capitalist development.

What is more, the pattern of development that is emerging is heavily regional in character. Over 25% of ASEAN trade takes place between its own members, and another quarter or more (taking the total to 53% of exports and over 56% of imports) takes place with Japan, China and Korea. Add in the near neighbours of India and Australia, and the totals come to comfortably over 60% in each case. The EU and the US take less than 25% of ASEAN's exports between them, and account for only just over 20% of ASEAN imports, with the US trailing the EU in each case (calculated from official ASEAN statistics, available at http://www.aseansec.org/13100.htm). Add in the growth record of the larger Asian economies over recent years, and the relative prospects for the future, and a first observation is that ASEAN enthusiasm for integration into the "global" economy, which is real, is better understood in terms of the prospects and characteristics of the region than in terms of external imposition. Again, the Asian Development Bank is unequivocally supportive of the strategy of "weaning the region away from excessive dependence on demand in the G3 [the US, the eurozone and Japan]", and uninhibited in supporting it (ADB 2009:116).

It looks, then, as if in the first instance the ASEAN project should be approached as the outcome of coherent and perhaps well founded (equally, contestable and ultimately contradictory) capitalist development projects thoroughly embedded in the individual countries concerned, and supported by more or less hegemonic coalitions drawing strength from regional links. And the reasons are not far to seek. Surrounded by large economies enjoying dynamic growth, enjoying demographic profiles weighted as heavily towards the young as those of Europe are to the old, unencumbered by the legacy of heavy welfare entitlements, and generally characterized by solvent and well-founded banks, and low levels of personal and national debt, as both the *Economist* and the IMF are at pains to point out (*Economist* 2009b; IMF 2009c, 2009d), they might be expected to take a different view of the potential for capitalist development from their peers in Europe and the USA. In this context, the collapse of the derivatives markets and over-extended credit system in the USA, widely dissected across Asia, and notably addressed at length in the 2009 Annual Report of the Asian Development Bank (ADB 2009:3–12), has punctured the myth of the superiority of American capitalism just as definitively as the sweep of Japanese troops across the region after 1941 destroyed forever the myth of the superiority of the colonial powers.

For all that, though, capitalism is still capitalism. Having briefly taken its measure, I turn to its critique.

Second Cut 1: The Politics of Global Competitiveness

It is widely accepted that in the late 1980s and early 1990s the Bretton Woods institutions were the leading protagonists of a narrow neoliberal doctrine that sought to impose on the developing world a dogma revolving around the subordination of states to markets, with its attendant policies of privatization, liberalization and deregulation; and that thereafter an internal critique, further impelled by the resistance of the "anti-globalization" movement, prompted its replacement by the "Post-Washington Consensus", equally committed to "market-friendly development", but more receptive to a positive role for the state, and more sensitive to issues of poverty and social inclusion.

This is dangerously misleading. First, the doctrine propagated by the Bretton Woods institutions in the period (more clearly articulated at first by the World Bank than the IMF) was *fundamentally* social rather than economic in character, and aimed at transforming *social relations* rather than (just) economic policy in the developing world. Second, far from being a project aimed by the North (or even its single most powerful state) against the South, it was a part of a universal class project, originating in the developed world and aimed as much at the citizens of the developed world itself as those of the developing world— the global neoliberal offensive which had its roots in the UK and the USA in the late 1970s. And as we have already seen, it was carried forward as much by the EU and the OECD as by the IMF and the World Bank.

Williamson's widely cited formulation of the "Washington Consensus" (Williamson 1990) (which incidentally made no claim to the status it has since been accorded) made no reference to the central idea of the class project at its heart—that, to quote the World Bank's 1990 World Development Report, the only route to the abolition of poverty was to "promote the productive use of the poor's most abundant asset—labor" (World Bank 1990:3). The engagement of the world's poor in productive labour (or the creation of a genuinely global proletariat) has remained the central objective of the project ever since. The logic of its broader social dimension was that it would equip the poor for their "incorporation into and subjection to competitive labour markets and the creation of an institutional framework within which global capital accumulation can be sustained, while simultaneously seeking to legitimate the project through participation and a pro-poor agenda" (Cammack 2004:190). Given this broad agenda, developed in detail over the early 1990s, it necessarily took the view that the state had to be an active agent of change rather than a passive conduit for uncontained market forces, arguing that competitive markets "cannot operate in a vacuum—they require a legal and regulatory framework that only governments can provide". Hence "It is not a question of state or market: each has a large and irreplaceable role' (World Bank 1991:1).

The World Bank/IMF project was focused primarily on what may variously be called poor and middle income countries, developing societies or "emerging economies". But it cannot be seen in isolation. In precisely the same period a parallel strategy was being promoted—principally by the EU and the OECD—for the developed economies as a group, and the member countries of the EU in particular. This strategy aimed at re-asserting the authority of capital over labour, and restoring the capacity for capital accumulation and the extraction of surplus value from the proletariat—a process of "reproletarianization" alongside the "proletarianization" of the developing world. As noted above, it came as a response to the faltering economic progress of the states of continental Europe in particular.

The key theme running through all of these proposals is not privatization, or liberalization, or deregulation, but *competitiveness*—the creation of national environments characterized by competitive product and labour markets, in a global system regulated in such a way as to boost the level of competition on a global scale (Cammack 2006). The OECD Jobs Strategy of 1994 aimed at addressing the need for reform in the *advanced* economies of the world—through institutional reforms that would modify behaviour in such a way as to create competitive labour and capital markets, and eliminate alternatives to productive labour (Cammack 2006:7). And wholehearted though the support of the Bretton Woods institutions for these objectives has been, other UN agencies (the UNDP and UNCTAD) have been just as deeply engaged in their promotion in the developing world (as we have already seen in the case of UNCTAD), in particular around the Millennium Development Goals and the Monterrey Consensus. Even so, it is the EU (through the Lisbon Agenda, its pre-accession and enlargement processes, and its structured interaction with developing states through Economic Partnership Agreements) and the OECD, through its dealings with its own members and its programme of engagement with non-members, that have been the most powerful advocates and disseminators of this broad programme aimed at (re)asserting the hegemony of capital over labour on a global scale.

The OECD was set up in the first place after all to promote the development of a world economy governed in accordance with liberal principles. Its ambition to expand its influence beyond its core membership of developed states was signalled in 2006 with the statement that the organization was "setting its analytical sights on those countries—nearly the whole world—that embrace the market economy" (Cammack 2006:3, Box 1.1) and in 2007 with the placing of the banner "For a better world economy" on its website. It claims, with some justification, to be the lead agency promoting the smooth running and further development of the global economy. OECD Executive Secretary Angel Gurría described it, on the eve of the current crisis, as "a hub of globalisation—a centre for discussion where both member and non-member governments can come together to find the tools necessary to better manage globalisation", and went on to say exactly what that meant:

> But better managing globalisation often requires making painful reforms. And these reforms frequently entail highly visible costs for some clearly identifiable groups, whereas the benefits come later and are less certain and more diffuse. How can governments implement much needed reforms and not lose the public's support? *The OECD is a strategic partner of decision-makers in the political economy of reform* (OECD 2007:5; emphasis mine).

This formulation—that the international organizations see themselves as strategic partners in the political economy of reform—fits the case of all the organizations mentioned so far. Far from being the instruments of US hegemony or of any other grouping of advanced states, they are committed to strategic political intervention aimed at supporting the emergence and consolidation across the world of political regimes committed to the maximum development of the capitalist world economy; and the "politics of competitiveness" promoted by the IMF and the World Bank differs not at all from that propagated by the OECD and the European Commission. In each case, the objective is the same: to secure the hegemony of capital over labour, locally and globally. And this in turn means that the disciplines of capitalist competition must be internalized and enforced.

For example, the World Bank's 2007 edition of *Global Economic Prospects*, sub-titled precisely *Managing the Next Wave of Globalization*, took as its starting point the assumption that this would feature "the growing weight of developing countries in the international economy, notably the emergence of new trading powerhouses such as China, India and Brazil", along with increased productivity arising from global production chains, in services in particular, and the accelerated diffusion of technology (World Bank 2007:vii). It unequivocally welcomed the rise of a unified global capitalist market, and identified growing inequalities, pressures in labour markets, and threats to the global commons as "dislocations" that needed to be managed. Predicting that the global labour force would increase from 3 billion to over 4 billion by 2030 (with practically all the increase in the developing world), and that over the same period developing countries' share of global output would rise from a fifth to a third (in retrospect a conservative estimate), the Bank stated baldly that "Developing countries, once considered the periphery of the global economy, will become main drivers" (2007:xiii). Its took for granted that firms and workers in the rich countries would have to adjust to the global sourcing of services, commenting that "workers previously sheltered from global competition are facing greater job insecurity, downward pressure on their wages, and potential costs of adjustment in moving from one job to another or in upgrading their skills to obtain new employment following displacement (2007:123). In the face of this prospect, its message was uncompromising, in line with its commitment to the logic of competitive global markets, whatever adjustment costs they might bring. The "rapid pace of change and flexibility demanded by competitive global markets" was not to be avoided. Rather, all countries, rich or poor, would have to "review their domestic policy and institutional frameworks to ensure that their advantages can be exploited and that affected workers are supported when they incur adjustment costs" (2007:125). The Bank is at one with the OECD, advising of the need for a politics of *global* adjustment to conditions of genuinely globally competitiveness: wherever in the world you may be, in other words, *de te fabula narratur*.

Underpinning these initiatives, then, is not a project for the developing world, or the emerging economies, or the developed world, but a *universal* project aimed at maximizing the level of capitalist hegemony, capitalist development and capitalist competitiveness throughout the global capitalist economy. It is promoted principally by and through the international organizations, but it is focused on enhancing the capacity of *governments* to promote capitalist development, and premised therefore on the need for *all* governments to seek to secure the conditions for accumulation—competition between capitalists and the hegemony of capital in general over labour. It is in this sense that the international organizations are "strategic partners of decision-makers in the political economy of reform". The objective is a global order entirely shaped by the logic of capital, in which states regulate labour and capital in a manner conducive to creating competitive markets at national level, and simultaneously enhancing competitiveness throughout the global capitalist system as a whole. It vindicates a theoretical perspective which takes the global market as its starting point (Burnham 1994; Cammack 2003; Holloway 1994). And if that implies the shift of the centre of global accumulation from the West to the East, so be it.

Second Cut 2: Global Competitiveness and the Current Crisis

This logic has been perfectly reflected in the response of the international organizations to the crisis—they have asserted the need to redouble efforts to assert the global hegemony of capital over labour. Less predictable, and certainly unsettling for anyone who expected the crisis to lead to a repudiation of those organizations and the agenda they have pursued over two decades, has been the brilliant success with which their efforts were rewarded (see Cammack 2009 for a fuller account). In particular, the two headline initiatives with which the IMF returned to the centre of the stage—the "abolition of conditionality" through the introduction of the Flexible Credit Line, and the commitment to reform to enhance the representation of emerging economies in the governance of the institution—were not what they seemed to be. Far from being concessions to their critics, they were crucial steps in the advancement of its global project, for whose implementation the crisis provided a perfect opportunity. As the IMF's internal analysis of the crisis concluded, "Bottom line ... *the damage wrought by the crisis provides an opportunity to make progress on seemingly intractable issues. The moment should not be missed* (IMF 2009a:13; emphasis mine). For the IMF, the crisis represents an opportunity to perfect the "global architecture", by improving its powers of surveillance and policy influence and increasing the resources behind them. Its analysis began not with a careful consideration of the merits or otherwise of the policies promoted in recent years, but with the assertion that the *traction* of IMF surveillance (its ability to persuade governments to listen to and act upon its advice) needed to be improved (IMF 2009a:1). According to this analysis, individual governments tended to respond to the crisis with unilateral measures, rather than in a collaborative and coordinated manner—and when the need for cooperation was finally recognized it came, regrettably, through the "improvised" mechanism of the G-20 meeting (November 2008), rather than through the IMF, "the institution mandated to coordinate efforts to preserve global financial stability" (p 8). For the Fund to reclaim this role, the report concluded, it needed to address "deficits in ownership and effectiveness", and it was this logic which underpinned the call for the reform of quota shares, and representation on the Board and the IMFC, intended to make the Fund "a trusted actor at the center of the system" (p 9).

It seized the opportunity at the same time to address what it saw as a major obstacle to its influence, commenting that "it is no secret that members resist approaching the Fund for financing due to the political stigma of such borrowing" (p 11). This was the strategic goal behind its commitment to what was a carefully *selective* reform of conditionality: "Consideration should be given to establishing an effective crisis prevention instrument catering to *high-performing members*. For other members, the scope for access to high-access precautionary arrangements should be clarified" (p 12; emphasis mine). The ensuing proposal for a Flexible Credit Line "to provide assurances to members with a strong policy track record and sound fundamentals of rapid, large and upfront access to Fund resources with no ex post conditionality" (p 12), which was widely received as a victory for campaigners against the rigidity of Fund conditionality, was *not* a waiving of conditionality, but a form of *advance conditionality* aimed to support and protect already *unconditional* adherents to the global project—a reward for unconditionality, in short. It would complement the second leg of the system, the use of strategically targeted conditionality to exploit an *external* crisis to leverage desired reforms from lower-tier countries "that do not qualify for the new instrument". Approved by the IMF Board on 24 March, the Flexible Credit Line was described as "designed to provide large and upfront financing to members with very strong fundamentals and policies", with the added comment that "as access to the FCL is restricted to those members that meet strict qualification criteria, drawings under it are not tied to policy goals agreed with the country" (IMF 2009e). The meticulously orchestrated photo opportunity alongside the April G20 meeting, which saw three willing accomplices, Mexico's President, Felipe Calderón, Finance Minister, Agustín Carstens, and Central Bank Governor Guillermo Ortiz Martinez (all unconditional devotees of the IMF) step forward to be feted as the first beneficiaries of the Flexible Credit Line was a carefully prepared coup de théâtre: the announcement that Mexico would be the first country to sign up to the IMF's new Flexible Credit Line (Cammack 2009:13–14).

The proposal to reform the governance of the IMF, following years of foot-dragging and debate, was a complementary offensive move to empower the emerging *capitalist* economies in the institution. It is a prime example of a "seemingly intractable issue" (promoted by the IMF itself but unwelcome to some leading developed states) on which movement was possible in the context of crisis. The report of the *Committee on IMF Governance Reform* (IMF 2009b), chaired by another "unconditional", South Africa Finance Minister Trevor Manuel, was published in the days leading up to the April 2009 G20 meeting. Its brief was stated as having been "to come up with a broad package of reform measures that would help bring the Fund back to the centre of the world economy" (Manuel 2009). An essential part of this, entirely consistent with the global focus of the project it shares with the OECD, is that the voices of the developing or emerging economies, many of them in East and Southeast Asia, should weigh more heavily. The IMF wishes to facilitate the shift of gravity of the global economy to Asia, and with it to strengthen the hegemony of capital over labour in the region.

The aim of perfecting and enhancing the reach of the global neoliberal project is equally in evidence at the OECD, whose 2009 edition of *Going for Growth* insisted that "the debacle in financial markets does not call into question the beneficial effects of recommended reforms of product and labour markets in this report" (OECD 2009:4). And wherever Gurría speaks, he takes the same consistent message:

> Let us be clear, the crisis is not an excuse to delay structural reforms. On the contrary, it is by addressing our structural challenges that we will get out of the crisis. As the world strives to regain economic

momentum, this is the moment to look at eliminating anti-competitive measures that reduce productivity ... It is essential that developing countries, in particular, tackle these obstacles to productivity and growth. Structural reforms that free up the ability of the informal sector to enter and compete in the formal economy will propel economies forward faster (Gurría 2009).

The international organizations continue, then, to press the case for global competitiveness. And they have succeeded (with the conspicuous support of the British Government in particular) in seizing the initiative in the global response to the current financial crisis. Neither the extent of their influence nor the global neoliberal thrust of their project is in doubt.

Second Cut 3: Embedding Competitiveness in Southeast Asia

The distinctive feature of the Southeast Asian states is that they need neither to be coerced (like the states that remain under "second-tier" IMF conditionality) nor protected from disaster (like the unconditional allies of the IMF such as Mexico and Poland threatened by the crisis). There are cases outside the region, such as South Africa, where national leaders committed to neoliberal integration into the global economy are succeeding, in a hotly contested struggle, in embedding their desired reforms (Hart 2008; Narsiah forthcoming), and others, such as Brazil, where leaders with equally impeccable radical credentials, now consigned to the past, have taken "ownership" of similar projects. But the strongest evidence for the successful embedding of such projects comes from Southeast Asia, and it presents a considerable analytical and existential challenge to advocates of other more radical forms of politics.

Indonesia offers a case in point. The IMF has recently praised its decentralization and empowerment of local governments as "one of Indonesia's most remarkable achievements in the past 10 years", with Indonesia's almost 500 sub-national governments managing close to 40% of all public spending (IMF 2009c:annex 2:4). Carroll's recent account of the *kecataman* (sub-district level) reform funded by the World Bank-funded Kecataman Development Programme gives an insight into the agenda involved. What began as a pilot project in 25 villages in 1997 has since extended to 38,000 communities, making it the largest community development project in Southeast Asia (Carroll 2009:452). Its principal feature is that within a tightly defined framework, it allows "local villager participation and choice in the allocation of funds" (p 448). Carroll describes the project as a "neoliberal Trojan horse", because "what is radical about it is the manner in which neoliberal reform is delivered, in essence attempting to rebuild citizenship, from the 'bottom up', in a liberal market compatible manner, using the provision of debt-based funding for productive economic and social infrastructure as an incentive" (pp 448–449): "Put another way, KDP, drawing upon the political technology of 'participatory development', constitutes a distinctly different and temporarily effective delivery device for extending capitalist social relations and the institutions that the development orthodoxy posits should accompany such relations" (p 449). Participatory budgeting, Indonesian-style, is in the business of creating "new competitive market citizens", and, for the time being, with some success (p 449). This is evidence of a sophisticated and nationally managed project, consciously aimed at producing the social relations and local institutions on which capitalist accumulation and reproduction depend. Further evidence of the embeddedness of the project is provided by Rudnyckyj's account of "Market Islam" and the "spiritual economy" that links Islam and neoliberalism in the country. Rudnyckyj describes Market Islam as merging Muslim religious practice and capitalist ethics (Rudnyckyj 2009a). I can offer only the briefest taste of the rich ethnography provided, but it hinges, in the case of Krakatau Steel, on a conscious strategy on the part of management to secure the transition from national developmentalism to "a new political economic landscape increasingly characterized by transnational competition": "The managers reasoned that through cultivating the religious virtues of the workforce they could enhance company productivity, eliminate corruption, become more internationally competitive, and perhaps prepare employees for privatization of this state-owned enterprise" (Rudnyckyj 2009b:105).

Nor is Indonesia an isolated case. Elias notes the commitment of the Malaysian regime to "provide an enabling environment to ensure more effective participation of women in national development"; "Women will be equipped with the necessary skills and knowledge to enable them to be more competitive and versatile to meet the needs of the knowledge economy" (Ninth Malaysian Plan, cited in Elias 2009:477). And in the case of Laos, Singh finds (admittedly in what Stuart-Fox (2005:29) describes as a country "virtually devoid of civil society"), by following up what appear to be wholly stage-managed participatory events around the Nam Theun 2 hydropower project, that villagers are well informed, and when addressed often unequivocal in their support for the national project ("We want the dam, we want electricity, we want music CDs, we want them quickly!", Singh 2009:502).

Conclusion

There is a vast literature on "varieties of capitalism" in the developed world, generally revolving around a dozen or so classic cases, but relatively little of a comparative character on "emerging varieties of capitalism" in Asia, and less still that is focused on emerging capitalist projects and their contestation. One only needs to reflect briefly on the specificities of China, India, Brazil and the Russian federation (the BRICs), Indonesia and South Africa (making up the extended BRIICS), or Argentina, Mexico, Saudi Arabia, South Korea and Turkey (the remaining "new" members of the G20), let alone on the variety exhibited between Malaysia, Thailand, the Philippines, Singapore, Laos, Cambodia, Burma/Myanmar, Brunei Darussalam and Vietnam (the rest of ASEAN) to realize the extent of the challenge if we are to apprehend "with sober senses" the coming form of global capitalism(s) and the struggles that do and will surround them. The World Bank, a recent and enthusiastic convert to uneven development, has produced its own recipe ("unbalanced growth, inclusive development"), both for the world as a whole, and for East and Southeast Asia in particular (World Bank 2009:xxi, 194–196; Huang and Bocchi 2009:338–341, 350–356). We need to develop a robust critique. I have suggested that a shift of perspective is needed if we are to do so, away in particular from the ideas that capitalism is owned by the "West", or that the international organizations are the unconditional servants of the USA or the advanced economies, rather than regional partners in a universal project aimed at securing the global hegemony of capital.

Endnote

[1] The members of ASEAN (in order of magnitude of GDP) are Indonesia, Thailand, Malaysia, Singapore, Philippines (the ASEAN 5), Vietnam, Myanmar, Brunei Darussalam, Cambodia, and Laos PDR.

References

ADB (2009) *Asian Development Outlook 2009: Rebalancing Asia's Growth*. Manila: ADB
ASEAN (2009a) *Roadmap for an ASEAN Community 2009–2015*. Jakarta: ASEAN
ASEAN (2009b) *Annual Report 2008–2009: Implementing the Roadmap for an ASEAN Community 2015*. Jakarta: ASEAN
Burnham P (1994) Open Marxism and vulgar international political economy. *Review of International Political Economy* 1(2):221–231
Cammack P (2004) What the World Bank means by poverty reduction, and why it matters. *New Political Economy* 9(2):189–211
Cammack P (2006) The politics of global competitiveness. *Papers in the Politics of Global Competitiveness*, No. 1, Institute for Global Studies, Manchester Metropolitan University, e-space Open Access Repository
Cammack P (2007) Competitiveness and convergence: The open method of co-ordination in Latin America. *Papers in the Politics of Global Competitiveness*, No. 5, Institute for Global Studies, Manchester Metropolitan University, e-space Open Access Repository
Cammack P (2009) All power to global capital! *Papers in the Politics of Global Competitiveness*, No. 10, Institute for Global Studies, Manchester Metropolitan University, e-space Open Access Repository

Carroll T (2009) "Social Development" as a neoliberal Trojan Horse: The World Bank and the Kecamatan Development Program in Indonesia. *Development & Change* 40(3):447–466

Centre for Economics and Business Research (2009) Western world drops below 50% of world GDP this year. 2 June, http://www.cebr.com/Newsroom/press_releases.htm Accessed 22 August 2009

Economist (2009a) From slump to jump. *Economist* 30 July

Economist (2009b) An astonishing rebound. *Economist* 13 August

Economist (2009c) On the rebound. *Economist* 13 August

Eichengreen B (1996) *Globalizing Capital: A History of the International Monetary System*. Princeton: Princeton University Press

Elias J (2009) Gendering liberalisation and labour reform in Malaysia: Fostering "competitiveness" in the productive and reproductive economies. *Third World Quarterly* 30(3):469–483

EU (2009) EU-ASEAN: Ever closer, Europa Press Release IP/09/834, Brussels, 27 May

Gainsborough M (2007) Globalisation and the state revisited: A view from provincial Vietnam. *Journal of Contemporary Asia* 37(1):1–18

Gainsborough M (2009) Privatisation as state advance: Private indirect government in Vietnam. *New Political Economy* 14(2):257–274

Grabbe H (2006) *The EU's Transformative Power: Europeanization through Conditionality in Central and Eastern Europe*. Basingstoke: Palgrave Macmillan

Gurría A (2009) Staying the course: Preserving competition in a time of crisis. Opening remarks by Angel Gurría, OECD Secretary-General, at the Global Forum on Competition, Paris, 19 February, http://www.oecd.org/document/27/0,3343, en_2649_34487_42211291_1_1_1_1,00.html Accessed 15 August 2009

Hart G (2008) The provocations of neoliberalism: Contesting the nation and liberation after apartheid. *Antipode* 40(4):678–705

Holloway J (1994) Global capital and the national state. *Capital & Class* 52:23–49

Huang Y and Bocchi A M (2009) Lessons from experience: Reshaping economic geography in East Asia. In Y Huang and A M Bocchi (eds) *Reshaping Economic Geography in East Asia* (pp 338–367). Washington: World Bank

IMF (2009a) *Initial Lessons of the Crisis for the Global Architecture and the IMF*. Washington: IMF

IMF (2009b) Committee on IMF governance reform: Final report. 24 March, http://www.imf.org/external/np/omd/2009/govref/032409.pdf Accessed 24 August 2009

IMF (2009c) Indonesia: 2009 Article IV Consultation—Staff Report; Public Information Notice on the Executive Board Discussion; and Statement by the Executive Director for Indonesia, IMF Country Report 09/230, Washington, 30 July

IMF (2009d) Malaysia: 2009 Article IV Consultation—Staff Report; Public Information Notice on the Executive Board Discussion; and Statement by the Executive Director for Malaysia, IMF Country Report 09/253, Washington, 14 August

Kittikhoun Q (2009) Small state, big revolution: Geography and the revolution in Laos. *Theory & Society* 38(1):25–55

Maddison A (2005) Measuring and interpreting world economic performance 1500–2001. *Review of Income and Wealth* 51(1):1–35

Manuel T (2009) Cover letter from Mr Trevor Manuel to Mr Dominique Strauss-Kahn, 24 March, Ref: M 3/1/1 (389/09), http://www.imf.org/external/np/omd/2009/govref/032409n.pdf Accessed 7 April 2009

Narsiah S (forthcoming) The neoliberalism of the local state in Durban, South Africa. *Antipode*

OECD (2005) *Economic Policy Reforms: Going for Growth 2005*. Paris: OECD

OECD (2007) *OECD Annual Report 2007*. Paris: OECD

OECD (2009) *Economic Policy Reforms: Going for Growth 2009*. Paris: OECD

Offe C (2003) The European model of "social" capitalism: Can it survive European integration? *Journal of Political Philosophy* 11(4):437–469

Painter M (2003) Marketisation, integration and state restructuring in Vietnam: The case of state-owned enterprise reform. Working Papers Series, No. 39, Southeast Asia Research Center, City University of Hong Kong

Rudnyckyj D (2009a) Market Islam in Indonesia. *Journal of the Royal Anthropological Institute* 15:183–201

Rudnyckyj D (2009b) Spiritual economies: Islam and neoliberalism in contemporary Indonesia. *Cultural Anthropology* 24(1):104–141

Singh S (2009) World Bank-directed development? Negotiating participation in the Nam Theun Hydropower Project in Laos. *Development & Change* 40(3):487–507

Smith A (1999 [1776]) *The Wealth of Nations* (Books I–III, A Skinner ed). London: Penguin

Stuart-Fox, M (2005) Politics and reform in the Lao People's Democratic Republic. Working Paper No. 126, Asia Research Centre, Murdoch University

UNCTAD (2008) *Investment Policy Review: Viet Nam*. New York: United Nations

UNCTAD (2009) *Voluntary Peer Review on Competition Policy: Indonesia*. New York: United Nations

Williamson J (1990) What Washington means by policy reform. In J Williamson (ed) *Latin American Adjustment: How Much Has Happened?* (pp). Washington: Institute for International Economics

World Bank (1990) *World Development Report 1990: Poverty*. New York: World Bank

World Bank (1991) *World Development Report 1991: The Challenge of Development*. New York: World Bank

World Bank (2007) *Global Economic Prospects: Managing the Next Wave of Globalization*. Washington: World Bank

World Bank (2009) *World Development Report 2009: Reshaping Economic Geography*. Washington: World Bank

Who Counts? Dilemmas of Justice in a Postwestphalian World

Nancy Fraser

Department of Political Science, The New School for Social Research,
New York, NY, USA;
FraserN@earthlink.net

Abstract: Who counts as a subject of justice? Not so long ago, it was widely assumed that those "who counted" were simply the citizens of a bounded territorial state. Today, however, as activists target injustices that cut across borders, that "Westphalian" view is contested and the "who" of justice is an object of hot dispute. This new situation calls for a new kind of justice theorizing, whose contours I sketch in this essay. Arguing, first, for a reflexive mode of theorizing, I introduce the concept of "misframing", which can subject the Westphalian "who" to critical scrutiny. Arguing, second, for the necessity of a substantive normative principle to evaluate competing "who's", I introduce the "all-subjected principle" as superior to three better known alternatives: namely, membership, humanism, and the all-affected principle.

Keywords: global justice, transnational injustice, Westphalian frame, all-subjected principle, all-affected principle

Who counts as a subject of justice? Whose interests and needs deserve consideration? When it comes to struggles for economic redistribution, cultural recognition, or political representation, who exactly belongs to the universe of those entitled to make justice claims on one another? In the decades following World War II, these questions were not live ones, as struggles for justice proceeded against the background of a taken-for-granted frame. In that era—let's call it the period of the Cold War—it generally went without saying that the sole unit within which justice applied was the modern territorial state. That "Westphalian" view framed the lion's share of justice-discourse across disparate political cultures, notwithstanding lip service paid to human rights, proletarian internationalism, and Third World solidarity.[1] Whether the issue was redistribution, recognition or representation, class differentials, status hierarchies or the legitimate exercise of political power, most claimants assumed the scope of justice coincided with the bounds of their political community. Only the members of such a community counted as subjects of justice for one another. The effect was to drastically limit, if not wholly to exclude, binding obligations of justice that cut across borders. By definition, then, this frame obscured transborder injustices.

The Westphalian understanding of the "who" went with a specific picture of political space, a Westphalian political imaginary. In this

Antipode Vol. 41 No. S1 2009 ISSN 0066-4812, pp 281–297
doi: 10.1111/j.1467-8330.2009.00726.x

imaginary, political communities appeared as geographically bounded units, demarcated by sharply drawn borders. Associating each such polity with a state of its own, the Westphalian political imaginary envisioned the state as exercising exclusive, undivided sovereignty over its territory; seeking to bar "external interference" in the state's "internal affairs," it also rejected the view that the state should be constrained by any higher, international power. In addition, this view enshrined a sharp division between two qualitatively different kinds of political space. Whereas "domestic" space was imagined as the pacified civil realm of the social contract, subject to law and obligations of justice, "international" space was envisioned as a state of nature, a warlike realm of strategic bargaining and *raison d'état*, devoid of any binding duties of justice. In the Westphalian imaginary, accordingly, the subjects of justice could only be fellow members of a territorialized citizenry.

It is true, of course, that this mapping of political space was never fully realized. Great Power hegemony and modern imperialism belied the notion of an international system of equal sovereign states. Yet this imaginary exercised a powerful sway, inflecting the independence dreams of colonized peoples, who mostly yearned for Westphalian states of their own. It is also true that international lawyers and cosmopolitan thinkers have sought over the course of three centuries to "pacify" international space, by subjecting it to legal regulation. Until recently, however, their efforts did not directly challenge the fundamental bifurcation between national and international space, nor the associated contrast between a territorially bounded realm, subject to the strictures of justice, and another, exterior region, subject, even in the best case scenario, only to far more modest and minimal normative requirements. The effect was largely to ratify the Westphalian mapping of political space.

Today, however, the Westphalian mapping of political space is losing its hold. For one thing, its presumption of exclusive, undivided state sovereignty appears increasingly counterfactual, given a ramifying human-rights regime, on the one hand, and spiraling networks of global governance, on the other. Equally questionable is the notion of a sharp division between domestic and international space, given novel forms of "intermestic" politics, practiced by new, trans-territorial non-state actors, including transnational social movements, intergovernmental organizations, and INGOs.[2] Also dubious is the view of territoriality as the sole basis for assigning obligations of justice, given patently trans-territorial problems, such as global warming or genetically modified agriculture, which prompt many to think in terms of functionally defined "communities of risk" that expand the bounds of justice to include everyone potentially affected.[3] No wonder, then, that activists contesting transnational inequities reject the view that justice can only be imagined territorially, as a domestic relation among fellow citizens. Positing post-Westphalian views of "who counts", they are subjecting the Westphalian frame to explicit critique.

Today, accordingly, both the "who" of justice and the mapping of political space are objects of struggle. As a matter of fact, the Westphalian "who" is now being challenged from at least three directions: first, by localists and communalists, who seek to locate the scope of concern in subnational units, such as "the Basque country" or the "Inuit peoples"; second, by regionalists and transnationalists, who propose to identify the "who" of justice with larger, though not fully universal, units, such as "Europe" or "Islam"; and third, by globalists and cosmopolitans, who propose to accord equal consideration to all human beings. Consequently, there are now in play at least four rival views of the "who" of justice: Westphalian, local-communalist, transnational-regional, and global-cosmopolitan. And these views increasingly collide. No sooner does one party issue a demand for justice, premised on one understanding of the "who", than others proceed to launch counterclaims, which are premised on rival understandings. The result is a veritable cacophony or heteroglossia of justice discourse, which I have called "abnormal justice" (see Fraser 2008b).

I have coined this expression by analogy with Thomas Kuhn's distinction between normal and abnormal science. For Kuhn, science is "normal" just so long as a single paradigm dominates inquiry to such an extent that dissent from it remains contained. Science becomes "revolutionary", in contrast, when deviations cumulate and competing paradigms proliferate. In the first case, inquirers share a basic set of underlying assumptions, which gives their work an orderly, progressive appearance. In the second case, a shared grammar is lacking, and scientific discussions come to resemble dialogues of the deaf (Kuhn 1996 [1962]). By analogy, I distinguish episodes of "normal justice", when most interlocutors share a sense of the basic parameters, including with respect to "who counts". By contrast, "abnormal justice" arises when such agreement is absent. It signifies a condition in which those who struggle for social justice assume competing views of such matters.[4] That, I claim, is our situation today.[5]

Under current conditions, of "abnormal justice", theorizing cannot proceed in the usual way. Unlike those who sought to theorize justice in the previous era, we cannot assume that we already know who counts. Far from simply assuming the Westphalian "who", as they did, we must explicitly pose the question of who counts as a subject of justice. We must ask: given the clash of rival views of the bounds of justice, how should we decide whose interests ought to count? Faced with competing framings of social conflicts, how should we determine which mapping of political space is just?

The trick, I submit, is to reckon simultaneously with the positive and negate sides of abnormal justice. On the one hand, a viable approach must valorize expanded contestation concerning the "who", which makes thinkable, and criticizable, transborder justices obscured by the Westphalian picture of political space. On the other hand, one must grapple as well with the exacerbated difficulty of resolving disputes in which contestants hold conflicting views of who counts. What sort of justice theorizing can simultaneously meet both of those desiderata? What sort of theorizing can both open up space for entertaining novel claims and also provide for the provisional closure needed to vet and redress them? The answer I shall propose here can be stated in brief: theorizing suited to abnormal times should be simultaneously reflexive and discriminating. Let me explain each part of this two-pronged proposal.

On Reflexivity as Meta-Political Critique: A Plea for the Concept of "Misframing"

In order to valorize expanded contestation, reflection on abnormal justice must be open to claims that first-order questions of justice (whether for redistribution, recognition or representation) have been wrongly framed. To ensure that such claims receive a fair hearing, one should assume at the outset that it is possible in principle that some ways of delimiting the "who" of justice are themselves unjust, whether because they exclude some who deserve consideration or because they include some who should be excluded. Thus, abnormal justice theorizing must be reflexive, able to jump up a level to interrogate the justice (or injustice) of competing frames. Only by becoming reflexive can one engage the meta-level where framing itself is in dispute. Only by becoming reflexive can one grasp the question of the "who" *as* a question of justice.

The need for reflexivity is especially acute when we confront new kinds of justice claims, which suppose non-hegemonic mappings of political space. Absent the ability to reflexively scrutinize established frames, theorizing tends to beg the question against those who would challenge Westphalian definitions of the "who" of justice. Theorizing suited to abnormal times must bend over backwards to avoid foreclosing novel claims. To validate contestation, it must turn reflexive.

How can one generate the reflexivity needed in abnormal justice? The strategy I shall propose extends the view of justice I have developed elsewhere. That view consists of a three-dimensional view of the "what" of justice, encompassing economic redistribution, legal-cultural recognition, and political representation, all of which are overarched by the normative principle of participatory parity.[6] Rather than rehearse that entire view here, I propose to zero in on the part of it that is most relevant to the problem at hand. To clarify abnormalities of the "who", I shall focus on the dimension of representation. My claim is, properly understood, that political dimension of justice can provide the reflexivity needed to clarify disputes over the "who" in abnormal justice.

The reason is that political dimension applies at two levels, which I call "ordinary political" and "meta-political" respectively. Usually, theorists focus on the ordinary-political level, which concerns the structures of political representation within a bounded political community. Here, in contrast, I want to focus on the meta-political level, which concerns the divisions between political communities, hence the design of the broader political space within which they are situated. Let me explain the difference between these levels.

The ordinary-political level is intuitively familiar. At this level, representation is largely a function of a polity's internal constitution, which sets the ground rules for the legitimate exercise of political power within its borders. The paradigm case, from the standpoint of mainstream political science, is electoral decision rules, which mediate the relations between voice and power in a bounded polity. Together with other fundamental features of political constitution, such decision rules establish the terrain of legitimate contestation within the polity. They set the terms on which those included in the political community air their claims and adjudicate their disputes. Shaping the terms on which members exercise political voice, ordinary-political representation takes the polity's external boundaries as a given.

In principle, of course, the relations of ordinary-political representation are matters of justice. At this level, one can ask: are the relations of representation just? Do the polity's decision rules accord equal voice in public deliberations and fair representation in public decision-making to all of its members? Are all who are counted as members able to participate on a par with all others? When the answer is no, we are confronted with what I call "ordinary-political injustices". Ordinary-political injustices arise within a political community whose boundaries and membership are taken as settled. Thus, ordinary-political misrepresentation occurs when a polity's decision rules deny some who are counted in principle as members the chance to participate fully, as peers. Recently, such injustices have given rise to demands for changes in the mode of ordinary-political representation, ranging from demands for gender quotas on electoral lists, multicultural rights, indigenous self-government, and provincial autonomy, on the one hand, to demands for campaign finance reform, redistricting, proportional representation, and cumulative voting, on the other.[7]

Important as such matters are, they do not exhaust the political dimension of justice. That dimension applies as well at what I am calling the meta-political level. Although less intuitively familiar, the meta-level concerns the design of the broader political space within which the bounded polities considered so far are embedded. At issue here are precisely those matters that were taken for granted at the previous level:

namely, the setting of boundaries and the delimitation of membership. Here, accordingly, the crux of representation is inclusion in, or exclusion from, the community of those entitled to make justice claims on one another. If ordinary-political representation concerns the allocation of political voice among those who are counted as members, then meta-political representation concerns the prior establishment of who counts as a member in the first place. It tells us who is included in, and who excluded from, the circle of those entitled to just distribution, reciprocal recognition, and fair terms of ordinary-political representation.

Like ordinary-political representation, meta-political representation is a matter of justice. At this level, too, one can ask: are the relations of meta-representation unjust? Do the boundaries of political membership wrongly exclude some who are actually entitled to voice? Does the division of political space *into* separated bounded polities deprive some of the chance to engage politically with others as peers on matters of common concern? When the answer is yes, we are confronted with what I call "meta-political injustice". Meta-political injustices arise when a polity's boundaries are drawn in such a way as to wrongly exclude some people from the chance to participate *at all* in its authorized contests over justice. In such cases, those who are constituted as nonmembers are wrongly excluded from the universe of those entitled to consideration within the polity in matters of distribution, recognition, and ordinary-political representation. The injustice remains, moreover, even when those excluded from one polity are included as subjects of justice in another–as long as the effect of the political division is to put some relevant aspects of justice beyond their reach. An example is the way in which the international system of supposedly equal sovereign states gerrymanders political space at the expense of the global poor. When that happens, the result is a special form of meta-political misrepresentation that I call *misframing*.[8]

Misframing is a reflexive idea. Pitched at the meta-political level, it permits us to interrogate the mapping of political space from the standpoint of justice. Taking the ordinary level as an object of scrutiny, the concept of misframing makes it possible to ask whether a given account of the "who" of justice is truly just. Enabling us to interrogate first-order framings of justice, this notion can help us parse disputes that encompass conflicting views of the "who". As a result, the concept of misframing possesses exactly the sort of reflexivity needed in circumstances of abnormal justice.

Although the term is certainly new, the idea of misframing has already some real traction in today's struggles over globalization. This notion implicitly informs the claims of many "alternative globalization" activists, even though, of course, they do not use the term. For example, activists associated with the World Social Forum effectively contend that the Westphalian frame is unjust, as it partitions political space in ways that block those whom they call "the global poor" from challenging the forces that oppress them. Channeling their claims into the domestic political spaces of relatively powerless, if not wholly failed, states, this frame insulates offshore powers from critique and control (Pogge 1999, 2001; Forst 2001, 2005). Among those shielded from the reach of justice are more powerful predator states and transnational private powers, including foreign investors and creditors, international currency speculators, and transnational corporations (Harris and Seid 2000; Hoogvelt 2001). Also protected are the governance structures of the global economy, which set exploitative terms of interaction and then exempt them from democratic control (Aman 2003; Boyce 2004; Cox 1996, 1997; Gill 1998; Helleiner 1994; Schneiderman 2001; Storm and Mohan Rao 2004). Finally, the Westphalian frame is self-insulating, as the architecture of the interstate system excludes transnational democratic decision-making on issues of justice (Bohman 1999; Dryzek 1999; Held 1995, 1999, 2000, 2003, 2004).

These claims are meta-political. Premised on the idea that first-order framings of justice may themselves be unjust, the concept of misframing permits claimants to pose the question of the frame *as* a question of justice. As a result it, it provides the reflexivity needed to parse disputes about the "who" in abnormal justice. By itself, however, reflexivity is not a solution. As soon as we accept that injustices of misframing can exist in principle, we require some means of determining when and where they exist in reality. Thus, a theory of justice for abnormal times requires a discriminating normative principle for evaluating frames. Absent such a discriminating principle, we have no way to assess the alternatives, hence no way to clarify disputes that encompass conflicting understandings of the "who".

On Discriminacy as Substantive Normative Critique: A Plea for the "All-Subjected Principle"

This brings me to the second prong of my two-part proposal concerning the "who". Having just argued for reflexivity, I shall argue now that theorizing in abnormal times must also be discriminating—in the sense of including a substantive principle that can evaluate competing frames. Such a principle is needed to cope with the negative side of abnormal justice. Having just acknowledged the positive side, by opening a space for entertaining novel views of the "who", I need now to accommodate the negative side, by envisioning the provisional closure that is necessary for adjudicating them. What might a discriminating principle for evaluating frames look like? Currently, there are three major candidates on offer. Let me examine them one by one.

The first proposal for evaluating frames of justice is the principle of *political membership*. Proponents of this approach propose to resolve disputes concerning the "who" by appealing to criteria of political belonging. For them, accordingly, what turns a collection of individuals into fellow subjects of justice is shared membership in a single political community. As they see it, therefore, the "who" of justice should consist of those who belong together as fellow members of a polity.

Actually, there are at least two different variants of the membership principle, which hold different interpretations of political belonging. In one interpretation, political belonging is (or should be) a matter of shared nationality. For proponents of this approach, such as Michael Walzer and David Miller, justice finds its strongest support when political membership is undergirded by a shared pre-political ethos, a common matrix of language, history, culture, tradition or descent. For these theorists, accordingly, the "who" of justice is simply the nation.

Other membership theorists reject that interpretation, however, as objectionably racialist, historically misleading, and generally unsuited to the polyglot, multicultural character of modern states. In their eyes, political membership need not rely on any substantive pre-political commonality. It is better conceived as a political relation all the way the down. On this second interpretation, which is endorsed by philosophers Will Kymlicka and Thomas Nagel, one belongs to a political community simply by virtue of citizenship. Citizenship alone, irrespective of national identity, is sufficient to establish the relationship required for standing as a subject of justice. Thus, the "who" of justice is simply the citizenry.[9]

One might wonder, parenthetically, where John Rawls fits in this scheme. Certainly, the author of *The Law of Peoples* belongs in the ranks of membership theorists, as he conceives justice as a relation among fellow members of a "people" organized as a domestic political community. But what sort of membership theorist is he? Everything depends on what Rawls means by a "people". Without pretending to parse the subtleties of his account, which I find equivocal, we can safely locate him somewhere in the grey area that lies between the nationality and citizenship variants of the membership principle (Rawls 2001).

Significant as they are, the differences between these variants of the membership principle are less important for my purposes here than the similarities. What they share is the conviction that what turns a collection of individuals into fellow subjects of justice is the condition of co-belonging to the same bounded political community. For all of them, moreover, that bounded political community turns out to be a modern territorial state. For the nationalists, every viable or "historical" nation should have such a state; for the citizenship thinkers, belonging simply means holding citizenship in such a state.

The underlying reasoning runs something like this. Justice is by definition a *political* concept. Its obligations apply only to those who stand to one another in a *political* relationship. So determination of the "who" of justice depends on what exactly counts as a political relationship. The answer, for membership theorists, nationalist or otherwise, is co-belonging in a bounded political community, conceived on the Westphalian model. Nagel provides the most thoughtful explication of this point. What makes a relation political, he claims, is common subjection to a political authority that exercises coercive power in its members' name and enlists their active cooperation or involvement. It is our connection to and through a coercive power that acts in our name and enlists our cooperation that makes us political fellows. Political relations arise, accordingly, by virtue of shared belonging in a territorially bounded unit with a sovereign state. Only relations among the members of such a unit count as political relations in the sense required to trigger obligations of justice.[10] Thus, the bounds of justice coincide with those established by the Westphalian frame. And the only legitimate "who" of justice is the Westphalian "who".

What shall we make of this approach? The first thing to note is that the membership principle grounds obligations of justice in a determinate social relation. Rejecting the view that justice can bind people who bear no relation to one another, it insists that justice applies only among those who stand to one another in a certain specific, morally relevant social relationship: namely, a political relationship of shared belonging to Westphalian state. As a result, the membership principle has the advantage of expressing a robust sense of human sociality. Refusing recourse to abstract appeals to "Humanity", it maintains that any defensible account of the "who" of justice must rest on real connections among those comprising it.

In addition, the membership principle has the advantage of realism. Its account of the morally relevant type of social relation jibes with widely appreciated features of existing institutional reality and widely held collective identifications. As such, it is no mere ought devoid of purchase on already existing commitments and self-understandings. Yet that last strength is also a weakness. In practice, the membership principle serves all too easily to ratify the exclusionary nationalisms of the privileged and powerful—hence to shield established frames from critical scrutiny.

But that is not all. By definition, this approach is barred from contemplating the possibility that in some cases the Westphalian framing of questions of justice may be unjust. Effectively foreclosing such misframing in advance, it is unable to provide a fair hearing for claims that assume non-hegemonic accounts of the "who". Forfeiting the reflexivity needed to entertain such claims, the membership principle fails to meet the requirements for theorizing abnormal justice. Thus, it is not a viable option for abnormal times.

No wonder, then, that many philosophers and activists have sought a more critical approach. For some, the preferred alternative is the *humanist principle*. Seeking a more inclusive standard, proponents of this second approach, such as Martha Nussbaum, propose to resolve disputes concerning the "who" by appealing to criteria of personhood. For them, accordingly, what turns a collection of individuals into fellow subjects of justice is common possession of defining features of humanity. Exactly what those defining features consist of is a matter of controversy, however, as humanist theorists differ among themselves as to whether to stress autonomy, rationality, language use, capacity to form and pursue an idea of the good, or vulnerability to moral injury, among other possibilities.[11] Fortunately, those debates need not detain us here. More important than the precise definition of "the human" is the idea that all those in possession of it belong together in a single "who" of justice. That idea is shared by all proponents of humanism, notwithstanding their other disagreements.

What should we make of the humanist principle as a vehicle for evaluating disputes over the "who"? The first thing to note is that this approach provides a critical check on exclusionary nationalism. Because it delimits the frame of justice on the basis of personhood, it is capable of entertaining claims that suppose non-hegemonic understandings of the subject of justice. Nevertheless, the humanist principle is not genuinely reflexive. After all, this principle operates at such a high level of abstraction that it can discern nothing of moral significance in any particular configuration. Staking out a view from the commanding heights, it accords standing indiscriminately to everyone in respect to everything. Adopting the one-size-fits-all frame of global humanity, it forecloses the possibility that different issues require different frames or scales of justice.

The root problem, I think, is that the humanist principle takes no account of actual or historical social relations. Cavalierly oblivious to such matters, it is, in this respect, the antithesis of the previous principle. Whereas membership theory sought to ground obligations of justice in what turned out to be an overly restrictive type of social relation, this one assigns such obligations with no regard whatever to such relations. As a result, it rides roughshod over the forms of life it wishes to regulate and over the self-understandings of those whom it claims to obligate. Effectively handed down from some lofty perch, high above the world of real human doings, the humanist insistence that everyone counts in every matter at every time, regardless of what anything does or thinks, carries an unmistakable whiff of authoritarianism.

Humanism's lofty abstraction may help explain, moreover, its historic affinity with imperialism. Although it would be wrong to posit a necessary relation here, there may well be a subterranean connection between the "view from nowhere" this approach assumes and the relatively powerful somewhere from which that view is usually assumed. This is not to say that the disadvantaged do not sometimes couch their claims in the idiom of shared humanity; they surely do. But, as Hannah Arendt shrewdly observed, that is typically the idiom of last resort, the one adopted when all else has failed, hence an expression of weakness or lack of other, more robust entitlement. On Arendt's (1973) reading, to appeal for justice in the name of abstract humanity is implicitly to admit that one is owed little or nothing on the basis of one's actual relationship to the powerful and privileged. The effect, when the actual relation is one of predation or exploitation, is to obscure some important facts about the world in which claims for justice arise. In that sense, the humanist principle can appear to express, indeed to ratify, the perspective of the powerful and the privileged.

In any case, the principle's one-size-fits-all globalism suffices to disqualify it as a viable approach to justice theorizing in abnormal times. To say that every question of justice always necessarily implicates everyone is every bit as a priori as to say that every question of justice is necessarily national. In both cases, the matter is always already decided in advance, and the capacity for reflexive questioning of frames is thereby surrendered. For equal if opposite reasons, then, neither the humanist principle nor the membership principle is able to parse disputes encompassing conflicting understandings of the "who" of justice. Neither can adequately handle problems of abnormal justice, so characteristic of the present era.

Understandably, then, many philosophers and activists reject both membership and humanism. Seeking to avoid approaches that pretend to settle every question in advance, they prefer a third principle for evaluating justice frames, namely, the *all-affected principle*. Endorsed by many who believe that the "who" of justice is neither always national nor always global, this principle promises to make it possible to conceptualize *transnational* justice. The root idea is intuitive and simple. Proponents of the all-affected principle propose to resolve disputes about the "who" by appealing to social relations of *interdependence*. For them, in other words, what makes a group of people fellow subjects of justice is their objective co-imbrication in a web of causal relationships.[12] Whoever is causally affected by a given action nexus has standing as a subject of justice in relation to it. Thus, the "who" of justice is a function of the scale of social interaction. As the latter varies from case to case, so does the former.

This approach, too, has several distinguishable variants. Peter Singer offers an empiricist-utilitarianism version of it, while Jürgen Habermas incorporates it into his famous principle "D" of discourse ethics. Here too, however, the differences are less important than what they share. The defining crux of this position is its identification of the "who" of justice with a "community of risk" figured in terms of causality. Those who count are those whose actions impact and impinge on one another.

What should we make of the all-affected principle as a standard for evaluating conflicting "who's"? The first thing to note is that this principle eschews the humanist strategy of defining a class of beings who share a common property, regardless of their interconnections. As opposed to that approach, it shares the membership-theoretical commitment to ground obligations of justice in actual relationships. At the same time, however, proponents of this third principle reject membership theory's understanding of the morally relevant kind of social relation. Finding both nationality and citizenship too restrictive, they seek to broaden the bounds of justice to include all whose actions affect one another.

At first sight, therefore, the all-affected principle appears to avoid the weaknesses of the previous two. It simultaneously provides a critical check on self-serving notions of membership, while also taking cognizance of social relations. Yet this principle is disturbingly objectivistic. By conceiving justice-triggering relations in terms of causality, it treats human beings on the model of colliding billiard balls, ignoring the constitutive force of social mediations. In its utilitarian incarnation, moreover, the all-affected principle is objectionably scientistic. By reducing the question of the "who" to the question of who is affected by whom, affectedness treats it as a simple matter of empirical fact, which could be settled by social science. Thus, this approach effectively authorizes social scientific experts to determine the "who" of justice.

In fact, however, the question of the "who" cannot be handed off to social-science experts on structural causality. Given the so-called butterfly effect, one can adduce empirical evidence that just about everyone is affected by just about everything. What is needed, therefore, is a way of distinguishing those levels and kinds of effectivity that are deemed sufficient to confer moral standing from those that are not. Social science, however, cannot supply such criteria. On the contrary, such judgments necessarily involve a complex combination of normative reflection, historical interpretation and social theorizing. They are inherently dialogical and political.

In general, then, the all-affected principle falls prey to the *reductio ad absurdum* of the butterfly effect. Unable to identify *morally relevant* social relations, it treats every causal connection as equally significant. Painting a night in which all cows are grey, it cannot resist the very one-size-fits-all globalism it sought to avoid. Thus, it too fails to supply a defensible standard for determining the "who" in abnormal times.

Given the respective deficiencies of membership, humanism, and affectedness, what sort of discriminating principle can help us evaluate rival frames in abnormal justice? I propose to submit allegations of misframing to what I shall call the *all-subjected principle*. According to this principle, all those who are jointly subject to a given governance structure have moral standing as subjects of justice in relation to it. On this view, what turns a collection of people into fellow subjects of justice is not shared citizenship or nationality, or common possession of abstract personhood, or the sheer fact of causal interdependence, but rather their joint subjection to a structure of governance, which sets the ground rules that govern their interaction. For any such governance structure, the all-subjected principle matches the scope of moral concern to that of subjection.[13]

Thus, this principle, too, rejects humanism's disregard of social relationships. Like membership and affectedness, it insists that justice obligations arise from social relations. Unlike affectedness, however, it rejects the view that mere causal interdependence constitutes a sufficiently robust relation to trigger obligations of justice. Like membership, rather, it insists that the relation in question must be political. Unlike membership, however, it rejects the view that identifies political relations exclusively with co-belonging in a Westphalian state. From the perspective of the all-subjected principle, justice-triggering political relations exist whenever a collection of people are jointly subjected to a governance structure that sets the ground rules governing their interaction.

Of course, everything depends on how we interpret the phrase "subjection to structure of governance". I propose to understand this expression broadly, as encompassing relations to powers of various types. Not restricted to states, governance structures also comprise non-state agencies that generate enforceable rules that structure important swaths of social interaction. The most obvious examples are the agencies that set the ground rules of the global economy, such as the World Trade Organization and the International Monetary Fund. But many other examples could also be cited, including transnational structures governing environmental regulation, atomic and nuclear power, policing, security, health, intellectual property, and the administration of civil and criminal law. Insofar as such agencies regulate the interaction of large transnational populations, they can be said to subject the latter, even though the rule-makers are not accountable at present to those whom they govern. Given this broad understanding of governance structures, the term "subjection" should be understood broadly as well. Not restricted to formal citizenship, or even to the broader condition of falling within the jurisdiction of such a state, this notion also encompasses the further condition of being subject to the coercive power of non-state and trans-state forms of governmentality.

Understood in this way, the all-subjected principle affords a critical standard for assessing the (in)justice of frames. An issue is justly framed if and only if everyone subjected to the governance structures that regulate a given swath of social interaction is accorded equal consideration. To deserve such consideration, moreover, one need not already be an officially accredited "member" of the structure in question; one need only be subjected to it. Thus, sub-Saharan Africans who have been involuntarily disconnected from the global economy as a result of the rules imposed by its governance structures count as subjects of justice in relation to it, even if they are not officially recognized as participating in it (Ferguson 1999).

The all-subjected principle remedies the major defects of the previous principles. Unlike membership, it pierces the self-serving shield of exclusionary nationalism so as to contemplate injustices of misframing. Unlike humanism, it overcomes abstract, all-embracing globalism by taking notice of social relationships. Unlike affectedness, it avoids the indiscriminateness of the butterfly effect by identifying the morally relevant type of social relation, namely, joint subjection to a governance structure. Far from substituting a single global "who" for the Westphalian "who", the all-subjected principle militates against any one-size-fits-all framing of justice. In today's world, all of us are subject to a plurality of different governance structures, some local, some national, some regional, and some global. The need, accordingly, is to delimit a variety of different frames for different issues. Able to mark out a plurality of "who's" for different purposes, the all-subjected principle tells us when and where to apply which frame.

Conclusion
In general, then, I am offering a constructive proposal for dealing with conflicts over the "who" in current conditions of abnormal justice. Specifically, I propose to submit claims against injustices of misframing to the all-subjected principle. This approach, I contend, can illuminate justice conflicts that encompass competing views of the "who".

More important than the specifics of this proposal, however, is its general conceptual structure. What is crucial here is that this approach is simultaneously reflexive and discriminating. It combines the reflexive questioning of justice frames with a discriminating evaluative principle. In this way, it reckons with both the positive and negative sides of abnormal justice. Thanks to its reflexivity, the concept of misframing validates contestation of the Westphalian frame. Because it is pitched to the meta-level, this concept permits us to entertain the possibility that first-order questions of justice have been unjustly framed. Thus, it opens space for non-hegemonic understandings of the "who". At the same time, thanks to its discriminating character, this approach offers a way of assessing the justice of rival "who's". By submitting proposed frames to the all-subjected principle, it enables us to weigh their relative merits. Thus, it provides some provisional closure for adjudicating disputes. All told, then, this approach holds considerable promise for clarifying disputes about the "who" in abnormal times.

Most important of all, however, is the general problem I have outlined here. Under conditions of abnormal justice, previously taken-for-granted assumptions about the "who" of justice no longer go without saying. Thus, these assumptions must themselves be subject to critical discussion and re-evaluation. In such discussions, the trick is to avoid two temptations. On the one hand, one must resist the reactionary and ultimately futile temptation to cling to assumptions that are no longer appropriate to our globalizing world, such as passé Westphalianism. On the other hand, one should avoid celebrating abnormality for its own sake, as if contestation were itself liberation. In this essay, I have tried to model an alternative stance, which acknowledges abnormal justice as the horizon within which all struggles against injustice must currently proceed. Only by appreciating both the perils and prospects of this condition can we hope to reduce the vast injustices that pervade our world.

Endnotes

[1] For an account of the Westphalian frame, see Fraser (2005, 2008a). Some readers have suggested that colonized people never accepted the legitimacy of the Westphalian frame, hence that this frame was never truly normalized. In my view, however, the great majority of anti-colonialists in the post-World War II era sought to achieve independent Westphalian states of their own. In contrast, only a small minority consistently championed justice within a global frame—for reasons that are entirely understandable. My claim, then, is that, far from contesting the Westphalian frame per se, anti-imperialist forces generally sought rather to realize it in a genuinely universal, even-handed way. Thanks to Ann Laura Stoler for forcefully raising this issue, although she will not be satisfied with my answer.

[2] "Intermestic" is a neologism coined by James Rosenau (1997), combining elements of "international" and "domestic" so as to indicate the blurring of that standard divide.

[3] The expression "community of risk" was coined by Ulrich Beck (1992).

[4] If one were faithfully to follow Kuhn's (1996 [1962]) terminology, one would speak rather of "revolutionary justice". But given that expression's associations, I prefer to take my cue from Richard Rorty and speak instead of "abnormal justice". Rorty (1979, 1989) distinguishes "normal" from "abnormal discourse".

[5] For the full argument, see Fraser (2008b).

[6] For my original two-dimensional view of justice, see Fraser (2003). For the revised, three-dimensional, view, see Fraser (2005, 2008a).

[7] For discussions of such issues, see Guinier (1994), Htun (2004), Kymlicka (1995), Rai (2002), Ritchie and Hill (2001) and Williams (1998).

[8] I first introduced the term "misframing" in Fraser (2005, 2008a).

[9] For the citizenship variant of the membership principle, see Kymlicka (2001) and Nagel (2005). For the nationality variant, see Miller (1995).

[10] For the full argument, see Nagel (2005).

[11] The most prominent proponent of this approach today is Martha Nussbaum. See, for example, Nussbaum (1996).

[12] Proponents of this approach include Peter Singer (2004); Thomas W. Pogge (2002) and Iris Young (2006). Until recently, I myself considered the all-affected principle the most promising candidate on offer for a "postwestphalian principle" of frame-setting, even though I criticized its standard scientistic interpretation and its "butterfly-effect"

indeterminacy, as explained below. Now, however, I believe that these difficulties are so serious that the better course of wisdom is to abandon the all-affected principle in favor of the alternative presented here. For my earlier views, see Fraser (2005, 2006, 2008a).
[13] The expression "all-subjected principle" is my own, but the idea can be found in Cohen and Sabel (2006) and Forst (2005).

References

Aman A C (2003) Globalization, democracy and the need for a new administrative law. *Indiana Journal of Global Legal Studies* 10(1):125–155

Arendt H (1973) *The Origins of Totalitarianism* (new edition). New York: Harcourt Brace Jovanovich

Beck U (1992) *Risk Society: Towards a New Modernity*. London: Sage

Bohman J (1999) International regimes and democratic governance. *International Affairs* 75(3):499–513

Boyce J K (2004) Democratizing global economic governance. *Development and Change* 35(3):593–599

Cohen J and Sabel C (2006) Extra Republican *Nulla Justitia? Philosophy & Public Affairs* 34:147–175

Cox R W (1996) A perspective on globalization. In J H Mittelman (ed) *Globalization: Critical Reflections* (pp 21–30). New York: Lynne Rienner

Cox R W (1997) Democracy in hard times: Economic globalization and the limits to liberal democracy. In A Mc Grew (ed) *The Transformation of Democracy?* (pp 49–72). Cambridge: Polity

Dryzek J (1999) Transnational democracy. *Journal of Political Philosophy* 7(1):30–51

Ferguson J (1999) *Expectations of Modernity: Myths and Meanings of Urban Life on the Zambian Copperbelt*. Berkeley: University of California Press

Forst R (2001) Towards a critical theory of transnational justice. In T W Pogge (ed) *Global Justice* (pp 169–187). Oxford: Blackwell

Forst R (2005) Justice, morality and power in the global context. In A Follesdal and T W Pogge (eds) *Real World Justice* (pp 27–36). Dordrecht: Springer

Fraser N (2003) Social justice in the age of identity politics. In N Fraser and A Honneth (eds) *Redistribution or Recognition? A Political-Philosophical Exchange* (pp 7–109). London: Verso

Fraser N (2005) Reframing justice in a globalizing world. *New Left Review* 36:69–88

Fraser N (2006) Democratic justice in a globalizing age: Thematizing the problem of the frame. In N Karagiannis and P Wagner (eds) *Varieties of World-Making: Beyond Globalization* (pp 193–215). Liverpool: Liverpool University Press

Fraser N (2008a) *Scales of Justice: Reimagining Political Space in a Globalizing World*. Cambridge: Polity

Fraser N (2008b) Abnormal justice. *Critical Inquiry* 34(3):393–422

Gill S (1998) New constitutionalism, democratisation and global political economy. *Pacifica Review* 10(1):23–38

Guinier L (1994) *The Tyranny of the Majority*. New York: The Free Press

Harris R L and Seid M J (2000) *Critical Perspectives on Globalization and Neoliberalism in the Developing Countries*. Boston: Leiden

Held D (1995) *Democracy and the Global Order: From the Modern State to Cosmopolitan Governance*. Cambridge: Polity

Held D (1999) The transformation of political community: Rethinking democracy in the context of globalization. In Shapiro I and Hacker-Cordón C (eds) *Democracy's Edges* (pp 84–111). Cambridge: Cambridge University Press

Held D (2000) Regulating globalization? *International Journal of Sociology* 15(2):394–408

Held D (2003) Cosmopolitanism: Globalization tamed? *Review of International Studies* 29(4):465–480

Held D (2004) Democratic accountability and political effectiveness from a cosmopolitan perspective. *Government and Opposition* 39(2):364–391

Helleiner E (1994) From Bretton Woods to global finance: A world turned upside down. In R Stubbs and G Underhill (eds) *Political Economy and the Changing Global Order* (pp 163–175). New York: St Martin's Press

Hoogvelt A M M (2001) *Globalization and the Post Colonial World: The Political Economy of Development*. Baltimore: The Johns Hopkins University Press

Htun M (2004) Is gender like ethnicity? The political representation of identity groups. *Perspectives on Politics* 2(3):439–458

Kuhn T S (1996 [1962]) *The Structure of Scientific Revolutions*. Chicago: University of Chicago Press

Kymlicka W (1995) *Multicultural Citizenship: A Liberal Theory of Minority Rights*. Oxford: Oxford University Press

Kymlicka W (2001) Territorial boundaries. A liberal-egalitarian perspective. In D Miller and S H Hashmi (eds) *Boundaries and Justice: Diverse Ethical Perspectives* (pp 249–275) Princeton: Princeton University Press

Miller D (1995) *On Nationality*. Oxford: Oxford University Press

Nagel T (2005) The problem of global justice. *Philosophy & Public Affairs* 33:113–147

Nussbaum M C (1996) Patriotism and cosmopolitanism. In M C Nussbaum (and respondents) *For Love of Country: Debating the Limits of Patriotism* (pp 3–20). Boston: Beacon

Pogge T W (1999) Economic justice and national borders. *Revision* 22(2):27–34

Pogge T W (2001) The influence of the global order on the prospects for genuine democracy in the developing countries. *Ratio Juris* 14(3):326–343

Pogge T W (2002) *World and Poverty and Human Rights: Cosmopolitan Responsibilities and Reforms*. Cambridge: Polity

Rai S M (2002) Political representation, democratic institutions and women's empowerment: The quota debate in India. In J L Parpart, S M Rai and K Staudt (eds) *Rethinking Empowerment: Gender and Development in a Global/Local World* (pp 133–145). New York: Routledge

Rawls J (2001) *The Law of Peoples* (new edition). Cambridge: Harvard University Press

Ritchie R and Hill S (2001) The case for proportional representation. In R Ritchie and S Hill (eds) *Whose Vote Counts?* (pp 1–33). Boston: Beacon

Rorty R (1979) *Philosophy and the Mirror of Nature*. Princeton: Princeton University Press

Rorty R (1989) *Contingency, Irony, and Solidarity*. Cambridge: Cambridge University Press

Rosenau J (1997) *Along the Domestic-Foreign Frontier: Exploring Governance in a Turbulent World*. Cambridge: Cambridge University Press

Schneiderman D (2001) Investment rules and the rule of law. *Constellations* 8(4):521–537

Singer P (2004) *One World: The Ethics of Globalization*. 2nd ed. London: Yale University Press

Storm S and Mohan Rao J (2004) Market-led globalization and world democracy. *Development and Change* 35(5):567–581

Williams M (1998) *Voice, Trust, and Memory: Marginalized Groups and the Failings of Liberal Representation*. Princeton: Princeton University Press

Young I (2006) Responsibility and global justice: A social connection model. *Social Philosophy and Policy* 23(1):102–130

The Communist Hypothesis and Revolutionary Capitalisms: Exploring the Idea of Communist Geographies for the Twenty-first Century

Erik Swyngedouw

Geography, School of Environment and Development,
University of Manchester, Manchester, UK;
erik.swyngedouw@manchester.ac.uk

Abstract: This essay starts from the presumption that "the communist hypothesis" is still a good one, but argues that the idea of communism requires urgent re-thinking in light of both the "obscure" disaster of twentieth century really existing socialism and the specific conditions of twenty-first century capitalism. I explore the contours of the communist hypothesis, chart the characteristics of the revolutionary capitalism of the twenty-first century and consider how our present predicament relates to the urgency of rethinking and reviving the communist hypothesis. Throughout, I tentatively suggest a number of avenues that require urgent intellectual and theoretical attention and interrogate the present condition in light of the possibilities for creating communist geographies for the twenty-first century.

Keywords: communism, the communist hypothesis, radical geography, radical politics, communist geographies

The communist hypothesis is that a different collective organization is practicable, one that will eliminate the inequality of wealth and even the division of labour. The private appropriation of massive fortunes and their transmission by inheritance will disappear. The existence of a coercive state, separate from civil society, will no longer appear a necessity: a long process of reorganization based on a free association of producers will see it withering away (Badiou 2008a:35).

On the cover of its issue of 17 February 2009, *Newsweek* announced boldly that "We are all socialists now". It referred to the unprecedented nationalization of banks and the multi-billion dollar rescue packages, demanded by the financial elites, the US federal state and many other governments around the world are pumping into an ailing capitalist economy. If we take Newsweek's point seriously, the choice we are presented with today is no longer the one Marx once held up, ie between barbarism and socialism, but rather between socialism and communism. I am sure the use of the word "communism" will raise a few eyebrows. The persistent outlawing of the name and its erasure from

Antipode Vol. 41 No. S1 2009 ISSN 0066-4812, pp 298–319
doi: 10.1111/j.1467-8330.2009.00727.x

the pages of self-respecting journals over the past two decades or so has been so effective that even its utterance is looked at with suspicion, distrust, and perhaps, a slight sense of curiosity. In an age in which anything and everything can be discussed, the very idea of communism as a positive injunction seems to have been censored and scripted out of both everyday and intellectual vocabularies. It is only tolerated in sensationalized accounts of the "obscure disaster"[1] of twentieth century "really existing socialism" or in romanticized Hollywood renditions of the life and work of communist heroes like Che Guevara. Of course, the work of Karl Marx, Antonio Gramsci or Louis Althusser is still discussed in arcane academic tracts, but this is much less the case for the political treatises of, say, Vladimir Lenin, Leo Trotsky, Rosa Luxemburg, Mau Ze Dong, or Ho Chi Minh. The idea of communism has either been stigmatized beyond recovery or relegated to the dustbin of failed utopias.

The argument I present here is not about the lingering remnants of political practices that go under the name of communism in various parts of the world (like China, Cuba, North Korea, Nepal, or parts of India). Rather, I intend to explore the communist hypothesis (as summarized in the quote above) and offer some tentative lines of enquiry needed to revive this hypothesis for the twenty-first century. The key point is not to tease out what the history of communist thought and practice may mean or whether it is still relevant today, but, much more importantly, to analyse how the present conditions look from the perspective of the Idea of Communism. Between 13 and 15 March 2009, more than 1000 people convened at Birkbeck College in London to attend a conference on the "Idea of Communism"; an event that gathered about two dozen philosophers from around the world to think "communism". "Move over Jacko, Idea of Communism is hottest ticket in town this weekend", *The Guardian* announced in its Thursday edition to express its surprise at the success of this sell-out event (Campbell 2009). As Alain Badiou noted in the foreword to the conference program:

> The communist hypothesis remains the good one, I do not see any other. If we have to abandon this hypothesis, then it is no longer worth doing anything at all in the field of collective action. Without the horizon of communism, without this idea, there is nothing in the historical and political becoming of any interest to a philosopher. Let everyone bother about his own affairs, and let us stop talking about it . . . what is imposed on us as a task, even as a philosophical obligation, is to help a new mode of existence of the hypothesis to deploy itself.

The two central metaphors that sustain the idea of communism are, of course, equality and democracy, held together by a fidelity to the belief that these can be realized geographically through continuous and sustained political struggle. The realization of these principles involves the self-organization and self-management of people, and, therefore, will eliminate the coercive state as the principal organizer of political life. Organized and self-confident social and political struggle would be the means by which the former would be realized. The communist hypothesis combines the negativity of "resistance" (to any relation or practice that perverts the presumption of (political) equality) with a belief in the immanent practicability of free and equal forms of socio-spatial organization. The origins of *Antipode*, 40 years ago, were very much indebted to these principles. As Dick Peet put it in Issue 1 of the journal:

> This group is characterized by a new level of commitment to the movement for social and economic equality...believes in radical change...The nascent New Left in geography can contribute to the cause in three fundamental ways. We can help design a more equitable society...To do this we need to take an entirely different set of premises and build new theories of the way things should be, the arrangements of people which are most conducive to a participatory democracy, the distributions of manufacturing and agricultural activities which lead to economic equality over space...in short a whole new geography truly based upon the precepts of equality and justice. Our second contribution must be to the achievement of radical change...Geographers can play particularly important roles in providing a constant barrage of criticism and proposals for change...Thirdly, we must organize for effective action...(Peet 1969:1–3).

There is an uncanny resemblance between Peet's clarion call for a revolutionary Left geography and Badiou's insistence, 40-plus years later, of the continuing relevance of the communist hypothesis. However, the political practice of achieving what both Peet and Badiou call for seems today more remote than ever, despite the positively verifiable geographical facts, tirelessly explored and theoretically accounted for in the pages of this journal, that we are further away than ever from socially equal and politically democratic forms of "being-in-common" (Nancy 1991) in a geographically highly diversified world.

The idea of communism retains a subversive edge—in spite of the failed experiments that went under that name in the twentieth century— precisely because the name still evokes the sense that a genuinely different world cannot only be imagined but is practically possible. Being-in-common in egalitarian and free ways that permit the self-development of each and all retains a great mobilizing potential. An urgent and demanding intellectual task is required to re-think the socio-spatial practices, the possible forms of political organization, and the transformative imaginary and material geographies that will give the idea of communism again a positive content. The courage of the intellect needs to be mustered to work through if, how, and in what ways a communism for the twenty-first century can be thought again. In the remainder of this essay, I shall offer some pointers for the formidable intellectual task ahead. I shall proceed in two steps. First, I outline the presumptions on which the communist hypothesis is based. Second, I briefly summarize the political fault lines that striate the current phase of capitalism. On the way, I shall chart tentatively what is left to think.

The Idea of Communism

Today, communism is just an idea, a hypothesis, and a scandalous and illegitimate notion, in the present sequence of things. The question is whether new and different significations can be inscribed in its name, rather than endlessly repeating the refrain of the ethico-moral bankruptcy of the former Communist bloc. Neither a rehearsal of the standard critiques nor a simple invocation of its utopian possibilities will do; what is required is nothing less than a radical invention of the new, on the basis of a sustained critical engagement with what was and is already embryonically there. It is useful, in this context, to recall Marx's definition of communism from *The German Ideology*: "Communism is for us not a *state of affairs* which is to be established, an *ideal* to which reality will have to adjust itself. We call communism the *real* movement which abolishes the present state of things" (Marx and Engels 1987:56–57; original emphasis).[2] Tentatively charting the contours of this real movement for the twenty-first century is the challenge for the contemporary collective communist intellect.

For me, communism is intimately connected to democracy. I am not referring here to democracy as a set of political institutions (parliaments, governments, and the like) and its associated political procedures (like elections at regular intervals in which a recognized set of individuals can participate if they wish to do so), but rather to the founding gesture of democracy (Swyngedouw 2009c). The democratic political, following, among others, Claude Lefort (1989) or Jacques Rancière (1995, 1998), expresses the contingent presumption of equality of each and everyone qua speaking—and hence political—beings. The contingent presumption of equality that marks "the democratic invention" stands in strict opposition to any given, and sociologically verifiable, order, including any given and instituted "democratic" order. The democratic political, therefore, exposes the un-egalitarian processes that rupture any given socio-spatial order. In other words, equality is the very premise upon which a democratic politics is constituted; it opens up the space of the political through the testing of a wrong that subverts equality (Rancière 2004). Justice, from this perspective, disappears from the terrain of the moral and enters the space of the political under the name of equality. For Etienne Balibar (1993), for example, the unconditional premise for justice and emancipation resides in the fusion of equality and liberty (what he names as "égaliberté"). However, neither freedom nor equality are offered, granted or distributed, they can only be conquered. The democratic political, therefore, is not about expressing demands to the elites to rectify injustices, inequalities or unfreedoms, but about the enunciation of the right to *égaliberté*. The idea of communism is thus premised on the unconditionality of equality in a given institutional and social arrangement that has always already "wronged" the very condition of equality (Rancière 2001). Put simply, a communist political sequence arises when, in the name of equality, those who are not equally included in the existing socio-political order demand their "right to equality", a demand that calls the political into being, renders visible what is invisible, and exposes the "wrongs" in the present order (Swyngedouw forthcoming-a).

Moreover, the presumption of equality is predicated upon asserting difference, differentiation, agonism, and dispute, while refusing to inscribe one particular antagonism as the One that prevents the realization of the presumption of equality. Finally, the presumption of equality assures that the place of power is kept structurally vacant (Lefort 1986) or, in other words, any one can claim the place of power. There is neither a transcendental figure (like "the King") nor a universal political subject (like the Proletarian or the Party) that can and should suture the place of power. A proper democratic political sequence, then, is of course one that demands equality in the face of clear and present exclusions that are part of any (democratic or otherwise) instituted order. A communist practice is one that fights for the positive realization of equality (as a historically–geographically contingent and, therefore, always contestable inscription, one that demands enduring verification and re-imagination) in the face of inegalitarian practices, and strives for the universalization of this egalitarian injunction from the basis of always historically and geographically situated inequalities.

Consider, for example, the emancipatory–egalitarian struggles of the proletarian subject in the nineteenth century, demanding political equality in a republican configuration that disavowed the persistent perversion of the egalitarian principle, which was nevertheless enshrined in the republican constitution. Or consider the struggle of women in the twentieth century for political recognition, the extraordinary fights of African Americans and the South African ANC for egalitarian democratic political emancipation. Today's struggles of immigrants (illegal or otherwise), demanding political equality, equally express the egalitarian democratic desires that underpin the communist hypothesis. It is these demands that the instituted "democratic order" with its allocation of places and functions systematically perverts in all manner of ways (Swyngedouw 2009a). These struggles are invariably located in concrete places but aspire to universalization and spatialization; they are predicated on political subjectivation, the becoming of a political subject through grounded emancipatory struggles. The presumption of equality that operates under the name of democracy is of course an integral part of the idea of communism. Re-thinking and re-claiming the political notion of democracy as equality is a central and vital task.

However, the demand for political equality is a necessary, but not sufficient, condition for the realization of the communist hypothesis. Political equality prefigures and permits the agonistic expression of differential claims, particularly with respect to the forms of social organization and the distribution of collective wealth (or surplus). Political equality assumes the capacity of each and everyone to govern, and affirms the capability of self-organization and collective decision-making. This opens up a second terrain—after equality—that sustains the communist hypothesis, ie the belief in the capacity of each (and not just of the state, its technocratic managers, or propertied elites) to govern and to decide the principles of appropriation, mobilization, and distribution of wealth and revenue. The communist hypothesis, therefore, prefigures the end of the coercive state as we know it and its replacement by forms of self-organization and self-management. Thinking through the relations between emancipatory struggles and the transformation of forms of governing the commons is indeed an urgent task. In particular, the articulation between different interlocking scales of regulation, self-management and organization on the one hand and their relation to changing state forms on the other remains a thorny issue.

The historical–geographical terrain for the realization of the communist hypothesis is of course the commons. The very name of communism not only invokes an egalitarian "being-in-common" of all qua multiple and multitude, but also includes the commons that is the earth, the world and, therefore, life itself. This latter sense of the commons refers fundamentally to the collectively transformed socio-ecological relations, such as water, air, CO_2, but also knowledge, information, affective labour, biodiversity regimes, resources, urban space, and the like. The commons of socio-ecological arrangements and their conditions of rights of use, transformation (metabolization), access and distribution, the modalities of their spatial organization, and the configuration, access (education), ownership and distribution of collective knowledge/information are now the key domains around which the communist hypothesis has to be thought and developed. In particular, it raises the question of property and property relations with respect to common resources like those exemplified above. Cloaking the political argument around the commons as one between public versus private property, I would argue, misses the point if the public sphere is defined as or restricted to the domain of the State. As I shall argue further below, the State has become (and arguably has always been) another instance of the private, distinct from private capital or individuals, but nevertheless private with respect to the commons, the ownership of the biopolitical conditions of life like the environment, resources, genetic and informational code-systems, knowledge, etc. The communist hypothesis is structured around the commons as the shared ownership of each and everyone under common stewardship. Communism, therefore, is a struggle against both the privatism of the state and that of capital—ultimately sanctioned by property relations that fragment, privatize and monopolize the commons—and for the production of collective institutions for the democratic management of the commons, thereby turning the commons into a new use value. The communist idea is, therefore, also about the transformation of the commons from private to collective, the abolition of private property (of the commons) and re-affirming the capacity of all qua collective—the communist intelligence—to govern the city, the commons in-common.

The struggle over and for the commons also highlights the now irreconcilable difference between current forms of social-democratic socialism (what Paul Virno defines as the socialism for capital—see below) and communism. As Toni Negri put it:

> The need to distinguish between 'socialism" and "communism" has again become obvious: but this time not because of the blurred boundaries between them, but because they are so opposed. Socialism is nothing other than one of the forms taken by capitalist management of the economy and of power, whereas communism is an absolutely radical political economic democracy and an aspiration to freedom (Negri 1990:167).

The communist hypothesis contains an historical invariant—it stands for the eternal return of the heroic-tragic historical-geographies of emancipatory struggles sustained by the eternally returning, albeit in different historical forms, desire/struggle for emancipation, freedom, and equality. Realizing the communist hypothesis entails a voluntaristic (subjective) moment to revive this communist invariant, that is the will of the individual to join up in common with others to realize politically the idea of communism (Hallward 2009). The communist idea is nothing without the will to do something new, without the will to become political subject. It insists on the continuous transformation of this singularity of the egalitarian will and movement to the universality of being-in-common as part of a commons.

Needless to say, the communist hypothesis is confronted with the existing state of affairs, the conditions of contemporary neoliberal capitalisms with their often extreme and multiple socio-spatial and socio-ecological inequalities, uneven political and economic development, extraordinary exclusions and autocratic global transformations, animated by the joint dynamics of multi-scaled state and quasi-state forms and the competitive struggle of individual capitals, organized as networks with varying spatial geometries, for surplus-value production and realization. Working through the communist hypothesis requires engaging seriously with this state of the situation and, in particular, with the fate of instituted post-democracy, the type and contours of the multiple emancipatory struggles and the changing conditions of the commons in the relentless reworkings of capitalism. In other words, a critique of political economy, reframed as political-ecology, is still urgently needed, a critique that also accounts both for the resurgences of emancipatory and egalitarian desires (the continuous re-emergence of the communist principles) and for deepening struggles over the privatization/dispossession of the commons.

The New Spirit of Capitalism: Capitalism's Revolutions

Cultures of Excess

Coming to terms with the "obscure" disaster of twentieth century communism not only necessitates a communist critique of the uneven and truncated failures of the socialist projects in the Soviet Union or China, but also of the failure (in emancipatory terms) of state control/management and of the repressive (in ethical, cultural, and moral terms) state capitalism in "the West" (including many of the post-colonial states). Only an in-depth understanding of the failures of the socialist management of capital may permit grappling with how the "New Spirit of Capitalism", which re-invigorated the capitalist class project after the 1970s, permitted to capture imaginaries and fantasies that had galvanized so much of earlier communist thought and political practice (emancipation, freedom, and equality). The 1968 events, both in the West and the East (like in Prague), were of course as much a revolt against the stale, repressive, and reactionary moral order of capitalism as against economic exploitation choreographed by capitalist relations or the excesses of state domination. Indeed, the bureaucratized "Fordist-welfarist" forms of capitalism were paralleled by a repressive moral order shared both by the social-democratic and socialist variants of state management. The revolts of the late 1960s and early 1970s targeted, among other demands, the suffocating "moral restraint" in sexual, gender, money, relationships, and other affective matters that had been an integral part of the capitalist socio-cultural order until then. The revolutionaries of the libertarian and romantic currents of the late 1960s demanded (successfully) all manner of affective liberations. Conservative constraint was replaced by the imperative to enjoy. The left's critique of everyday life in the stale suburbanized living of the extensive spectacle of western capitalism as well as in the Stalinist bunker spaces of living in the intensive spectacle (see Debord 1967) became exquisitely incorporated—and de-politicized—in what

Boltanski and Chiapello call *The New Spirit of Capitalism* (Boltanski and Chiapello 2007; Sennett 2007). Both economic elites and radical cultural critiques and practices revelled in embracing new forms of excess. Liberation was experienced as the search for surplus value as well as surplus enjoyment. The injunction to enjoy became the cultural expression of the latest round of capitalist transformations (Žižek 1999, 2006); an injunction that also "liberated" the traditional elites of the bourgeois injunction to "care".

Political equality weakened as a central concern. The new capitalist cultural political-economy of excess fused seamlessly with demands for equality that became defined as the equality of difference (and justice framed as the right to be different or, rather, as the right to enjoy one's specificity). Democracy, in turn, became defined and pursued as the freedom to exercise individual choice and preference rather than the unconditional given of each and every one as equal qua speaking beings. Consuming became the highest freedom and expression of emancipation. Indeed, consuming identity became the hard kernel that secures enjoyment, freedom, and difference in a market that treats everyone as equal. Market equality replaced political equality.

Equality as difference and freedom as the enjoyment of excess became the cultural expression of new forms of fragmented, networked, diffuse, and multi-centred capitalisms (Hardt and Negri 2001). A presumably non-authoritarian and inclusive capitalism, which skilfully displaced— both geographically and organizationally—the more overt mechanisms of repression, exploitation, exclusion, and submission to the global South, hegemonized the signifiers that once belonged to communism. Some of the Left's 1960s critique became incorporated in and subsumed under a revolutionary capitalism. Indeed, not the communist idea and practice, but capitalist "perestroika" became the most revolutionary and exhilarating game in town. Mao's call for permanent revolution, which was smothered in China's transition to capitalism while being the condition of the latter's possibility (Russo 2006), had been taken up by the newly emerging (and older transforming) western elites in a class project to revamp capitalism and capitalist class power. This "cultural" transformation of capitalism signals nothing less than a passive revolution of the kind that Gramsci identified in the early 1930s with the emergence of "Fordism", a form of neutralization of originally counter-hegemonic demands by new organizational and managerial forms of capitalism (Mouffe 2009).

Capturing the State: Socialism for the Elites
Indeed, the onslaught of neoliberalisms, which is the signifier that stands for the successful class struggle of the bourgeoisie to regain the upper hand over the dispossessed of the world, has all but wiped out

working class politics. As Harvey contends, "[neo-liberalism] is a class project, masked by a lot of neo-liberal rhetoric about individual freedom, liberty, personal responsibility, privatization and the free market. These were means, however, towards the restoration and consolidation of class power, and that neo-liberal project has been fairly successful" (Harvey 2009; see also Harvey 2005). This class victory is now plain to see in the present conjuncture marked by intensifying sequences of financial-economic crises. In the 1970s, the then dominant Marxist political theory that conceptualized the state as the executive branch of the capitalist class required sophisticated re-formulation (most notably in the work of Nicos Poulantzas and Bob Jessop) to tease out both the increasingly obscured class character of the "Keynesian" welfare state as well as the possibilities the state offered for socialist transition. Today, there is nothing obscure any more about the mission of state intervention. Bankers on the verge of bankruptcy successfully call on the national state for immediate, urgent and desperate measures. Unprecedented public deficits are produced for future generations to carry. This, of course, short-circuits the possibilities for alternative state policies, while those losing their homes, jobs or whatever flimsy security they had largely remain in the cold. This has now become a process that is fully transparent and legible, barely wrapped in a general discourse of protecting the "common" interest.

This is an extraordinary process of accumulation by dispossession orchestrated through the state in the name of salvaging a capital-financial system built on spiralling fictitious capital circulation and formation. Without much organized protest, financial capital basically took command of the state's capacity and forged it in its own interest, a political *coup d'état* that indeed returned the state to be the executive managers of the collective interests of the economic elites. Indeed, this is a return of socialism and of the socialist state, but a socialism that assures the interests of capital (see Virno 2004), and certainly not the interests of those at the bottom of the pile. The creation of a permanent state of exception has now become indeed part of the normal function of the state (Agamben 2005). If the emergent post-crisis order is one structured around socialism for capital, then the future is not about the political choice between market and state, but rather between socialism and communism.

I contend that this "privatization" of the State renders any political project articulated around the state problematic. As I have argued elsewhere, neoliberalization processes are accompanied by multi-scalar reorganizations of the mode of governing, which re-orders socio-political power geometries as well as the institutional modalities of governing, towards a form of governmentality that banishes the democratic supplement, resulting in more autocratic (quasi-)state forms (Swyngedouw 2005, 2007). This suspension of the properly democratic, and the consolidation of post-democratic forms of institutional arrangements is supported by post-political tactics of depoliticization (Swyngedouw forthcoming-a). Contemporary capitalism is indeed increasingly authoritarian, as Peter Sloterdijk maintains, with a choice between China's "party dictatorial" mode, the Soviet Union's 'state dictatorial" mode, the USA's 'sentiment dictatorial" mode and finally the "media dictatorial" mode of Berlusconi's Italy (Sloterdijk 2005).

Financializing Everything and Dispossessing Natures/Bodies

The procedures of neoliberalization do not only constitute simple class tactics of mobilizing the state for the class project, but also signal a profound transfiguration of inter-capitalist relations. There is a clear shift in intra-class relations from industrial/commodity producing capital to financial capital, a process usually referred to as financialization. While there is considerable dispute exactly over what constitutes financialization, I take it to be a condition whereby the accumulation process is increasingly sustained by the circulation of capital through all manner of financial transactions (of the $M\text{-}M^+\text{-}M^{++}$ kind), rather than by commodiy production (of the $M\text{-}C\text{-}M^+$ kind) (see Krippner 2005). The accompanying changing power relations are clearly expressed in the current climate of economic crisis and, in particular, in the differential ability to mobilize state power by different fractions of capital. It is vital to recognize that financial capital is, of course, not separate from other circuits of capital accumulation, the key is to grapple with their mutually constituted condition of possibility, their interrelationships, and tensions. In light of this, the new forms of mobilization of nature and its incorporation within the circuits of capital through new forms of articulation between financial and "real" capital is urgently required.

I would argue that one of the central transformations in the political ecology of contemporary capitalism resides in the changing dynamics and new relations associated with property and property relations. In *The Economic and Philosophical Manuscripts*, Marx already alluded to the tensions and struggle between two forms of capital, ie between immobile versus mobile capital (Marx 1967). The former is land and resource based and surplus was accumulated primarily through various forms of rent extraction; the latter is based on the property of circulating capital and surplus generated through surplus value production. While the latter is productive of value through the mobilization of labour, the former is extractive in terms of transferring labour values into rents and/or interest. In the past few decades, financialization has indeed accelerated the reversal of inter-capitalist relations back to a greater role of surplus generation through rent extractions of a variety of kinds. Financialization as a particular form of circulating capital, premised upon transforming geographically specific, relatively fixed, and particular conditions into abstract circulating fictitious and interest yielding capital, has become a key form of what David Harvey calls accumulation by dispossession. Capitalism's spectacular resurgence, strongly related with this extraordinary re-assertion of rent/interest yielding "stuff", centred on land-based speculation, the privatization of environmental commons like water, gene pools, CO_2, minerals, and the like, intellectual property regimes, bio-genetic ownership, affective and cognitive labour (like software code), and so on.

This rent/interest extraction form of financial capitalism also increasingly relies on the mobilization and appropriation of collective or common immaterial labour or, as Michael Hardt calls it, "biopolitical" capital (Hardt 2009):

> In the final decades of the twentieth century, industrial labor lost its hegemony and in its stead emerged "immaterial labor," that is, labor that creates immaterial products, such as knowledge, information, communication, a relationship, or an emotional response... As an initial approach, one can conceive immaterial labor in two principle forms. The first form refers to labor that is primarily intellectual or linguistic, such as problem solving, symbolic and analytical tasks, and linguistic expressions. This kind of immaterial labor produces ideas, symbols, codes, texts, linguistic figures, images, and other such products. We call the other principle form of immaterial labor "affective labor"... [it] refers equally to body and mind. In fact, affects, such as joy and sadness, reveal the present state of life in the entire organism, expressing a certain state of the body along with a certain mode of thinking... Affective labor, then, is labor that produces or manipulates affects... A worker with a good attitude and social skills is another way of saying a worker adept at affective labor (Hardt and Negri 2004:108).

These are the sorts of labour that produce reproducible goods like information, codes, affects, designs, images; they are reproducible in a biopolitical sense—they can be produced (albeit in new and always changing ways) through the biopolitical production of life itself, hence Hardt and Negri's insistence on defining these forms of immaterial labour as "biopolitical" capital. New forms of property arise from that, usually referred to as "intellectual property" rights. While formal property of affective "goods" is difficult to establish, all manner of dispossession tactics, outside of the economic sphere but articulated through legal, state and other institutional arrangements, are operative, opening up a vast terrain of tension, continuous contestation, and occasional subversion (code sharing, pirating, hacking, social economy initiatives, and the like). Software code, information networks, images, knowledge, smiles, good teaching, are difficult to privatize directly and hence need extraordinary mechanisms. What is vital to distinguish here is that the product is "immaterial", not the labour. Financialization (see the dotcom bubble) and direct dispossession (through violent regimes of establishing private property rights) have become the key tropes through which the common intellect of affective labour becomes incorporated and reproduced within the circulation of capital.

The spiralling forms of immaterial labour, upon which much of contemporary capitalism (particularly in the global North) rests, opens up new forms of "class" conflict that does not revolve around the ownership of the means of production, but directly around the ownership of the products of affective labour, mediated through the monetary nexus and the right to the rents produced through collective affective/immaterial labour. All manner of political conflict, both symbolic and material, revolves around the control and expression of these forms of affective labour and the surplus they produce or, in other words, social struggle unfolds increasingly around the collective/common versus private character of affective capital. An interesting example of this is the current mobilization of University of London students and academics around the privatization of knowledge, centred on the demand that publicly funded research should not be published in outlets that are privatized and to which access is restricted.

Both the financialization of space/nature (land and other socio-ecological "resources") as well as the financialization of reproducible biopolitical affective goods are the dominant forms of the new culture of capital, conditions that require urgent attention as they signal a nodal point in thinking through the idea of communism for the twenty-first century. As Marx and Engels already observed in the Communist Manifesto, expropriation or dispossession is of course not the objective of a communist regime. It is capitalism's expansion that is predicated upon expropriation and dispossessing. Reclaiming ownership of the privatized commons under collective management is, of course, an integral part of the communist demands.

The flip-side of biopolitical production is of course biopolitical management, that is the management and regulation of the security and welfare of the people, the management of fear or, more precisely, the management of the fear of fear (see Graham 2009). It is in this form that the properly ideological regime of the new spirit of capitalism is directly evident. Whether the fear of globalization and loss of competitiveness, the fear for an ecological Armageddon, Political Islam or the flood of (il)legal immigrants, the cultivation of the fear of fear is the central trope through which the integrity of the state is maintained while, at the same time, the apocalyptic imaginary that accompanies these discourses is one without the promise of redemption; it is an apocalypse without issue. It is one that can neither be fulfilled nor overcome, only postponed (Jay 1994). The politics of fear are central to the post-politicization or de-politicization that has characterized the past few years (Badiou 2008b).

The communist hypothesis radically breaks with fear—communism is about the faithful belief and relentless call for and struggle over the staging of equality and freedom, sustained by the conviction that this is immediately realizable and immanently practical.

Revolutionized Uneven Geographies of Capitalism

The support structures that permit the proliferation of affective labour are deeply material, albeit geographically unevenly organized. In the contemporary new spatial divisions of labour, material production is increasingly (although by no means all) carried out in China, India and other newly emerging capitalist spaces. Forms of direct labour exploitation, based on ultra-Taylorist modes of labour organization under strictly and multiple exploitative conditions, have become the material engines of world production. While the proletariat as a political force may be disappearing in the global North, the proletariat, both sociologically and politically, is being constituted on an extraordinary scale in the new spaces of capitalism, and with it, growing labour unrest and conflicts as the following example of China illustrates:

> By 2006 the Chinese working class numbered 764 million, with 283 million living in the cities. Bitter labour disputes, anger at rising food prices and pollution have taken a growing number of people onto the streets. In 1994 an estimated 740,000 joined street demonstrations. By 2004 the number rose to 3.7 million. Strikes rose from 1,909 in 1994 to 22,600 in 2003 and the number of strikers has grown from 77,704 to 800,000 . . . 30,000 workers in over a dozen factories in the Dalian Development Zone struck in 2005 (Solidariy.net.au—accessed 7 April 2009).

In addition, much of the affective labour (care, catering, security, and the like) and its material support structures in the global North are organized through internationally migrant labour, often sustained by illegal immigration, refugees or other precarious forms of life. The (il)legal migrant has become the ideal de-regulated (undocumented) body as mere labourer. An extraordinary form of inter- and intra-national exclusion and inequality is structured through these new affective forms of labour organization and appropriation. Both these emergent forms of political subjectivity require urgent theoretico-political attention.

Globally speaking, therefore, the demands for equality and the staging of freedom will in all likelihood articulate around the proletarian political subject in the spaces that are configured as the "assembly lines of world", while struggles around common property, dispossession, citizenship rights, control of affective labour, bio-political equality and the like are emerging and proliferating in the global North as well as among many of the structurally dispossessed in the slums of the world's mega-cities. In sum, the new faces of capitalism revolve increasingly around processes of changing property relations, articulated around both cognitive/affective and material commons, and primarily meditated and choreographed by financialization and its process of rent/interest extraction.

However, the current financial crisis shows the ineffectiveness, if not inability, of capital to govern or manage the commons, signalling a growing contradiction between the conditions of private property on the one hand and the organization of the commons on the other. Communism is radically about foregrounding the commons and the abolition of the exclusive private property of the commons upon which contemporary capitalism rests or, in Tony Negri's words, communism is about the democratic management of the commons.

This discussion of the commons brings us directly to one of the vital, but ultimately fundamentally disavowed (yet discursively hegemonically mobilized; Smith 2008), condition of our time, ie the ecological quagmire. The ecological question relates directly to the commons, our common life world. The attempts to mainstream the ecological problem are marked by three interrelated processes. First, the ecological turn of capital; second, the nurturing of a particular discourse of the environment; and third, the continuing financialization/privatization of the environmental commons, whether in the form of CO_2, bio-pools, water and other resources, human and non-human genetic codes, and the like, including of course the gigantic privatization of the greatest of all common ecologies, the urban process. The "environmental wedge", as Noel Castree suggests, re-orientates the political mind-set (Castree 2009). For the first time in history, human–non-human interactions may produce socio-ecological conditions that are inimical to the continuation of human and other life forms. Although we may not know all the ecological consequences of human's socio-ecological labour, the possibility of interventions to spiral out into too risky a terrain has now become a plain reality. Yet, capitalism cannot and will not stand for an unconditional demand for a transformation to a different egalitarian socio-ecological order, despite the call to arms from a variety of elites, ranging from Prince Charles' apocalyptic warning that we only have 18 months left to do something to Al Gore's biblical *An Inconvenient Truth*. The fantasy that immediate and urgent action would be taken was of course terminally shattered by the unconditional demand to take immediate and urgent action to "save the banks" (other demands, most notably the alleged pending environmental catastrophe, can wait—democracy was instantaneously suspended, the environment disappeared from the agenda as the "real" of capital imposed its own urgency). The restoration of capital was predicated upon restoring the fantasy of confidence and making money circulate again as capital. The inability or incapacity to manage the commons of socio-ecological assemblages, probably not even in the elite's own interest, is an extraordinary situation. The point, here, is not to fall into the urge to save nature—which does not exist anyway as a stable marker or reference (Swyngedouw 2007, forthcoming)— or to retrofit socio-ecological conditions to an assumedly more benign earlier historical condition (which is of course an inherently reactionary demand)—but to call for an egalitarian and democratic production of socio-ecological commons.

Moving Bodies/Fixed Bodies

What the new spirit of capitalism points at is the general privatization of the commons: the commons of the intellect/affect, the commons of external nature, and the commons of internal biopolitical/bio-genetic nature. The unprecedented enclosure of the registers of the commons through privatization points to a final and, arguably, crucial conflict and contradiction, namely the dialectic of inclusion and exclusion: the separation between those who are part and those who are not. The figure that literally inscribes the markers of the proliferation of walls, demarcations, separations and the multiple insides/outsides of the current geo-political order is the moving body and, in particular, the body of the illegal immigrant, the refugee, the idealized neoliberal subject, the one without political inscription, without papers (and therefore without rights):

> Nowadays, when the welfare state is gone, this separation between citizens and non-citizens still remains, but with an additional paradox that non-citizens represent the avant-garde within the neo-liberal project, because they are indeed positioned within the labor force market without any kind of social rights or state protection. Thus, if we examine this problem in such a way, the *sanspapiers* and the *erased* are the avant-garde form of sociality which would prevail if the neo-liberal concept is to be fully realized, if it would not be important anymore if someone is a citizen or not, if everybody would be defined only according to their position in the labor market and the labor process (Pupovac and Karamani 2006:48).

While running the risk of unacceptable overgeneralization, the refugees in Darfur, the Albanese diaspora in Greece and Italy, mass illegal migration from Africa to Europe, the Latino exodus to North America are marked by distinct geographies of exclusion and encampment. This undefined "rabble", those who are non-existent in proper political terms, *homines sacri*; those who do not have a voice to speak, do not have the right to be, yet are everywhere, often itinerant, are the signifier par excellence of the travesty of really existing "democracy". The flip side of these itinerant bodies are those who cannot move, imprisoned behind walls, material (like Gaza and West-Bank) or symbolic (those with no or the wrong papers), or concentrated in slums, favelas, asylum centres, or labour camps (like in China). This large and growing army of excluded stand in for the "scandal of democracy", the fact that indeed not everyone is equal and the bio-political state is here the central demarcating agent of inclusion and/or exclusion. A radical democratic demand, therefore, is the one around which the illegal immigrants rally: "we are here, therefore we are from here". Of course, this egalitarian demand does not only pertain to the place of utterance, but to all other places to which these multi-scaled bodies "belong" (see Swyngedouw and Swyngedouw 2009).

Under conditions of abject exclusion, violence can become the only conduit for voicing radical discontent. Indeed, we cannot ignore the rise of subjective violence over the past few years: the burning French "banlieues" (see Dikeç, 2007), the rioting students and other youths in Greece's main cities in December 2008, the food riots that spread like wildfire in mid-2008 (in the midst of a massive hike in both food and oil prices), the sequence of urban rebellions in places as different as Italy, Denmark, Moldavia, South Korea, or Haiti, and the like, or the string of ritualistic anti-globalization protests and their perennial promise of violence. The resurgence of such forms of subjective violence, ie when participants engage voluntarily in acts recognized as violent, seems to be a permanent feature of the new geographies of a post-political world. Subjective violence is of course always measured with respect to a state of apparent non-violence, a benign condition of absence of violent conflict. This absolutist measuring rod disavows the multiple expression of objective violence, that is the de-subjectified normal condition of everyday violence, often of the most brutal and repressive kind (see Žižek 2008b). Consider for example the death-toll in Iraq, the genocidal march of HIV in sub-Saharan countries and parts of Asia in the absence of accessible retroviral drugs, the death of an unknown number of refugees that try to reach the shores of Europe or the USA. Or the fact that 1.5 billion people worldwide do not have access to water, a situation that is the world's number one cause of premature mortality, of people dying before their sell-by date has passed. Closer to home and less dramatic, one can think of the violence inflicted by the repossession of homes, rising unemployment, disappearing savings, etc. These forms of objective violence, normal everyday conditions in the existing state of the situation and which are not measured against a condition of non-violence are strictly parallel to the regular outbursts of subjective violence. Universally condemned by the political elites, these are desperate signs of the levels of discontent, screams for recognition, and express profound dissatisfaction with the existing configuration, while testifying to the political impotence of such gestures and signalling the need for a more political, that is politicized, organization of these anarchic expressions for the desire for a new commons.

What is Left to Think? Excavating the Future of the Communist Hypothesis, Mobilizing the Courage of the Intellect, and Trusting the Voluntarism of the Will

We are living in times that are haunted and obsessive in equal measure. On the one hand, our time is haunted by the spectre of once "really existing socialism". The idea of communism is indeed tainted by the failure of its twentieth century manifestation, a condition that, towards the end of the previous century, left the Left in a state of utter paralysis, politically and intellectually. This is not to say that the "obscure disaster" of twentieth century communism does not require urgent and critical attention. On the contrary, this is one of the tasks ahead, one that has to be undertaken in light of the communist hypothesis. But in equal measure are we living in obsessive times, obsessive commitments to "do something", "to act" in the names of humanity, cosmopolitanism, anti-globalization or alter-globalization, the environment, sustainability, climate change, social justice, or other empty signifiers that have become the stand-in to cover up for the absence of emancipatory egalibertarian political fantasies. The failure of such obsessive activism is now clearly visible. Humanitarianism is hailed to legitimize military intervention and imperial war, the environment becomes a new terrain of capitalist accumulation and serves ideologically as a "new opium for the masses" (Žižek 2008a), cosmopolitanism is cherished as the cultural condition of a globalized capitalism, and anti-globalization manifestations have become the predictable, albeit spectacular, short-lived Bakthinian carnivals whose geographical staging is carefully choreographed by the state. Communist thought has disappeared, to be replaced by relentless, yet politically powerless, resistance (rather than transformation), social critique and obsessive acting.

The relationship between our critical geographical theories and the political as egalitarian-emancipatory process has to be thought again. It is undoubtedly the case that the three key markers of twentieth century communist politics—state, party and proletariat— require radical reworking. I would insist that neither the state nor the party are any longer of use to think the communist hypothesis. This should not be read as an invitation to ditch forms of institutional and political organization. On the contrary, it calls for a new beginning in terms of thinking through what institutional forms are required at what scale and what forms of political organization are adequate to achieve this. The notion of the proletariat as a political subject equally needs radical overhaul in light of a new critique, not of political economy, but of political ecology (see above). In a context of mass dispossession and privatization of the commons, the political fault lines become drawn around this axis, around which all manner of new political (proletarian) subjectivities arise. The name of the "proletarian" stands of course for the political subject who, through egalibertarian struggle, aims to take control again of life and its conditions of possibility. Communism as a hypothesis and political practice is of course much older than the twentieth century and will, in one guise or the other, continue in the future. Excavating the historical-geographical variations and imaginations of the communist invariant requires re-examining and re-evaluation. Communism as an idea manifests itself concretely each time people come together in common, not only to demand equality, to demand their place within the edifice of state and society, but also to stage their capacity for self-organization and self-management, and to enact the democratic promise, thereby changing the frame of what is considered possible and revolutionizing the very parameters of state and government, while putting new organizational forms in their place. There are plenty of historical communist political sequences, marking the communist invariant, from the rebellion of the "ochlos" (the rabble), demanding their rightful place as part of the "demos" in the governing of the polis in ancient Athens to the French revolutionaries who declared equality and freedom for all in the revolutionary constitution of 1789. Or consider, for example, the 1870 Paris Commune—the first emblematic moment when the proletariat showed, to the horror of the bourgeoisie, their capacity to self-organize and self-govern, the early Soviets, the Shanghai commune of 1966, brutally smashed by the forces of the Chinese State despite Mao's earlier calls for a permanent revolution (but which had to be performed according to the rules of the State and not taken literally as the Shanghai communards did), or late-nineteenth-century Canudos, a self-governing mini-state, brutally destroyed by the Brazilian military (Levine 1995), and brilliantly immortalized in Vargas Llosa's novel, *The War of the End of the World* (Vargas Llosa 2004).

The key task, therefore, is to stop and think, to think communism again, to think through the communist hypothesis and its meaning for a twenty-first century emancipatory, free, and egalitarian politics. While the pessimism of the intellect over the past few decades, combined with the scepticism of the critical theorist, usurped the will for radical change, the realization of the communist hypothesis requires a new courage of the intellect to break down barriers and taboos, to dare to think universalizing emancipatory and democratic politics again, to trust the demands formulated by those who have no voice, who have no part; to trust the will for change and to embrace the task of testing radically the truth of the communist hypothesis; a truth that can only be established through a new emancipatory political sequence.

The communist hypothesis forces itself onto the terrain of the political through the process of subjectivation, a coming into being through voluntarist actions, procedures and performances, of collective embodiments of fidelity to the presumption of equality and freedom. It is a fidelity to the practical possibility of communism, but without ultimate guarantee in history, geography, the Party or the State. Communism is an idea without ultimate ground, but with extraordinary emancipatory mileage. The proletarian (or revolutionary) subjects are those that assemble together, not only to demand freedom and equality but to take it, to carve out, occupy, organize the spaces for the enactment of this politics, already experimented with in localized practices of militant groups. The historical-geographical invariant of the communist hypothesis requires serious intellectual engagement in order to tease out what an equal, free and self-organizing being-in-common for the twenty-first century might be all about. This is a formidable task to be asked of the communist (common) intellect. It will require serious theoretical reconceptualization, a restoration of the trust in our theories, a courageous engagement with painful histories and geographies, and, above all, abandoning the fear of failing again. The fear of failing has become so overwhelming that fear of real change is all that is left; resistance is as far as our horizons reach—transformation, it seems, can no longer be thought, let alone practiced. The injunction scripted by the communist hypothesis is one that urges communist intellectuals to muster the courage to confront the risk of failing again. There is no alternative. We either manage what exists to the best of our humanitarian abilities or think through the possibilities of re-imagining and realizing the communist hypothesis for the twenty-first century. This will have to take the form of a "communist geography, a geography of the "real movement which abolishes the present state of things"" (Mann 2008:921). *Antipode* has always been on the side of the latter; let it stay there.

Acknowledgements

I am grateful to Noel Castree, David Harvey, Nik Heynen, Maria Kaika, Geoff Mann, and the referees for ideas, arguments, and critical comments on earlier drafts of this essay. I would also like to thank my wonderful colleagues at the University of Manchester for helping to create a space where these thoughts can be thought. Of course, I alone am responsible for both the opinions and arguments developed in the essay.

Endnotes

[1] The terms "obscure disaster" is taken from Alain Badiou and refers to the disavowed legacy of actually existing twentieth-century "communisms" by the contemporary Left. Badiou argues that a critical-philosophical engagement with the causes, conditions of possibility and lessons to be drawn from this "disaster" is urgently required as part of a political project to found a communism for the twenty-first century.
[2] With thanks to Geoff Mann for suggesting this inclusion.

References

Agamben G (2005) *State of Exception*. Chicago: University of Chicago Press
Badiou A (2008a) The communist hypothesis. *New Left Review* 49:29–42
Badiou A (2008b) *The Meaning of Sarkozy*. London: Verso
Balibar E (1993) *Masses, Classes, Ideas: Studies on Politics and Philosophy Before and After Marx*. London: Routledge
Boltanski L and Chiapello E (2007) *The New Spirit of Capitalism*. London: Verso
Campbell D (2009) Move over Jacko, Idea of Communism is hottest ticket in town this weekend. *The Guardian* 12 March, http://www.guardian.co.uk/uk/2009/mar/12/ philosophy Accessed 14 August 2009
Castree N (2009) The environmental wedge: Neoliberalism, democracy and the prospect for a new British Left. In P Devine, A Pearman and D Purdy (eds) *Feelbad Britain: How to make it better* (pp 222–233). London: Lawrence & Wishart
Debord G (1967) *La Société du spectacle*. Paris: Buchet-Chastel
Dikeç M (2007) *Badlands of the Republic: Space, Politics and French Urban Policy*. Oxford: Blackwell
Graham S (2009) *Cities under Siege: The New Military Urbanism*. London: Verso
Hallward P (2009) The will of the people: Notes towards a dialectical voluntarism. *Radical Philosophy* 155:17–29
Hardt M (2009) "The common in communism". Paper presented at The Idea of Communism, Birkbeck College, London, 13–15 March
Hardt M and Negri A (2001) *Empire*. Cambridge: Harvard University Press
Hardt M and Negri A (2004) *Multitude*. London: Penguin
Harvey D (2005) *A Brief History of Neoliberalism*. Oxford: Oxford University Press
Harvey D (2009) Is this *really* the end of neoliberalism?, http://www.counterpunch.org/ harvey03132009.html Accessed 22 July 2009
Jay M (1994) The apocalyptic imagination and the inability to mourn. In G Robinson and J Rundell (eds) *Rethinking Imagination: Culture and Creativity* (pp 30–47). New York: Routledge
Krippner G R (2005) The financialization of the American economy. *Socio-Economic Review* 3:173–208
Lefort C (1986) *The Political Forms of Modern Society: Bureaucracy, Democracy, Totalitarianism*. Cambridge: Polity
Lefort C (1989) *Democracy and Political Theory*. Minneapolis: University of Minnesota Press
Levine R M (1995) *Vale of Tears: Revisiting the Canudos Massacre in Northeastern Brazil, 1893–1897*. Berkeley: University of California Press
Mann G (2008) A negative geography of necessity. *Antipode* 40:921–934
Marx K (1967) *Economic and Philosophical Manuscripts of 1844*. Moscow: Progress
Marx K and Engels F (1987) *The German Ideology: Introduction to a Critique of Political Economy*. London: Lawrence & Wishart
Mouffe C (2009) "Enige Ideen zu Radikalpolitik Heute". Paper presented at Updating Radical Democracy: Uber Hegemonie und radikale Demokratie, Rosa Luxemburg Foundation, Berlin, 12 May
Nancy J-L (1991) *The Inoperative Community*. Minneapolis: University of Minnesota Press
Negri A (1990) Postscript, 1990. In F Guattari and A Negri (eds) *Communists Like Us: New Spaces of Liberty, New Lines of Alliance* (pp). New York: Semiotext(e)
Peet R (1969) A new left geography. *Antipode* 1:3–5
Pupovac O and Karamani S (2006) On the margins of Europe: An interview with Rastko Močnik. *PRELOM—Journal for Images and Politics* 8:39–57
Rancière J (1995) *On the Shores of Politics*. London: Verso
Rancière J (1998) *Disagreement*. Minneapolis: University of Minnesota Press

Rancière J (2001) Ten theses on politics. *Theory & Event* 5(3), http://muse.jhu.edu/journals/theory_and_event/v005/5.3ranciere.html Accessed 14 August 2009

Rancière J (2004) Introducing disagreement. *Angelaki* 9:3–9

Russo A (2006) How to translate Cultural Revolution. *Inter-Asia Cultural Studies* 7:673–682

Sennett R (2007) *The Culture of the New Capitalism*. London: Yale University Press

Sloterdijk P (2005) Damned to expertocracy http://www.signandsight.com/features/238.html (last accessed 12 April 2009)

Smith N (2008) Afterword to the third edition. In N Smith (ed) *Uneven Development* (pp 239–266). Athens: Georgia University Press

Swyngedouw E (2005) Governance, innovation and the citizen: The Janus face of governance-beyond-the-state. *Urban Studies* 42:1991–2006

Swyngedouw E (2007) Impossible/undesirable sustainability and the post-political condition. In J R Krueger and D Gibbs (eds) *The Sustainable Development Paradox* (pp 13–40). New York: Guilford

Swyngedouw E (2009a) The zero-ground of politics: Musings on the post-political city. *NewGeographies* 1:52–61

Swyngedouw E (2009b) The antinomies of the post-political city: In search of a democratic politics of environmental production. *International Journal of Urban and Regional Research* 33(3):601–620

Swyngedouw E (2009c) Where is the political. *Antipode* under revision

Swyngedouw E (forthcoming) The trouble with nature: Ecology as the new opium for the masses. In P Healey and J Hillier (eds) *Conceptual Challenges for Planning Theory*. Aldershot: Ashgate

Swyngedouw E and Swyngedouw E (2009) The Congolese diaspora in Brussels and hybrid identity formation: Multi-scalarity and diasporic citizenship. *Urban Research & Practice* 2:68–90

Vargas Llosa M (2004) *The War of the End of the World*. New York: Faber and Faber

Virno P (2004) *A Grammar of the Multitude*. New York: Semiotext(e)

Žižek S (1999) *The Ticklish Subject: The Absent Centre of Political Ontology*. London: Verso

Žižek S (2006) *The Parallax View*. Cambridge: MIT Press

Žižek S (2008a) *In Defense of Lost Causes*. London: Verso

Žižek S (2008b) *Violence*. London: Profile

An Economic Ethics for the Anthropocene

J. K. Gibson-Graham

Department of Geosciences, University of Massachusetts, Amherst, MA, USA;
graham@geo.umass.edu

Centre for Citizenship and Public Policy, University of Western Sydney,
NSW, Australia;
katherine.gibson@uws.edu.au

Gerda Roelvink

Centre for Citizenship and Public Policy, University of Western Sydney,
NSW, Australia;
g.roelvink@uws.edu.au

Abstract: Over *Antipode's* 40 years our role as academics has dramatically changed. We have been pushed to adopt the stance of experimental researchers open to what can be learned from current events and to recognize our role in bringing new realities into being. Faced with the daunting prospect of global warming and the apparent stalemate in the formal political sphere, this essay explores how human beings are transformed by, and transformative of, the world in which we find ourselves. We place the hybrid research collective at the center of transformative change. Drawing on the sociology of science we frame research as a process of learning involving a collective of human and more-than-human actants—a process of co-transformation that re/constitutes the world. From this vision of how things change, the essay begins to develop an "economic ethics for the Anthropocene", documenting ethical practices of economy that involve the being-in-common of humans and the more-than-human world. We hope to stimulate academic interest in expanding and multiplying hybrid research collectives that participate in changing worlds.

Keywords: Anthropocene, ethics, community economies, hybrid research collective, more-than-human

In 2008, the Geological Society of London announced a new geological epoch, the Anthropocene, in which humankind is foregrounded as a geological force or agent:

The Holocene epoch—the interglacial span of unusually stable climate that has allowed the rapid evolution of agriculture and urban civilization—has ended and . . . the Earth has entered "a stratigraphic interval without close parallel in the last several million years." In addition to the buildup of greenhouse gases, the stratigraphers

Antipode Vol. 41 No. S1 2009 ISSN 0066-4812, pp 320–346
doi: 10.1111/j.1467-8330.2009.00728.x

cite human landscape transformation which "now exceeds [annual] natural sediment production by an order of magnitude," the ominous acidification of the oceans, and the relentless destruction of biota. This new age, they explain, is defined both by the heating trend (whose closest analogue may be the catastrophe known as the Paleocene Eocene Thermal Maximum, 56 million years ago) and by the radical instability expected of future environments . . . Evolution itself . . . has been forced into a new trajectory (Davis 2008).

The end of the Holocene, the coming of the Anthropocene, the displaced trajectory of evolution—these apocalyptical images toss us onto a meta-historical playing field without a clue as to how to play the game (Chakrabarty 2009). Suddenly we are not just billions of individuals and millions of collectivities but a single species alongside other species, one whose survival is threatened by its own behavior. References to millions of years, which used to make our brief lives seem inconsequential, now endow us with gargantuan agency and an almost unbearable level of responsibility—intuitively beyond our capacities for rational or concerted action. Never mind that climate scientists instruct us that such action, undertaken over the next few years, is the only thing that can possibly avert a catastrophe.

In response to scientists' warnings, solutions are being proposed and put in place—cap-and-trade arrangements, experiments in green technology (particularly energy) and development, international treaties, corporate pledges (many already reneged upon), changes in lifestyle and consumption. Efforts to generate political momentum for change are intensifying, including cautions about imminent tipping points and predictions such as Davis's of a "planet of slums, with growing food and energy crises" (2008) punctuated by small climate-protected pockets of the wealthy (Steffan 2008). These attempts at stimulating outrage and action frequently involve naming and blaming capitalist industrialization, in both its systemic and personified forms. The head of NASA's Goddard Institute for Space Studies, for example, recently proposed to a congressional committee that CEOs of fossil energy companies be tried for "high crimes against humanity and nature" (*Tomdispatch* 2008).

Frustrated that confronting the world with terrifying "facts" is not enough to galvanize appropriate action, climate scientists have begun to call upon social scientists to come up with new approaches to social change. And here the debate rages over whether technology alone can solve our problems or whether fundamental shifts in values are required (Steffan 2008). Techno-skeptics point to the history of energy efficient innovations that have resulted in cheaper appliances, leading to more widespread appliance use and large overall increases in energy consumption (Hobson 2008). Proponents of values shifts are similarly unconvincing. As Hobson argues, we don't seem to know how to create such shifts, nor do we know that they are effective. Information campaigns don't engender changes in values, and changes in values don't automatically yield changes in behavior (2008:7), which are ultimately what we are seeking—ways of living differently with the earth. Val Plumwood is eloquent and arresting here: "If our species does not survive the ecological crisis, it will probably be due to our failure . . . to work out new ways to live with the earth, to rework ourselves . . . We will go onwards in a different mode of humanity, or not at all" (2007:1).

From this perspective, responding to the challenges of the Anthropocene is not simply about humans finding a technological or normative fix that will control and restore the earth. It is about human beings being transformed by the world in which we find ourselves—or, to put this in more reciprocal terms, it is about the earth's future being transformed through a living process of inter-being. But how do we put ourselves (and the earth) in the way of such transformations? How do we get from an abstract ontological revisioning to a glimmer or a whiff of what to do on the ground? No answer arrives when we ponder this question—just a spacious silence and a slowing down.

Silence and slowness are openings, of course, opportunities for the body to shift its stance, to meld a little more with its surroundings; chances for the mind to mull over what floats by on the affective tide, or to swerve from its course as momentum decreases. Undoubtedly these are openings for learning. Not learning in the sense of increasing a store of knowledge but in the sense of becoming other, creating connections and encountering possibilities that render us newly constituted beings in a newly constituted world. Latour along with others has called this "learning to be affected" (2004:205; see also Hinchliffe 2003, 2007). Effectively we are created as bodies/beings by the entirety of human and non-human conditions of the world that affect us and from which we learn—if we are open to doing so.[1] Momentous as it may sound and mundane as it may actually be, this learning is a process of co-constitution that produces a new body-world.

So what does this mean for "an economic ethics for the Anthropocene?" We are all familiar with posthumanist ontologies that imagine "an entangled world of living [and non-living] things in which are relaxed the lines marking off the human from the non-human" (Anderson 2007:34, insert added). If we can read these new ontologies as evidence of "learning to be affected" and thus as part and parcel of a newly sensitized and conditioned world; if we can understand them as Deleuzian philosophy, "a means of going on rather than a cerebral, ivory tower pastime" (Whatmore 2004:1360); if we can treat them as symptoms rather than precursors of change, we may be able to see that an ethics for the Anthropocene has already emerged. And from there it might not be such a stretch to discern an emerging "economic" ethics in the projects and activities of communities worldwide. It would then be our role to theorize this nascent formation and make its practices and promises visible, thereby participating in a new phase of its existence.

It is here that we can finally begin this essay.

*****

For several decades now, we have been involved in a project of rethinking economy, opening to and being practically affected by the wide diversity of economic activities that offer possibilities of livelihood and well-being, within and beyond the ostensibly global purview of capitalist development. We have also opened to our necessary interdependence with the rest of humanity (Nancy 1991) and to the possibility of building economic communities in which that interdependence is acknowledged and enlarged. Theoretically, as well as through action research in a number of locations, we (alongside others) have experimented with the ethical dynamics of building community economies in the air and on the ground.

But it took the near simultaneous deaths of the Holocene and eco-feminist Val Plumwood to shock us into a posthumanist project of learning to be affected (Roelvink and Gibson-Graham 2009). (Not that the raw and processed materials for such a project weren't available all around us, in our discipline, in the academy, and in the world more generally.)[2] In this essay we begin the process of opening our economic thinking and enactments to encompass what Jean-Luc Nancy has called the "being-in-common" (1991:4) of all being(s), human and non-human, animate and inanimate, processual and fluid as well as categorical and definite in conception (see also Bingham 2006).

The essay unfolds in three sections. The first section explores learning to be affected as an ethical process in which bodies and worlds are co-constituted; we introduce the hybrid research collective as the central character, the body-world that learns. The second section explores the economic ethics that is emerging among hybrid collectives that have learned to be affected by the conditions of the Anthropocene; here an ethics of interdependence embodied in "community economies" comes into view. The third section highlights the role of research collectives in the experimental community economies of rural and outback Australia—noting the role of academics, the proliferation of economic possibilities, and the transformed landscapes and species of a new econo-sociality. We conclude the essay with a call to academic action.

Learning to be Affected: An Ethical Practice of Co-transformation

What is required in order to be "a receiver" of communicative and other kinds of experience and relationship is openness to the other as a communicative being, an openness which is ruled out by allegiance to reductive theories. To view such differences as simply "theory choices" is to overstate the intellectualist and understate the performative aspects involved, which is captured somewhat better in the terminology of posture or stance. Is it to be a posture of openness, of welcoming, of invitation, towards earth others, or is it to be a stance of prejudged superiority, of deafness, of closure? (Plumwood 2002:175–176).

With her reference to an open stance, Val Plumwood brings us to the edge of embodiment. We are at the brink, in this welcoming posture, of recognizing earth others as not-other than ourselves; and we are just a hair's breadth away from acknowledging our co-constituted being as body-world. Eve Kosofsky Sedgwick (2003) takes us, in her book *Touching Feeling*, to a similar edgy location. Always attuned to the body and its postures, she asks us to reconsider the "paranoid" critical stance so prevalent among social scientists, which tends to confirm what we already know—that the world is full of devastation and oppression, and that transformation is an unlikely if not hopeless project. She suggests instead an open reparative stance that refuses to know too much, that makes space for hope and expands possibility. Unlike the critical stance, which is often suspicious and dismissive, the reparative stance is receptive and hospitable, animated by care for the world and its inhabitants (Gibson-Graham 2006:6).

What Sedgwick is concerned to preserve is the world of possibility that is performatively squelched and narrowed by critical modes of apprehension. In advocating an open "reparative" stance, she implicitly recognizes the (trans)formative potentials of a bodily posture, the way it may promote or allow change, in this case, contribute to a "repaired" or newly cared for world. Unlike the well-defended critical stance, the open reparative posture is conducive to learning, itself a transformative process, and perhaps especially to the kind of bodily learning that Latour (2004) calls "learning to be affected". We have grasped onto this evocative notion for a number of reasons: it provides an accessible place to start—the body—in addressing environmental crisis; it offers a greater field of possibility (and no more uncertainty) than technological and normative approaches; and, most importantly, it distances us from the subject–object dualism that separates humans from a disparaged or discounted non-human world. Performing this dualism has arguably led us into planetary crisis, and "un-performing" it may turn out to be a key practice in an ethics for the Anthropocene.

Starting with the Body: Learning to be Affected

Drawing on Vinciane Despret's reading of William James, Latour suggests that "to have a body *is to learn to be affected*, meaning 'effectuated,' moved, put into motion by other entities, humans or non-humans" (2004:205; original emphasis). To illustrate this constitutive process of living and learning, he takes us to the perfume industry, focusing on the training sessions through which one acquires a "nose" that can differentiate subtle variations in smell. An odor differentiation kit, consisting of a range of fragrances, is used to train noses, thereby becoming "part of" or "coextensive with the body" (207):

> It is not by accident that a person is called "a nose" as if, through practice, she had *acquired* an organ that defined her ability to detect chemical and other differences. Through the training sessions, she learned to have a nose that allowed her to inhabit a (richly differentiated odoriferous) world. Thus body parts are progressively acquired at the same time as "world counter-parts" are being registered in a new way. Acquiring a body is thus a progressive enterprise that produces at once a sensory medium *and* a sensitive world (Latour 2004:207; original emphasis).

Latour contrasts the "learning to be affected" vision of body-world co-constitution with the familiar (ingrained) ontology where

> . . . there is a body, meaning a subject; there is a world, meaning objects; and there is an intermediary, meaning a language, that establishes connections between the world and the subject. If we use this model, we will find it very difficult to render the learning by the body dynamic: the subject is "in there" as a definite essence, and learning is not essential to its becoming; the world is out there, and affecting others is not essential to its existence. As to the intermediaries—language, odour kits—they disappear once the connection has been established since they do nothing but convey a linkage (2004:208).

By contrast to this static (dead?) rendering of body/subject and object/world, Latour's perfume industry example depicts a dynamic, changing, living body-world, proliferative and differentiating rather than stable and monolithic. As he introduces other "intermediaries" into the example, including scientific debates between "physiologists about the olfactory and gustatory receptors" (211) and strategies for marketing perfume, Latour argues that the more entities involved the greater the opportunities for registering difference and "the wider [more highly differentiated] the world becomes" (211, insert added). Rather than narrowing down options and inputs, "learning to be affected" embraces multiplicity and diversity as creating more possibilities for registering and enacting the world. Latour refers to this world as "the multiverse", no less singular than a universe (note the definite article) but constituted by beings becoming sensitive to differences (213).

We are interested in thinking about learning to be affected as an ethical practice, one that involves developing an awareness of, and in the process being transformed by, co-existence. We are also interested in the ways that an ethics of learning to be affected might be operationalized in a wider arena. In *Disclosing New Worlds*, Spinosa, Flores and Dreyfus offer fascinating examples of society-wide and even global changes that have been initiated and informed by this sort of learning. One of the most compelling of these concerns Mothers Against Drunk Driving (MADD), a citizen action group that the authors portray as transforming the culture of responsibility in the USA (1997:88–94). MADD was formed by a group of women who had experienced the death or serious injury of a loved one due to drunk driving. They came together to share their pain and anger, which only grew as their collective inquiry identified the profound disconnect between the huge losses they had suffered and the minimal level of responsibility for those losses attributed to drivers. At the time of MADD's formation, there was considerable social tolerance of drunk driving—in the (modified) words of the public service ad, friends *did* let friends drive drunk. Drinking was often viewed as a form of "earned" relaxation for hard-working Americans, and the injuries and deaths related to drunkenness tended to be seen as horribly unlucky accidents—basically absolving perpetrators of responsibility. MADD drew public attention to the place of drinking in American social life, and to the avoidance of responsibility that accompanied it.

MADD's strategy was to talk to a wide range of citizens, including lawyers, medical professionals, educators and corporate executives (1997:91). The mismatch between the mothers' powerful emotions and the relatively casual treatment of drunkenness created a sensitivity in them that enabled them to differentiate the subtle ways in which drunk driving was differently absolved across many communities (91–92). Most of the medical community, for example, seemed to accept that a few daily drinks would have little impact on health. MADD showed physicians not only that regularly drinking hard liquor was hazardous to your health—a minority view in medicine at the time—but also that mixing drinking and driving could damage another's health. This began a shift among medical professionals toward advocating responsible drinking, since it would save lives in a number of ways (92).

Instead of focusing on a single practice or law, MADD initiated learning to be affected among interdependent others in a "plurality of subworlds that could contribute to their cause" (92). Eventually laws were passed increasing penalties for drunk driving and decreasing acceptable levels of blood alcohol for drivers. Bars and party hosts were held responsible for letting drunks drive and designated drivers became widespread. But Spinosa, Flores and Dreyfus credit MADD with something more far-reaching than simply generating a practice of responsible drinking. They see the group as initiating a society-wide ethic and practice of "full responsibility" (91) that informs safe sex practices, dietary awareness, smoking behavior, and exercise regimes. The process of learning that began with a small group of mothers deeply affected by loss and lack of accountability became a generalized way of living with ourselves and each other.

From our perspective, we can discern in this example the co-constitution of a new body-world in which alcohol, blood, brain, pathologies and sex differences are connected in new ways with far-reaching manifestations in law, medicine, behavior, and instruments of measurement. Literally we have acquired new bodies in which the breathalyzer is a sense organ, pregnancy and alcohol don't mix, and a range of cancers are associated with moderate rates of alcohol consumption.

Learning Together: The Hybrid Collective

The activities of MADD remind us that research can play a central role in ethical practices of learning to be affected and "disclosing new [more differentiated] worlds" (Spinosa, Flores and Dreyfus 1997; insert added). In our own action research projects and intellectual communities, we have embraced research as a collective (human) endeavor; we are now being pushed by events and ontological explorations to expand our collective research process to include the non-human entities that make up a world. In Latour's perfume industry example, it is not just the pupil that learns and is thereby created/transformed/differentiated. A hybrid collective including the professor, an odor kit, the pupil, the laboratory setting, and the "*collective body* of science" (Latour 2004:209, original emphasis) interacts in a process of co-transformation and co-constituted action. It is, as we see in the story of MADD, a hybrid collective that learns.

A hybrid research collective is an assemblage that, through research, increases possibilities for (being in) the world (Callon and Rabeharisoa 2003; Roelvink 2008; Roelvink forthcoming). The concept was developed by Callon and Rabeharisoa through their analysis of a muscular dystrophy patient organization in France. The story of this hybrid entity begins with a medical and scientific community that had no interest in muscular dystrophy. To put it bluntly, people with muscular dystrophy were dehumanized—all viewed as the same terminal case. In the late 1950s, families and patients affected by the disease joined together in the Association Française contra les Myopathies (AFM) to undertake research on the disease. They distributed questionnaires, collected testimonies, kept diaries and photographic records, and made films. Through their research AFM differentiated life with muscular dystrophy, showing variation in the effects and development of the disease. The AFM also raised funding for research and, through this funding and their initial research, were able to partner with scientific and medical researchers to undertake further research.

The hybrid collective that emerged went on to conduct many different research projects, rapidly transforming knowledge of the disease:

> The more knowledge about . . . the disease advances, the more complex the picture becomes. The number of actants involved (all kinds of proteins, antibodies, enzymes, etc.) multiplies and causal links proliferate. As a result, differences between individual patients intensify, and the number of specialists that can be mobilized increases. This opens the way for strategic options. (Callon and Rabeharisoa 2003:199)

As research projects further differentiated the disease, creating new possibilities for partnership with specialists, "the range of possible therapeutic options [became] broader and more diversified" (199). Patients not only gained from therapeutic options but were transformed through the collective in other ways. Because of the sensitivity to life with muscular dystrophy instilled by MD research—enabling people with the disease to have differentiated bodies (in Latour's sense of the word)—patients became "personalized" for clinicians and researchers "while gaining depth and complexity" (199). And as patients interacted with a variety of specialists, scientists, laboratories, prostheses, genetic materials, and even a worm whose genome was used as a model, they were learning to be affected: "Their own understanding of the disease [was] . . . enriched with an array of new human and non-human entities that they learn[ed] to describe and with which they [became] accustomed to sharing their existence" (199–200, insert added). One might go so far as to say (and Callon and Rabeharisoa do) that they learned to think of these entities as "part of themselves" (199).

Among all the human and non-human actants, the gene is singled out by Callon and Rabeharisoa as holding the collective together (at least for many of the MD research projects). The gene, for example, enabled fundraising that could appeal to a number of different disease communities in addition to muscular dystrophy (200). Moreover, the gene enabled patients' identities to be transformed so that they could be seen as citizens with a small genetic difference: "Genes are not content just to make particular and general interests compatible; they also produce solidarity and compassion. When circulating through various spheres (scientific, political, medical, and economic), they no longer divide; they connect, create interdependency, and produce a common humanity that includes those who tended to be excluded" (200–201).

The increasingly differentiated world brought to life through the hybrid MD collective offers many new possibilities for living and acting. Patients now have a range of experiences open to them and medical scientists have developed new areas of expertise and career paths. Genes are actively implicated in an ever-expanding array of biological and social outcomes: "One researcher will accompany the discovery of a gene by creating an animal model and then testing gene therapy; a second will continue the gene hunt by studying other diseases; a third will concentrate on proteins and their functions; and so on. Each choice can be part of a different set of alliances" (199). Drawing on Paul Rabinow, Callon and Rabeharisoa describe these co-transformations as yielding a new "bio-sociality" (2003:199).

Taking off from this characterization, we could perhaps say that through our own (hybrid) research collectives we have been attempting to produce a new "econo-sociality". Over the past two decades we have worked with community researchers drawn from all walks of life as well as NGOs, government agencies, small businesses, academic researchers and students in a variety of locations in the USA, Australia and the Philippines (Gibson-Graham 2006). Our action research around the world has attempted to reclaim the economy as a site of ethical decision-making and practice. In all our research conversations the economy, rather than being seen as "out there" in the stock markets and corporate headquarters of global cities, has been "domesticated", brought down to size and made visible as a site of everyday activities and familiar institutions.

A powerful image that has emerged from these conversations is that of an iceberg with formal market transactions, wage labor and capitalist enterprise at the tip, underpinned by a myriad of submerged but sustaining alternative and non-market transactions, alternatively paid and unpaid labor, alternative capitalist and non-capitalist enterprises (see www.communityeconomies.org). We have used this image and the diverse economy diagram in which it is encoded (Gibson-Graham 2006:71) as an inventory kit—not unlike the perfume industry's odor kit—to produce economic actors attuned to their multiple economic roles. This kit locates *everyone* as contributing to (and part of) the economy in different and multiple ways: the grandmother who gifts her caring labor to mind a grandchild so that the parents can join the paid work force, the corporate executive who volunteers several hours a week at a local food bank, the trash-picker who recycles the rubbish of a city in the majority world, the poor farmer who harvests his neighbor's rice as part of a time-honored reciprocal labor relationship and the policeman who turns a blind eye to the movement of illegal drugs within a neighborhood in return for kick-backs. The heightened economic sensibility that arises from using this kit has spun off discussions about the ethical choices that confront people in daily life, as they participate in a diverse economy of interdependent "being-in-common".

Retrospectively, we can understand our research experience as involving a hybrid research collective learning to be affected by economic diversity. Such learning provokes a questioning of all the inherited givens that see, for example, the unemployed as economically inactive, the household as a dependent site of consumption, minimally capitalized self-employed businesses as unviable, cooperatives as backward-looking, capitalist corporations as unable to care for the environment, and unionized workers as defending collective well-being. The diverse economy catapults multiplicity and economic differentiation to the fore and helps us to counter the ingrained belief that capitalist economic relations are the only driving economic force. Once this one-way street toward development becomes just one among a number of avenues, economic innovation proliferates. New possibilities for enterprise development emerge from discussions around the inventory kit; as these possibilities are pursued, new enterprise forms are created, which lead to greater differentiation of the inventory kit and the possibility of developing new types of enterprises in different locations. In our action research people and agencies have been transformatively affected and new body-worlds (or body-economies) have been created, ones that are dynamic and differentiating rather than stuck and singular. Localities that were defined in terms of deficiency and need have been re-experienced as sites of surplus possibility where alternative pathways to shaping economies are continually opening up.

Taken together, these processes of co-constitution are producing a new econo-sociality (what we have called a community economy) at the core of which is the negotiation of interdependence. The diverse economy inventory kit assists with clarifying the ethical choices involved. Will a local government continue to grant free access to a closed pre-school building so that a group of volunteers can keep their Santa's workshop open? The kit helps local officials to locate all the economic activities (barter with the corporate sector, volunteer training labor, work-for-the dole, gold coin donations for access to materials, gifts of paints and timber, recycling of waste paint, production for use by local residents, sale of surplus product) that flow through and around the workshop and contribute to the integration and resilience of the local community (Cameron and Gibson 2005). Will a farming community continue to value and engage in the longstanding practice of reciprocal labor exchange? The diverse economy kit helps community researchers recognize this form of labor as a key contributor to livelihoods in the agricultural sector, and to propose that it be drawn upon as a resource for the fledgling phase of social enterprise development (Community Economies Collective and Gibson 2009).

While these examples suggest how close we have come to practicing an economic ethics of human interdependence, they also indicate how distant we still are from an ethics for the Anthropocene. In small and local ways, the human being-in-common of our action research has changed the world, including ourselves and our research collectives; and in more extensive ways, it has changed (that is, contributed to) the world of possibility. But we are just beginning to be affected by the coming of the Anthropocene, and have barely glimpsed the world of economic possibility it carries with it. In the next section we attempt to extend our thinking to the ethics of more-than-human interdependence, seeking out already existing projects that are learning/acting/being *with* a more-than-human world.

Ethical Coordinates of Interdependence: Building Community Economies for the Anthropocene?

In our project of rethinking economy, we hoped to open the eyes of economic activists (and everyone else) to projects and possibilities of non-capitalist development *here* and *now* (Gibson-Graham 2006:ch 7). Rather than pose the time-honored but often paralyzing question of "what is to be done" to produce change, we chose to marshal examples of "what is already being done", thereby contributing to the credibility and strengthening of alternative economies. In a similar move, here we take a closer look at diverse experiments all around us to see that many hybrid collectives are enacting ethical practices of learning to be affected by the Anthropocene. In these experiments humans already have a sense of their more-than-human lives as works-in-progress. By joining these experimental collectives—in other words, by bringing our perspective and analysis to bear—we hope to increase their legibility as economic projects, engaged in inventing and practicing an econo-sociality that involves the human in relations of mutuality with the more than human.

We have focused our reading of contemporary experiments that are building "community economies" on four ethical coordinates of econo-sociality (see Gibson-Graham 2006:ch 4):

- commons (how a commons is produced and sustained),
- consumption (whether and how products and surplus are to be consumed),
- necessity (what is necessary to personal, social and ecological survival), and
- surplus (how surplus is appropriated from and distributed to humans and the more than human).

The ethical coordinates function as a rudimentary language of economy. In what follows we extend our use of these coordinates to survey and sort out the tangled spaces of ethical negotiation in which interdependence between humans and non-humans is being acknowledged and transformed. Some brief examples may help to convey the range (if not the magnitude) of these transformative interactions.

Commons

Anthropologist Stephen Gudeman has taught us that a "community economy makes and shares a commons" (2001:27). Many experiments worldwide are currently extending community beyond the human species. In September 2008, the voters of Ecuador accepted a world-precedent-setting constitution that protects indigenous (and all) peoples' connection with their more-than-human world. The constitution includes a Bill of Rights that gives:

> nature the "right to exist, persist, maintain and regenerate its vital cycles, structure, functions and its processes in evolution" and mandates that the government take "precaution and restriction measures in all the activities that can lead to the extinction of species, the destruction of the ecosystems or the permanent alteration of the natural cycles" (Pena 2008).

This document will guide laws that recognize and validate an indigenous world view in which the duality of "private" and "commons" dissolves. To the extent that the constitution is respected, those economic activities that interfere with nature's cycles will be banned or regulated and others that promote the diversity and resilience of species, ecosystems and natural cycles will be supported. The Ecuadorian Bill of Rights was co-drafted by the Community Environmental Legal Defense Fund, which has assisted communities in the USA to put in place first-in-the-nation laws that treat ecosystems not as property but as rights-bearing entities (Community Environmental Legal Defense Fund 2008). A movement is underway that could potentially transform what has been seen as "common property" (and well or badly treated as such) into "members of the community" that have rights and a "voice" in ethical economic decision-making.

At the same time that nations and localities are extending rights to the more than human, collectives around the world are taking action to share, replenish, and live *with* a commons:

> We in our conventional lives today export all our harms to a Commons we don't ever see. WestWyck brings the Commons to your front doorstep and you can't avoid the fact that your actions have a direct impact on your water supply and the quality of your soil." Michael Cann, resident of a Melbourne inner city eco-village in which organic and human waste is treated on-site, grey water is recycled, rain water caught and used and solar power captured for heating and power (Dolan 2008:58).

The eco-village experiment is international in scope. Each village explores the limits of their ability to live sustainably under vastly different local conditions. In drought-prone Australia, Michael Cann and his co-residents are learning to live and garden with water and solar power in ways that respect the seasonal rhythms and variable quantities of the former and the daily rhythms and unboundedness of the latter. While producing novel options for urban design, WestWyck is also producing a new human body—one that turns on the tap and experiences connection to reservoirs, the hydrologic cycle, and the needs of neighbors and more-than-human others. As a complex assemblage of worms, water, waste, bacteria, energy, space, tanks, sunshine, children, vegetable growers, plants and, no doubt, unaccounted for guests like possums and cockroaches, WestWyck is a (hybrid) neighborhood community economy that is producing a new local commons while participating in an international experiment to invent a new econo-sociality.

Consumption

Many communities are making individual and social consumption the focus of concerted action and in doing so are reconfiguring felt responsibilities and connections between humans and the more than human. In a poor urban neighborhood of Metro Manila some 200 workers, mainly women, are members of a cooperative that collects plastic juice containers from streets and garbage cans, cleans them and sews them into colorful and stylish carry-alls that are sold in fair trade outlets around the world (Milgram 2005). In a rural Philippine municipality in Mindanao, a social enterprise has been established to make coconut coir into matting for erosion control, fiber for mattresses, plant hangers, and furniture. The primary raw material of the enterprise is waste coconut husk that once clogged waterways and destroyed marine habitats (Community Economies Collective and Gibson 2009:124). In 1996 the Australian Capital Territory became the first government in the world to set a goal of no waste going to land fill. The commitment to zero waste by 2010 has just been revised, but in 2005 residents were already recycling or reusing 75% of what was once thrown away (Australian Bureau of Statistics 2007). In the recycling and reuse sectors a diverse range of enterprises have sprung up—not-for-profit charitable enterprises, volunteer organizations, social enterprises, capitalist firms, cooperatives, child can collectors and barter networks.

The relatively new attachment to recycling is evidence of a shift toward living *with* that has occurred as the degraded earth and its inundated creatures have imprinted themselves on our twenty-first century bodies and psyches, in large part due to the efforts of the environmental movement. Around an emerging ethic of consumption with its technologies, bodily habits, moralities and waste possibilities, economic communities are formed, new commons emerge, and economic possibilities proliferate.

Necessity

What do humans, other species and ecosystems *need* in order to survive with some kind of dignity? This (anthropomorphic?) question increasingly intrudes upon what were formerly purely "economic" deliberations. The needs of animals, plants, soils and water sources, for example, have become a matter of concern that is reorganizing the food production industry. Reorganization has been moved along by rogue infectious agents such as the prions that cause mad cow disease (Whatmore 2002) and the algae that grow in stagnant water holes but also by the environmental and animal liberation movements. The need for chickens to scratch the earth, move about, take dust baths, nest at night and lay eggs in comfort is acknowledged and accommodated in the growing organic free range poultry industry. While the price of the eggs and poultry meat from this sector cannot compete with that of mainstream producers, the presence of this niche has put pressure on the mainstream to improve the living conditions of its birds.

Gerardo Ramos of Holyoke, Massachusetts has initiated a small business around more-than-human needs, responding to the plight of dying coral reefs by focusing his education and livelihood on them. Though he never completed high school, Ramos has taught himself to read the English-language textbooks and articles that have made him an expert on coral reef habitats. His business, Marine Reef Habitat, supplies institutions, individuals and businesses with fresh and saltwater tanks, fish and corals. Eventually, with the stock of corals generated through coral farming, and his savings supplemented by donations, Ramos intends to restore the coral reefs of his native Puerto Rico, where he used to swim and fish as a child before the reefs were decimated by pollution.

Surplus

Traditionally, Marxists and labor advocates have been militantly concerned about the exploitative capitalist class process in which surplus (value) is appropriated by non-producers from the workers who produce it. What if we added to our concern about the exploitative interdependence between producers and non-producers a concern for the unaccounted-for exploitation of the non-human world? Because the contribution of the more than human is not taken into account, in practice it ends up in the residual we identify as surplus. This is true for exploitative and non-exploitative enterprises alike—capitalist firms, worker cooperatives, independent producers, etc. To recognize and account for the needs of the non-human world would be to raise the social allocation to "necessity" and reduce the social surplus generated and finally appropriated.[3] It would mean the growth of activities focused on regeneration and maintenance of the environmental commons and the dignity of animal life as an integral part of production. It would mean a fundamental change in the nature of business thinking and practice. Indeed, with a smaller surplus available for investment, the whole economics of growth might be called into question, and an opening created for a new "economics" focused on sustenance and interdependence.

Such a shift seems impossible when posed in macro terms, but the beginnings of a change are clearly visible at the firm and industry levels. A New Hampshire electronics firm, for example, was at first resistant to regulation by the US Environmental Protection Agency and only reluctantly allocated a distribution of surplus to comply with clean air and water regulations. Ten years later the picture had entirely changed: the department that was initially assigned the task of compliance had become the center of innovation and cost-saving in the firm, and also the area where employees were most desirous of working. New people with environmentalist values had joined the company and older personnel had left or been influenced to change (James Hamm, personal communication). While the impact on surplus was probably positive, the example reminds us that new distributions of surplus are always taking place (if often toward executive compensation) and such distributions are increasingly targeted to meeting the needs of the more than human (see, for example, Gibson-Graham and O'Neill 2001).

Reflections

The community economy coordinates focus attention on ethical practices that produce economic connection and change. Distinct but interrelated, the coordinates prompt us, for example, to trace the ways that attending to the *needs* of the more than human reallocates *surplus*, shifts patterns of *consumption*, and replenishes a *commons* (or not). They constitute rudimentary elements of an economic theory—categories that separate out points of analytical interest (these could be called entry points) while at the same time enabling us to map and differentiate the ethical space of an economy. They help to distance us from the structural dynamics that have plagued economic theorizing, allowing us to represent an economy as a space of negotiated interdependence rather than a functional (or dysfunctional) growth machine. They also offer a tool for discerning an emerging economic order and participating in its performative consolidation (Callon 2007).[4]

We have collated and displayed here just a few among the multitude of ethical projects that are arguably and even demonstrably bringing a more-than-simply-human economy into being. At the same time, in this essay and elsewhere, we've been engaged in a number of related activities, including bringing an experimental (learning) rather than critical (judging) stance to ethical projects; amplifying and integrating small projects and disparate processes (via the community economy concept, for example); coming up with schematics and categorizations (like the coordinates and the inventory kit) that can orient research and proliferate economic possibilities; interpreting and disseminating key ideas and innovations; translating and making connections between different knowledge systems and communities; developing a pedagogy and protocols for "listening" to what was previously inarticulate; extending the collective to students, colleagues and other communities; transforming the collective's concerns into tangible and transportable objects of public policy; fostering credibility and working against inevitable attempts to discount the viability and significance of collective achievements (Santos 2004). We see these activities as an academic contribution to hybrid research collectives that are building community economies. In what follows we track several such collectives that are engaged in co-creating a community economy for the Anthropocene.

Emergent Hybrid Research Collectives in Rural and Outback Australia

Deborah Bird Rose is an academic anthropologist who works with Indigenous Australians in what we see as a hybrid research collective that is teaching us how we might be nourished in our world while participating in nourishing earth others:

> My work with Aboriginal people indicates an alternative. Rather than humans deciding autonomously to act in the world, humans are called into action by the world. The result is that country, or nature, far from being an object to be acted upon, is a self-organising system that brings people and other living things into being, into action, into sentience itself (Rose 2005:303).

Rose's research in Northern Australia with Aboriginal people reveals intricate practices of mutual life-giving whereby the needs of humans, animals and country are attended to simultaneously. She documents practices that have hitherto been recorded in Dreamtime stories and traditional Law. In our terms, she codifies key ethical negotiations of an active community economy. Consider, for example, the principle of mutual benefit whereby benefits ramify beyond immediate use—the river fig provides firewood for humans and fruit for birds, ants, fish and turtles. When harvesting bush tucker some food is left behind or distributed to others because it is "food for everyone", and this action returns benefit (297). As one of Rose's teachers, Riley Young Winpilin, explains:

> . . . when you go fishing and the [river] figs are ripe, you can eat some for yourself, and then throw some into the water to attract the attention of turtles. One reason you would want to attract the attention of turtles is that the time when the figs are fruiting is also the time when turtles are becoming fat, hence especially good to eat (296; insert added).

Rose draws on the many stories related by her Aboriginal co-researchers to demonstrate the place-based and ecosystem-bounded aspects of a communication system that connects humans and earth others. "Country tells what is happening; it announces its own patterned eventfulness and invites engagement" (298):

> The country tells you when and where to burn. To carry out this task you must know your country. You wouldn't, you just would not attempt to burn someone else's country. One of the reasons for burning is saving country. If we don't burn our country every year, we are not looking after our country (April Bright, quoted in Rose 2002:78–82).

Firestick farming, or mosaic burning of grassland, helps animals and insects to thrive, gives good hunting for humans, and sustains biodiversity. But how to burn one's country is an embodied knowledge relevant only to that particular interconnection of earth and species. Outside one's country the body's sensory and practical capacities are underdeveloped:

> One of the floodplain people describes the experience of coming home in this way: "You see the birds [referring to a totemic species], you see the country, and your senses come back to you. You know what to do and where to go (Rose 2005:299).

Listening to country, observing its interconnected changes and being called into action to produce mutual benefit—these are ethical practices of a more-than-human community economy. The hybrid research collective that includes Rose is bringing this economy to our attention, recognizing the ethics of interdependence that, despite colonial settlement, is still active in the landscape.

Economic anthropologist Jon Altman (2003) works in a hybrid research collective with biological scientists, ecologists and Aboriginal people in remote Arnhem Land, also in the north of Australia. Altman has explored the economic, social and ecological benefits of Aboriginal reoccupation and harvesting of traditional lands and suggests that Aboriginal methods of farming can be understood as maintaining a biodiverse commons. Increased recognition of the diversity of Aboriginal land management techniques has generated new economic possibilities. Altman argues, for example, that Aboriginal land management could be resourced in the same way that national park management is resourced and the discourse of welfare dependency could be supplanted with a recognition of the important public roles played by Aboriginal communities. He notes that at present "smoke inhalation in Darwin associated with late dry season wildfires generates significant health costs" (2003:76–77). Employing Aboriginal firestick farmers to manage the land around Darwin could "be supported as a preventative health measure that may be more cost effective than later health interventions" (76–77). Here the principle of mutual benefit practiced by Aboriginal people would be extended to urban dwellers while wild life habitats would be maintained and the transfer of traditional knowledge between Aboriginal generations would be ensured. In this more-than-human community economy Altman imagines the replacement of state income support with on-country income security that fuels the proliferation of community enterprise. Supporting people to stay on the land might ensure the sustainability of an indigenous art industry in which art is "produced on country". And land-based livelihoods remunerated in kind could be supplemented by new jobs in wild life management, wild life harvesting and pest eradication (2003:75).

We can see parallel hybrid research collectives forming around some adventurous Australian farmers who have allowed country to speak to them and have been called to buck mainstream agricultural science and experiment with radically different ways of working with the land. European settlers brought their knowledge of green pastures and flowing brooks to the dry island continent and proceeded to clear the land and manage the waterways to reproduce a version of the country they knew. Horse breeder and farmer Peter Andrews learned at an early age to be affected by the effects of these practices on his father's outback farm near Broken Hill. After witnessing the devastation caused by dust storms he realized that:

> ...without the scrub that had always protected it, the land was exposed to the weather. The winds could now rip and tear at the earth. It was my first lesson in how, within a decade or two, people could drastically affect a landscape that had been operating successfully for tens of thousands of years (Andrews 2006:16).

Andrews later conducted archival research into pre-colonial landscapes, noting that while the journals of early European explorers "are filled with descriptions of swamps and marshes . . . today ninety per cent of wetlands have disappeared" (2006:6). He became increasingly alarmed that practices of clearing waterways and grazing animals along stream banks had deepened stream incisions and increased the flow of water through the landscape, stripping the land of nutrients and causing erosion and salinity problems. Over many years he experimented with slowing the water flow on his property, becoming a self-taught agricultural scientist:

> As far as I could tell there was no body of scientific knowledge I could turn to that threw any light on what I was doing . . . Tarwyn Park, with its paddocks, creeks, weeds and salinity problems, became my laboratory (Andrews 2006:33).

Eventually he devised a system of farming known as Natural Sequence Farming (NSF) which involves impeding water flow with plants and other barriers and increasing water retention in the landscape (Andrews 2006). Former CSIRO head John Williams speaks for Andrews about the simplicity and obvious benefits of this system:

> ...what Peter's saying is, well, instead of letting the water run down the stream into the dam and then we pump it back and irrigate, why don't we, as a society, hold the water in the landscape and use it where it is? (Williams 2005)

NSF is not dependent on expensive new technology but on a new way (for most Australian farmers) of being *with* the land:

> The investment required is in training for the landholder to interpret the natural processes of the landscape and time spent by the farmer in "reading the country" and applying the NSF principles to the particular property and landscape features of their region (Newell and Reynolds 2005).

Switching to a farming practice that attends first and foremost to the needs of the land for water, plants for nutrient and soil for cover, but that doesn't lose sight of the needs of introduced animals for pasture and farmers for income, may actually reduce the consumption of industrial inputs (Hudson 2005:244). In the case of NSF, Newell and Reynolds (2005) argue that the system simply requires "intelligent redistribution" of on-site resources with small amounts of outside inputs targeted to redress occasional imbalances. Moreover, "where neighbouring landholders in a sub-catchment adopt NSF, even more rapid progress to increased profitability and environmental sustainability can be achieved, as NSF adopts a whole-of-catchment approach to farming" (Newell and Reynolds 2005).

Despite his evident success, Peter Andrews suffered years of resistance from the agricultural science and land management communities. Land ecologist David Goldney recalls first traveling to meet him with a group of bureaucrats "who laughed about Peter all the way there and...derided him all the way back":

> But I saw something there that just kept drawing me back. And then I had to try and fit this stuff in to my existing scientific understanding. That took me 10 years to do it. Now I think we can explain the process, you know in half an hour or less, ten minutes given the right sort of video help (Goldney 2005).

Academic scientists have now recognized that Andrews' learning and experimentation has resulted in an increasingly differentiated landscape of greater bio- and ecological diversity which is more resilient to drought (Williams 2005). John Williams co-organized an international workshop on thermodynamics (or energy flows) to explore Andrews' ideas, noting that after 3 weeks of discussion and debate among participating scientists there was a strong consensus supporting Andrews' activities on ecological grounds (2005). A hybrid research collective has now formed around Andrews' farm (Wentworth Group of Concerned Scientists 2009; Williams 2005).

Through Andrews and his unconventional ways, scientists, bureaucrats and business people are learning to be affected by the Australian environment. The Wentworth Group of Concerned Scientists (2009), an independent organization interested in innovation and sustainability, has proposed five key changes based on Andrews' work that the Federal and State governments can implement immediately:

- Clarify water property rights and the obligations associated with those rights to give farmers some certainty and to enable water to be recovered for the environment.
- Restore environmental flows to stressed rivers, such as the River Murray and its tributaries.
- Immediately end broad-scale land clearing of remnant native vegetation and assist rural communities with adjustment.
- Pay farmers for environmental services (clean water, fresh air, healthy soils)...on behalf of the rest of Australia.
- Incorporate into the cost of food, fibre and water the hidden subsidies currently borne by the environment.

The first two recommendations are currently being acted upon with the Federal government spending $50 million in 2007–2008 to purchase water allocations from farmers that will amount to 35 billion extra litres of water for the Murray Darling Basin rivers (Wong 2008).[5]

John Weatherstone is another farmer who has learned to listen to country and discovered a new economy of working *with* the land. From the 1960s, his merino sheep stud, Lyndfield Park, was an exemplar of state-of-the-art farming, enjoying high stock carrying capacity and productive cash cropping. As Weatherstone remembers, "the whole focus of scientific research and government policy was production-oriented" (2003:6). Australian farmers were exhorted to make their land work harder to produce more food and fiber for the "starving millions of the world waiting to be fed and clothed" (6).

For Weatherstone, the long-term impacts on the land of following mainstream agricultural practice were devastating. During the 1982–1983 drought Lyndfield Park was transformed to dust and he was faced with the horrible task of killing new born lambs as there was no way to meet their needs for food and water. Standing at the edge of his property he watched the remaining soil and organic matter blow away, while only a few feet from his fence the weedy overgrown border of a nearby highway gave evidence of adequate soil and moisture retention. He pinpoints this moment as when he resolved to radically change his farming practices and, in the face of much criticism, begin "repairing the country".

Weatherstone's program of repair involved creating a diversified community economy in which the land and a variety of species live together in recognized interdependence. He reduced stocking rates, planted a range of tree species (not all native) chosen to ensure flowers at all parts of the year, improved pastures with perennial grasses, decreased cultivation, switched from ploughing to seed drilling, and reduced use of toxic chemicals. Key to the farm's survival has been species and economic diversification and a focus on mutually benefiting activities, such as planting honey locust trees that reduce fire risk, offer foliage for fodder and shade, help maintain fertile soils, provide timber and honey, and enhance the beauty of the landscape (Weatherstone 2003:10). The farm currently generates income from beef cattle, forestry and a seed business. It has become a native habitat for over 51 species of native birds. The scientific community has taken notice and Lyndfield Park is now a leading example of farming innovation. In 2001–2002, Weatherstone was awarded a Land and Water Australia community fellowship to tell his story. He works with scientists and other visitors to evaluate the farm and generate new ideas for experimentation (Weatherstone 2003:17). In the process, he has gained a diversified identity that extends well beyond his original role of feeding the nation and world.

In October 2006, in the midst of continuing drought, one of us visited Lyndfield Park from nearby Canberra and found a green and pleasant oasis—paddocks of trees with cattle grazing on the lush grass, flowering trees full of birds, and many interested visitors gathered in the converted shearing shed to hear how Weatherstone and his wife achieved this turnaround. All around were the barren, drought-stricken paddocks of neighboring farms. That night on the TV news, hundreds of farmers pressured the Federal government for larger handouts to weather the current "once in a 100 year drought".[6]

The hybrid research collectives involving Deborah Bird Rose, Jon Altman, their Aboriginal co-researchers, Peter Andrews, John Weatherstone, their scientific and business co-researchers, and many others are showing us that there is a way to live *with* earth others even in the dry conditions of the Australian Anthropocene. In these collectives academic researchers are learning to listen to country and to non-academic researchers and being called to translate, inventory, codify, formalize, formulate policy, communicate to ever wider publics, extend the boundaries of collectives, and make connections between them. All these collectives are constituting a new econo-sociality in which the *needs* of the more than human are valued and prioritized. *Surplus* is directed toward more-than-human needs, *consumption* habits are modified with respect to these needs, and the *commons* shared by

Journal compilation © 2009 Editorial Board of *Antipode*.

all species is replenished and renewed. These practices can be seen as the elements of an economic ethics for the Anthropocene.

Conclusion

As we celebrate the 40th anniversary of the birth of *Antipode*, it is inspiring and heartening to note the theoretical and political distances that radical geographers (and others on the left) have traversed in the past 40 years. Even a brief inventory yields a sense of dramatic shifts in how we are able to think about things. Perhaps most notably, we have loosened the hold of structural visions that channel transformative change into narrow openings and scarce opportunities; we have gained a sense of power as distributed and ramified rather than as (always) concentrated and monolithic; we have rethought scale beyond nested hierarchies in which the global generally prevails; and we have opened to the being-in-common of humans and the more-than-human world.

There are also many new ways to think about how things change. We have a broader notion of (political) agency, no longer restricted to a mass collective subject and potentially involving variously sized collectives of human and non-human actants. Small actions and networks can be seen to have sweeping global effects, and rapid large-scale change can emerge from diffuse local transformations. Theory has taken on a new relation to action—to understand the world *is* to change it. As a performative practice, academic research *is* activism; it participates in bringing new realities into being. Our role as academics has thus dramatically changed. We are less required to function as critics who excavate and assess what has already occurred, and more and more pushed to adopt the stance of experimental researchers, opening to what can be learned from what is happening on the ground. To put this in the form of a mandate, we are being called to read the potentially positive futures barely visible in the present order of things, and to imagine how to strengthen and move them along.

Faced with the daunting prospect of global warming and the apparent stalemate in the formal political sphere, this essay has put the hybrid research collective at the center of change. Research here is framed as a process of learning involving a collective of human and more-than-human actants—a process of co-transformation that re/constitutes the world. Starting with Latour's "body" to give a sense of this differentiating, co-creating process, we moved to the MADD collective to convey the rapid and far-reaching changes (now codified in law) that can arise from a small group of learners. We moved next to the muscular dystrophy story of Callon and Rabeharisoa, which provides a striking example of the proliferation of actions and identities that a hybrid research collective can engender in a brief period of time.

It is this vision of how things change that grounds our "economic ethics for the Anthropocene". What we can see all around us, if we put on the 3-D glasses provided here, are ethical practices of economy that involve the being-in-common of humans and the more-than-human world. Each of these practices is involved in building a community economy, in which sustenance and interdependence are key values and ethical negotiations center on the interrelated issues of necessity, surplus, consumption and commons. Each is more or less embedded in a hybrid research collective, which is more or less effectively learning to be affected, and more or less successful at proliferating alliances and avenues of action. What we would hope to stimulate is an academic interest in expanding and multiplying these hybrid research collectives, and thereby participating in a world-changing process.

Acknowledgments

We would like to thank the editors for their invitation to contribute to this anniversary issue. In particular, we are grateful to Wendy Larner for her encouragement, enthusiasm and flexibility. Thanks also to two anonymous reviewers for their comments and suggestions. This essay is dedicated to the memory of Val Plumwood whose death prompted us to extend our thinking to the more than human and whose legacy continues to inspire new thoughts and practices.

Endnotes

[1] According to Latour, such learning is not optional: "If you are not engaged in this learning you become insensitive, dumb, you drop dead" (2004:205). Our hope is to make such learning more intentional.

[2] In geography Harvey (1974, 1996) and Smith (1984) pioneered the "production of nature" thesis based on an historical geographical materialism which posits a relational ontology of nature and society in dialectical connection. Placing human labor *within* nature they went a long way towards collapsing the dualism that has structured so much economic and ecological thinking and action. Writing more recently, Braun (2006) and Castree (2002), among others, have voiced concerns about the remnant privilege accorded to logics of capitalist determination in this formulation and have moved towards a new materialism of immanent causality which sees capitalism as performatively constituted through hybrid assemblages of human and non-human actants. We bring our own critique of capitalocentrism to our interactions with this rich tradition of scholarship.

[3] We are accustomed to thinking about surplus (value) as the basis of capitalist profits. The term "social surplus" has been proposed as a way of thinking about the aggregate surplus labor produced within all the different class processes making up an economy (capitalist, communal, independent, feudal, slave, household based, etc) (Chakrabarti and Cullenberg 2003; DeMartino 2003; Gibson-Graham 2006). DeMartino defines social surplus as "the residual that arises from the fact that those who perform the labor necessary to provision society produce more than they themselves consume" (2003:8). We assume that he is referring here to multiple class processes as earlier he writes that "antiessentialist Marxism refuses to acknowledge the (ontological) dominance of any particular class process. It encourages us to expect that each and every economy (no matter its self-designation) will comprise of diverse class forms and that these will be

articulated in various and unpredictable ways (rather than just merely in a structure of dominance)" (2003:7).

[4] The coordinates can be seen as having multiple potential functions, not unlike the gene in the muscular dystrophy example above (Callon and Rabeharisoa 2003:200–201). Tracing ethical negotiations around the coordinates can connect activist communities; foster acknowledged interdependency and solidarity; proliferate economic possibility; create new identities; and prompt new research questions and the formation of hybrid research collectives.

[5] Geographer Jessica Weir (2008) is concerned, however, that rivers continue to be viewed as flows, an image that perpetuates a plumbing system mentality and ignores the Aboriginal and ecological communities supported by water. Weir has conducted research with the Murray Lower Darling River Indigenous National Alliance to formulate a different understanding of river systems, one that can be used by Aboriginal communities in their negotiations with government authorities and environmental groups about an Indigenous water allocation (Weir and Ross 2007:187).

[6] Writing in February of this year as the country burns, eco-philosopher Freya Mathews asks us to learn to be affected by our environment and to "stop using the word 'drought', with its implication that dry weather is the exception. The desiccation of the landscape here is the new reality. It is now our climate" (2009).

References

Altman J (2003) People on country, healthy landscapes and sustainable indigenous economic futures: The Arnhem Land Case. *The Drawing Board: An Australian Review of Public Affairs* 4:65–82

Anderson K (2007) *Race and the Crisis of Humanism*. New York: Routledge

Andrews P (2006) *Back from the Brink: How Australia's Landscape Can Be Saved*. Sydney: ABC Books.

Australian Bureau of Statistics (2007) *Australian Capital Territory in Focus: Waste Management*, http://www.abs.gov.au/AUSSTATS/abs@.nsf/Latestproducts/A33E74BE4D1B16D0CA2573A1007B33F6?opendocument Accessed 28 February 2009

Bingham N (2006) Bees, butterflies, and bacteria: Biotechnology and the politics of nonhuman friendship. *Environment and Planning A* 38:48–498

Braun B (2006) Towards a new earth and a new humanity: Nature, ontology, politics. In N Castree and D Gregory (eds) *David Harvey: A Critical Reader* (pp 191–222). Oxford: Blackwell Publishing

Callon M (2007) What does it mean to say that economics is performative. In D MacKenzie, F Muniesa and L Siu (eds) *Do Economists Make Markets?* (pp 311–357). Princeton: Princeton University Press

Callon M and Rabeharisoa V (2003) Research "in the wild" and the shaping of new social identities. *Technology in Society* 25:193–204

Cameron J and Gibson K (2005) Alternative pathways to community and economic development: The Latrobe Valley Community Partnering Project. *Geographical Research* 43:274–285

Castree N (2002) False antitheses? Marxism, nature and actor-networks. *Antipode* 34:111–146

Chakrabarti A and Cullenberg S (2003) *Transition and Development in India*. New York: Routledge

Chakrabarty D (2009) The climate of history: Four theses. *Critical Inquiry* 35: (Winter):197–222

Community Economies Collective and Gibson K (2009) Building community-based social enterprises in the Philippines: diverse development pathways. In

A Amin (ed) *Plural Economy, Plural Provision: The Social Economy in International Perspective* (pp 116–138). London: Zed Press

Community Environmental Legal Defense Fund (2008) Ecuador approves new constitution: Voters approve rights of nature, http://www.celdf.org/Default.aspx?tabid=548 Accessed 12 February 2009

Davis M (2008) Living on the ice shelf: Humanity's meltdown. *Tomdispatch* 26, http://www.tomdispatch.com/post/174949 Accessed 15 December 2008

DeMartino G (2003) Realizing class justice. *Rethinking Marxism* 15:1–31

Dolan K (2008) Urban showpiece. *Green Sustainable Architecture and Landscape Design*, 7:57–63

Gibson-Graham J K (2006) *A Postcapitalist Politics*. Minneapolis: University of Minnesota Press

Gibson-Graham J K and O'Neill P (2001) Exploring a new class politics of the enterprise. In J K Gibson-Graham, S Resnick and R Wolff (eds) *Re/Presenting Class: Essays in Postmodern Marxism* (pp 56–80). Durham: Duke University Press

Gudeman S (2001) *The Anthropology of Economy: Commodity, Market and Culture*. Oxford: Blackwell Publishers

Goldney D (2005) Interview with land ecologist Professor David Goldney. The Australian Story, The ABC, Program Transcript 6 June 2005, http://www.abc.net.au/austory/content/2005/s1384171.htm Accessed 27 February 2009)

Harvey D (1974) Population, resources, and the ideology of science. *Economic Geography* 50:256–277

Harvey D (1996) *Justice, Nature and the Geography of Difference*. Blackwell Publishers: Massachusetts and Oxford: Cambridge

Hinchliffe S (2003) "Inhabiting"—landscapes and natures. In K Anderson, M Domosh, S Pile and N Thrift (eds) *Handbook of Cultural Geography* (pp 207–225). London: Sage Publications

Hinchliffe S (2007) *Geographies of Nature: Societies, Environments, Ecologies*. London: Sage Publications

Hobson K (2008) "Values, behaviour and the hope of "creative maladjustment" in the Anthropocene." Paper presented in the Fenner School Seminar Series, Fenner School of Environment and Society, The Australian National University, Canberra, 4 December

Hudson R (2005) Towards sustainable economic practices, flows and spaces: Or is the necessary impossible and the impossible necessary? *Sustainable Development* 13: 239–252

Latour B (2004) How to talk about the body? The normative dimension of science studies. *Body and Society* 10:205–229

Mathews F (2009) Fires the deadly inevitability of climate change. *The Age* 10 February, http://www.theage.com.au/opinion/fires-the-deadly-inevitability-of-climate-change-20090209-8289.html Accessed 6 July 2009

Milgram B L (2005) Juicing up for fair trade. *Cultural Survival Quarterly* September:47–49

Nancy J-L (1991) Of being-in-common. In Miami Theory Collective (ed) *Community at Loose Ends* (pp 1–12). Minneapolis: University of Minnesota Press

Newell P and Reynolds C (2005) Natural Sequence Farming: Principles and applications http://www.nsfarming.com/Principles/principles2.html, Accessed 24 February 2009

Pena K (2008) Opening the door to food sovereignty in Ecuador. *Food First News and Views* 30:4, http://www.foodfirst.org/en/publications/newsandviews Accessed 6 July 2009

Plumwood V (2002) *Environmental Culture: The Ecological Crisis of Reason*. London and New York: Routledge

Plumwood V (2007) A review of Deborah Bird Rose's *Reports from a Wild Country: Ethics of Decolonisation. Australian Humanities Review* 42:1–4

Roelvink G (2008) Performing new economies through hybrid collectives. Unpublished PhD dissertation, The Australian National University

Roelvink G (forthcoming) Collective action and the politics of affect. *Emotion, Space and Society*

Roelvink G and Gibson-Graham J K (2009) A postcapitalist politics of dwelling: Ecological humanities and community economies in conversation. *Australian Humanities Review* 46:145–158

Rose D (2002) with D'Amico S, Daiyi N, Deveraux K Daiyi M, Ford L and Bright A *Country of the Heart: An Indigenous Australian Homeland*. Canberra ACT: Aboriginal Studies Press

Rose D (2005) An indigenous philosophical ecology: Situating the human. *The Australian Journal of Anthropology* 16:294–305

Santos B de S (2004) The World Social Forum: Toward a counter-hegemonic globalisation (part 1). In J Sen, A Anand, A Escobar and P Waterman (eds) *The World Social Forum: Challenging Empires* (pp 235–245). New Delhi: Viveka Foundation

Sedgwick E (2003) *Touching Feeling: Affect, Pedagogy, Performativity*. Durham: Duke University Press

Smith N (1984) *Uneven Development*. Oxford: Blackwell

Spinosa C, Flores F and Dreyfus H (1997) *Disclosing New Worlds: Entrepreneurship, Democratic Action, and the Cultivation of Solidarity*. Cambridge, MA: MIT Press

Steffan W (2008) Surviving the Anthropocene. Paper presented in the Fenner School Seminar Series, Fenner School of Environment and Society, The Australian National University, Canberra, 16 October

Tomdispatch (2008) Tomgram: Mike Davis, welcome to the next epoch. *Tomdispatch* 26, http://www.tomdispatch.com/post/174949 Accessed 15 December 2008

Weatherstone J (2003) *Lyndfield Park: Looking Back, Moving Forward*. Booklet produced by Greening Australia and Land and Water Australia, Braddon, ACT: Worldwide Online Printing

Weir J (2008) Connectivity *Australian Humanities Review* 45:154–164

Weir J and Ross S (2007) Beyond native title: Murray Lower Darling Rivers Indigenous nations. In B Smith and F Morphy (eds) *The Social Effects of Native Title: Recognition, Translation, Coexistence* (pp 185–202). CAEPR Research Monograph 27: ANU E Press

Wentworth Group of Concerned Scientists (2009) *Wentworth Group of Concerned Scientists*, http://www.wentworthgroup.org/index.php Accessed 11 February 2009

Whatmore S (2002) *Hybrid Geographies: Natures, Cultures and Spaces*. London: Sage Publications

Whatmore S (2004) Humanism's excess: Some thoughts on the "post-human/ist" agenda. *Environment and Planning A* 36:1360–1363

Williams J (2005) Interview with John Williams, former CSIRO Head of Land and Water. Australian Story, http://www.abc.net.au/austory/content/2005/s1385834.htm Accessed 11 February 2009

Wong P (2008) Government water purchase secures rights to 35 billion litres for the Murray Darling. Senator the Hon Penny Wong, Minister for Climate Change and Water media release 23 May, http://www.environment.gov.au/minister/wong/2008/pubs/mr20080523.pdf Accessed 11 February 2009

Index